Ageing and Mental Handicap

James Hogg, Steve Moss and Diana Cooke

There has been growing recent interest in the topic of ageing and mental handicap, for two principal reasons. First, the life expectancy of people with mental handicap has risen significantly over the last decades and many, once infancy has been survived, may expect a life span similar to that of non-handicapped people. Secondly, a growing commitment on the part of government and service providers to make provision for people with handicaps in the community rather than in institutions, has focused attention on this group.

This book is one of the first on this subject. It examines epidemiology and mortality, and medical and psychiatric issues compared with non-handicapped older people. It considers how people with mental handicap change in intellectual and adaptive function with age, the nature of family relationships relevant therapeutic programmes, and policy and the development of services. The book represents a major review of a hitherto neglected topic and should interest gerontologists, psychologists and professional health, social and educational staff concerned with the welfare of older people with mental handicap.

Ageing and Mental Handicap

James Hogg,
Steve Moss and
Diana Cooke
*Hester Adrian Research Centre,
University of Manchester, UK*

London New York Sydney
CROOM HELM

First published in 1988 by Croom Helm Ltd
11 New Fetter Lane, London EC4P 4EE
Published in the USA by
Routledge Chapman and Hall Inc.
29 West 35th Street, New York NY 10001
Croom Helm Australia
44–50 Waterloo Road, North Ryde,
2113, New South Wales

Printed in Great Britain at
The University Press, Cambridge

ISBN 0 7099 5718 1

British Library Cataloguing in Publication Data

Hogg, James
Ageing and mental handicap.
1. Mentally handicapped old persons
I. Title II. Moss, S. (Steve) III. Cooke, Diana.

ISBN 0–7099–5718–1

Library of Congress Cataloging-in-Publication Data

Hogg, J. (James)
Ageing and mental handicap / James Hogg, Steve Moss, and Diana Cooke.
p. cm.
Bibliography: p.
Includes index.
ISBN 0–7099–5718–1
1. Mentally handicapped aged. I. Moss, Steve. II Cooke, Diana. III. Title.
[DNLM: 1. Mental Retardation—in old age. 2. Mental Retardation--rehabilitation. WM 300 H716a]
RC451.4.A5H64 1988
362.3′0880565—dc19 88–14936
DNLM/DLC CIP

CONTENTS

ACKNOWLEDGEMENTS

The opportunity to undertake this extensive review was afforded in the first instance by a grant from the Joseph Rowntree Memorial Trust. Special thanks must therefore go to the Trust for this support, and to the Trust's Director, Robin Guthrie and to the Trust's Advisor at that time, Malcolm Johnson, for their encouragement and interest.

The opportunity to explore directly some of the issues affecting families with older sons and daughters with mental handicap came through a grant from the MENCAP City Foundation. This generous support is acknowledged and the outcome of the work is reflected in Chapter 8 of this volume.

In our efforts to familiarise ourselves with issues in this area we spent a considerable time in Oldham Metropolitan Borough meeting both service providers and their clients. We would like to thank all who gave their time to educating us. Much of what they provided appears in our illustrative study in Chapter 1. In that Chapter we mention several people by name and here will note only two people who played a special role in this venture. Sally Cheseldine, of the Community Mental Handicap Team, gave us our entrèe into Oldham introducing us to the relevant service providers and clearing up many misconceptions that emerged in our first draft of Chapter 1. Dan Stansfield, Principal Officer responsible for mental handicap in Oldham Social Services Department, also gave us significant support and has continued to make additional work in Oldham possible.

Outside of Oldham we had also required assistance from Calderstones Hospital and here Tom McLean (Unit Director of Nursing Services) gave all the support we could wish for. Brian Shields (Charge Nurse) unstintingly gave us all statistical information we requested. Our thanks to both of them.

Several dozen colleagues in the United States and Canada have provided detailed reports on the development of their own service plans. We have not been able to do justice to these contributions but trust that the citations that we do offer reflect our appreciation of their communications and go some way to ensuring our approach to the topic cannot be accused of insularity. We must acknowledge in particular Matthew P. Janicki, Director for Aging Services, State of New York Office of Mental Retardation and Developmental Disabilities, who has facilitated our contact with those workers in North America and the invaluable part played by the National Institute on Aging's Newsletter of which he is Editor.

Our own colleagues in the Hester Adrian Research Centre have also given their time to reading parts of this volume. Special thanks go to Hazel Qureshi and Margaret Flynn. Margaret Flynn, too, must be thanked for allowing us to use material that she herself is still in the course of publishing.

The complex operation of producing the camera-ready copy for this volume has been undertaken by Christine Houghton in collaboration with the second author. Special thanks are due to her for the high quality of her work and meticulous organisation throughout the production period in which the volume was written.

Finally, we gratefully acknowledge permission to use the following figures:

Fig. 1.1: "Percentage of the population aged 65 and over for selected countries", from V. Carver and P. Liddiard (Eds.) (1978) "An Ageing Population", Open University Course P252. Copyright permission: The Open University Press, Milton Keynes.

Table 3.1: "Prevalence of diagnoses in health surveys of 50 and 60 year old men in Uppsala, Sweden", from U. Waern (1978) "Health and Disease at the Age of Sixty. Findings in a health survey of 60 year old men in Uppsala and a comparison with men 10 years younger",

Uppsala Journal of Medical Sciences, Volume 83, 153-162. Copyright permission: Uppsala Journal of Medical Sciences.

Table 3.2: "Mean prevalence rates of major disease categories in a sample of a French managerial population at retirement", from Vallery-Masson et al (1981) "Retirement and Morbidity: a three year longitudinal study of a French managerial population", Age and Ageing, Volume 10, 271-176. Copyright permission: Bailliere Tindall Ltd, London.

Fig. 3.1: "International comparison of annual age-specific hip fracture rates in women (A) and men (B)" from J.C. Gallagher et al (1980), "Epidemiology of Fractures of the Proximal Femur in Rochester, Minnesota", Clinical Orthopaedics and Related Research, Volume 150, 163-171. Copyright permission: J.B. Lippincott, Harper & Row, Philadelphia, Pennsylvania.

Fig. 4.1: "Some alternative patterns of growth of mental age and associated changes in IQ";
Fig. 4.2: "Mean semi-longitudinal MA growth functions for the five levels of handicap. Numbers on the curves refer to numbers of subjects measured";
Fig. 4.3: "Age changes in IQ for the five levels of handicap computed semi-longitudinally", from M.A. Fisher and D. Zeaman (1970) "Growth and Decline of Retardate Intelligence", in N.R. Ellis (Ed.) International Review of Research in Mental Retardation, Volume 4. Copyright permission: Academic Press, Orlando, Florida.

Fig. 4.4: "Personal self-sufficiency. Mean factor scores for ten age groups. Each line represents a specific level of measured intelligence";
Fig. 4.5: "Community self-sufficiency. Mean factor scores for ten age groups. Each line represents a specific level of measured intelligence";
Fig. 4.6: "Personal-social responsibility. Mean factor scores for ten age groups. Each line represents a specific level of measured intelligence", from K. Nihira (1976) "Dimensions of Adaptive Behavior in Institutionalized Mentally Retarded Children and Adults: Developmental Perspective", American Journal of Mental Deficiency,

Volume 81/3, 215-226. Copyright permission: American Association for Mental Deficiency, Washington DC.

Fig. 5.1: "Schematic model of the social support system of the elderly", from M. Cantor and V. Little (1985) "Aging and Social Care" in R.H. Binstock and E. Shanas (Eds.) "Handbook of Aging and the Social Services", 2nd Edition. Copyright permission: Van Nostrand Reinhold Company Inc., New York.

Fig. 7.1: "Characteristics of various residential settings as measured on six different scales by Baker *et al.* (1977)", from B.L. Baker, G.B. Seltzer and M. Mailick Seltzer (1977) "As Close as Possible: Community residences for Retarded Adults". Copyright permission: Little, Brown and Company, Boston.

Chapter One

AGEING AND MENTAL HANDICAP - BACKGROUND AND AN ILLUSTRATIVE REPORT

1 INTRODUCTION

Since the turn of the century most industrial countries have seen a marked shift in the age structure of their populations. People are living longer and having fewer children, with the result that the proportion of older people has been steadily rising. This "greying" of society is predicted to continue well into the 21st century, with a consequent pressure on services to the elderly that is becoming of increasing concern to policy planners. In Britain, the numbers of those aged 75 or more will rise by 23 per cent between 1976 and 1996, while the proportion of very elderly people (aged 85 and over) will increase by 42 per cent in the same period (Walker, 1981). Similar trends for other countries are presented by Hendricks and Hendricks (1978) (see Figure 1.1) and Myers (1985).

One of the fundamental determinants of increasing longevity has obviously been the improvement in quality of medical care. People are now much more likely to survive serious illness in old age than they were 50 years ago. For people with mental handicap, some of whom tend to be more susceptible to illness than their non-handicapped peers, these medical advances have had an even greater impact. Advances in perinatal care have resulted in a much greater proportion of impaired children surviving the first year of life, so that Fryers (1984) is able to report a current death rate of only 10 per cent among children with Down's syndrome, compared with 50 per cent in earlier studies (Carter, 1958; Hall, 1964; Oster, 1953; Record and Smith,

1955). Mortality rates among adults similarly declined in the early part of this century

Figure 1.1:

Percentage of the population aged 65 and over for selected countries

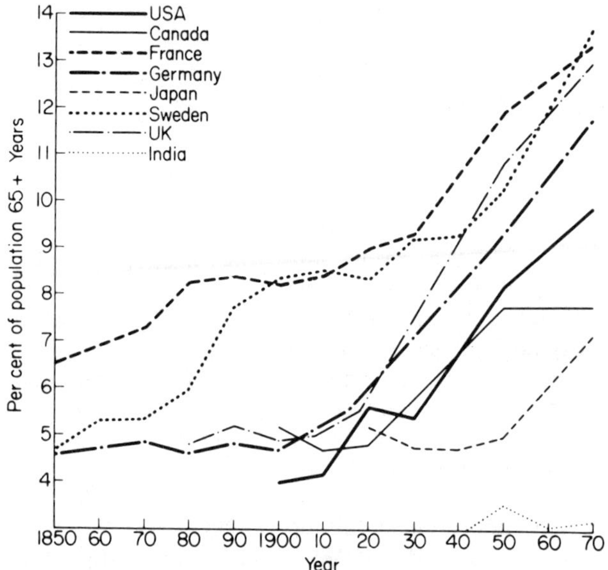

Sources: United Nations, *The Aging of Populations and Its Economic and Social Implications*, Population Studies, no. 26 (New York: United Nations 1956); United Nations, *Demographic Yearbook, 1973*, 25th ed. (New York: United Nations 1974). (Adapted from numeric data.)

as former major causes of death were brought under control. Tuberculosis, pneumonia and influenza were responsible for 50 per cent to 60 per cent of deaths among people with severe mental handicap, a death rate which was around 13 times that of the non-handicapped population (Conley, 1973). Studies which are widely separated in time illustrate clearly this change in lifespan. Dayton *et al.* (1932) found 28 per cent of the people alive at 10 years to have survived to 60. Forty years later, Balakrishnan and Wolf (1976) reported a corresponding survival rate of 46 per cent.

As a result of this dramatic increase in longevity, policy makers must now plan on the basis that approximately half of all people with mental handicap will reach the conventional age of retirement. Indeed, the concern with the topic of ageing, as measured by the number of published articles relating to older people with mental handicap, has burgeoned over the past ten years. However, the fact that the majority of the relevant literature dates from less than ten years ago, suggests it is not merely an increase in the numbers of older people with mental handicap that has stimulated the interest. Rather, there has been a growing awareness that the needs of this client group have been overlooked. They suffer the "double jeopardy" of belonging to two groups whose members are disadvantaged in Western Society, i.e. being both aged and having a mental handicap (Sweeney and Wilson, 1979). Ageing, even for non-handicapped people, usually brings the abrupt termination of "useful activity" at the age of retirement, while little value is attached to those positive features which senior citizens may possess to a greater degree than other members of society, e.g. wisdom and experience. An expectation of economic dependence is also the reality for many older people. Walker (1981) states that elderly people comprise the majority of those living in poverty in the UK, with around half of this group having incomes below the poverty line. In the USA, about 20 per cent of elderly people have incomes below the federal minimum (Hendricks and Hendricks, 1978).

Elderly people with mental handicap are liable to be even more disadvantaged than their non-handicapped peers. As Dickerson *et al.* (1979) point out "By middle age (40-55) persons experience loss of parents and some friends, loss of some of his sensory awareness (bifocals, hearing aids, etc.). We regard this as a normal loss pattern. However, for the retarded this loss pattern becomes a double or triple jeopardy. If he has lived at home with his parents, this loss may result in a change of home space. Thus, mentally retarded persons who become older may tend to become part of the life occupant category in long-term care institutions such as nursing homes. There the patients who are mentally retarded tend to be grouped with patients who are senile. (This seems to be another factor in how the mentally retarded elderly person becomes invisible. They get lumped together with these elderly senile persons and their behaviors are not differentiated.)" (p.12).

In the USA, the growing awareness of the need to plan services for, and research the needs of, older people with mental handicap has led to changes in Federal and State legislation. The Older Americans' Resources and Services (OARS) Act enshrines the rights of all senior citizens, including those who have a mental handicap. It is apparent, however, that most State and private agencies have no special plans or provisions for older people with mental handicap (Janicki, Ackerman and Jacobson, 1984; Sweeney and Wilson, 1979), although there are notable exceptions (e.g. Durow and Pierson, 1975). One result of these detailed investigations into State and private agency plans has been a heightened awareness of unmet needs and insufficient numbers of suitably trained staff. Social Services are increasingly being reviewed from the perspective of cost effectiveness and output, where this is defined as effect on the client. The question is no longer how many units of service were expended, but what happened to the client as a result of those services and how much did they cost (McAllister, 1975).

In the UK, the specific needs of older people with mental handicap have received little attention. In 1985 we were able to find only 13 references concerned with the needs of this older group of clients. There is an extensive literature on all aspects of ageing in non-handicapped people, but very little overlap between the two subject areas. Indeed, this lack of overlap is not peculiar to the UK. It is notable, for instance, that there is no reference to retardation or handicap in one of the most recent and major of the textbooks on ageing (Binstock and Shanas, 1985). However, this lack of overlap is probably not surprising when one considers the very different life histories and expectations of many people with mental handicap compared with those of non-handicapped individuals. Much of the literature on ageing in non-handicapped people is concerned with disengagement from the active roles of earlier adult life such as work and parenthood and with the consequent changing roles in relation to family and friends. Thus, Fennel *et al.* (1983) state: "From quantitative data we know that among elderly people living in the community, proximity to and contact with children increases with age. We also know that in some cases parents and children have been involved in moves which bring them into greater proximity. At the same time, we know that reliance on the family for help increases in extreme old age."

In comparison, many older people with mental handicap have lived an institutional life for many years. Some of these people no longer have family or friends living in the community, or are no longer in touch with them. In these cases there is the danger that a move to the community will bring isolation, unless appropriate statutory networks of care and support are available. There is no doubt that these statutory provisions should exist, but it can be seen that sociological analyses of informal care networks relying on a lifelong history of family involvement may be of limited relevance.

It is to be hoped that eventually the majority of people with mental handicap will live their adult lives in the community, using generic services for elderly people in their later years when necessary. At present, however, there is an urgent need to examine policy issues and priorities for service provision to this client group. The current policy of community relocation is likely to have profound effects on the lives of many people who undergo this transition. We are therefore presented with two interacting considerations. On the one hand, people with mental handicap are living longer. At the same time they are also being asked to consider the possibility of making major moves towards independence, sometimes when they are already well beyond the conventional age of retirement.

2 DEFINING THE POPULATION OF OLDER CLIENTS

There has been much discussion in the literature of what definition we should use to characterise a person with mental handicap as "old" or "elderly". Many service providers consider that this line should be drawn lower than for the non-handicapped population (Hamilton and Segal, 1975). Thus, Daniels (1979) advocates an age criterion of 55+, while Janicki (1984) and Seltzer (1984) are in favour of including all people over 50 years of age. Some authors have suggested lowering the age criterion to 45 years (Thomae and Fryers, 1982), or even to 40 years (Fancolly and Clute, 1975; Kriger, 1975).

A number of authors advocate retaining the statutory age boundaries (i.e. 60-65) which apply to the non-handicapped population (Ballinger, 1978; Deshayes, 1979; Gress, 1979; Rowitz, 1979). It is noticeable, however, that the majority of these papers are written from a medical standpoint where statutory service eligibility may be an important consideration.

Evidence of premature ageing associated with Down's syndrome (see Chapters 2 and 3) does lend support to the view that, for some people with mental handicap, a lower age criterion is appropriate. It is important to bear in mind, however, that in the absence of a universally accepted index of ageing, any age criterion is essentially arbitrary. Thus, Sweeney and Wilson (1979) point out that many people with severe mental handicap are physiologically or neurologically impaired in their early lives. This makes it difficult to know whether a particular biological phenomenon is to be considered a symptom of "ageing" rather than environmentally induced disease, insult or trauma. Thomas *et al.* (1979) suggest that "It is not enough for a person to 'look old' and to be given a label of 'aging or aged'. In this day of consciousness-raising on every topic, professionals in both gerontology and developmental disabilities need to take a long look at their subjective, often presumptous, expectations of client behavior" (p.46).

Within our study of service provision in Oldham Metropolitan Borough described below, it was necessary to employ an age criterion in order to give some context to the interviews with service providers. For this purpose we took <u>50 years</u> as a lower age limit, although this did not preclude discussion of the needs of any younger clients who were thought to be suffering from premature ageing.

3 POLICY BACKGROUND

Approaches to the care of people with mental handicap have undergone major changes over the past decade. There has been a massive shift away from the notion of custodial maintenance in large isolated institutions to an acceptance of the fact that these people have a right to live a normal life in the community. As a result, patterns of service provision are showing an increasing emphasis on normal life styles and their integration as much as possible into community routines (Bruininks *et al*, 1981).

The process of providing appropriate residential placements for mentally handicapped people encompasses three interrelated elements: 1) The prevention of admission by finding and developing alternative residential facilities in the community: 2) Deinstitutionalisation of existing clients, and: 3) The establishment of a responsive residential environment which protects human rights (Bruininks *et al.*, 1981).

In England and Wales, mental handicap policy has for over thirty years been directed to a shift towards community care. The report of the Royal Commission in 1957 strongly supported the community option, recommending a mandatory requirement on local authorities to provide appropriate services. The subsequent legislation, the Mental Health Act (1959) adopted most of the Commission's recommendations, but did not require local authorities to make community provision; it merely empowered them to do so. The White Paper "Better Services for the Mentally Handicapped" (DHSS and Welsh Office 1971) offered a statement of the principles that should guide community services and guidance to local authorities and health authorities on service development in line with Government objectives. Inadequacies in community and hospital services were identified and a 20 year programme of transfer of services from hospitals to the community set out. The recent report by the Audit Commission (1986) notes that this transfer implied a considerable expansion in social service provision since in August 1959 the Minister of Health had directed under the National Health Service Act (1959) that local authorities should buy residential and accommodation services for people with mental handicap.

Impetus has been given to the transfer and the nature of service provision more clearly defined through a variety of intiatives since publication of the White Paper, notably the establishment of the National Development Group for the Mentally Handicapped and the setting up of the Jay Committee (DHSS 1979). Further monitoring and advice has come from the National Development Team. It is of interest to note that thinking regarding the implementation of the community care policy has continued to evolve over this period and far more radical objectives have been set many local authorities than were ever envisaged in 1971. However, marked differences exist between different authorities in both the way in which the policy is being realised and the extent of commitment to the policy. DHSS publication "Care in Action" (DHSS, 1981) urged authorities to aim for smaller, more local units, and set as the main aim the development of each individual's capabilities at independent living. However, establishing homes in small group houses or in relatively independent residences such as housing association accommodation has become the required objective of some Regional Health Authorities and local authorities as we shall see later in this chapter. Variations in quality of provision are documented by the Audit Commission (1986), and problems in the realisation of the policy analysed here and in a variety of other studies (e.g. Donges 1982). A fuller comment on these difficulties which affect older people with mental handicap in significant ways will be made in Chapter 9 of this volume.

Legislation to enhance the quality of services received by people with mental handicap in the community has also been introduced in the wider context of provision for disabled people generally. The Disabled Persons (Services, Consultation and Representation) Act 1986 if fully implemented will lead to a more formal assessment of the needs of older adults with mental handicap with respect to help in the home, recreational facilities, assistance with transport, aids and adaptations, holidays, meals and access to a telephone. At the time of writing, this legislation, though on the statute book, has yet to be implemented. (For a valuable summary of this Act and its implication see Bingley and Mitchell

(1986)).

Although a major focus of these various policy statements has been closure of large mental handicap hospitals, it is important to remember that the resulting patterns of service provision are equally relevant to the lives of those clients who have <u>never</u> lived in an institution. Richardson (1981) estimates that, at age 22, 20 per cent of people with severe mental handicap were living at home with their parents. Some of these individuals may be sufficiently able to live a totally independent life when the time comes, but it seems likely that many of them will require some form of supportive residential alternative when their parents can no longer look after them. Nowadays it is to be hoped that, wherever possible, the chosen living situation is an appropriate community dwelling, although it is clear that this policy has not been adopted in the past. This fact is reflected in the figures for increasing institutionalisation as a function of increasing age.

Heron (1983) has pointed out that, because of the total independence of the Health and Local Authority administration, Britain provides a unique structural model of service delivery. As a result, the government policy directives on community care, coupled with the variable nature of priorities for expenditure at local level, have produced a number of different patterns of district service provision. Indeed, Heron (1983) suggests that there is an almost infinite variety of ways in which community service expansion and relocation of clients from the large hospitals could be handled. We will return later to some of these differing strategies.

The current situation, therefore, is of a general commitment to the run-down of large institutions and a concomitant expansion of community services. The way this policy is interpreted, however, depends on a complex interaction between the various interested parties, RHA, DHAs, LAs and voluntary bodies and on current spending priorities. Finance is, of course, one of the main determinants in the transfer of services and in this respect the local authorities are somewhat concerned. The role of finance and financial administration is analysed by the Audit Commission (1986).

With regard to the subject of this book, it should be noted that the policy of care in the community is as applicable to elderly people generally, as to people with mental handicap. Guidance has not, however, been as specific with regard to implementation of the policy for older people. In Care in Action (DHSS 1981), however, objectives are set emphasising the maintenance of the person in their home with adequate care services, active rehabilitation and treatment, and maintenance of acute and long-stay facilities where required.

The preceding brief discussion touches upon broad trends with respect to the life expectations of people with mental handicap, their present position within the framework of services and the fact they will be living their later life in a world in which the nature of that service provision is going to change in certain fundamental ways. In order to reflect the reality of this situation more fully, we will now describe the situation in one Borough and the main hospitals which will be discharging people with mental handicap into it.

4 AGEING IN OLDHAM

4.1 The Background

To make some of these issues concerned with ageing and elderly people with mental handicap more real, we would like to offer an informal account of the lives of such people in one area of the North West of England, Oldham Metropolitan Borough. To anyone unacquainted with the towns of this area, it is worth pointing out that Oldham is the real name of an actual town, despite the coincidence of name and the subject of this book. The choice of this Borough arose from the availability of co-operative colleagues, geographical accessibility, and good links with the large institutions that will be discharging Oldhamers to their home town.

There are many reasons why the choice was a happy one. We made contact with both service providers and clients during the summer of 1985. This was during a period of general reappraisal of services for people with mental handicap and a particular examination of the nature of provision for older people in this population. This was apparent at all levels of services and was leading to the development of specific projects directed at aspects of ageing.

Having said this, however, two factors soon became apparent to us. First, the fact of attaining a particular birthday does not at any stage automatically lead to a person being classified as "aged, mentally handicapped" as distinct from "mentally handicapped". In terms of their characteristics, needs or the provision of services, we cannot consider a person with mental handicap who is over 50, 60, 70 or even 80 years of age as being in some distinctly different category from younger peers. For this reason our account has to focus on these individuals as part of a wider network of services provided for people with mental handicap in the Borough, and this will necessitate at the outset some general account of these services. Second, though we have described this study as informal, it emerged in a considerably more organised form than we had initially intended. We soon found that to organise our information we had to collect numbers in relation to both facilities and age bands. We had to be able in some measure to identify individuals so we could trace them across different aspects of the service network. In order to understand trends we had to relate these figures to projected changes in the Borough, including the reincorporation of Oldhamers from facilities outside the town. What emerges is not a fully fledged survey, though we do go some way beyond the impressionistic picture we originally intended.

At the time that these visits took place, Oldham was one of the ten Metropolitan Boroughs that made up Greater Manchester, the town itself being located North East of the City of Manchester itself. In 1981 the population was 220,1017 (OPCS 1984). With respect to the older population generally, the percentage of people of pensionable age (Age 60 for women and 65 for men) was close to both the Regional (North West) and National proportions, i.e. Oldham 17.2, North West 17.5, National 17.7 per cent. The picture was similar for the 75 and over population, the equivalent figures being 5.2, 5.6 and 5.7 per cent.

The White Paper "Better Services for the Mentally Handicapped" estimated that, for a population the size of Oldham, there would be 650-700 people with mental handicap, while estimates based on the Guys Health

District Survey would lead to estimates of 200 children and 600 adults. The actual figure provided from the Oldham Register was 538, including some Oldhamers living outside the Borough. The shortfall between estimates and number on the Register is of special interest in this context, as it is likely that those not identified are people with mental handicap who are middle-aged and possibly living with ageing parents. Such families will not have received services for some years (Oldham Social Services Department 1984). Below we offer estimates of the number of people over 50 years of age who may be in this hidden group.

Before pursuing the question of numbers in more detail, it is useful to summarise the philosophy of the service providers as stated in both the Community Mental Handicap Team's own policy statement (Oldham Social Services Department 1984) and their "Parents' Handbook". This is in line with both national United Kingdom policy and enlighted practice elsewhere in the world. It is informed by the North West Regional Health Authority Model District Plan. Four basic views underlie developing practice:

1. Every person with mental handicap has the potential for development and has the right to live as ordinary a life as possible with the greatest degree of choice and independence that he or she can achieve.

2. Care for the person with mental handicap is a joint function of family and community. The Social Services Department itself is only one of several agencies that are seen as responsible for care. Hence, joint planning with the Departments of Health, Education and Housing is essential. To be effective the views of individuals with mental handicap and their families must be taken into account.

3. Services should be located in the community and be comprehensive, should lead to normalisation and should be individualised. Skilled personnel rather than specialised buildings are seen as the most appropriate way of achieving this end.

From the point of view of planning, this

philosophy necessitates the development of services that will prevent admission to long-stay hospitals and provision to relocate those already in hospital in Oldham itself.

This last point brings us to a central issue to which we alluded briefly above, i.e., the fact that some individuals on the Oldham Register are located outside the Borough, some in the long-stay hospitals. To these can be added those known Oldhamers who, though not on the Register, are also due to return to Oldham from such hospitals. At this point then, before proceeding with a more detailed account of what is happening in Oldham itself, we must take a broader look at the wider, Regional, context of hospital closure.

The North Western RHA's (1985) policy on hospital run-down recommends: "Accommodation should be in ordinary domestic housing dispersed throughout the community, with the degree of supervision appropriate to each person's needs, provided and organised in clusters based on neighbourhoods...A wide variety of ordinary housing is required, dispersed throughout the community, together with a wide range of support and supervision. The type of accommodation should be ordinary for its neighbourhood. It is not necessary to build houses specially for handicapped people although it may be necessary for some alterations to be made for people with physical handicaps" (NWRHA, 1985). No discrimination against older residents is intended in realisation of this plan which notes: "A number of residents in their 70s and 80s have been resettled very successfully already. It is inappropriate to argue that because services have deprived a person of ordinary home-living for a long time then they should continue to be deprived for the rest of their lives." (p.12.)

In passing, it is illuminating to contrast this approach with that developed in 1973 by the South East Thames RHA when the decision was made to close Darenth Park Hospital. The Board's recommendations were that each area should have a residential centre of about 72 places, divided into houses or flats for 6-8 people, smaller, 24 place hostels in the community and group homes to make up the provision of each District to the level required by <u>Better Service</u> norms (Korman and Glennerster, 1984).

Such contrast in provision will have implications for resources, the nature of the service and, through these factors, the lives of all groups of people with mental handicap, including the ageing and elderly. With respect to the philosophy and strategy stated by the Oldham Community Mental Handicap Team, there is close agreement with Regional philosophy, a state of affairs that should smooth the way to Regional Health Authority acceptance of plans for individual Oldhamers to return to the town. This is not necessarily the case elsewhere where plans at the local level are not consistent with those demanded by the RHA. For our present purposes, our interest in Oldhamers in long-stay hospitals has been limited to the two large institutions which can be regarded as the main, though not only, settings from which individuals will return.

4.2 An Estimate of Numbers

Let us now return to the question of numbers of people and specifically to the proportion of individuals who are over 50 years of age. In order to see these people in a wider historical context, it is worth noting that at the time of our visits those who were 50 to 59 years of age were born between 1926-1935, those from 60 to 69 years, between 1916 and 1925, and those over 70 years, before 1915. Using the Oldham Register of June 1985 and complementary information collected by us in the Authority the breakdown in Table 1.1 can be given. This gives a grand total of 75 people over the age of 50 years living in the Borough itself. The figures for the "Identified at home group" are based on information on place of residence supplied by the two ATCs/SECs. The estimate is based on the assumption that there are 160 adults not on the register. We have taken the proportion of people in each age band that would be expected on the basis of Midwinter's (1972) figures on people with mental handicap living in the community and extrapolated from these.

4.3 Service Provision for Older People in Oldham

As we stated above, to consider the position of older people with mental handicap in Oldham, it is necessary

Table 1.1:

<u>People over 50 years of Age Living in Oldham Metropolitan Borough</u>

AGE:	50+	60+	70+	80+
LOCATION:				
Hostels	19	18	1	0
Home Making Scheme	5	1	0	0
At home (identified)	9	5	0	0
At home (estimated)	6	3	1	0
Independent	4	3	0	0
TOTAL:	43	30	2	0

to take a broader look at the general service context. This we will do, and will then "place" the over-50s within this framework.

Community services are provided by specialist teams. They operate in three Core Teams, 1 to 3, working from the Community Mental Handicap Team base, Woodfield Centre. Core Team One is concerned with children, and therefore our own interest focussed on Teams Two and Three. Team Two is concerned with adults living in the community, including some with parents well into their 80s. Team Three concentrates on rehabilitation and maintenance, serving adults who are resident in the area. This team aims to give clients a more independent life in the community. Team members work with staff in residential settings to assess residents' capacity for independent living, prepare them to move out and support them in their own homes. Input to the Core Teams comes from Social Workers, Psychologists and Community Nurses, and we will consider their interacting roles in relation to the ageing population of people with mental handicap in Oldham.

4.3.1 Social Work Input.

Overall responsibility for social services for people with mental handicap rests with Dan Stansfield, Principal Officer Social Services Department. The leader of all three Social Work components of the Core Teams is Richard Woolrych. Brenda Lees (together with Maureen Martin) is the Social Worker primarily concerned with the Social Work aspect of Core Team Two. Discussion with her about older clients with mental handicap revealed concern regarding individuals living at home with their parents or other relatives. Essentially we are considering the 24 "at home" people identified and estimated above. As we shall see, such people, paradoxically, face potentially greater problems than those who are in hostels or are being prepared for leaving hospital. According to Brenda Lees, these problems stem from two sources. First, people with mental handicap who have lived with their parents all their lives have not, generally speaking, gained experience in self-care skills. As a result, the death of a parent or disablement through illness can cause a crisis in the life of the person with mental handicap, due to his or her inability to cope. Obviously, if the person is already known to the Social Service Department (SSD), this event can be planned for, (assuming the cooperation of the parent). Sometimes, however, people do not come to the attention of Social Services until a relatively late stage. In extreme cases this will be on the death of a caregiver, but sometimes it is a third party, neighbour or friend, who alerts the Department to a potential problem. Wendy's mother, for example, was in her 90s when she died. Social Services were not informed of the death; it was only when Brenda Lees read of it in the local paper that the situation came to the attention of social services.

Expectation regarding future care can also be unrealistic. In one instance, according to the mother, it had been agreed that a daughter would look after her brother who was mentally handicapped after the mother's death. However, when both the parents died within a few weeks of each other, the sister said that she was unable to cope, having a family of her own. The parents willed the house to their daughter, along with a request to allow the son to continue living in it. Clearly society here confronts a dilemma. Should the sister and her family be expected to provide support for the brother for what may be both their lifetimes, or renounce any right to the property?

Over the years, too, the relationship between carer and cared-for tends to become symbiotic, or even reversed. Brenda Lees mentioned several cases where the mother had become so disabled herself that it was <u>she</u> who actually relied on her son or daughter with mental handicap for her day-to-day care. Mark, who lived with his aged mother, came to the attention of the Social Service Department when he stopped attending the Adult Training Centre/Social Education Centre. It turned out that he was having to do literally all the physical tasks necessary to keep her and the house going. Up to the time she became ill, the mother always got up to get her son off to work. With the onset of her chest complaint she was then taking at least one hour to recover after getting up, so she was attempting to cope by rising at 6.00 am. Eventually this became impossible. The mother refused any help. She pointed to the tidy house as evidence of her continuing capability, but it emerged that it was her daughter who was coming in to tidy up.

The second problem is the attitude of older parents. They were brought up in a time when views of mental handicap and social welfare were very different. Social welfare was seen, at best, as charity, the acceptance of which indicated failure and a sense of shame. At worst, it was something imposed on people, irrespective of their wishes. For many of these older parents the name of of their "local" long-stay hospital, "Calderstones", is still inextricably linked to stories of children being taken away and locked up. As a result, visits from social workers and offers of help tend to be looked on with deep suspicion by older families. They see it as the thin end of the wedge, the ultimate aim being to get their son or daughter into an institution.

In one instance attempts had been made to visit the home of an older woman with mental handicap. Interviews were sometimes conducted through a crack in the door. The client lived with her brother as well as mother, the brother being particularly uncooperative, refusing to join in discussions at all. The Social Worker assumed that it was he who took over the job of dressing his sister after mother had become too feeble, and she pointed out the unacceptability of this arrangement. Though subsequently aware of the death of the mother, the social worker has no information on the present whereabouts of her client, although she assumes that a sister has taken her, rather than the brother whom she knew to be unwilling. Difficulties present themselves in knowing how to proceed. Should the social worker attempt to make contact when not requested to do so? Would the client be functioning at too high a level to fit in with the clients usually found in local authority old-peoples' Part Three accommodation if this option were considered?

A more explicit instance of suspicion regarding threatened institutionalisation can also be cited. The manager of the ATC attended by one 58 year old man with mental handicap received a message that the man had been seen walking in front of buses. Up to that time he had been quite able to deal with public transport, but as a result of these incidents it was decided that he should start using the Local Authority transport. His mother, who had actually asked for such transport over two years before, was very suspicious, seeing this as a ploy to get her son into a hostel by showing that he was incompetent. The main problem in engaging in effective social work is the very independence of this older group of people. Brenda Lees encourages younger parents to contact and meet the older ones. She feels that an introduction to modern attitudes to service provision comes better from other parents than from herself.

Family members often make assumptions about other relatives taking over responsibility on the death of the parents. This is frequently not justified and needs forward planning to avoid a crisis developing.

Social work intervention can only move at the pace the family is prepared to accept. Since older mothers tend to be very resistant to offers of help, this can be very slow indeed. Core Team Two tries to get the family to look realistically at their situation and to plan for changes, or a move to a new residential situation.

It is important to appreciate how different was the social and service milieu in the past with regard to mental handicap when considering these families. As noted above, fear of institutionalisation was very real, and often distorted patterns of life were established. Brenda Lees describes one mother of 75 with a son of 55. On the birth of her son the mother had advice from a relative that he should never see his reflection, never be around machinery, and never use a razor. As a result, she has spent the last 50 years with no vacuum cleaner or washing machine, and her son waxes his beard to remove it. Attempts to alter this way of life have been totally unsuccessful.

These difficulties are compounded by a range of deficiencies in community services to which our attention was drawn. First, the needs of people with mental handicap are not responded to by the Housing Department since the factor of stress or problems arising from the mental handicaps do not contribute to the points system on which allotment of accommodation is based. Active collaboration with the Housing Department to alleviate this situation is on-going at both the level of Social Workers and Rehabilitation Officer and between the Principal Officer responsible for mental handicap and the Director of Housing. Second, medical services are seen as inadequate relative to those provided for children. Indeed, there is a feeling that there is actual discrimination against older people with mental handicap, the long waiting list for orthopaedic services being cited. Further, monitoring of the appropriateness of prescriptions is considered inadequate. One notable exception to this state of affairs that was commented on in many discussions was that of psychiatric care where services for older people with mental handicap in the District Hospital were highly praised. Third, problems with allowances were also commented on, particularly the mobility allowance with its criterion of physical disability. Less problematical, though not invariably so, is that of attendance allowance, received by some families dealing with parents and relatives in the family home. In general, allowances related to the fact of increasing age were regarded as satisfactory.

The account we have given emphasises the specific problems of ageing people with mental handicap and their families. Clearly families do cope and provide a good family life through much of adulthood. Equally, however, problems do exist, in some cases in extreme and even tragic form. Only detailed and formal analysis of the balance of problems and their relation to ageing would permit a definitive statement on needs and resources.

One of the resources that contributes to dealing with the problems of the individual with mental handicap whose families encounter difficulties is the ***Olive Claydon Assessment Centre.*** The focus of this centre, which was set up seven years ago, is to assess individuals with mental handicap with respect to suitability for various types of placement and to provide initial training in implementing the intended plan. Assessment is extended over a six to 18 month period for up to 25 non-residential clients, generally in the younger age range. The centre has also been involved in assessment of clients in the *Home Making Scheme* which we describe below.

When older families cannot cope with their son or daughter with mental handicap, assessment of the individual and the resources required to maintain them is undertaken. Doris, a woman in her earlier fifties, could not be maintained in the home by her father when her mother became hospitalised. Following assessment at the Centre, she moved to a hostel for preparation for a return to her father with adequate input from a community nurse. In this and in other instances the emphasis is on assessment of both the older individual and the resources required to maintain the person in the most independent and ordinary life possible. For this reason staff of the Centre work closely with Social Work, Psychological and Nursing staff from Core Team Two. Within this arrangement the main input comes from the psychologists while Brenda Lees (Social Worker) liaises between the assessment centre and those involved in the next environment to which the person moves.

Core Team Three deals with adults with mental handicap living independently or in hostels. Their clients live predominantly in the Borough, though some live elsewhere, while some of these are in long stay hospitals. The Social Work component of this team consists of Martin Haigh (Social Worker) and Sue Griffiths

(Rehabilitation Officer). The Social Work component of Core Team Three does not deal with residents of Calderstones Hospital who are the responsibility of the *Home Making Team.*

Discussions regarding placement in the community follow yearly meetings of the multidisciplinary Core team arranged by the Hostel or ATC. These can involve Social Workers, Psychologists, Nurses and peripatetic home-helps. At such meetings a decision is taken regarding eventual community placement, dependent upon the client's own willingness and how realistic such placement is. Sue Griffiths and community nurses subsequently work with the selected client in his/her hostel until the necessary skills have been acquired. The hope that her support after the move could be reduced has not proved the case, sustained involvement being required to avoid the client getting into difficulties with everyday living. It was felt that there was a lack of adequate community support staff and that this led to the requirement that those living independently needed a high level of living skills. Transfer to the community would be facilitated if more staff were available.

In the judgement of this team, age is not seen as a potential barrier to community resettlement. They had been associated with relocation of at least four clients around pensionable age, 57, 64, 64 and 66 years. All moved to warden-controlled accommodation of the kind used by frail but not mentally handicapped elderly people. Two other individuals had followed this route prior to Sue Griffith's appointment. For younger people, it was a problem to become involved in the community given lack of employment opportunities and the often inappropriate nature of Adult Training Centre activities. More involvement in Further Education Colleges and other forms of education were deemed desirable. In some instances voluntary work was suggested, e.g. as in the case of a client who works in a children's nursery. In contrast, the feeling was that it was easier for older people to live a constructive life through retirement activities. It should be added, however, that others in Oldham with whom we discussed this possibility felt that lack of money severely curtailed such opportunities during retirement.

The picture presented by the social workers in

Core Team Three is markedly different from that of Team Two. No specific problems related to ageing were commented on and the process of relocation out of hostels was influenced primarily by competence not age. There is, then, a paradox. The more apparently normalised life of older people with mental handicap, often maintained by their families in the community without services, presents a greater problem to social services when age-related factors come into play, than is the case for those in the non-normalised environment of the hostels. This picture is confirmed if we consider staff views in the three Oldham hostels to which we turn in section 4.4.

4.3.2 Psychological Input.

The psychological service consists of three full time clinical psychologists under the immediate direction of Maggie Gibb. Their broad aim is, of course, consistent with the wider CMHT aims, and the NWRHA Model District plan, i.e. to promote independent living in the community and prevent institutionalisation. At a more detailed level support is given to families, and both support and training to direct care staff and other professionals. The psychologists, too, contribute to the planning and development of services and the creation of appropriate environments for people with mental handicap.

With respect to adult services, each of the two core teams described above has a psychologist working alongside Social Workers and Community Nurses. At weekly meetings of the Teams, the psychologist takes on the role of key worker for some individual clients and becomes jointly involved with other key workers when this is requested. The psychologist acts as adviser in programme planning and in the development of services when these are found to be deficient.

With respect to the facilities in Oldham described later in this chapter, the psychologists have a number of functions. With respect to Adult Training Centres, they act as key workers for some individuals and advise staff on the development of suitable programmes. They also arrange informal discussion groups with ATC staff on general issues such as leisure, self-advocacy and normalisation. In addition specific training courses may be put on in ATCs as well as other centres, e.g. the Olive Claydon Assessment Centre. Similar input to the three hostels in Oldham is provided by the psychologists, as well as to the *Home Making Scheme.* (This input is described when we consider that scheme.)

The roles and activities described above are concerned with all adults in the Borough, of course. With respect to ageing and elderly people with mental handicap, the psychologists' role is again to facilitate independent living, but also to enable such people to cope with important transitions in their life. Special interest has been shown in evolving a pre-retirement course, "The Step Forward Group", which we describe more fully below (4.5). Similarly, the issue of bereavement becomes a key issue as the parents and relatives of the person with mental handicap themselves age and die. Together with a nurse or social worker, the psychologist will give support in the home of both a practical and emotional kind.

4.3.3 Community Mental Handicap Nursing Input.

Community Mental Handicap Nurses are part of the Core Teams. Three are attached to each of the three Core Teams, and three more are responsible for resettlement of those returning from long-stay hospitals. Overall responsibility for this group rests with the Director of Community Nursing, Dorothy Simpson, while David Brunskill is Senior Clinical Nurse. Each team of three nurses deals with approximately 25 clients. As described by David Brunskill and Claire Gormanly (of Core Team Three), the role of the Community Nurse can be partially distinguished from that of the social worker by the intensive focus on the client rather than the wider pattern of relations between client, family, friends and services. The nurse spends more time living and working along side the clients in their homes, hostels or ATC/SECs. At a more specific level, behavioural assessments of strengths and weaknesses are made and goal plans developed. Where appropriate, these are directed to facilitating independent living with the CMHN progressively reducing his or her support.

With respect to community nursing, there has been

a growing awareness of the needs of elderly clients. In particular, specialisation has developed in relation to the needs of elderly parents of adults with mental handicap. It was emphasised that there is a need to "get the ball rolling" long before the parents can no longer cope. Here again, joint input by community nurse and social worker is called for with the former giving the intensive programmed input. Issues of bereavement and separation can also demand the professional attention of the nurses in the home.

Where a community nurse encounters problems of dementia in older clients, the preferred treatment will be through the GP and local psychiatric services. David Brunskill emphasised the need for changes in local services to cope with these problems where experience with this client group may be lacking. Failure here can still lead back to referrals to long stay hospitals. One important development in this respect is the formation of a forum between psychiatric staff and nurses under the auspices of the Mental Illness Joint Care Planning Team which should have special relevance to older people with mental handicap.

In many respects this role is seen not as a *nursing* role. Specific medical problems of clients living with their families will be dealt with by the Health Visitor who works along side the three Teams or the District Nurse, and ultimately through the General Practioner and other generic medical services. Therefore, the CMHNs work in close collaboration with Shirley King (Liaison Health Visitor) who, though based in Core Team 1, also works with adults. Her role is essentially to identify resources in the community for other members of Core Team Three, notably with respect to dentistry, chiropody, dietary expertise, medical services, and for younger people, family planning. Her involvement with clients is less than for the CMHT members though this becomes more intense when elderly people are considered. She has been involved in the pre-retirement groups noted above and described in 4.5 below.

Collaboration is, of course, essential with respect to other Core Team members. Is is felt that there are strong similarities between the Nurse's role and that of the Social Worker, despite the somewhat differing focus noted above. With respect to their role in assessment, the psychologist, Sally Cheseldine, is involved from the outset. Joint visits are made by two people, who may be nurses, psychologists or social workers.

4.4 Older People in Hostels

There are at present three hostels in Oldham, with the following distribution of people over 50 years of age:

Table 1.2:

AGE BAND:	50-59	60-69	70+
LOCATION:			
Wellington Lodge	5	10	1
Nuffield House	6	3	0
Willow House	8	5	0

From the point of view of our own exercise, Wellington Lodge is of special interest. This is a large Victorian house still bearing many of the features of its earlier life as a private home. As the Officer-in-Charge, Jill Milne, told us, until five years ago it provided for ambulant elderly people, into which group, three, new, older residents (ages 59, 63 and 70) with mental handicap were introduced. For these people the effect of integration was not beneficial. They began to display the withdrawn behaviour of the existing residents. A decision was taken to move the original residents to a new home and to make Wellington Lodge a home exclusively for older people with mental handicap. This transition took place in 1981, the original three responding positively to the introduction of their mentally handicapped peers with great pride in their own ability to "know the ropes". These transfers came from the other two hostels in Oldham, from the District Hospital and from a hospital for people with epilepsy in Lancashire (now closed).

Referrals come through the CMHT as well as from hostels and hospitals throughout the Borough. The

Officer-in-Charge invites prospective residents to visit the Lodge and have tea or to stay for a week or weekend. Ample time is given to discuss whether they wish to come on a permanent basis. The residents' ages are 40+ (1), 50+ (5), 60+ (10) and 70+ (1). The nature of the house is such that it is not possible to deal with people with severe physical handicaps and potential residents with such problems would be located elsewhere.

The backgrounds and personalities of these residents were diverse. Arnie, aged 57, has spent 24 years living in a locked ward at Oldham and District Hospital. On arrival at Wellington Lodge he had 'borrowed' clothes from the other residents' lockers, so used was he to communal clothing. Bedrooms remained 'wards' for some time. However, despite a past history of violence he had settled well into the Lodge. Terry (aged 62) came from Willow House. Until Christmas 1984 he had worked in a local mill as a labourer, then having to take voluntary redundancy. Ernest (aged 62) had lived with his sister who died in an accident and had moved via another hostel to Wellington Lodge. Henry (aged 58) had not been to the SSD when he lived in the community with his sister and brother-in-law prior to moving to Wellington Lodge 12 months ago. These individuals reflect the diversity of backgrounds of residents, none of which have presented any long term bar to assimilation in the Lodge. Though some residents have come from their families and the families of many of the others live in the area, contact is slight. In all instances residents' parents are dead, and in all only four receive visits from their relatives.

Residents share eight bedrooms, one of which is single, four doubles and one with three-person occupancy. The sex of a new admission is therefore taken into account, though opposite sex sharing is a possibility (of which no residents are availing themselves at present). Two residents (ages 67 and 65) at present wish to marry. Counselling is being undertaken, but Jill Milne is emphatic that should the couple marry it will not be publicised as some out-of-the-way event.

Assessment of adaptive behaviour is undertaken employing the standard assessment procedures used in other hostels. This permits continuity of assessment when transfers are made. Areas of special concern are broadly social skills and self-help activities such as ironing, cleaning and bedmaking. Residents share in most domestic activities, though not in cooking, an area to which Jill Milne feels they could well contribute. She also acknowledges the need for sex education for the 'engaged' couple described above as well as for other residents. With respect to other skills, a less formal approach is adopted. "Academic" teaching has been undertaken by Barbara Glover for the past four years (an arrangement set up by the Head of Literacy at the Community Centre in Oldham). For two hours each week a range of skills are taught - basic writing skills, numeracy, currency (coinage and value), time, colour and so on. It is moving to talk with a sixty year man who is able to sit and read - however simple the material may be - for the first time in his life. There is justified pride in such an achievement, and it is notable that staff in the hostel were fully acquainted with the programmes underway and were able to give help and support when required. Additional support is given by some 30 pupils from Hulme Grammar School. No formal record keeping is undertaken on these activities.

More broadly, Wellington Lodge's ethos is directed against childish behaviour on the part of residents, e.g. expectations regarding Father Christmas. Similarly, unacceptable public behaviour is discouraged. However, within the Lodge there are ample opportunities for leisure of a conventional domestic kind, gramophone records, wireless and television, as well as table games, snooker etc. Impromptu games and dances are also options when domestic activities have been completed.

Outside of the Lodge, holidays have in the past been spent at ordinary hotels in two separate groups at seaside resorts. Staff accompanying the residents on holiday in the past received 40 hours each week in wages but paid their own travel and hotel accommodation. No overtime was paid. Though in 1984 the Local Authority agreed to pay staff expenses, this contribution has subsequently been withdrawn. As a consequence, the residents of Wellington Lodge will not be having extended holidays and outings will be limited to day trips.

This lack of resources for holidays is paralleled by lack of funds for individuals to enjoy their spare time outside the hostel, particularly in relation to shows or cinema. The high hopes residents have of the quality of their life when they receive the state pension are doomed to disappointment when they realise there are deductions to cover their residential costs. Contact has also been made with two clubs for people with mental handicap, the Terence O'Grady Club and a Gateway Club. Those running the latter have, however, suggested the Lodge residents are really too old to attend.

Almost half of the residents attend Adult Training Centres/Social Education Centres, six going to Arthurs and Kenyon and two to Oakbank (see below). Another resident attends Oldham and District Industrial Therapy Unit. Hostel and Centre staff exchange visits for reviews, though it is clear that there are differing perspectives regarding the competencies of the individuals. Jill Milne has also established a link with Havenside Community Centre at Moorside. Here some residents can spend two mornings working on arts and crafts. Six go on a Monday and five on Wednesday. Four more have begun afternoon woodwork classes yielding some impressive pieces for the Lodge itself.

In line with the overall policy of care in the community, two developments are at present underway. First, as individuals, some residents are under consideration for placement in independent or ordinary housing. Indeed, some have already moved on making this transition successfully. Preparation in relevant skills is undertaken through training both in Wellington Lodge and in the community. Second, some degree of integration with generic services for elderly people is being considered. In conjunction with *Age Concern*, plans for an integrated hostel for elderly people with mental handicap and mental illness as well as frail elderly people are being considered.

The issue of use of generic services also has a bearing on medical care. Care from the local General Practice is arranged and referrals for specialist consultations follow in the usual way. Psychiatric support has been of high quality and four residents are under treatment for a range of conditions. None, however, show signs of dementia.

Psychiatric opinion is also required with respect to an additional problem, i.e. the ability of a resident to manage his or her own money. Three residents have their money tied up in the Court of Protection, one to the tune of £15,000. Judgement that an individual is competent to deal with his or her money is made by the psychiatrist as part of the on-going endeavour to enable residents to get access to their money.

Nuffield House is in marked contrast to Wellington Lodge with respect to physical appearence and residents. In contrast to the Lodge's homely, Victorian atmosphere, Nuffield House consists of a series of linked prefabricated buildings which local legend has it were used originally as barracks for prisoners of war. This is not the case, however, as the buildings were in fact purpose built as a residential hostel. The immediate area has become rundown as mills close and are demolished. Both buildings and setting are regarded as sufficiently unacceptable that it is planned to close the hostel and move its residents to ordinary housing in two years time. We will discuss the implications of this change for overall numbers moving into the wider community in the final section.

As a facility not specialising in elderly people with mental handicap, the majority of the 30 residents are under 50, six being over 50 and three over 60, all three, in fact, being 61 years of age. The broad context with respect to the origins of the residents, links with the SSD and other community agencies, is comparable to that of Wellington Lodge. The same assessment procedures are employed, and social and self-help training undertaken. Selected residents are considered for moves to independent community living or life in warden-controlled accommodation, and this process is not limited to younger people. Mrs. Haslam, the Acting Officer-in-Charge, with a background in geriatric nursing and Social Service work with elderly people, told us of two residents, a woman of 60 and a man of 65, both of whom had moved on into warden controlled flats. It is also clear, however, that though the number of older residents is less than in Wellington Lodge, two of the nine are more disabled than those in the Lodge. Mary, a 58 year old woman with Down's syndrome, has clearly degenerated both physically and mentally, spending her days in the hostel being cared for, but apparently unoccupied. Brenda was 61, frail in appearance and at that time with a broken arm.

The other seven over-50s attended the ATC/SEC (Arthurs and Kenyon) that occupies part of the same site. In this setting they were not seen as problematical, but again, in the area of leisure, difficulties were noted. These related to economic restrictions with respect to outside entertainment for those who could get about. For those who were house-bound, keeping them occupied in a constructive way presented major problems. In Mrs Haslam's judgement, Gateway Clubs are indeed unsuitable for many older residents and she suggested the development of over-50s clubs for those who would benefit from them.

While the review procedure for community placement from Nuffield is clear, the factors that influence transfer to Wellington Lodge are less so. Deterioration was seen as a major influence in considering this option, yet it appears that all Lodge residents are more able bodied than the two disabled women in Nuffield described above.

Willow House is physically quite different from both the other hostels. Built in 1966, it was one of the first purpose-built hostels in the country. It is set in a pleasant residential area consisting of housing of similar age. As explained by Stan Bartram, Officer in Charge, when originally opened, the hostel made provision for residents with a range of conditions including mental illness, delinquency and drug abuse. People were often accepted because of no available placement elsewhere. From 1978 onwards, however, it began to deal exclusively with people with mental handicap who are now its sole residents.

Many aspects of this third hostel are directly comparable to Nuffield House. This is so with respect to assessment, social skills training, orientation to the wider community, ATC/SEC involvement and leisure. However, special provision is made for people who are profoundly retarded and multiply impaired, with 14 downstairs places and special bathing and lifting equipment available. On the first floor are flats for more able people where residents are responsible for their own affairs with the exception of cooking their own main meals. Four places are for short stay placements.

Eight of the 25 residents are between 50-59 years and five between 60-69 years. Stan Bartram does not feel that these residents present any special problems. While opportunities for open employment have declined, all but one of these older residents attends an ATC/SEC. This is a 50 year old man with Down's syndrome, Maurice, who is becoming infirm and losing his sight. At the time of our visit he sat cross legged engaging in visual stereotypies. No specific programmes or treatment are considered necessary for him at this stage.

The view of carers in the three hostels differs markedly from the view expressed regarding older people living in the community. As a group the former are not judged to have social or emotional problems, or indeed special medical or psychiatric problems. This positive judgement must in part arise from the success of hostel staff in providing for them and in ensuring that generic services are made available. However, we would suggest that identifiable problems do exist even though staff do not in any sense feel unable to cope with these. Of the 38 hostel residents at least six require some form of psychiatric treatment, four as described in Wellington Lodge and the two Down's syndrome individuals who appear to have degenerative conditions. A further resident of Nuffield House appears very frail, and from conversation with her, perhaps not fully in touch. As we will show, the degree of disability in older people in the community will undoubtedly increase with hospital closure and this state of affairs will become more serious.

Second, in the relatively self-contained world of the hostels a range of potential social problems are mitigated. Most noticeable is the problem of leisure, particularly when the individual is unemployed or not attending an ATC/SEC. Lack of finance restricts outside activities though some people show considerable enterprise employing free travel passes to explore their local transport system. Here the communal nature of life in the hostels cushions these difficulties, ensuring the opportunity for developing friendship patterns and guaranteeing staff support.

In many respects it might be argued that both the issue of mental frailty and restriction of social opportunities do not differ from the experiences of the wider ageing population generally. This is certainly true, though specific problems associated with the fact of mental handicap will inevitably exacerbate this ordinary situation. Given this, however, it is important that we do not lose sight of this state of affairs simply because a majority of older people with mental handicap are not presenting overt problems in the hostel setting.

In contrast to the positive view of life in the hostels, we have suggested that professionals perceive major problems associated with ageing where the person with mental handicap lives with elderly parents. These problems exist not only with respect to their contemporary family life, but also with respect to the changing situation as the parents cease to be able to cope. This is not necessarily a problem, but can in extreme cases lead to major difficulties.

With respect to the movement into ordinary housing, it is clearly easier for professionals to control and cope with staff already living in residential facilities. Here, carefully constructed programmes can be implemented, sometimes over a time scale of years, and the transition effected with a high level of monitoring. In contrast, to effect change in the family situation is far more difficult without full family co-operation. In addition, even to identify future clients can be highly problematical.

4.5 Work and Retirement in the Community

Residents of all three hostels attend one of the two ATC/SECs. Indeed, of the 38 hostel residents over 50 years of age, 27 attend either Oakbank ATC/SEC or Arthurs and Kenyon ATC/SEC. Others have attended and have retired. Physically, and in terms of organisation, these two Centres are in marked contrast and provide distinctive environments for those who attend, with different consequences for older individuals. We will comment on the general character of Oakbank and Arthurs and Kenyon and then the place of older people within them.

Oakbank is a 90 place Centre, 18 of which are allocated for individuals who are profoundly retarded and multiply impaired. There are a further six places in what is described as Willow House Annex. The Centre is situated in an old residential area and was purpose built 20-25 years ago. The rooms were built with no dividing walls and there are no corridors, so moving from place to place necessitates walking through the rooms themselves. Privacy is therefore impossible. When Mrs Conley, the Officer-in-Charge, took over, she attempted to alleviate this problem by setting up large room dividers so that people working in the open areas are not directly overlooked by people passing through.

The facilities are being slowly built up as money permits. Most impressive was the partially constructed "special needs" unit. At the moment this is merely an empty room, but elaborate lifting and conveying gear has already been installed. This will make the moving of physically disabled people very much easier. As a result of the money being spent, Oakbank will become the principal Centre dealing with clients who are multiply impaired. Elsewhere, cooking facilities are being installed to enable clients to do some cooking for themselves. Other examples of recent capital expenditure included an impressive array of televisions, videos and games.

The atmosphere at the Centre is relaxed and friendly and obviously reflects the high level of mutual respect between staff and clients. One of the older clients told us that he acts as a stand-in to answer the phone when no staff are available, and apparently other clients also act in this capacity. Despite limitations of the physical environment, efforts are made to respect privacy. Thus, everyone is expected to knock on the "door" (ie room divider) before entering a group situation. At lunch times clients are welcome to use Mrs Conley's room freely, and during our visit this period developed into an informal meeting with some of the older clients. Lunch itself is organised in the same groups that clients work in, (about six groups in all). Clients do all the table setting, serving and clearing away.

The Centre is seen mainly as a Social Education Centre - very little contract work being undertaken. The education programme is designed to give opportunities for all clients, including those who are ageing and those who are profoundly retarded and multiply impaired. Clients work in small groups whose membership does not change from day to day.

Thirteen clients are over 50, nine being 50+ and four 60+. Of the fifty year olds, five live at home (three with sisters, one with parents and one alone). The other four live in Willow House. Of the 60+ group, one lives alone with support from his sister, two in Willow House and one in Wellington Lodge. Oakbank has no specific policy regarding age of clients. Mrs Conley stated that she sees the clients as individuals and is usually unaware of a person's age until they have a birthday party. (All birthdays are celebrated in this way, with all organisation and preparation done by the clients.) Clients are given the option to retire from work at any time, or stay on as long as they like. We were given the example of one man who retired to look after his sister who was dying of cancer. After her death, he moved to Willow House, returning to the ATC/SEC two years later. The option to stay on is also regarded as giving some relief to elderly parents who are often looking after the client. Policy with respect to ageing is seen as being concerned not only with Centre activities, but also with what is occurring elsewhere in the client's life.

The second ATC/SEC, Arthurs and Kenyon, is located on the same site as Nuffield Hostel. It was one of the first industrial training units to be established in England, in December 1954. Such was the innovatory character of its change of use that a report appeared in the *Hospital Journal* and *Picture Post* in the early 1950s. This training unit originally catered for people who were mentally ill as well as those who are mentally handicapped, and "Arthurs" and "Kenyon" were separate facilities for men and women respectively. Such segregation has long ceased and Arthurs is now a Social Training Unit for 48 younger men and women, while Kenyon is more vocationally orientated. The Social Training Unit concerns itself with literacy, budgeting, cookery and general independence training. Kenyon consists of a sewing room where soft toys are made and repairs undertaken though not on a contract basis. Both light and heavy industrial work is undertaken. In addition to these activities, clients on "this side", i.e. Kenyon, have access to a prevocational unit and a general interest room where various tools are available.

There is no special unit catering for people who are profoundly retarded and multiply impaired, though there is a special group of more severely handicapped people.

All of the 157 are involved in one of the two sections, 48 in the social training unit and 88 in the vocational sections. While the majority have a mental handicap, the earlier mixed composition of the Centre is reflected in the fact that there are still 21 people with mental illness attending Arthurs and Kenyon. All in the Social Training Unit, however, are mentally handicapped. Of the people with mental handicap, nine fell in the 50-59 age band and eight in the 60-69 band. The majority of these lived in their own home either alone (two 50 year olds and one of 60), with a sister (two 50 year olds), or parent (one 60 year old). Six clients (four 50+, two 60+) lived in Wellington Lodge and three in Nuffield House (two 50+, one 60+). Two others (50+ and 60+) were in the Home Making Scheme (see below) and the remaining two in unspecified hostels. Thus, there is great variation in the residences and degrees of independence in this group that reflect all the domestic settings discussed in the report apart from long-stay hospitals.

While the move from social training to vocational activities can be seen as a positive progression, it does carry with it in this setting the suggestion that the the client is unlikely to benefit from further social education. There is an age-related factor here that tends to suggest that the move occurs in some cases when the client is considered too old to benefit from further social training. Thus, the over 50s are concentrated exclusively in the vocational units in Kenyons. These older people have the opportunity for work or leisure in this setting, though it was suggested that some decline to engage in either set of activities.

This state of affairs naturally leads on to the issue of retirement from work and indeed from the Centre itself. As with Oakbank, the formal decision to retire is in principle up to the older client. However, advice on the desirability of retirement <u>is</u> given to clients as also is advice on continuing work if the client inappropriately moots the issue of retirement. Policy regarding retirement for older people with mental handicap is not consistent nationally and opinions differ widely on how and whether retirement should be required. In discussing retirement policy with Centre staff and then seeing how this policy is viewed by hostel staff and, by report, by parents, we gained the impression that at this local level some clarification is called for. How can the option of retirement be presented to a person without some suggestion that this is what should now happen? Certainly hostel staff feel that, however unintentionally, pressure is placed on older clients to retire. It may in fact be less ambiguous to adopt a specific policy of retirement related to the statutory age in the wider community. We describe in the next section one such policy implemented in a long-stay hospital.

Whatever policy decision is adopted, it is clearly desirable that when retirement is approached, preparation should precede this event. This has been emphasised by Frances Hunt of *Age Concern* who in conjunction with Sally Cheseldine and other members of the Oldham CMHT has established a formal pre-retirement course: **"Step Forward"**. While aware of the lack of clarity with respect to retirement in services in Oldham, both have urged the importance of such preparation. The meetings for people with mental handicap have been held in an ordinary District Health Authority (DHA) house. Cheseldine (1985) describes the topics covered in "Meeting the Needs of Older People with Mental Handicap": Health in Retirement; Money Management; Benefit Entitlement; Home Safety; Voluntary Organisation; Cooking on a Budget; Tester Visits to Various Leisure/Adult Centres.

The material in these broad topics had to be adapted for people with mental handicap. Contributions to the course were made by all three CMHT professions as well as a Home Safety Officer and head of a Further Education College.

The eight participants were selected on the basis of perceived needs, i.e. those who frequently had little to do in the day and/or had limited social contacts. Those attending the course came from both the community and Wellington Lodge, and were sufficiently independent to travel to the house alone. Their ages ranged from 55 to 68 years. At present an evaluation is being undertaken through analysis of pre- and post- course interviews. The aim is to see how far specific information has been assimilated and how far the course has had an impact on the lives of the participants (Cheseldine 1985). In Frances Hunt's judgement, the basic needs of older people with mental handicap with respect to retirement are probably not fundamentally different from many of those of older people without such a handicap.

A more broadly based view of the ageing process and preparation for retirement has been developed by Jill Milne ("Mentally Handicapped People Retiring in a Residential Setting: A programme for developing opportunities for elderly mentally handicapped people and preparing staff for their role in provision", 1983). Here the assumption is that older people with mental handicap have untapped potential with respect to the abilities they can develop and the extent to which they can cope with work and leisure. The retirement programme is therefore part of the wider view of increasing this competence through education and training in order to ensure that all their resources are brought to bear on their lives in retirement. To create the right conditions for this adaptation, appropriate staff training and supervision are seen as essential conditions for making sure that preparation for retirement and life during retirement itself are optimised. Seen in this way, preparation for retirement is not "simply" a matter of individual training, but the creation of a whole context that will make this stage of the person's life progressive and worthwhile.

An important aspect of this context is the nature of day care provision. Neither homes nor hostels are necessarily geared to cope with the presence of the retired person for 24 hours a day. Statutory services in the North West are limited in this respect, though *Age Concern* does have centres in Oldham (and elsewhere) into which people with mental handicap are being introduced. This is being done gradually and the example was cited of the introduction of an elderly woman with her 30 year old son with mental handicap into a day centre in order to give nonhandicapped attenders the opportunity to accept such a person. Frances Hunt also drew attention to older people with mental handicap who had become volunteers, and pointed out that such people had real potential regarding their contribution to various agencies.

4.6 Outside the Community

We have already indicated that many Oldhamers live outside the Borough, a significant number in Calderstones Hospital, a medium size group in Brockhall Hospital, and a number of individuals scattered around the North West. To give a fuller account of the diversity of lives led by older people with mental handicap, we must also say something about these people.

For purposes of this discussion we will concentrate mainly on Calderstones Hospital which is located in the country about 30 miles from the centre of Oldham, near the village of Whalley in Lancashire. Within the acknowledged limitations of a large, rural, long-stay hospital, staff share many of the ideals regarding the education and training of the 981 individuals at present in the hospital. It has been accepted by staff, however, that the stated aim of enabling the resident "...to develop... to his maximum potential in order that he may lead as full, independent and unrestricted life as possible, consistent with what is best for him and for the society in which he may reside", is most appropriately realised by transfer to the community. Policy is to return, where possible, residents to their original towns, of which Oldham is one, while developing suitable programmes in the hospital, some of which, as we shall see, relate to ageing. Within the whole hospital population, Table 1.3 below gives the numbers for given age bands over 50 years. The grand total of 501 represents just over half of the total population of 981, i.e. 51.1 per cent.

We can say a little more about these older residents by reference to Hospital assessments based on National Development Team (NDT) categories (NDT 1985). In brief, these categories reflect in a broad way the degree of handicap and type of care required:

Group I

Criteria: Competent in all areas of self-help, ambulant, continent, no behaviour problems, not disruptive in any way.

Could be discharged home to hostel immediately without any special facilities necessary for management, apart

Table 1.3:

Age Band	Males	Females
50-59	98	68
60-69	80	66
70-79	82	61
80-89	21	21
90+	1	3
TOTAL	282	219

from those normally provided in a local authority hostel. Some may be appropriately placed in group homes.

Group II

Criteria: Continent, ambulant, almost completely self-sufficient with mild problems of behaviour which could be corrected with a short period of treatment and self-help training. A number could be considered for self-care training units.

Should be suitable immediately for discharge home or to a hostel, where, after a short period of pre-discharge training they would be suitable for discharge to a group home or other form of independent living in the community.

Group III

Criteria: Continent with lapses at night. Some are mildly over-active with occasional mild behaviour problems. All are said to be easily managed and would benefit from specific training. If discharged to a hostel, staff ratios would need to be higher than those in groups I and II.

Considered suitable for care in the community after intensive training, and with greater supervision than is usually required by those in Groups I and II.

Group IV

Criteria: Severe double incontinence, multiple physical handicaps, severe epilepsy, extreme hyperkinetic behaviour, aggression to self and others.

The majority require some form of long-term residential care with a higher staff ratio than is required by those in Groups I, II and III.

In terms of these categories the percentages at each of our age bands, based on hospital assessments, is as follows:

Table 1.4:

Percentage of Calderstones Hospital Residents Over 50 Years of Age in Relation to NDT Categories:

	NDT CATEGORY			
AGE	I	II	III	IV
50-59	3.0 (5)	19.3 (32)	39.2 (65)	38.6 (64)
60-69	6.2 (9)	25.3 (37)	28.8 (42)	39.7 (58)
70-79	7.7 (11)	12.6 (18)	32.9 (47)	46.9 (67)
80-89	14.3 (6)	7.1 (3)	23.8 (10)	54.8 (23)
90-99	0 (0)	50.0 (2)	25.0 (1)	25.0 (1)

We can clarify this picture by considering the distribution of additional impairments with respect to age. First, given that 51 per cent of the hospital population is over 50 years, we can compare the presence of such impairments in the over and under 50s as given in the hospital records. With respect to blindness, there is no indication of a marked increase in relation to age. Of those in the hospital described as "blind", 54.3 per cent are over 50, a small deviation from the 51 per cent expected if there was no effect of age. The same position obtains with respect to physical handicap, where the over 50s show 50.4 per cent of moderate and 48.4 per cent of severe physical handicaps, i.e. there is no greater likelihood of them being physically handicapped than is the case for the under 50s. With respect to mobility, there is a small age trend indicating that problems are greater in the over 50s than the under 50s: 56.4 per cent vs 43.6 per cent. 42.2 per cent of the over 70s are reported as having mobility problems. Deafness, on the other hand, shows a clear age trend, 63.2 per cent of those described as deaf being over 50. At 50+, 4.2 per cent are deaf, at 60+, 8.9 per cent, at 70+, 9.8 per cent, at 80+, 19.0 per cent and at 90+, 33.3 per cent (though in the last case this is only one of three people).

Although the NDT categories are extremely broad and imply that particular characteristics are invariably correlated, e.g. "extreme hyperkinetic behaviour" and "multiple physical handicaps" appear together in Category IV, when this is not necessarily the case, this information on the older Calderstones population obviously has implications for their lives in the hospital and their eventual reincorporation into the community.

Given the large proportion of elderly clients in Calderstones, it is not surprising that many wards and services are devoted wholly to this group. The hospital has, for two reasons, followed a policy of grouping by age. First, cohorts have grown up together and now have established patterns of friendship. Second, age on admission is regarded as an important criterion in deciding on an appropriate ward placement. There are at least 20 wards with a predominance of people over 60.

The medical needs of these older residents were not perceived as being any greater than those of other residents. A physician visits the wards daily but is usually not required as it is rare that anything more than a minor problem is encountered. Nevertheless it was acknowledged that problems related to chronic infirmity did exist and that facilities were not sufficient to deal adequately with these. There were no reports of dementia among older residents.

Education courses of various kinds are being run constantly. There are presently 68 day and evening classes per week, funded by Lancashire Education Authority. Older people apparently attend particular classes for years on end primarily to maintain longstanding friendships with their teachers, rather than out of a particular interest in the subject matter. Recently the hospital was offered six evening class places at Whalley, but could not take them up due to lack of transport.

As mentioned above in passing, friendships develop and endure in this setting. Two couples are presently living together and there have been three previous marriages. Two blind people were also going to marry and were awaiting resettlement, but one had to return from the training flat to the hospital. There are only a few mixed wards because of the difficulty of modifying the existing building design to include separate bathrooms. The resettlement flats are, however, all mixed. Several members of staff have been trained in sexual counselling.

In contrast to the somewhat variable situation with respect to retirement in Oldham itself, a formal policy decision was taken in 1984 that all residents retire from work activities at the age of 60. This means that there is a whole range of work-type activities they no longer attend, but instead are offered a variety of leisure facilities and less demanding occupations. Thus older residents cease their basic training and take up pursuits such as leisure clubs and eurythmics. All people who have retired have gone on to these structured leisure programmes. Originally these activities were envisaged as drop-in centres, but in practice many residents end up staying all day, putting in at least as many hours as they previously spent at work. Difficulties in occupying retired residents resulted when they became increasingly frail. In addition, ways had had to be found to give the opportunity for retired residents to make up the incentive money they lost when ending work. Many retired residents continue to act as if they are still attending work. The staff told us that some people need constant reminders that they "no longer need to attend".

With respect to the role of the volunteer network, Calderstones has almost more volunteer help than is needed. Thus Trinity Youth Club in Clitheroe has for 12 years been involved in virtually all hospital activities, from helping on the wards to mobility within the grounds and leisure. There is also considerable interest from local schools, but no input from either MENCAP or Age Concern. There is concern that this intensity of focus on the hospital may be lost as residents move into the community and become dispersed, an on-going process to which we now turn.

4.7 Moving into the Community

In our meetings with both the Core Teams and Hostel Staff we heard of many successful moves from family homes and hostels into the community by older people with mental handicap. For example, Hanna had, at 64, moved from Wellington Lodge into the community and John from Nuffield House to a warden-controlled house. Several other people were at various stages in preparation for such a move. Indeed, longer term policy is aimed at closure of the hostels, with Nuffield House to be closed in 1988. An even more significant contribution to this stream will be the return of Oldhamers from the long-stay hospitals and other settings outside the Borough. While a small number are in scattered, identifiable institutions (seven in Brockhall and one in Cranage Hospitals, two in Lisieux Hall) the large majority are in Calderstones Hospital.

We referred above to the North Western Regional Health Authority plan for hospital closure, noting that residents would be discharged without specific regard to their age. We pointed out that taken across the hospital over 51 per cent of residents were over 50 years. Here we will now consider the pattern of discharge realised and anticipated over the period 1983-1988, and characteristics of the group with respect to age and ability.

The Regional plan proposes a pattern of discharge of residents for all major Districts from which they originally came. It must be emphasised that the

Table 1.5:

Projected Pattern of Discharge of Oldhamers to Oldham Metropolitan Borough from Calderstones Hospital: 1983-1988

Year	1983	1984	1985	1986	1987	1988
Event						
Death	-	3	2	2	2	1
To resettle	-	12	12	12	12	16
Admissions	-	3	2	1	1	1
Total Remaining	92	80	68	55	42	26

projections shown in Table 1.5 are illustrative and not a rigidly predetermined plan, though they inevitably will provide an informal yard stick against which to assess progress. In reality, our working figure for 1985 is 67, not 68, 27 of whom are over 50 years. This percentage, 40.3 per cent, is less than the 50 per cent over fifties for the whole hospital, implying that some Districts will have relatively more older people to make provision for than others.

The age distribution and NDT Category for these people are as shown in Table 1.6. It may be seen that the majority of these residents fall in Categories 3 and 4, 23 out of 27. We have no directly comparable NDT data for the hostel residents in Oldham, but our observation of them would suggest that, with a few exceptions, they are not as impaired as this older hospital group. The percentage of these older residents exhibiting mild behaviour problems is actually greater than for the younger Calderstones residents, 12 (44 per cent) vs 10 (25 per cent), though only one resident over 50 exhibited a severe behaviour disorder (3.7 per cent) vs 7 (17.5 per cent) of under 50s. Again, we do not have comparable figures for Oldham itself. However, despite the generally unproblematical picture of

Table 1.6

Age Groups and NDT Categories for Oldhamers over 50 years of age in Calderstones Hospital:

NDT Category:		1	2	3	4
Age Band	Total				
50-59	13	0	1	5	7
60-69	5	0	0	4	1
70-79	7	0	3	4	0
80-89	2	0	0	0	2

behaviour in the hostels, several examples were given of mild problems, e.g. abuse of other residents, to suggest that hospital residents over 50 years of age actually do not present more serious behaviour problems than those in hostels.

We can, however, also consider the return to the community with respect to those who have already left the hospital and returned to Oldham. The usual procedure for resettlement of a resident from Calderstones involves consultation between the LA and DHA. A plan is formulated, and forms filled in, one for each resident, which are vetted by the RHA for conformity to the Model District Plan. Tom McLean, Director of Nursing Services at Calderstones, acts as advisor to the RHA in this process. The release of funding from Hospital to Community is now calculated in direct response to named people being moved into the community.

With respect to Oldham, however, a single project, the *Home Making Scheme*, involving funding through a lump sum was initated following two and a half years of negotiation between the NWRHA and Oldham Social Services Department. A pilot scheme to resettle 16 Oldhamers in their Borough was agreed in July 1983. This had the approval of the Social Service Committee and was submitted to the Joint Care Planning Team. A commitment was given to the development of as normalised a life as possible, in ordinary houses in the community.

The scheme started in March 1984 when the first group of four residents moved to Oldham. These were selected by the Resettlement Team in Calderstones, rather than members of the Home Making Team themselves as they had yet to be appointed. The appointment of Janet Holmes and Susan Henderson came when the first four residents were living in the resettlement training bungalow in the hospital grounds. A nurse from the resettlement team then introduced Susan Henderson to these residents and the other 81 Oldhamers. From these, a second group of three was selected, one of whom decided that he wished to live alone and has been supported by the scheme to live independently - he receives regular visits from Susan Henderson, and can call on Homemakers as necessary. The person living independently moved out in May 1984, and the two people he chose not to live with moved out in March 1985. The next four were also selected at this time, subsequently leaving in October 1985. At the time of our interviews, three of the four groups had returned to Oldham, and a fourth was in preparation. This group of three residents left the hospital subsequently. By the end of the pilot phase, 15 residents had moved out, one of whom subsequently died. Thus, 14 of the originally intended 16 had come out by the end of 1985. Parenthetically, we might note that the projected figure in the RHA plan was 24 residents by this date, though as indicated, this was only intended as a very rough projection and no time pressure was exerted on the Resettlement and Home Making Teams to meet such a target. It is emphasised that the pace of discharge must be determined by the time taken to prepare the residents for the transition. Parents are free to be involved in the resettlement process, although the travelling and time commitment involved in making frequent trips to Calderstones has made this very difficult for many people. The last group has had more involvement due to the fact that meetings have take place at the core house in Oldham rather than Calderstones.

The core house was established in Oldham to provide a temporary base for clients who can use it for short periods in the early stages of their transition to Oldham. For many it is their first experience of being in an ordinary house for many years. In order to set up the clients' houses, the requirements of the scheme were communicated to the Local Housing Department and to Housing Associations. In the event, three houses are Local Authority tenancies and two are from Housing Associations. All are let directly to the tenants as a group and all groups submitted housing applications while still in the hospital. Staff supporting the 14 tenants consist of one social worker, one (residential) Officer-in-Charge, two ATC Instructors, and sixteen Homemakers, 20 people in all (as of July 1985). Formal links exist with other SSD and health professionals such as the CMHT.

With respect to day-to-day activities, nine spend part of their time at ATCs using the rest of their time learning to run their new home with Homemaker supervision. The final group of four had not yet made final decisions. Some tenants were attending further education classes while two were involved in voluntary work. Only one individual has found employment and this was only temporary. While staff have reintroduced tenants to local leisure facilities, financial restrictions here and in relation to holidays have curtailed activities as in the hostels.

When the scheme was initially set up it was envisaged that the 24 hour support would be gradually withdrawn as clients became more accustomed to community living and more proficient in self help skills. This has not so far been possible. Janet Holmes believes this is because of the very long adjustment period necessary. They are looking to the idea of reducing staff time by paying close attention to "low-risk" times - eg 12.00 midnight to 7.00 am. Also, it appears that each individual has times of greater and lesser need, and in this respect the relationships between clients are important. Thus, one danger in leaving certain combinations of clients unattended is that one may come to dominate the others. Janet Holmes and Susan Henderson list all the risks for each person before they make the move to the community

A daily diary is filled in by staff and, where possible, by clients. Goal plans are formulated by the

Home Making team. Clients are assessed every six months using a modified version of the CMHT psychologist's assessment, although it is anticipated that these will be needed less frequently as they settle into their new mode of living.

Unlike hostels, staff have nothing to do with clients' finances. Clients have their own money to go out, although they very often need to be introduced to the range of purchases available, since they may have previously had few interests. Staff do not get reimbursed for out-of-pocket expenses incurred during, for instance, taking clients to the pub, although there are some returns on items like cinema outings. The Home Making scheme pays for staff use of house facilities.

Generally speaking the resettlement has run very smoothly. Initial reactions from neighbours have on occasion been hostile, but soon settle down. One neighbour wrote complaining about the change of use of the building, but the change was still authorised. One or two of the houses have reported incidents of children mocking clients in a cruel fashion. One neighbour complained about one tenant making noises in the street.

As already noted, both the Local Authority and the Hospital's stated policy is to have no age bar on relocation. Individual cases can readily be cited supporting this claim, the oldest person to move into the community so far being a woman of 80. When she moved, a staff member moved with her to give daytime support. Although it is not possible to undertake a statistical comparison between the age and ability composition of tenants and the hospital residents generally, the weighting in the Home Making group does appear to be towards more able younger residents (and indeed, men rather than women, 10 to 3, in June 1985) with only three out of 13 being over 50 and the oldest 61. Additional handicaps, too, do not add up to profound retardation and multiple impairment. Among the tenants we find:

- 1 deaf (very limited hearing and also diabetes)
- 2 partially sighted
- 4 claiming mobility allowance, although reasonably ambulant
- 1 Zimmer frame and wheelchair user

- 3 with epilepsy

An evaluation of the Project to date has been undertaken by the CMHT psychologists with respect to the physical situation, living arrangements, general activities and relationships among tenants. With regard to the first three areas the outcome is positive with tenants living in an essentially normalised context, albeit with considerable support from staff. With respect to relationships among tenants less success is claimed. "In the first house established, there was very little evidence of true friendships having developed among the four men." "In the second house there was some evidence to suggest a fairly friendly relationship between the two men although this also became strained at times." "In the third house, it was unclear for what reasons two men were sharing the house. They appeared to have very little in common and the relationship between them appeared strained and to have worsened with time." (Robinson and Steward, 1985, The Home Making Scheme: Progress Report, Oldham Metropolitan Borough Council, Social Service Dpartment.) Wider social contact was limited for all houses.

It is of significance that some aspects of the situation appear to have been readily normalised while others have not developed as wished. Normalisation with respect to decor and house location are readily achieved and are in the immediate control of both tenants and staff. Normalisation of the social ecology is far harder to achieve and is a little understood process. It is clear that despite the meticulous, prolonged and sensitive efforts to achieve good social groups, relationships are strained. To these individuals the ready solution of moving elsewhere that most of us would adopt are not available, and it may be that futher normalisation can only be effected through provision of a wider range of flexibly achieved options.

It is doubtful if any generalisations can be made either about the factor of increasing age in formation of the groups or in their maintenance. The Home Making Team did not consider older residents of Calderstones to be completely cut off from their Oldham roots, though there does seem to be some evidence of relocation producing stress. Thus one man has started to have fits again after being free of them for years. The oldest client to move out, 61 years old, although not showing stress has failed to develop any new interests. He likes to go back to Calderstones to talk to his old friends and see the work he used to do. Staff have tried to get him interested in the local day centre, and he now attends woodwork classes at Havenside. Calderstones staff also report that some people suffer relocation trauma, but did not consider this was age-related.

Taken with the limited evidence for success in the social groupings in the homes, it is possible that some older people in Hospitals will have even greater difficulties in forming new relationships, just as can occur when nonhandicapped elderly people are relocated. Tom McLean hopes that, as clients move out, some staff will move with them, and attract unqualified people in the location of the housing cluster. He feels, however, that staff transfers over long distances will have to involve promotion in order to be attractive.

Not all of those making the move into independent life in Oldham have done so from Calderstones via the Home Making scheme. In our discussions with hostel and ATC/SEC staff many examples were cited of older people who had made such a transition either into warden controlled flats or settings involving reduced dependence on service providers. In her study of community placement, Flynn (1986) has described the lives of 16 such individuals in Oldham, seven of whom are over 50 years (three of these over 60 years). We draw here on two of her accounts of which convey some of the concern her work expresses regarding their lives.

Mr Dawson is now in his mid-fifties and until the death of his parents some years before had lived in the family home. He had moved from there to lodgings and then back to the home where he lived with considerable support from other members of the family. From there he moved into a hostel where he lived for eight years. Much of the instability in his life over this period resulted from drinking, this contributing to further management problems in the hostel. From the hostel he moved to a council rented house where he lives with considerable support from his brother who lives in a neighbouring street. It is apparent that life in this setting presents several difficulties. He is subject to intimidation by local youths which has in large measure been dealt with by his brother's intervention with "...a couple of lads from work." Very close supervision of management of finance and house keeping is required by Mr. Dawson's social worker if he is not to drink his wages away. The social worker also acknowledges that Mr. Dawson is lonely, though with respect to community placement he is regarded as moderately successful. His brother, however, is less enthusiastic, seeing Mr. Dawson as an intrusion into his own family that he has had to endure all his life.

In contrast, Miss Spencer, who is 61, lives in a comfortable bedsit in a two storey block of warden controlled bedsits. Like Mr. Dawson, she has moved many times since the death of her mother, from family home to old peoples' home, to private residential facility, to general hospital (because of nutritional problems), to a hostel for people with mental handicap (Willow House). There she remained for fourteen years, moving first to a three woman tenancy in which she was unhappy because of personal incompatibility, then to her bedsit. This is well looked after and she expresses general satisfaction with her life in her home. She receives support from her peripatetic home help. Though dependent on such support for her own decision making, this placement is regarded as a success.

As one would anticipate, the degree of success in making the transition to community living whether through the Home Making Scheme or via the other paths in Oldham that facilitate such a transition is highly variable. The tailoring of programmes to individual needs is not an exact science and the degree of support required is not readily predictable. However, for the small number of older people who have made this transtion, age *per se* has not been a bar. This conclusion, however, must not be over-generalised as the oldest people involved in these schemes have been early to mid 60s. The extent to which the pattern of successes and difficulties identified with younger individuals with increasing age remains to be established.

From the above information it is possible to give an approximate picture of what needs will have to be met in Oldham with respect to older people with mental handicap in the coming years.

4.8 Developing Patterns for Older People with Mental Handicap

We can now consider the general position regarding future provision for older people with mental handicap in Oldham with respect to the demands to be made on services. This can be approached most directly by representing some of the figures given above with respect to those already in Oldham and those that we expect to move there in the next few years. In relation to the timetable of the Regional plan for hospital closure and the projected closure of Nuffield House, 1988 would be the hoped-for date. In reality this process might extend beyond into the 1990s. We are, however, considering this change as occurring over a three to five year period.

First, let us resummarise the position with respect to people with mental handicap who are already in Oldham Borough but not in hostels:

Table 1.6:

Numbers of People over 50 years of Age Living in Oldham Borough:

Age:	50+	60+	70+	80+	Total
Location:					
Home Making	5	1	0	0	7
Independents	4	3	0	0	7
Home	9	5	0	0	14
Home (est)	6	3	1	0	10
Total:	24	12	1	0	37

Let us now consider those who are projected as coming into the community, i.e. residents of Calderstones and Brockhall Hospitals, other residences outside the Borough and residents of Nuffield Hostel. Here we add in figures concerning other Oldhamers on the Register but outside the Borough:

Table 1.7:

Oldhamers who will return to the Borough, who are over 50 years of Age:

Age:	50+	60+	70+	80+	Total
Location:					
Calderstones	13	5	7	2	27
Brockhall	4	2	1	0	7
Other	4	4	4	0	12
Nuffield House	6	3	1	0	10
Total:	30	14	15	3	56

Clearly these figures can only be rough as we cannot be certain that all these people will choose to return to Oldham. It is possible that this "loss" will, however, be compensated for by indivduals who leave the other two hostels and move into the community, for plans are already being developed in this respect. Given that the policy will be to locate all 56 in ordinary housing, this means that the number of people over 50 living in ordinary housing will be 94 as against the present 37, an increase of 148 per cent, a figure that may be reduced somewhat as mortality takes its toll.

It is equally clear that a large proportion of the additional people will be far more severely handicapped than those already in ordinary housing. This can be inferred from the NDT data from Calderstones that we have presented and the presence of hearing impairment and problems in mobility in particular. Thus, 23 out of 27 Calderstones residents over 50 years fall in NDT categories III and IV. We should also note that there will be some increase in dementing people, though given the nature of our informal study we have only identified the one women in Nuffield House described above. Thus not only will there be a substantial increase in the percentage of people, but the degree of disability will be much greater with consequent implications for service provision.

Several elements of such provision have been identified and commented on. First, an input to training and everyday maintenance will be critical and will be at least of the order described in the Home Making scheme and in Flynn's study. In a significant proportion of cases even greater intensity of such maintenance will be called for in terms of staff time. Second, additional costs will be incurred with respect to modification to homes, equipment and adjunct services such as laundering clothing and bedding. Some preparation has already been made with respect to day care in the development of the special needs unit at Oakbank ATC/SEC. Third, simply at the level of numbers, GP rolls will be increased and other medical services will have to meet both physical and psychiatric needs.

It is clear that this increase in numbers and general level of disability will have funding implications. The most recent estimate of costs per client is £14,680 each year. This costing assumes "...a need to continue with present staffing levels on the very rough and ready basis that any economies resulting from reduced staffing levels for some groups will be absorbed by those groups containing a more severely dependent member." We would suggest that this hope may be over-optimistic, i.e. that there will be absolute increases in the money needed to maintain some of the more dependent older clients. Thus, the figure of £1,379,920 needed to maintain 94 elderly people in Oldham may be exceeded. The extent to which this figure represents an actual increase in costs depends on the shortfall between it and the extent of RHA funding and savings on closure of Nuffield House. A sobering additional thought is that these figures "only" cover the group with which we are concerned, and a somewhat larger number of under-50s will also be requiring a similar service.

The challenge, then, is a considerable one. In varying ways throughout the country Local Authorities will confront the need to provide a service for older people with mental handicap, a challenge that is indeed being faced throughout much of the world.

Chapter Two

EPIDEMIOLOGY

Considerable attention has been paid in the literature to the topics of mortality and prevalence. Such statistics permit us to estimate the size of the service population, and to make projections of future changes. With regard to the population of elderly people, whether handicapped or non-handicapped, it is clear that any changes in the near future are going to be in the direction of increasing numbers rather than reductions. As Jacobson, Sutton and Janicki (1985) point out, increases in the size of the service population present potential crises for human service systems. Increases in the absolute size of the elderly population will require a corresponding increase in the allocation of resources, and it is essential that such changes are made in time to meet the needs. In this respect, changes in the allocation of resources to older people with mental handicap deserve particular attention. At the present time, about 90 per cent of older people with mental handicap live in institutions of one sort or another. This compares with a figure of about 5 per cent for non-handicapped people (Blake, 1981). Institutional care is expensive, so it is not surprising that service providers are anxious to shift the burden of care onto the community where possible, which usually means the client's immediate family (Finch and Groves, 1980; Walker, 1981). For people with mental handicap, this shift to community care is a relatively new phenomenon. The novelty of this process, coupled with the fact that a large proportion of people with mental handicap are now surviving to old age, presents considerable uncertainty for the level of future service provision. What _is_ clear, however, is that the number of elderly clients is increasing, and that this group of people probably represents a population who are particularly vulnerable to institutional admission or readmission due to the impact of functional impairments related to the process of ageing (Jacobson *et al.*, 1985). It is thus vitally important to make the best possible projections of client numbers and predicted longevity.

1 MORTALITY AND LONGEVITY

There is obviously a sense in which a person's age at death is an utterly reliable statistic. Despite this, however, a number of points have to be borne in mind when interpreting figures from surveys of specially selected populations.

First, and probably most important, are the criteria which have been used to define the population being observed. In the present context this relates to two considerations. First, what are the criteria being used to define someone as having a mental handicap, and, second, where has this population been drawn from? The first of these points, the definition of handicap, bears directly on the perceived mortality, and hence age structure, of the population. People with severe mental handicap tend to suffer from a greater number of medical problems and have a shorter life expectancy than people with a mild level of handicap. It can therefore be seen that criteria for including clients in a mortality study should be clearly stated. Indeed, there is a good case for arguing that a major part of the research effort should be directed towards clarification of the sample definition. Only in this way can meaningful and accurate interpretations be made from the resulting data. In practice, however, such efforts have been rarely undertaken. Studies sometimes divide the observed population into "severe" and "mild" categories, without clarifying the method used to achieve these classifications. If the categories are derived solely from hospital records there is good reason to doubt the reliability with which this process is achieved (Crisp, 1985). Obviously there is no way that information from previous studies can be retrospectively made more accurate. Caution has been urged, however, in the interpretation of these kinds of data.

The second of these points, the source from which the observed population has been drawn, is likely to have a considerable impact on the overall structure, characteristics and average level of handicap of the sample. People living in hospital <u>may</u> be resident simply because the policy of institutional closure is still proceeding and will take a long time to complete. On the other hand, there is evidence that many people living in hospital are more dependent or more fragile than many clients living in the community. At the present time, the extra level of care required by these people is more likely to be available in the traditional hospital environment. As a result, the population characteristics of hospital residents and community residents are markedly different. The poorer health of many people living in hospital is reflected in the fact that mortality rates tend to be higher than for community residents or for a representative cross-section of people with mental handicap. It should also be noted, however, that it is not always the people in <u>poorer</u> health who remain in institutions. Stroud *et al.* (1984), in a survey of four different types of care setting, report that all the sample members who scored in the <u>mild</u> range lived in the <u>institutions</u>. Stroud *et al.* suggest the reason for this is a generational effect. When these people were young it was generally accepted by most families that an institution was the proper place for a person with mental handicap. Today these high-functioning people remain there through choice. They consider it their home, and most have refused community placement even when group home placements have been available in their county of origin.

In addition, two factors are likely to result in elderly clients being over-represented in institutional populations. First, the process of ageing increases the probability of developing a condition which demands hospitalisation or intensive nursing care. Second, there is evidence that the process of community relocation has an age bias towards younger clients, (see the figures for Calderstones Hospital presented in Chapter 1). The older residents tend, for one reason or another, to stay behind. Since the policy of community relocation has been operating for ten or fifteen years, figures for the age structure of hospital populations over this period have shown a corresponding increase in the proportion of elderly clients. It is important to bear these two points in mind when interpreting mortality statistics from institutions. On the one hand, mean age at death may be rising, due to improvements in medical care. On the other hand, the mean age may be falling, since the population increasingly comprises fragile people in poor health. Also, the number of people dying in a given institution may be rising, simply because a larger proportion of the residents is elderly.

To the extent that institutional populations are "captive" it is likely that information on the residents will be more complete than for people living in the community (Tarjan *et al.* 1973). However, the above points need to be kept firmly in mind when evaluating the results of institutional mortality surveys.

The statistics used to express longevity and mortality can also give some confusion. One of the most frequently quoted indices in this connection is the mortality rate. This measure has three essential elements (Lilienfeld and Lilienfeld, 1980):

1. A population group exposed to the risk of death
2. A time period
3. The number of deaths occurring in that population during that time period.

Thus, Lilienfeld and Lilienfeld (1980) give the example of calculating a mortality rate for the whole population of the USA in 1980. In that year there were 1,892,879 deaths in a population of 212,946,226. This yields an overall mortality rate of 8.89 per 1000 people.

This figure represents the overall non-specific mortality rate with respect to age. In other words, all deaths are included, irrespective of the age the person had attained. Studies of survival in people with mental handicap, however, often quote mortality rates by age bands. Thus, calculation of a mortality rate for 50-60 year old people with mental handicap would proceed by taking the total number of deaths in the sample of people within that age band, and dividing it by the total number of people in that age band who were alive during the middle of the period. These age-specific mortality rates can then be compared with corresponding rates for other populations, usually non-handicapped people. Thus, a mortality quotient of 1.0 would indicate an identical mortality rate for the two populations within that particular age band. A quotient of 1.7 would indicate that the handicapped group has 1.7 times the number of deaths of the corresponding non-handicapped age group.

The mathematics involved in these calculations are straightforward. An important point to bear in mind, however, is that the relation between increased mortality rate and associated reduction in life-expectancy cannot be directly calculated. An example will clearly demonstrate this. Forssman and Akesson (1970) give the overall mortality rate for people with mild mental handicap as 1.7 times that of the general population. In terms of life expectancy, however, this corresponds to an expected reduction of only 2 per cent.

A further word of caution. A rise in the mean age of a population does not necessarily mean a rise in the number of elderly people. A mean rise could equally be caused by an increased number of people surviving to a lower age, say adolescence or middle age.

A clear way to portray the age structure of a population is to plot age against population size. Even with this kind of representation, however, there is one final and most important point to be made about the interpretation of mortality statistics. Changes in overall age structure of a population can be produced by changes in fertility as well as by improvements in medical care. Indeed, Siegel (1980) points out that actual or potential changes in the number of births far exceeds the effect of changes in survival. In making this statement Siegel was obviously referring to the general population, since medical advances have led to dramatic reductions in mortality for some groups of people with mental handicap. It is not possible to predict the extent to which continuing improvements in the standard of medical care will further increase the longevity of people with mental handicap, although it does seem likely that a law of diminishing returns will operate. Changes in overall population structure will, however, continue to be a major contributing factor to the number of older people with mental handicap who are seeking services. A look at the 1981 Census figures for the population of the UK demonstrates clearly the expected magnitude of these fluctuations. Two peaks in the distribution are clearly visible, the post-war boom of the 1940s and an even greater peak in the 10-20 age group. In 1981 there were 2.7 million people in the age range 45-49. Assuming a national death rate of ten per thousand in this age group (Richards and Siddiqui, 1980), the number of people now in the 50-55 age group remains substantially unaltered from this figure. In fifteen years this age band will correspond to the post-war boom period, when the number of people in this group will rise nearly 50 per cent to approximately 4.0 million. A further fifteen years will see an even greater rise to 4.5 million. Whatever improvements in lifespan are seen over the next 30 years, these changes in overall population structure will have a corresponding effect on the number of older people with mental handicap.

1.1 Mortality Surveys

As already mentioned, mean age of a population is not a very useful statistic for expressing the expected lifespans of older residents, since changes in admission and discharge policies can greatly influence these figures. Many studies do, however, give information on age at death and numbers of people surviving beyond 50 years of age. Carter and Jancar (1983) analysed resident records from the Stoke Park group of hospitals for the period 1930-1980. During the first 25 year period 93 per cent of females and 99 per cent of males died before the age of fifty. In comparison, the second 25 year period saw only 40 per cent of women and 57 per cent of men dying before this age. Mean age at death showed a corresponding change, from about 18 years in the period 1931-35, to 59 years in 1976-1980. Mortality rates for the whole hospital population improved from 18.8 per thousand in 1931-35 to 14.3 in 1976-80. The current figure compares reasonably favourably with that of 11.9 for the general population.

Forssman and Akesson (1970) report the results of a survey on all people living in institutions or going to day schools for people with mental handicap in Sweden. The information was collected during the years 1955-59, and covered 12,903 individuals. During that period they found the proportion of people over 50 years of age to be 13.2 per cent. Longevity of people in five-year age bands from 0 to 60 was compared with corresponding rates for the general population. Over the age range 5-60 Forssman and Akesson found a stable relation between the two sets of figures, indicating a small reduction of life expectancy of between 3 and 7 per cent. Beyond the age of 60, however, life expectancy of people with mental handicap showed a much more sizeable reduction of 15 per cent compared with the general population.

Richards and his co-workers (Richards, 1969; Richards and Sylvester, 1969; Richards and Siddiqui, 1980) have analysed extensively the records from St. Lawrence's Hospital over the period 1963-78. They report (Richards and Siddiqui, 1980) that percentage of people over 55 years of age increased steadily throughout the period. For females, the percentage increased from 23.4 to 40.9, while the proportion of males increased from 15.9 to 24.7 per cent.

The pattern of mortality in people with Down's syndrome indicates a somewhat shorter lifespan than other people with mental handicap (Richards, 1969). The death rate for people with this condition is high in early childhood, drops to a level lower than that of other people with severe handicap, and then rises rapidly in the midle years (Richards, 1976). Collmann and Stoller (1963) present a life-table for people with Down's syndrome living in the Australian state of Victoria during the period 1942-57. The calculated mortality quotients show a death rate at age 10 which is 2.65 times that of the general population. By age 50, however, the comparative death rate is <u>40</u> times greater. Very few of the people with Down's syndrome lived beyond 50 years of age at that time.

By the beginning of the present decade many more people with Down's syndrome were surviving beyond 50, although the mortality rate continues to show a sharp rise over the age of 40 (Richards, 1969; Thase, 1982). In comparison with other people with mental handicap, individuals with Down's syndrome have equal or slightly longer life expectancies up to middle age, but then show a rapid decline.

Comparisons of community and hospital populations consistently show a higher death rate for the institutional group (McCurley *et al.*, 1972; Miller and Eyman, 1978). However, this difference is due chiefly to the different population stuctures in respect of age, level of handicap and current medical status (Richards, 1969). There is likely to be a complex interaction between characteristics of the service population such as health status and level of handicap, and administrative variations including admission and deinstitutionalisation policies. This makes it difficult to isolate the relative contributions of each factor (Lubin and Kiely, 1985). At the present time there is no clear evidence that an institutional life style *per se* has any effect on longevity.

The general conclusion fron these surveys is that life expectancies for people with mental handicap have been constantly increasing during the past 50 years. Advancements in perinatal care have resulted in a much greater proportion of impaired children surviving the first year of life, so that Fryers (1984) is able to report a current death rate of only 10 per cent among children with Down's syndrome, compared with 50 per cent in earlier studies (Carter, 1958; Hall, 1964; Oster, 1953; Record and Smith, 1955). Mortality rates among adults similarly declined in the early part of the century as former major causes of death were brought under control. Tuberculosis, pneumonia and influenza were responsible for 50 per cent to 60 per cent of deaths among people with severe handicaps, a death rate which was as much as 13 times that of the non-handicapped population (Conley, 1973). Studies which are widely separated in time illustrate clearly this change in lifespan. Jacobson *et al.* (1985) quote figures from two studies separated by more than 40 years. Dayton *et al.* (1932) found that 28 per cent of the people alive at 10 years survived to 60. In comparison, Balakrishnan and Wolf (1976) reported 46 per cent to have survived.

This overall reduction in mortality, coupled with changes in the admission and relocation policies of hospitals, is fundamentally altering the age structure of institutional populations. The evidence from prevalence studies, reviewed the next section, indicates that the vast majority of older clients still live in institutions, relatively untouched by the process of relocation into the community.

Despite increases in longevity, the life expectancy for people with mental handicap continues to be lower than for the general population. The more severe the level of handicap, the greater is the chance that an individual's life span will be short. Forssman and Akesson (1970) found an overall reduction in life span for people with mild mental handicap to be only 2 per cent. In comparison, their observations on clients rated as severely handicapped showed a 7 per cent reduction. People with a profound level of handicap are considerably more at risk from respiratory disease than individuals in the mild or severe categories. Thus, Chaney, Eyman and Miller (1979) found that 75 per cent of people with profound handicap die from this cause, compared with 58 per cent of the less handicapped. The reduction in life expectancy caused by Down's syndrome has also been well documented (e.g. Deaton, 1973; Collmann and Stoller, 1963; Forssman and Akesson, 1965).

In discussing the relation between mortality and level of handicap, Tarjan *et al.* (1973) point out that the prevalence of severe and profound levels of handicap is greatest in the younger age groups and decreases with age. Organic conditions and genetic syndromes are usually identified by the age of five years, so the decrements in age-specific prevalence essentially result from the higher than average mortality associated with these conditions. Mild mental handicap, on the other hand, has a low prevalence during the preschool years, rising sharply during the school years and dropping rapidly thereafter. This essentially functional category of handicap, i.e. resulting from (a) a reduced ability to learn and demonstrate adaptive skills, and (b) a low measured IQ, is often not accompanied by somatic signs. This lack of associated genetic or medical conditions accounts for the reduced mortality.

1.2 Sex Differences in Mortality Rates

It is well known that, in the general population, women live longer than men. Indeed, the social implications of a long period of widowhood and consequent social isolation gives cause for concern (Siegel, 1980). For people with mental handicap this sex bias appears to be substantially the same (Carter and Jancar, 1983; McCurley *et al.*, 1972; Primrose, 1966). However, the generally shorter life spans and different patterns of mortality necessitate a careful evaluation of the available information. At the present time the presence of a sex-differential in mortality may not carry with it the same implication of social isolation in old age which it does for the general population. This is because most older clients already live in institutions of one sort or another. On the other hand, increasing numbers of people with mental handicap are living independently, or in groups which are sufficiently small that one can envisage a situation in which all the group members are elderly. For this reason it is important to consider the likely effects of differential mortality rates on the male/female composition of an elderly client population.

Surveys giving data on relative mortality rates over a period of time consistently demonstrate two features. First, females live longer than males; second, lifespan for men has increased markedly over the past 50 years, while female longevity has shown a much smaller proportional improvement (Richards, 1969; Richards and Siddiqui, 1980; Richards and Sylvester, 1969). Thus, Richards and Sylvester (1969) found the mean age at death for men to have risen from 32.8 years in 1946-50 to 47.7 in 1961-65, i.e. an increase of fifteen years. In comparison, the mean lifespan for women in 1946-50 was already 50.9 years, rising to 52.6 by 1961-65.

A closer look at this apparent differential, however, suggests that the picture may be somewhat more complicated. Jacobson *et al.* (1985) present data from registries in New York and California. They conclude that the gender distributions actually reveal more males in the 55-64 age band, and more females over the age of 65 years. In other words, women are more likely to reach an age which would be described as elderly, but show at least as great a risk of death in their earlier years. This conclusion is supported by the observation of Polednak (1975) who found the mortality rate from respiratory disease to have a higher overall level for women than for men. Also, Richards and Siddiqui's (1980) analysis of mortality trends in people with Down's syndrome showed a greater number of females surviving beyond the age of 50, but a greater overall mean age for <u>males</u>.

1.3 Causes of Death

Extensive documentation is available on causes of death among institutional populations of people with mental handicap (Carter and Jancar, 1983; Chaney, Eyman and Miller, 1979; Deaton, 1973; Forssman and Akesson, 1970; Lubin and Kiely, 1985; McCurley *et al.*, 1972; Polednak, 1975; Richards and Sylvester, 1969; Thase, 1982). Apart from giving a wealth of detail on the particular populations under consideration, it is notable that one cause of death predominates in all these studies. Respiratory infection accounts for about half of all deaths within institutions for people with mental handicap (Carter and Jancar, 1983; Tarjan *et al.*, 1968). In comparison, only 5-7 per cent of deaths in the general population are attributable to this cause. Conversely, the biggest killers among the general population, cardiovascular conditions and cancer, account for only 15 per cent of institutional deaths among people with mental handicap (Carter and Jancar, 1983). This presumably reflects the fact that heart disease and cancer show a strong age relation. The lower mortality rate results from the fact that there is a smaller proportion of elderly people than is found in the general population.

Despite the comparatively low level of cancer-related deaths, there is evidence that these cases are on the increase among people with mental handicap. Carter and Jancar (1983) found the death rate from cancer to have increased markedly over the period 1931-80. Carter and Jancar conclude that the increase in due mainly to the increasing longevity of clients. They do, however, note that there is a particular increase in certain gastro-intestinal cancers. This may, they suggest, reflect factors other than the increasing longevity alone.

The mortality of people with Down's syndrome is known to be very high in early childhood, decreasing thereafter, and then rising again in middle age. The commonest primary causes of death in young children are respiratory infections and congenital heart malformations (Carter, 1958; Forssman and Akesson, 1965; Record and Smith, 1955; Richards, 1969). Thus, Hurst and Logue (1970) found 50 per cent of their sample of people with Down's syndrome to have died from congenital heart disease. Once early childhood has been survived, however, causes of death among people with Down's syndrome demonstrate a similar pattern to that of other people with mental handicap (Richards, 1969). Respiratory disease is therefore the commonest cause of death in older people with Down's syndrome. It has also been noted, however, that people of all ages who have Down's syndrome are more at risk of death from leukaemia than are members of the general population. It has been suggested by Fryers (1984) that there are two reasons for the preponderance of respiratory mortality. First, people with severe handicap tend to suffer a variety of additional medical problems which shorten life and specifically render them susceptible to respiratory infection. Second, they are likely to suffer from an inadequate level of self care, which will also increase the possibility of infection. Fryers concludes: "However, probably the most important factor in differentiating the pattern of deaths in severe intellectual impairment from the rest of the population is the difference in age structure. Although they may never achieve quite the same pattern, all these factors are changing and we can expect them increasingly to approach normal patterns" (p. 141).

2 THE PREVALENCE OF OLDER PEOPLE WITH MENTAL HANDICAP

Estimating the numbers of people with mental handicap is an exercise which presents considerable problems to the epidemiologist. A number of surveys published over the past 60 years make estimates of this kind, although it is only very recently that any work has appeared which is devoted specifically to the elderly client population (Janicki and MacEachron, 1984). The main impetus for conducting studies of this kind has been a desire to make projections of future population size for the purposes of service planning. Apart from making direct projections, figures from demographic surveys can also be used to make extrapolations beyond the actual population sampled. Thus, Sweeney and Wilson (1979) estimated the numbers of older people with mental handicap in a given geographical region by relating an overall prevalence rate for mental retardation in adults to the age structure of the general population. They then compared this figure with the number of such clients known to service providers. This comparison indicated a marked discrepancy between the estimated number of older clients and the number that were actually in touch with services. On the basis of these figures, Sweeney and Wilson concluded that older people with mental handicap were "denied, ignored or forgotten" in respect of service provision.

Before accepting a conclusion of the kind made by Sweeney and Wilson it is obviously essential that the estimate of client numbers is accurate. A detailed discussion of epidemiological methods is beyond the scope of this book. Instead, some of the basic problems will be outlined. Interested readers may like to consult one of the standard texts on this subject (e.g. Lilienfeld and Lilienfeld, 1980).

An accurate measure of the true prevalence of mental handicap in relation to age requires:

(a) A clear and rigorously applied definition of the population under consideration. Many studies fall short of this requirement. For instance, prevalence rates are sometimes quoted for "mild" and "severe" handicaps, without indicating how these classifications were applied to individual clients.

(b) A method of surveying the client population that ensures no groups or individuals who should have been included have in fact been overlooked. For institutional populations this presents no real problem. Not all people living in the community, however, may be known to service providers. As a result, surveys relying on agency contact tend to underestimate the prevalence.

Estimates of the number of older clients have sometimes been made from studies completed 20 or 30 years previously. In these cases there are a number of potential sources of variation and error which need to be considered when projecting from a young population to an older one, or from a study conducted many years ago to the present day. These variables include differential mortality of people with handicaps, changes in fertility of the overall population, improvements in perinatal care, increasing efficiency of early screening and differential migration. (In a situation of substantial population shift, people with mental handicap are more likely to remain static).

Of these various problems the most important is probably the lack of a commonly agreed definition of mental handicap. Unlike many medical conditions, mental handicap is essentially socially defined. Each study has tended to use its own definition, with the result that reported prevalence rates differ greatly. Thus Conley (1973) reports two studies whose estimate of prevalence differ by a factor of 46.

Studies focusing on <u>severe</u> handicap as opposed to mild or moderate handicap tend to yield more reliable estimates of prevalence since the population is more easily defined and identified (Lubin and Kiely, 1985). Nevertheless, problems of definition do exist with respect to all categories of mental handicap. Such categories are essentially socially defined, and even where IQ is employed as one criterion, as in the American Association on Mental Deficiency classification system, some measure of social adaptation is invariably employed. In their conclusion to a review of the positive value of psychometric testing in the field of mental handicap, Berger and Yule (1986) note that "...a diagnosis of mental handicap should never be made on the basis of an IQ score alone."

When considering community populations one way of ensuring that all clients are included is to conduct a door-to-door survey of the entire neighbourhood. A household survey of this kind obviously has the advantage of approaching closer to the ideal of estimating true prevalence, so it is not surprising that estimates from this type of research tend to yield higher rates (Malin *et al.*, 1980). Indeed, the limitations of agency surveys were highlighted by Richardson and Higgins (1965) in their study of Almanace County, North Carolina. Both agencies and households were surveyed. Rates based on the household survey were twice as high as those resulting from agency contacts. On the other hand, other issues also need to be considered. Tizard (1964) distinguishes true prevalence from what he refers to as an "administrative prevalence rate". This he defines as "the numbers for whom services would be required in a community which made provision for all those who needed them", implying that not all of the prevailing population would necessarily require provision. The problem of working from the true prevalence rate to an administrative one is that no such move can be made without the implication of an underlying policy of care. Thus Malin *et al.* (1980) advocate caution in dealing with surveys which quote "X per 100,000 population" being in "need" of some sort of provision. They point out that what is really being said is "there are X per 100,000 of this sub-population, and we think that they need service provision".

In the USA administrative prevalence and true prevalence differ greatly, at least for older clients, (e.g. Sweeney and Wilson, 1979). In the UK, on the other hand, the existence of the National Health Service and comprehensive Social Services ensures that a very large proportion of clients are known and supported, although there is still likely to be a shortfall between total client numbers and those known to service providers.

It is not proposed to present a detailed review of figures from the various prevalence studies that have included older clients in their sample. Excellent reviews can be found in Conley (1973) and Kushlick and Blunden (1975). Instead, what is shown in Table 2.1 is a set of estimates of the <u>actual number</u> of clients with mental handicap over 50 years old to be found in the entire population of England and Wales, based on the figures from each of these studies and from appropriate Census figures. The studies are shown in date order.

The figures for Lewis (1929) indicate a much higher proportion of people with a moderate degree of handicap compared to those in the severe category. This probably reflects differences in the system of classification being used at that time. It is also notable that Fryers' (1984) estimate for the prevalence of severe handicap is nearly three times as high as any of the others. This situation comes about mainly because

Table 2.1:

Estimates of the number of people with mental handicap in England and Wales, extrapolated from the results of six studies

Study and sample	UK Population (millions)	Estimated 50+	
		Severe	Moderate
Lewis (1929). Six urban and rural areas of England and Wales	39.9	6,223	28,980
Kushlick (1961). Salford (from Mental Health Service Registers)	46.3	13,507	10,097
DHSS (1972). Census of hospital residents in England and Wales	49.0	13,650	8,224
Fryers (1984). Salford (from register)	48.5	42,755	-
Hogg and Moss (1987). Oldham (from hospital, hostel and Social Service records)	48.5	29,294*	-

*People in the Oldham study represent all individuals known to mental handicap services. They are not classified according to level of handicap.

Fryers' prevalence rates for the over 60s are around three per thousand, compared with between 0.4 and 0.5 for the other studies. Why should such a large discrepancy have occurred? One major factor is undoubtedly the immense reduction in population which Salford has seen over the past 50 years. As Fryers points out, it is probably true that a falling population leads to inflated prevalence rates of any group which is less mobile than the population in general. Thus, declining inner cities tend to have high proportions of elderly, disabled and immigrant people. It is not therefore surprising that the "double jeopardy" of being both elderly and handicapped is more strongly manifested in a geographical region of this character.

From the point of view of service planning, the important conclusion to draw is that substantial numbers of people with mental handicap are now surviving into old age. On the basis of current research Jacobson *et al.* (1985) suggest that: "it is reasonable, therefore, to estimate that 40 per cent or more of those persons who are mentally retarded survive to the age of 60".

Chapter Three

MEDICAL AND PSYCHIATRIC ISSUES

The effects of age on people's physical and mental health have major implications for service planning. Indeed, the presence or absence of good health is one of the most important factors in determining the extent to which a person is capable of maintaining an independent life. In this chapter we consider the various sources of information which may help to inform service planners who are working with older people with mental handicap. It will be seen that there are many gaps in our knowledge, and a consequent need for appropriate research in a variety of topic areas.

1 PHYSICAL MEDICINE

The physical health of older people obviously reflects the fact that they (a) generally suffer from a greater number of medical conditions than younger people, and (b) increasing severity of handicap is associated with an increasing number of medical complications. Beyond these two established facts, however, the fundamental question is: do people with mental handicap suffer from a greater number of *age-related* medical problems than their non-handicapped peers, and do age-related medical problems differ in kind between the two populations? In respect of service planning, these would appear to be crucial issues. The review which follows includes the majority of published sources relating to this topic.

While a number of papers appear to address these issues by drawing attention to particular medical needs of older clients, many have failed to present data which would readily provide any answers. Thus Gress (1979), writing from a nursing perspective, reviews the US legislation relating to older citizens and to people with mental handicap. However, their medical needs, referred to in the title of his paper, are not assessed. A similarly sympathetic response to the needs of this group is expressed, from the point of view of the General Practitioner, by Allardice and Crowthers (1975). Again, however, there is no indication of the likely extent of these needs. In a recent book on older people with mental handicap (Janicki and Wisniewski, 1985) there is an extensive chapter devoted to musculoskeletal ageing (Rudelli, 1985), but not a single reference in which the processes have been related specifically to people with mental handicap. The same limitation applies to a chapter in the same book on nutrition, ageing and mental handicap (Huber, 1985). Thus, despite the detailed information presented within these articles, there is little basis for concluding that older people with mental handicap require any further attention than their non-handicapped peers. Naturally, people with mental handicap do suffer from increasing infirmity with age. Edgerton and Berkovici (1976), in their 12 year follow-up of residents discharged from Pacific State Hospital, found clear evidence of age-related deterioration in health. In 1960, all cohort members were in good health, with few individuals being troubled by serious or chronic illness or injury. Twelve years later, however, nine of the remaining 30 people who could be traced had major disabling ailments, and one was terminally ill.

From an epidemiological standpoint, the health of older people can be assessed from two types of data. Mortality studies can take advantage of the most reliable general estimates provided by the census bureaux of most advanced countries (Bourliere and Vallery-Masson, 1985). There is a vast literature relating to disease-specific mortality. One must remain aware, however, that mortality statistics provide only one of the sources of information on health. They give no direct information on the quality of life of people who survive. Also, it should be noted that the apparent precision of information available from death certification is sometimes misplaced. There is no doubt that the ability to diagnose certain conditions has increased with the advent of sophisticated technology, and that there is a concern to shift death certification from vague and ambiguous categories such as "senility" to ones that are as explicit as possible (McMahon *et al.*, 1960). On the other hand, Muir-Gray (1985) points out that precision and accuracy have to be clearly distinguished from one another, and he gives evidence that the desire to become more precise has led to inaccuracy in death certification in old age. At one time it was common for doctors to assign cause of death to "senility", the ninth revision of the International Classification of Diseases still having "old age" as a cause of death. However, the proportion of deaths ascribed to simple "old age" has fallen, so that it now appears that a larger number of people die principally as a result of the ageing process than the number who are classified as doing so.

As with the general literature, most of the studies of health in people with mental handicap have been mortality studies, (reviewed in Chapter 2). Thus, Richards (1976) entitled a chapter "Health and Longevity", but made reference only to cause of death. Nevertheless, it is worth noting in this context the preponderance of respiratory mortality found in studies of this kind, since it is matched by a similarly high level of non-fatal occurrences amongst people with mental handicap. McDonald (1985) has suggested that the probability of respiratory and middle-ear infections is increased if the client is bed-ridden, a state which in itself is more likely to occur in people of greater age. The increased incidence is the result of a variety of causes including backflow from the process of being fed on one's back, obstructed drainage of Eustachian tube secretions, impaired coughing and sneezing reflexes, and difficulties with sucking and swallowing which increase the likelihood of regurgitation into the nose and ears (Blackwell, 1979). McDonald points out the importance of correct position for feeding in reducing these problems. In general, McDonald concludes that inadequate or insufficient attention to potentially lethal infections and respiratory disorders has led to the high mortality rates seen in the past, (reviewed in Chapter 2). She advocates a focus on prevention and aggressive medical intervention to improve health and survival in people with mental handicap.

Medical

With regard to non-terminal medical conditions, two studies have reported on the needs of children with mental handicap (Smith, Decker, Herberg and Rupke, 1969; Wright *et al.*, 1962), while Leck, Gordon and McKeown (1967) report on the medical and nursing care being received by 1652 clients living in mental handicap hospitals. This last study is particularly extensive, involving a series of studies over a 9 year period. The client group included all Birmingham residents living in hospital, each individual being assessed by a doctor and a nurse. The survey gives details of treatment being received, and of unmet medical needs. The general conclusion was that half the residents needed no medical treatment of any kind, and that two thirds had no need even of basic nursing. Unfortunately, Leck and his colleagues analysed their findings in respect to only two age groupings: under 16 years and over 16 years.

The fact that Leck *et al.*'s (1967) study extended over a nine year period gives an indication of the time and resources necessary to gain detailed information of this kind. It is difficult to use retrospective information from medical records, due to potential unreliabilities of recording. Also, one must bear in mind that the level of medical input in the client's past history may not accurately reflect medical *needs* at that time. Indeed, McDonald (1985) has recently drawn attention to the existence of medical problems due to neglect or poor management (Adams, 1972; Blackwell, 1979; Nelson and Croker, 1978; Smith, Decker, Herberg and Rupke, 1969). Notably, she makes reference to the high incidence of orthopaedic disabilities including scoliosis, contractures and dislocated hips which is found in non-ambulatory institutionalised patients (Brown, 1963; Hoffer, 1981; Rinsky, 1981). The vast range of conditions to which elderly people are susceptible, and the correspondingly large amount of information, makes a comparison of disease-specific mortality in handicapped and non-handicapped people a highly specialised and technical subject. On the other hand, the main concern for care providers who are dealing with older clients is the likely range and prevalence of serious medical conditions in *living* people, rather than the likely cause of death in the future. For these reasons, the remainder of this section focuses on morbidity rather than mortality.

1.1 Morbidity in the General Population

Unlike the data on mortality, there are few studies giving reliable information on the prevalence of major diseases in middle aged and elderly people (Bourliere and Vallery-Masson, 1985). Among the more recent is that of Waern (1978) on men aged 50 and 60 years of age in Uppsala. Table 3.1 summarises the general findings, from which it can be seen that there is a general increase in morbidity with age, particularly in the categories of circulation, endocrine and metabolic disorders. Corresponding to this increased morbidity is a very large rise in the intake of drugs. In the younger group, 9.6 per cent of the subjects reported a daily intake, compared with 38.1 per cent of the older men.

Table 3.1:

Prevalence of diagnoses in health surveys of 50 and 60 year old men in Uppsala, Sweden (Waern, 1978).

Groups of diagnoses according to the International Classification of Diseases (3rd. Rev. Ed.)

Group of diagnoses	50-year-old men (n=2322) Subjects %	60-year-old men (n=331) Subjects %
Circulatory diseases	5.9	31.3
Mental disorders	1.5	3.0
Endocrine, metabolic	1.2	12.1
Nervous diseases	0.8	3.6
Musculoskeletal disorders	0.7	7.9
Respiratory diseases	0.3	2.4
Tumours	0.2	1.5

A similar study on 70 year old people in Gothenburg (Svanborg, 1977) shows a sharp increase in the prevalence of circulatory diseases, musculoskeletal disorders and mental illness. About 3 per cent in this age group suffered from advanced handicap or disease to such an extent that institutional care was necessary. High rates for cardiovascular and musculoskeletal disease have also been found by Vallery-Masson *et al.* (1981) in a study of a male managerial population (see Table 3.2). It is notable, however, that the prevalence rates given by Vallery-Mason *et al.* are very much higher than those of Waern, particularly in the musculoskeletal category, where Waern gives a figure of 31.3 per cent prevalence in 60 year olds compared with Vallery-Masson's estimate of 78 per cent. Such an increase is most unlikely to be due simply to the increased age of Vallery-Masson's sample (65 years as against 60 years). Rather, it indicates the problem of comparing different studies whose methodologies, diagnostic criteria and classification are not standardised, although it must also be borne in mind that ethnic factors can also play a role in determining disease-specific mortality. In the USA, for instance, hypertension is twice as prevalent among black as among white adults (Bourliere and Vallery–Masson, 1985).

Table 3.2:

Mean prevalence rates of major disease categories in a sample of a French managerial population at retirement

Affected system	Non-retirees (n=51)	Retirees (n=105)
Musculoskeletal*	79	73
Cardiovascular	55	41
Digestive*	37	41

*Every subject suffering from a chronic disease of the two systems concerned was included.

Despite the problems in comparing studies of mortality, there is no doubt that circulatory diseases are the most common of the major disease categories in elderly people, of which the majority are heart conditions (Williams, 1985). In patients over 65 years old, heart disease accounts for more than 70 per cent of all cardiovascular deaths in many countries including the UK (Scottish Health Service, 1981) and the USA (Rodstein, 1956). A high prevalence of heart disease has been observed in many health surveys of elderly people (Acheson and Acheson, 1958; Droller and Pemberton, 1977; Kennedy, Andrews and Caird, 1977; Kitchin, Lowther and Milne, 1973; Martin and Millard, 1973). Community surveys have shown a high prevalence of heart disease in relatively fit elderly people. Forty per cent in the age group 65-74 and 50 per cent of people 75 years and over show clear evidence of heart disease (Kennedy, Andrews and Caird, 1977).

In terms of prevalence, musculoskeletal disorders rank second to circulatory disorders. All adult men and women lose bone as they grow older, especially women after the menopause. However, the borderline between the normal physiological loss and the senile *osteoporesis syndrome* is hard to delineate. Bourliere and Vallery-Masson (1985) suggest that a useful index of the prevalence of osteoporesis is the occurrence of hip fracture. The 10 year study of the population of Rochester, Minnesota (Gallagher *et al.*, 1980) has yielded some of the most reliable figures available. The results show a doubling of the fracture rate in each decade of life after 50 years of age (Figure 3.1). The fracture rate is much higher in women than in men, and by 90 years of age 32 per cent of women and 17 per cent of men have suffered a fracture.

Within this book there is insufficient space to discuss the wide range of other physical conditions which affect older people. For the purpose of comparing the general population with older people with mental handicap, however, it is important to make some mention of respiratory conditions. This is a class of conditions to which people with mental handicap are particularly prone, (see Chapter 2). Among elderly people in the general population the majority of disorders are chronic bronchitis and emphysema, neoplasia and pneumonia. In terms of the distress or "burden" (Black and Pole, 1975) caused by such disorders, measured in terms of inpatient days in hospital, outpatient referrals, lost work days and GP consultations, respiratory problems are second only to mental disorders. This chronic burden is also reflected in mortality statistics, where neoplasia, pneumonia and chronic bronchitis account for the majority of deaths (Davies, 1985). There is a steady rise in deaths from age 50, and in people aged 85 it accounts for 25 per cent of all deaths.

Figure 3.1:

International comparison of annual age-specific hip fracture rates in women (A) and men (B)

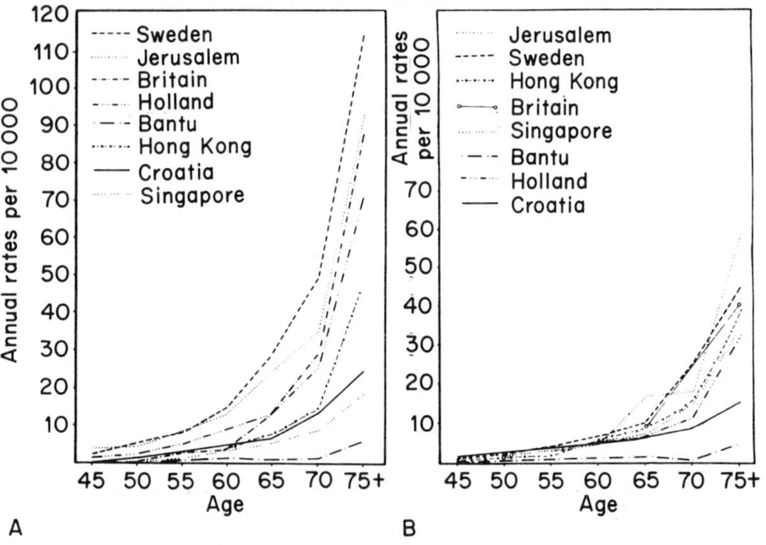

1.2 Morbidity in people with mental handicap

Most of the available epidemiological information on medical status of older people with mental handicap comes from the needs assessment survey of people with mental handicap living in New York (Jacobson, Sutton and Janicki 1985; Janicki and Jacobson, 1982; Janicki and MacEachron, 1984). The survey was conducted between 1978 and 1982, and identified 7,823 clients aged 53 years or greater. Data from this survey (Janicki and MacEachron, 1984) are reproduced in Table 3.3 below. From this table it can be clearly seen that increasing age results in a greater likelihood of medical disorders in all the named categories, with the exception of "neurological". In reference to this specific category, Jacobson, Sutton and Janicki (1985) present a somewhat more detailed breakdown of the findings. They state that the rate of cerebral palsy was lower by 50 per cent among people aged 60 and over, compared with those in the 22 to 59 year age group. Similarly, the rate for epilepsy declined by 35 per cent. The probable reason for this observed reduction is that people with serious physiological anomalies resulting in neurological impairments are likely to evidence high mortality. Thus, average health status of people who survive to a greater age is likely to be higher than that of the whole age range.

Table 3.3 Percentages of clients showing various medical problems. (Janicki and MacEachron, 1984)

	Age Group		
Characteristic	53-62	63-72	73+
Cerebral palsy	8	5	3
Epilepsy	20	14	12
Musculoskeletal	25	28	35
Hearing/Vision	29	32	45
Respiratory	3	4	7
Cardiovascular	19	32	57
Neurological	40	34	30

A smaller scale study (N = 742) in Alberta (Badry *et al.*, 1986c) yielded the breakdown of health problems by three age categories shown in Table 3.4. This confirms the findings of Janicki and MacEachron that cardiovascular and musculoskeletal problems increase significantly with age.

Table 3.4:

Percentages for health impairments across three age groups. (Badry *et al.*, 1986)

Characteristic	Age Group 45-54	55-64	65+
Cardiovascular	12.8	14.9	24.5*
Digestive	6.0	8.3	7.5
Oedema	3.0	5.8	8.8
Endocrine	6.3	11.6	12.3
Genito-Urinary	2.2	3.8	4.4
Growth Impairment	1.9	1.7	0.4
Hemic Lymphatic	1.1	2.1	0.4
Musculoskeletal	15.7	19.8	32.0*
Neoplastic disease	0.4	1.2	3.1
Neurological	5.2	5.4	7.4
Obesity	18.3	15.3	13.6
Paralysis	8.3	6.3	3.1
Other	14.6	15.0	13.2

n = 742

*Indicates significant differences between that age group and the other two age groups

Information from mental handicap registers in California, Massachusetts and New York (Jacobson, Sutton, and Janicki, 1985) suggest that the major changes are seen in the areas of hearing impairment, vision impairment and loss of mobility. Comparing a group of 55-64 year olds with a group aged 65 and over, Janicki *et al.* found a 25 per cent increase in these problems for the older group.

The prevalence of chronic physical conditions has also been examined using information from mental handicap registers (Commission on Professional and Hospital Activities, 1978). The information in Table 3.5, presented by Janicki *et al.* (1985) shows modest increases in the number of problems for most of the observed categories. However, the general prevalence of problems does not differ greatly for the two groups. Janicki *et al.* (1985) conclude that: "By inference, with some exceptions for treatment of neurological and to a lesser degree endocrine problems, the health care needs of this population should be comparable to those of the general population" (p. 126).

Table 3.5:

Percentage of people with mental handicap in three U.S. States, California (CA), Massachusetts (MA), New York (NY), showing various physical impairments

	Age 55-64			Age 65+		
Condition	CA	MA	NY	CA	MA	NY
Cerebral palsy	13	5	6	11	3	4
Epilepsy	21	18	17	15	20	12
Hearing impairment	19	24	14	29	32	26
Vision impairment	22	23	16	27	29	21
Mobility impairment	*	16	16	*	21	23

*Unreported

Stroud *et al.* (1984) included some information on physical conditions in their survey of older clients in N.E. Ohio. The four groups (1/ Institutionalised, 2/ Deinstitutionalised, 3/ Community (i.e. never having lived in an institution) 4/ Unserved by mental handicap services) were found to be similar in terms of the number of chronic conditions and mobility. It was found, however, that there were wide variations in the number of medications taken by members of the different groups. Of the people resident in institutions, 45 per cent took two or more medications, compared with only 14 per cent of the community group. The authors suggest that this is due to the greater availability of medication for residents of a total-care facility. The institutional group also used the *fewest* prosthetic devices such as glasses, dentures and hearing aids. Stroud *et al.* suggest various reasons for this including (a) institutional residents may be unable to afford them, (b) the aids may not seem to be so necessary in an environment where many of the residents are relatively disabled, (c) the aids may have been available at one time, but were not used or needed for the institutional way of life.

It is not clear how Stroud *et al.* collected their medical information, or how they chose the categories and scope of the data. It appears that a single schedule was devised for the complete survey, covering physical condition, social competence, cognitive development and service utilisation. The interviews were conducted by Qualified Mental Retardation Professionals (QMRPs), who are not medically trained. Information on medical conditions was collected in relation to a number of chronic conditions including heart, lung, ear, eye, circulation and seizures, the variable being "level of care received". It is not specified how "level of care" was assessed, although it is clear that this approach cannot yield reliable data since (a) some individuals may be suffering from conditions which are undetected, and (b) some conditions may be receiving a level of care which is inappropriate to the severity of the condition.

In the UK, information collected by the authors from hospital records (Table 3.6) is in general agreement with the findings of Janicki and his co-workers. Calderstones Hospital, described in Chapter 1, has nearly 1000 clients in residence. The table presented below gives the proportion of residents suffering from a variety of medical conditions according to two age groupings: Under 50 years and 50+ years. It can be seen that, as with the figures presented above, there is a sharp drop in the proportion of people suffering from epilepsy, while hearing impairment shows a sharp rise. Mobility and vision problems show only modest increases. Diabetes, heart conditions and respiratory problems show an expected increase in frequency for the older group. The increase in heart problems is particularly marked. The recorded frequencies of 0.4 per cent for the younger group and 4.8 per cent for the older clients corresponds to only two cases out of 483 people in the younger group, but 24 people in the older group.

Table 3.6:

Percentage of Calderstones residents with various medical conditions

	Age	
Condition	Under 50	Over 50
Epilepsy	34.8	15.2
Hearing impaiment	5.6	9.3
Vision impairment	7.1	8.2
Mobility problems	19.6	24.6
Diabetes	0.8	2.8
Respiratory problems	0.0	1.2
Heart conditions	0.4	4.8

In a recent study, Day (1987) has surveyed the physical and mental health of people with mental handicap over 65 years of age, resident at Northgate Hospital in the North East of England. He found that 23 per cent had no medical or surgical problems, while 33 per cent had one or more conditions with an average of 1.92 conditions for those affected. Not surprisingly, Day found that residents in the older group had more problems, with 87 per cent aged 75 years or over having one or more medical or surgical conditions. Within the 65+ age group as a whole the most common conditions included mobility problems (34 per cent), cardiorespiratory disease (24 per cent), impaired vision (24 per cent), hearing impairment (21 per cent), and urinary incontinence (12 per cent). Day remarked on a surprising lack of association of age with urinary incontinence. In comparison, the frequency of cardiorespiratory disease rose considerably in the over 70s.

Given the relative unreliability of much of the available medical data on morbidity in people with mental handicap, the most reliable comparison of people with and without mental handicap is probably between the figures of Janicki and MacEachron (1984) for people with mental handicap in New York State, and those of Waern's (1978) study of the general population in Uppsala. Table 3.7 shows the comparative prevalence rate from these two studies for the comparable categories of circulatory, musculoskeletal and respiratory disorders.

Comparison of such figures is made very difficult by the lack of standardisation in identification procedures. This must account for the apparently vastly greater prevalence of musculoskeletal disorders in people with mental handicap. It will be remembered (see above) that this class of conditions is particularly difficult to define. Indeed, Vallery-Masson *et al.* (1981) recorded an even higher level for this type of disorder (78 per cent) in their study of non-handicapped people. Circulatory disorders appear to be roughly equivalent in the two groups, while respiratory problems show the expected greater prevalence in the handicapped group. Overall, however, the variation of prevalence rates, particularly in the musculoskeletal category, casts doubt on the validity of any firm comparative conclusions. It therefore seems premature to infer that the health care needs of older people with mental handicap are comparable to those of the general population (Janicki and MacEachron, 1984).

Table 3.7:

Comparative prevalence rates for people with and without mental handicap on three major disorders

	Non Handicapped*		Mentally Handicapped**	
	Age		Age	
Condition	50	60	53-62	63-72
Circulatory	5.9	31.3	19	32
Musculoskeletal	0.7	7.9	25	28
Respiratory	0.3	2.4	3	4

*From Waern (1978)

** From Janicki and MacEachron (1984)

It must be borne in mind that the prevalence of major disease categories does not tell the whole story concerning health care of older people. The terms *disease* and *illness* are often used synonymously but in fact refer to different things. A person may have a disease but have no symptoms and feel perfectly well, as with certain kinds of cancer. On the other hand, some people feel unwell but have no identifiable disease. Some of the people who feel ill may actually feel better when told they have no disease, although many older people continue to have symptoms and feel ill even though no physical explanation can be found. Illness varies very much from one social group and one culture to another, and for older people illness is a different experience than it is for younger people (Muir-Gray, 1985). Whether it can become, in addition, a different experience due to mental handicap remains an unanswered question.

Finally, the information presented here has

permitted a basic comparison of handicapped and non-handicapped people's physical health with respect to three major disease categories. It is important to bear in mind, however, that these are not necessarily the conditions which bring the greatest *problems* to older people. Muir-Gray (1985) makes the point that the most *handicapping* conditions in old age are arthritis, stroke, Parkinson's disease, blindness and dementia. With the exception of the last category (see next section) there is insufficient information currently available to compare the two populations on these conditions. A comparative study which includes this kind of information is urgently needed, since handicap due to age-related conditions is a major factor in planning appropriate servies.

2 MENTAL HEALTH

It will come as no surprise to the reader that there are very few studies of psychiatric disorder which have concentrated specifically on older people with mental handicap. Apart from the general lack of attention which the older client group has received until recently, however, there is a further specific problem associated with work which attempts to study psychiatry in mental handicap; namely, the difficulty of distinguishing specific psychiatric symptoms from the variety of behaviour problems exhibited by some people with mental handicap. Those efforts which have been directed towards this daunting task will be reported here. There is no doubt, however, that this topic area is in its infancy, with much important work to be done in the future.

A dominant theme of this book is that older people with mental handicap are primarily *older people*, rather than individuals with mental handicap. It therefore seems appropriate that this discussion of psychiatric symptoms associated with ageing should start with a consideration of the knowledge that can be gained from work on older, non-handicapped people. It must be borne in mind, however, that psychiatric disorder in old age can be caused by both biological and environmental factors, or more likely a complex interaction between the two. For this reason it is necessary to be cautious in generalising between the two population groups. Sudden isolation through loss of a spouse is less likely to occur to people with mental handicap, since few of the more severely handicapped are married. On the other hand, some of the changes in society's attitude normally attendant on old age, e.g. loss of status and lack of support, have been borne by people with mental handicap for their entire lives. Thus, when considering the effects of environmental factors on psychiatric disorder there are at least as many similarities as dissimilarities between older people with and without mental handicap.

2.1 Psychiatric disorder in old age

Studies of elderly people living in the community indicate that this group suffers from definite psychiatric symptoms in a high proportion, perhaps 20 per cent, of the general population over 65. Their psychiatric symptoms are often accompanied by physical illnesses, and they are often disabled by their symptoms. Fifty per cent of US hospital and nursing home beds are occupied by psychiatrically ill elderly people (Gianturko & Busse, 1978), yet the use of psychiatric outpatient services by the elderly is low, and less than 5 per cent of this age group reside in institutions. It therefore appears that there may be many older people in the community who need psychiatric help but do not receive it. Thus, Bergmann (1978) in his comparison of hospital and community resident elderly refers to the "low social visibility" of the latter group in respect of psychiatric disorders.

Two principal reasons have been suggested for this discrepancy between service need and take-up in the community elderly. First, systems of health care have generally evolved on a model more suitable for a younger, more assertive, vigorous and affluent age group, whose disorders tend to be more consistent with traditional organisation of professional and specialist services. Second, complaints of elderly people often do not fit neatly into the compartments (such as "psychiatric", "medical" or "social") which are generally built into a health care system (Gurland, Copeland, Kuriansky, Kelleher, Sharpe, & Dean, 1983). As Shamoian (1985) points out, in elderly people particularly, medical illnesses can mimic psychiatric disorders, which in turn can present as physical problems. Thus, it is frequently found that somatic, rather than psychiatric, symptoms dominate the picture, so that the elderly depressed person may complain only of a headache, backache or joint pains. The complexity of these interacting factors presents considerable problems to the psychiatrist. Accurate differential diagnosis necessitates an accurate appraisal of the relative contributions of physical status, physical symptoms and psychiatric symptoms before appropriate treatment can be prescribed.

Psychiatric disorder, particularly dementia, can be a major contributory factor towards the need for hospitalisation of an elderly person. As Busse (1973) points out, 86 per cent of people over 65 years of age in the USA have one or more chronic conditions. Where this condition is exacerbated by the presence of a psychiatric problem there is a greatly increased probability that the resulting level of disability will overwhelm coping capacity of the individual, of family and friends, and community services. At this point the probability of institutionalisation increases greatly.

Redick, Kramer & Taube (1973) have pointed out that the gathering of systematic epidemiological data on mental disorders is hampered by a lack of:

a) Standard case-finding tools for detecting people in the general population
b) Differential diagnosis techniques that make it possible to assign each case to a specific diagnostic group with a high degree of reliability
c) Reliable methods of establishing date of onset

The problem is particularly difficult in the case of elderly people since the diagnosis of geriatric disorders is highly complex. As Stromgren (1963) states: "The abnormalities under consideration very often have no clear-cut borderlines. In many cases the onset is so insidious that it is impossible to state the time at which a person is passing from the 'healthy' group to the ill group".

Much of the basic data have come from surveys of psychiatric facilities. These data, however, only allow us to estimate the morbidity rate within a population which has presented for services. Furthermore, admissions to and discharges from specific types of facility are determined by a variety of administrative, policy related and socioeconomic factors. Consequently, variations in the rates of usage are a function not only of incidence and prevalence of mental disorders, but also of these selective factors (Bergmann, 1978).

Shepherd & Gruenberg (1957) investigated the age-specific incidence of hospital admission for neurosis using records of hospital admissions and discharges and also of "new cases" registered with a health insurance plan under the title of "Service for psychoneurosis". They found a peak in early maturity, followed by a rapid decline from age 40 onwards. However, other studies based on general practice samples have not supported this conclusion (Bremer, 1951; Primrose, 1962; Watts & Watts, 1952). Shepherd *et al.* (1966) showed that, while patient consulting rates did *not* decline steeply with age, the consultation rate for *new* psychiatric cases after the age of 55 declined very steeply indeed.

Rates for psychiatric disorder in stratified community samples can be used to give an estimate of incidence which is independent of the decision to seek treatment. Such surveys typically return higher rates for neurotic disorders than studies based on GP records. Kay *et al.* (1964) found 12.5 per cent of the elderly population of Newcastle-on-Tyne to have a neurotic or personality disorder of at least moderate severity. Furthermore, 5 per cent of elderly people had a neurotic condition starting after the age of 60, with no evidence of previous psychiatric conditions.

Bergmann (1978) suggests that the discrepancy between community and general practice figures is at least partly related to variations in general practitioners' awareness of psychiatric conditions. Williamson *et al.* (1964) compared awareness of GPs with the ascertained prevalence in their practices. It was found that dementia remained very much undetected, depression and affective disorders coming second, and neurosis third. Conditions which are readily detected include severe alcoholism and paranoid states. This suggests that "nuisance value" is an important factor in bringing cases of psychiatric disorder to the attention of services. The fact that dementia is so poorly detected is obviously of critical relevance to the needs of older people.

Goldberg and Huxley (1980) have discussed the factors which determine whether someone with a neurotic disorder becomes a "case". They point out that the severity of symptoms is not necessarily directly related to degree of incapacity or interference with day-to-day life. Both interpersonal factors and external social factors may determine whether a given set of symptoms results in presentation to a doctor. Once someone has been referred to a psychiatrist it is likely that they will receive a differential diagnosis of their particular condition. It is interesting to note, however, that psychiatrists are more confident about making differential diagnoses (ie determining in which *category* a person's disorder belongs), than in determining whether a person qualifies as a "case". This fact emerged in a community study of elderly people in New York and London (Gurland *et al.*, 1983), in which individuals with possible psychiatric problems were interviewed to determine the true extent of possible psychiatric disorder. Gurland found that the psychiatrists were obviously more used to making a differential diagnosis, starting from an assumption that the person *is* a case since they have presented for treatment. Diagnostic manuals are not good at providing explicit criteria for case determination. This indicates clearly that the likelihood of "caseness" will depend on predeliction of particular population for seeking psychiatric treatment, and availability of such treatment. These are factors which are obviously relevant when one is considering the need for, and take-up of, psychiatric services among people with mental handicap.

To overcome the problems of case-determination, Gurland *et al.* advocate the use of a rigorous diagnostic system based on objective criteria. The system they developed for their study (CARE) involves components which relate both to the pattern of symptoms and their severity, so that both these criteria can be used to describe cases or chart progress. Non-clinical states are classified as well as clinical ones. Symptom patterns, social adjustment, positive mental health, stress, associated conditions and course of illness are all taken into account in the diagnostic criteria. The criteria distinguish between symptoms which are the product of psychiatric disturbance and those which are the result of physical illness.

2.2 Studies of General Prevalence

Estimating the proportion of people over 65 who will develop mental disorders requiring medical attention is difficult, since the basic tools to provide accurate annual morbidity statistics on incidence and prevalence do not exist. Those surveys which do exist are difficult to compare since there are differences in the definition of a mental disorder, case finding techniques, diagnostic procedures, classification and measures of prevalence. A minimum level of 2 per cent prevalence is suggested by the fact that data on patient care episodes show at least 1.5 per cent of 65+ were under psychiatric care from either inpatient or oupatient services. Much higher estimates come from community surveys of psychiatric morbidity on General Practice lists (Shepherd *et al.*, 1966) or random samples of the general population (Pasmanick *et al.*, 1959). Thus Shepherd *et al.* (1966) found psychiatric morbidity rates within a general practice to be 11 per cent for men and 15 per cent for women. Diagnostic categories were not presented by age group, but, overall, the following conditions were included: formal psychiatric illness (psychosis, psychoneurosis and personality disorders), psychosomatic conditions, organic illness with a psychiatric overlay and psychosocial problems. Assuming a level of 10 per cent, Redick *et al.* estimate the numbers of 65+ who were in need of or receiving psychiatric services in 1980. They conclude that 80 per cent would not be receiving the service they required.

Redick, Kramer & Taube (1973) define a "patient-care episode" as the number of residents in inpatient facilities at the beginning of the year plus the total additions to these facilities during the year. Using this measure they found age specific rates vary with age, being lowest for the under 18s (928 per 100,000), highest for 18-64 (2,451 per 100,000), and dropping to 1,595 per 100,000 for the over 65s. However, despite the apparent lowering in the older population, 85 per cent of the over 65s were <u>inpatient</u> episodes. This suggests that service resources used by older people may actually be far higher than these figures indicate.

In the USA Redick *et al* found 15 per cent of institutionalised elderly (123,555) were resident in psychiatric hospitals. A survey of nursing homes and related facilities conducted by the National Center for Health Statistics showed that in 1963 404,000 people over 65 lived in this kind of facility. Of these, 118,200 were reported as suffering from senile psychosis, 26,500 were senile without mention of psychosis, and another 63,700 were declared to have non-specific mental or nervous trouble.

There is a strong association between physical ill health and neurotic and affective disorder arising in old age. The higher mortality of elderly patients with a neurotic disorder has been demonstrated by Kay and Bergmann (1966). Bergmann's (1978) findings indicate that the onset of neurosis in later life may in some cases be an indicator of life threatening or serious ill health. Bergmann (1978) therefore suggests it is safest to consider all neurotic illnesses beginning in later life as possible organic conditions, until a thorough investigation has been carried out.

Within the general population there are marked differences in incidence of psychiatric morbidity according to marital status and living arrangements. For people over 65 years old admission rates are highest for divorced and separated people, followed by those who have never married or are widowed, with the married having the lowest admission rate (Redick, Kramer & Taube, 1973).

2.3 Depression

The true incidence of depression among elderly people is unknown. Data vary from study to study, depending on population and criteria, although it is generally thought that 15-20 per cent of elderly people suffer from depressive symptoms (Shamoian, 1985). However, only 15-20 per cent of this depressed group will receive treatment. Shamoian points out that elderly people often deny their depression and are reluctant to seek psychiatric assistance. Their denial and unwillingness to seek assistance is complicated by frequent misinterpretation of the signs and symptoms of depression as disparate symptoms of normal ageing.

Many depressed elderly patients present with cognitive dysfunction which can be mistaken for dementia. Cognitive functions diminish in elderly depressed people and return to normal when the underlying depression is effectively treated. About 12 per cent of elderly people diagnosed as suffering from a dementing condition are thought to actually have a pseudodementia resulting from undiagnosed and untreated depression (Shamoian, 1985). Unfortunately there are no unequivocal tests for distinguishing pseudodepression and dementia. Differential diagnosis depends on the patient's history, clinical observation and the response to antidepressant treatment.

Goldberg *et al.* (1970) found that 32 per cent of their sample initially selected for referral to Social Services suffered from depression ranging from a rating of above average severity to severe. Goldberg notes that very few patients were actually receiving psychiatric treatment and that practitioners were generally not aware of clients' psychiatric needs.

Pervasively depressed elderly people show an increased use of medical services; they take more psychotropic medications and are given multiple drugs more often. They see their doctor repeatedly, receive more special investigations, and are admitted to hospital more frequently. Gurland *et al.* (1983) found little specific treatment of depression, and concluded that opportunities for more vigorous treatment were probably being missed.

Within the course of Gianturko and Busse's (1978) longitudinal study of elderly people they found depressive episodes increased in frequency and depth with advancing years. Throughout the course of the study the proportion of depressed people stayed consistently around 20-25 per cent. By the end of the 10th evaluation panel, only 30 per cent of people had no depressive episode, 40 per cent had one episode and 30 per cent had two or more. They found that depression shows a recurrent pattern, ninety per cent of those depressed at round one having at least one other depressive episode. (It should be noted, however, that the method of case-determination was not specified, so that a diagnosis of depression may have been influenced by the outcome of previous assessments.)

There is some evidence of sex differences in respect to symptoms of depression. The community study of Gurland *et al.* (1983) found men to have lower rates for depression prior to age 75 (ratio 2:3), with the sexes converging at age 75-79. Gianturko and Busse (1978) suggest that further support for this apparent increasing depression in men comes from figures for suicide. Suicide in white males age 15-24 is quoted as 7.4 per 100,000. This rate increases steadily with age, so that for age 65-74 the rate is 45.5.

It is notable that the majority of respondents in Gianturko and Busse's study were able to trace most depressive episodes to specific life events. This finding suggests one should be cautious in generalising results to a population of people with mental handicap, since for many of these people the course of life events will have been very different from non handicapped individuals.

The concept of *personal time dependency* (Gurland *et al.*, 1983) is of particular relevance to the study of depression. It refers to a state of dependency requiring time-consuming help from another person. In Gurland's study people were defined as *personal time dependent* if they (a) had mental or physical disabilities which cause (b) inabilities to perform tasks which (c) require someone to spend time providing the services in direct contact with the dependent person, and (d) the withholding of such services would seriously threaten the dependent person's continued existence in that setting. On this basis, 30 per cent of elderly people living in the community in London were judged to be *personal time dependent*. Gurland *et al.* found pervasive depression among *independent* elderly at a level of 10 per cent, and among *personal time dependent* at a level of 20 per cent. Similar results were found by Kay *et al.* (1973) in a survey of the needs of a random sample of elderly people seen in the community. These were divided into those showing impaired ability to cope with day-to-day life and those needing no services. The former group showed a greater proportion of functional psychiatric disorders, of which 87 per cent had a neurotic disorder of at least moderate severity.

The role of isolation in contributing to depression in elderly people has received considerable attention.

However, an important point which emerges from such studies is that it is important to distinguish between objective circumstances and subjective states - between isolation and loneliness (Friis & Manniche 1961; Pagani 1962; Townsend, 1957). Lowenthal (1965) demonstrated that isolation itself (ie few social contacts) is of little psychopathological significance. A factor analytic study on a random population of community residents derived an isolation factor which was independent of a general illness factor, psychiatric diagnosis factor and socioeconomic factors. Tunstall (1966) also emphasised the distinction between isolation and loneliness, pointing out that, in his sample, only a quarter of isolated elderly men and women were "often lonely". Similarly, Gurland *et al.* (1983) found that living alone and current isolation were <u>not</u> associated with depression in either London or New York.

2.4 Dementia

Dementia is the disorder which is most obviously associated with the process of ageing. It is frequently the precipitating factor in the decision to hospitalise an elderly person who can no longer cope alone, or whose needs are too great to be met by family caregivers. Among nonhandicapped people living in the community Gurland *et al.* (1983) found 2.5 per cent of Londoners and 5.8 per cent of New Yorkers over 65 years old to be suffering from a clinical level of dementia. Given the interest that has developed with respect to dementia and mental handicap, particularly the occurrence of dementia in people with Down's syndrome, we will enter into some detail on the nature of the condition and its diagnosis. The study of dementia is obviously of great relevance to any group of people who are of advancing age. It is important to stress, however, that the observed *increase* in prevalence does *not* extend to other groups of people with mental handicap except those with Down's syndrome. Thus, several authors have noted that dementia rates for hospital residents with mental handicap are similar to those of the general population (Day, 1987; Kay *et al.*, 1964; Parsons, 1965; Reid and Aungle, 1974; Tait, 1983). In the most recent of these studies, Day found 6 per cent of hospital residents over

65 years of age to be suffering from dementia, and a further 6 per cent showing early signs of the disorder.

Bracco & Amaducci (1980) describe dementia as "a progressive deterioration of mental functions, without clouding or disturbances of perception, resulting from diffuse or disseminated disease of the cerebral hemispheres during the adult life". The degree of altered function ranges from a barely discernible deviation from the normal to a virtual cerebral death, and results from a general rather than focal damage of the cerebral hemispheres. There is a loss of previously acquired capacities, so it is necessary to judge the patient's symptoms in comparison with premorbid activities.

Early in the process of dementia a variety of barely perceptible disorders may present, such as alteration in drive, mood, enthusiasm, capacity to give and receive affection and creativity. Hollender (1977) suggests several behaviour observations which should alert the examiner to the possibility of dementia; the patient who expresses lack of interest in a topic, indicating that his sons or daughters are the ones who "keep up with that sort of thing"; the patient who expresses too much satisfaction from trivial accomplishments; the patient who struggles too hard to turn out performances which earlier would have required little effort; the patient who says he will come back to that question later, but neglects to do so.

In the USA the Diagnostic and Statistical Manual of Mental Disorders, or DSM-III (American Psychiatric Association, 1980) clearly defines the diagnostic criteria for dementia, which include:

A. Loss of intellectual abilities of sufficient severity to interfere with social or occupational functioning

B. Memory impairment

C. At least one of the following:
   1. Impairment of abstract thinking as manifested by concrete impairment of proverbs, inability to find similarities and differences between related words, difficulty in defining words and concepts, and other

similar tasks.

2. Impaired judgement
3. Other disturbances of higher cortical function, eg, aphasia, apraxia, agnosia, and constructional difficulty.
4. Personality changes, i.e. alteration or accentuation of premorbid traits.

D. State of consciousness not clouded (ie does not meet the criterion for delirium or intoxication, although these may be superimposed)

E. Either 1 or 2:

1. Evidence from the history, physical examination or laboratory tests of a specific organic factor that is judged to be aetiologically related to the disturbance.
2. In the absence of such evidence, an organic factor necessary for the development of the syndrome can be presumed if conditions other than organic mental disorders have been reasonably excluded and if the behavioural change represents cognitive impairment in a variety of areas.

According to the DSM-III, the diagnosis of primary dementia, either presenile or senile, is made if the disorder demonstrates the core clinical feature of dementia based on the criteria described above and if it has an insidious onset with uniformly progressive deteriorating course - and all other specific causes of dementia have been excluded by history, physical examination, and laboratory tests.

A complete diagnosis of Alzheimer's disease requires observations in two distinct areas. First, there are certain characteristic behaviour changes which must be clinically observable; second, the brain tissue shows particular patterns of degeneration. This latter aspect can only be investigated by post-mortem. Some details relating to these two aspects of diagnosis are given below.

2.4.1 Clinical Diagnosis

Sim (1965) describes three stages in the development of the clinical symptoms. The initial stage is characterised by depression, loss of memory, distress over the loss of function, reduced efficiency and loss of order, and an often flippant attitude. As the condition worsens the depression becomes correspondingly deeper, there is obvious confusion and disorientation, and the patient becomes increasingly unable to perform tasks, particularly if there is any stress involved. In the late stage increasingly bizarre behaviour is likely to occur, involving forced laughing and crying, forced groping and grasping, rigidity, gait disturbance, and seizures (Sjogren, 1950) In addition, Parkinsonism, incontinence, epilepsy, delusions and hallucinations also occur.

At the primary care end of the assessment spectrum (ie initial detection of the condition by a GP or health visitor), the techniques seem somewhat crude, although contact with the individual in his/her home environment permits the gathering of important information including observations of the patient's normal behaviour patterns, and knowledge of premorbid behaviour from relatives. Thus Arie (1973) stresses that "An organic psychiatric syndrome should always be assessed initially at home because it is an old person's capacity to function in her normal surroundings that needs to be assessed. Members of the family and neighbours should be interviewed - and one cannot overstress that a reliable history obtained from others is paramount in assessing dementia." Arie's view is that the examination should be chiefly directed to the assessment of cognitive functions, largely by finding out the patient's grasp of everyday life. Wilson & Brass (1973) claim that a very short series of questions can detect and roughly measure intellectual impairment in old people living at home. Their 10 questions were, in brief, Town? Address? Date? Month? Year? Age? Year of birth? Month of birth? Prime Minister? Previous Prime Minister? Arie states that, in most cases, a diagnosis of dementia, senile or arteriosclerotic, can be made at home. This is because the history in an elderly person of progressive deterioration over months or years is so typical that when it coincides with clinical findings, both physical and mental, the diagnosis can be regarded as conclusive.

Other screening tests advocated for the initial detection of dementia include the Set test (Isaacs & Kennie, 1973), and the Mini Mental State (Anthony *et al.*, 1982). The Set test is performed by asking the subject to name as many items as he/she can recall in each of four successive categories or sets - colours, animals, fruits, and towns. One point is awarded for each correct item offered, with a maximum of 10 in each set and a maximum total score of 40. In healthy old people from a mining community Isaacs & Akhtar (1972) obtained a mean score of 31.2. Ninety five per cent of subjects scored over 15 on the test. A score of under 15 is thus considered abnormal. In their study a low score on the Set test corresponded closely with a clinical diagnosis of dementia. (Twenty of the 22 subjects who scored less than 15 were clinically demented.) The Mini Mental State Examination (MMSE) is a very brief test of several cognitive functions. It assesses a subject's orientation to time and place, instantaneous recall, short term memory, serial subtractions, reverse spelling and the use of language. Anthony *et al.* (1982) report good levels of correct classification among hospital patients, and suggest that scores of 0-23 are indicative of delirium or dementia.

Generally speaking, medical opinion seems to hold that accurate history taking, clinical examination and observation are sufficient to conclude a diagnosis of dementia (Hecht, 1980). There are certain factors, however, that indicate a fuller investigation. These include: (a) when the onset has been acute or subacute, suggesting a superimposed acute confusional state or a potentially reversible cerebral or metabolic lesion; (b) when dementia appears in a younger patient, e.g. below 65 years – this group tends not to have senile dementia and there is a higher proportion of reversible causes; (c) when the course of the disease is markedly fluctuant as opposed to relentlessly progressive. Hecht goes on to state that "a blanket regimen of diagnostic tests for all patients is wasteful in terms of money and the amount of useful information obtained".

Papers reporting more sophisticated assessments of dementia are unanimous in stressing the necessity of a tripartite evaluation of the presenting psychiatric syndrome, associated and/or contributory medical illness and social functioning. Thus dementia is viewed, for practical purposes, as consisting of (a) memory and cognitive impairment - the core feature of dementia; (b) functional and structural impairment of the brain; and (c) behavioural manifestations that affect the patient's ability for self care, interpersonal relationships and adjustment in the community. These three components are grossly related but do not closely parallel each other. In some cases memory and cognitive impairment is rather severe although there is little evidence of brain impairment. In other cases the reverse may happen - there is little memory and cognitive impairment in the presence of significant brain impairment.

As part of a clinical assessment a routine neurological examination is frequently conducted, although the presence of abnormal reflexes and neurological signs such as apraxia, agnosia and aphasia provides little objective information when assessing the severity of brain impairment in Alzheimer dementia (Wang, 1981). Pneumoencephalography is used to estimate the extent of cortical atrophy and ventricular dilation, since this corresponds fairly well with the severity of dementia. The method involves the introduction of air into the ventricular spaces, since air is much less radio-opaque than liquid. This method used to be the first choice to establish a diagnosis of dementia, but involves considerable discomfort and the risk in some patients that marked mental deterioration may subsequently develop. It has now been superseded by Computerised Axial Tomography. Cerebral blood flow is frequently measured if there is a suspicion of cerebral vascular disease, and there are a number of methods available. These include nitrous oxide inhalation, the carotid injection and the Xenon inhalation method, the latter two relying on isotopic radiation. Brain biopsy is the ultimate method for establishing a diagnosis of Alzheimer's, although it is of little help to the patient! Also, as already noted, the relationship between neurological signs and behavioural symptoms is not a close one (Gurland *et al.*, 1983)

A very detailed account of assessment of Alzheimer's disease is provided by Rosen (1983). Her approach includes history taking, behavioural observations, and a test battery leading to a profile of scores. Some of the principal points are as follows:

2.4.1.1 History Taking. The first part of the evaluation involves taking a detailed history from a reliable informant, usually the spouse or offspring. The symptom most commonly noted early in the course of the disorder is impaired memory for recent events. Problems of language may also be reported, including word finding difficulty, failure to express thoughts clearly and impaired comprehension of speech. Depending on the degree of dementia other symptoms may include disorientation to time and place, inability to handle finances, impaired driving ability, becoming lost in a familiar environment, and problems in the management of daily living activities.

Changes in non-cognitive behaviours vary among patients. Some show increased motor activity and agitation, while others become increasingly sedentary and appear apathetic. Diminished concentration may be evident. Sleep disturbance is manifested primarily as nocturnal confusion, where the patient awakens in the middle of the night and behaves as if it were daytime.

2.4.1.2 Behavioural Observations. Patients in the early stages of dementia with word finding difficulty compensate for this problem with circumlocution or substitution of a semantically related word. As the disorder progresses some patients become increasingly dysfluent, while others remain fluent but often produce nonsensical or irrelevant speech. Semantic and phonemic paraphrasias may appear, and in the late stages echolalia and palilalia may develop. Many patients also show difficulty comprehending complex questions, and rephrasing or simplifying the question may elicit appropriate responses.

Despite these language problems, some patients retain appropriate conversational and social skills. However, they frequently experience difficulty in following the conversation between two people, and thus appear withdrawn.

Most patients experience difficulties recalling both personal and non-personal recent events, including daily activities, experiences with family members, and significant news stories.

One of the most consistent characteristics of these patients is difficulty understanding performance requirements on complex tasks (eg WAIS Digit Symbol Substitution). They require repeated step-by-step instructions and are often unable to perform the task independently.

2.4.1.3 Test Battery. (a) Global mental status: This is an adaptation of a brief mental status examination shown to correlate significantly with histopathological signs. The test includes such items as orientation, recall, recitation of months backwards and a five minute delayed recall of name and address.

(b) Intellectual functioning: The WAIS is used for this purpose. Full scale IQ is compared with an estimate of the premorbid level of functioning based on the patient's level of occupation and education to determine if there has been a significant decline. More specific to Alzheimer patients, and not necessarily characteristic of other types of dementia, is that the verbal IQ is greater than performance IQ by a minimum of 15 points. There are at least two reasons for this particular differential. First, it appears that old knowledge initially remains less affected by the disorder than other intellectual abilities. Second, the lower scores on the performance subtests may be attributed to the typical finding of extreme difficulty in executing the Digit Symbol Substitution subtest and a constructional apraxia for the block design. The relative contribution of (a) experience to verbal IQ performance and (b) neurological functioning to performance IQ, are discussed in the following chapter with respect to ageing effects in general.

(c) Memory functions: The impairment of memory appears in recall of both verbal and visual materials. Immediate recall of verbal material may be unaffected in the early stages of Alzheimer's disease, so that performance on digits forward may be intact, and very intelligent patients may not be markedly deficient in recall of the Logical Memory stories. Although immediate recall may not appear to be very impaired, a striking deficit in long term memory is most revealing.

To assess long term memory, a 10 minute delayed recall of both the stories and forms (from the WAIS) is administered. On the stories the patient may not recall that the task was given, may be unable to respond to a cue, and show a loss of four or more points from their immediate recall score. Delayed recall of the forms usually reveals loss of parts of the form, increased distortion, or inability to recall an entire form.

(d) Constructional ability: The Block Design subtest and Rosen Drawing test are administered in order to evaluate the manipulatory and graphomotor components of constructional ability. A disturbance is usually apparent in both types of task. In copying geometric forms there is usually an association between accuracy and overall severity of dysfunction. Patients in the early stages have the most difficulty with obliquely oriented forms and perspective. As the disorder progresses, impairments appear in copying a diamond and simple overlapping figures. Eventually deficits are notable in execution of the simplest forms. Many patients begin to "close in" on the forms, that is, they draw around or within the form or incorporate part of the model in their copy. On the manipulatory task many patients only construct two or three of the 4-block designs.

(e) Language: Language abilities are assessed on selected subtests of the Boston Diagnostic Aphasia Examination. Deficits in language appear to be more variable among patients than impairments in memory and IQ. The most typical problem in Alzheimer's patients is failure to name objects correctly. In the early stages of the disease this tends to show up with objects whose word-frequency is low.

2.4.1.4 Differential Diagnosis. In all cases of suspected dementia it is necessary to determine whether the condition is functional or organic, since this obviously has implications for management and prognosis (Miller, 1977). The chief differentiation appears to relate to memory: "it can be stated with confidence that any memory impairment in the functional psychoses is certainly much less severe than that which occurs in dementia" (Miller, 1977). New-word learning tests are much in favour for this type of assessment. With more severe dysfunction, dementia may be confused with psychosis, and this is apparently much more difficult to differentiate (Bracco & Amaducci, 1980). Apart from the difference in memory and orientation, the examiner should also look for certain biological features which are more typical of depression. These include anorexia, weight loss, constipation and early waking. A crucial point is the rate at which the syndrome appears, being insidious and slowly progressive in the case of dementia. Although disorders of thought are prominent in dementia, it can usually be differentiated clinically from a primary disorder of thought, i.e. schizophrenia. In the latter it is possible to demonstrate preservation of orientation, memory and intellectual functions. The schizophrenic's thought is affected by sudden and inexplicable twists, tolerance for conflicts is striking, and conclusions are reached on a logically unacceptable basis. In dementia the thoughts expressed take more of a meandering course. One can follow their progression but they appear to lead nowhere.

2.4.2 Histopathology

The ultimate diagnosis of dementia involves a post-mortem examination of the brain tissue. Certain characteristic changes must be present before a firm diagnosis of Alzheimer's disease is confirmed. These changes are of three types. "Senile plaques" are found throughout the tissue of the brain, but particularly prevalent in the hippocampus, cingulate gyrus and frontal lobes (Burger and Vogel, 1973; Olson and Shaw, 1969). They consist of a core of hollow fibres surrounded by various types of cell processes, both normal and degenerating. Amongst these surrounding fibres are also found characteristic twisted tubules of approximately 20nm diameter with nodes every 80 nm (Ohara, 1972). "Neurofibrillary tangles" are the second distinguishing feature of pathology in Alzheimer's disease. These, as their name suggests, are clumps of neuron fibres which have become twisted together. The extent to which this process has occurred can be expressed in terms of the "Adjusted Tangle Index" (Ball and Nuttall, 1980). Degeneration is seen to have affected substantial numbers of nerve cell bodies, leading to the destruction of the nucleus. This third manifestation is referred to as "granulovacuolar degeneration".

In addition, a number of other tell-tale signs are frequently seen in conjunction with these three main indices. Amongst these are substantial neuron loss, leading to a reduced density of fibres (Crapper *et al.*, 1975; Ellis *et al.*, 1974), and mineral deposits of iron and calcium on the blood vessels (Burger and Vogel, 1973).

2.5 Psychiatry in Mental Handicap

The literature on psychiatric aspects of mental handicap is very limited. Heaton-Ward (1977) points out that two of the major psychiatric text books devote only a few lines to people with mental handicap. This, despite the fact that people with mental handicap may be <u>more</u> prone to mental illness than non-handicapped individuals, and that in some syndromes associated with mental handicap, mental illness is part of the symptom complex (Penrose, 1972). Thus, Tredgold (1908) estimated that mental illness was 26 times as common in people with mental handicap as in the general population. Also, people with mental handicap are likely to express indirectly depressive affect. Aggressive acting out, withdrawal, and/or somatic complaints may be observed instead of classic depressive complaints such as feelings of hopelessness. Reid (1982) describes a variety of behaviours which are the result of depression in people whose level of handicap makes it difficult to verbalise their feelings. Such behaviours include somatic symptoms like headache and abdominal ache, hysterical fits, agitation, florid delusions and disturbances of physiological functions such as sleep, appetite and bowel movements. Regressive behaviour is also not uncommon. Reid describes the case of a depressed woman with mild mental handicap who said she could not walk, and began to negotiate the stairs on her bottom like a baby.

The diagnosis of psychiatric disorder in people with mental handicap is complicated by the reduced linguistic ability which is often found (Reid, 1983). Psychiatric diagnosis is essentially based on information obtained from clinical interviewing. Accounts from informed observers and outside sources *are* very important, but are supplementary to the interview itself.

For patients in whom verbal ability is severely restricted, or entirely absent, access to mental state is necessarily inferential. With dementing disorders Reid suggests it is usually still possible to make a confident diagnosis on the basis of objectively observed decline in intellectual abilities over a period of time. In schizophrenic and paranoid syndromes, however, where the diagnosis depends on subtle nuances of meaning and experience such as hallucinations and delusional phenomena, the problem is daunting. Reid believes that it is not possible to diagnose schizophrenia in people with an IQ of less than about 40.

The considerable literature on reliability of psychiatric diagnosis between individual psychiatrists attests to the fact that it is difficult enough to define and classify mental illness in people *without* mental handicap. As Crisp (1976) points out, there are no absolute criteria for the diagnois of depression. Also, the diagnosis of schizophrenia varies widely from one school to another, being more widely used in the USA, for example, compared with France (Deniker, 1976).

Further difficulties arise when existing diagnostic criteria are applied to people with mental handicap (Heaton-Ward, 1977). Thus, the *Encyclopaedia of Psychiatry* defines psychosis as "Mental illness which is severe, produces conspicuously disordered behaviour, cannot be understood as an extension or exaggeration of ordinary experience and whose subject is without insight". Heaton-Ward suggests that "On this basis, all those of our profoundly retarded patients (IQ approximately 20 or less) and some of our severely retarded patients (IQ approximately 20-35), who have no intelligible speech, in whom emotional lability, noisy outbursts, continuous or periodic disorganised, purposeless activity, including aggression, destructiveness and self mutilation are the rule, could be considered psychotic" (p. 527).

As a result there appears to be considerable disagreement between authors as to the diagnosis of psychiatric disorder among people with mental handicap. Thus, Gordon (1918) noted that depression was more common than mania, while Duncan (1936) claimed that mania was four times as common as melancholia.

The central problem in considering mental illness

in relation to mental handicap is to distinguish the symptoms of mental illness from those behaviours which are characteristic of mental handicap in that particular individual. To this end, Heaton-Ward stresses the need for accurate and complete records to make any distinction between behaviour characteristic of the client and behaviour which is the result of an additional psychiatric disorder.

Despite these daunting problems in diagnosis the attitude to psychiatric treatment of people with mental handicap has changed markedly. Thus, in 1955, Tredgold suggested that the undifferentiated nature of the personalities of many people with mental handicap made the usual differential diagnoses of mental illness very difficult. Similarly, in 1967 Gardner queried whether it was possible for people with mental handicap to manifest an affective disorder. Since that time, disorders of this kind have been reported by a number of authors, who have demonstrated that such conditions usually respond to treatment with appropriate antimanic, antidepressant and prophylactic agents such as lithium (Reid, 1982).

Eaton & Menolascino (1982), and Reiss (1982) have reported surveys of people with mental handicap attending community-based mental health clinics in Nebraska and Chicago. The results of both surveys support prior observations (Menolascino, 1970; Philips, 1967; Reid, 1972) that people with mental handicap are subject to a wide range of emotional disturbances, and that the symptoms of specific psychiatric disturbance are essentially the same for people with and without mental handicap.

Reiss and Benson (1985) report that people with mild and moderate levels of handicap are often very aware of negative social conditions which have affected their lives for long periods of time. The following conditions are mentioned: *Labelling, rejection and ridicule, segregation, infantilisation, social disruption, restricted opportunities and victimisation.* Reiss and Benson's studies indicate that, at least for people with less severe levels of handicap, such negative social attitudes can be contributory factors in the development of psychiatric symptoms. We return to the way in which people cope with stigma in our review of

Edgerton's work in Chapter 5.

Sovner and Hurley (1983) similarly conclude that mental illness in people with mental handicap should not be regarded as fundamentally different from that occurring in non-handicapped individuals. Twenty five published reports were reviewed regarding the presence of depression and mania in people with mental handicap. Diagnoses were validated against the DSM-III criteria, from which it was concluded that people with mental handicap manifest the full range of affective disorders. Developmentally impaired social functioning influenced clinical presentation, but did not affect symptomatology. For people whose level of handicap is mild or moderate Sovner and Hurley advocate diagnosis by standard interview techniques and criteria. In cases of greater handicap, diagnosis can be based on changes in behaviour, in conjunction with family history of affective illness.

Despite this general change in attitude to psychiatric services for people with mental handicap there is continuing diagreement about diagnostic procedures. Corbett (1979) and Reid (1982) are confident of their ability to diagnose affective disorder in people with mental handicap, but Reid (1982) points out that this view would not be held by all psychiatrists working in the field. The use of standardised psychiatric evaluation instruments may eventually provide some improvements in the level of agreement between individual psychiatrists. It is essential, however, that reliabilities for suçh instruments are measured on people with mental handicap as well as non-handicapped individuals. To date, there is no available reliability study of this kind.

2.5.1 Prevalence of Psychiatric Disorder in People with Mental Handicap

Prevalence rates vary considerably according to the definition of the population under consideration and the criteria for determining presence of a psychiatric disorder. In this respect, the category of *behaviour disorder* causes particular problems. The category of *personality disorder* is considered to be a manifestation of mental illness rather than mental handicap. However, the high prevalence of behaviour disorders in people with mental handicap means that it is sometimes extremely difficult to decide whether a particular pattern of behaviour qualifies as a genuine psychiatric disorder. As a result, studies which include behaviour disorders as *psychiatric* problems result in high prevalence.

Day (1985) highlights this problem by demonstrating the notable difference between the pattern of diagnosis for comparably aged handicapped and non-handicapped people. In people with mental handicap, behaviour disorder comprises the largest single category, accounting for over half the presentations in the long-stay residents, and a third of the admissions from the community. Excluding alcohol and drug abuse, this represents a prevalence of *fifteen* times that of non-handicapped peers. Day points out that the lower level of behaviour disorder in non-handicapped people is partly accounted for by the fact that most behaviour problems do not lead to hospital admission because they are dealt with in other ways, e.g. through the penal system.

If behaviour disorders are included, the prevalence of psychiatric disorder among people with mental handicap is high, maybe as high as 60 per cent in hospital populations (Craft, 1971; Leck, Gordon & McKeown, 1967; Primrose, 1971; Reid, 1972). However, if people whose only form of disorder is a behaviour disorder are excluded, then the prevalence of psychosis and neurosis combined appears to be as low as 8-10 per cent (Heaton-Ward, 1977).

The DHSS survey of 1972 (DHSS, 1972) showed 32 per cent of population of hospitals to have a behaviour disorder of some degree, of which half were thought to be severe. Kirman (1979) urges caution, however, in drawing conclusions from estimates of this kind. They probably reflect the institutional setting and understaffing as much as intrinsic problems in the resident population.

Williams (1971) estimated 59 per cent of patients at the St Birinus group of hospitals to be psychiatrically disordered, while Forrest and Ogunremi (1974) found a level of 10 per cent for serious psychiatric disorder in the residents of Gogarburn Hospital in Edinburgh. Day (1985) surveyed 357 hospital residents, and found 30 per cent to have a psychiatric disorder. Of these, a high proportion of behaviour disorders (over 50 per cent) and low proportion of neuroses was observed. In a study of 122 people with severe and mild levels of handicap Gostason (1985) concluded that 18 per cent of the group with severe handicap were suffering from a severe or incapacitating level of mental illness. This compares with only 3 per cent of the group with mild handicap. Corbett's (1979) Camberwell study surveyed all adults and children with mental handicap who were in contact with services. Of the 400 adults surveyed it was concluded that a psychiatric diagnosis could be made on 46 per cent of clients. Corbett is at pains to point out, however, that the process of diagnosis is not straightforward. He reports that the largest group of people with marked behavioural symptoms could not be classified under any of the conventional categories of psychiatric disorder.

There are a number of further considerations to be borne in mind when interpreting findings from studies of psychiatric morbidity. Corbett (1987) points out that it is important to distinguish between those studies giving lifetime prevalence rates (as in Corbett's Camberwell study) with those which report only current psychiatric illness. This is likely to account for some of the discrepancies in prevalence reported by different studies. Another source of variation is the failure to distinguish between (a) psychoses occurring for the first time in adult life and (b) the long term effects of childhood psychosis, (a term commonly used to describe the symptoms of childhood autism). Such a distinction is sometimes difficult in the absence of a proper account of the person's developmental history, although it is likely to have an important effect on reported prevalence. Forrest and Ogunremi (1974), for example, have suggested that the bulk of adult psychopathology occurs in individuals who have suffered from childhood autism, while Corbett (1987) found in Camberwell that around 17 per cent of adults with mental handicap showed symptoms of childhood autism, a figure which may be even higher among those with severe mental handicap.

2.5.2 Psychoses

Reid (1982) points out that there has been a long history of the concept of manic depressive disorder among people with mental handicap. Thus, Hurd (1888) described cases of mania, folie circulaire and attempted suicide, and Ireland (1898) described three "imbecile lunatics" who were clear cases of melancholia. Herskovitz and Plesset (1941) considered that all psychoses to which people of normal intelligence are susceptible may also affect people with mental handicap. From their study, however, they conclude that functional psychoses do not usually occur in people with an IQ less than 50.

Reid also points out that a diagnosis of manic depression can be disputed within people with severe handicap. In his study of Strathmartine and Royal Dundee Liff Hospitals (personal communication quoted by Heaton-Ward (1977), Reid's diagnosis of the condition was based on changes in patterns of behaviour and sleep, observed by people who knew the client well. In one case there were phases of "mischievous activity" lasting 10 to 20 days, accompanied by early morning waking, self injury and irritability. The second patient had an apparently depressive spell lasting eight weeks, during which food was refused and weight lost, with a characteristic pattern of early waking observed. In the third patient, phases of noisy over-activity, weeping and depression, each lasting about two weeks, developed into a more prolonged state of depression during which self injury was attempted and attention-seeking behaviour manifested.

Heaton-Ward (1977) considers the basis for diagnosis of affective disorder in people with mental handicap to be somewhat speculative. Despite these difficulties, however, Heaton-Ward is confident of his diagnosis of affective psychosis in eight male and eight female residents of Stoke Park, of which seven satisfied his criterion for a diagnosis of manic-depressive psychosis. This represents a prevalence rate of 12 per thousand residents, identical to Reid's figure for Strathmartine. Rates for other hospitals vary, however, and Heaton Ward suggests this is due to differing methods of identifying cases.

Heaton-Ward does not provide a detailed age breakdown of these patients. It is stated, however, that age of onset was in the third, fourth and fifth decade in males, and the fourth, fifth and sixth decade in females. Symptoms described as: noisy, boisterous over-activity with obscene language and aggression to other residents and staff during the manic phase. Paranoid features occurred during both manic and depressive phases, but more commonly in the latter, in which delusions of bodily malfunction were also common. Several depressed patients expressed ideas of guilt and unworthiness.

Corbett (1979) has reviewed various studies of prevalence rates for affective disorder in people with mental handicap. He concludes that around 5-10 per cent of admissions to mental handicap hospitals suffer from schizophrenia or manic-depressive psychosis. Corbett's upper figure of 10 per cent is supported by several other studies. In a survey of mental health problems in Baltimore, Lemkau *et al.* (1942) reported a prevalence rate of 9 per cent for psychotic conditions in people with mental handicap. In Denmark, Moller (1965) found that 10 per cent of children in a mental handicap centre were psychotic, while Payne (1968) found an identical level of 10 per cent in a study of 216 people with mental handicap aged 5-76 years. Payne concluded that psychoses occur at all levels of handicap and are of long duration. Dupont (1981) presented an analysis on the basis of register information on 22,000 people with mental handicap in Denmark. Among the 6000 people classified as severely handicapped, 11.3 per cent had psychosis as a supplementary diagnosis.

Hucker, Day, and George (1979) note that, at the onset of psychosis, the possibility of a psychiatric illness is often not considered. This they illustrate by the case of a middle-aged man with a mild degree of handicap. He lived with his parents and worked in open employment. He developed an acute paranoid psychosis in response to obvious stress; as a result he became socially withdrawn, developed hysterical fits and paralysis of both legs and demonstrated immature behaviour. His parents, although aware of the condition, assumed it was a manifestation of the handicapping condition. However, he responded well to treatment with phenothiazine and returned to work after two months.

2.5.3 Depression

Reiss and Benson (1985) suggest that "The depressive symptoms of sadness, loneliness and crying bouts imply a considerable amount of emotional suffering" (p. 331). This is supported by the findings of Jacobson (1982) in a survey of patient records in New York State showing that 6.2 per cent of adults with mild mental handicap showed evidence of depression.

In an investigation of the psychosocial correlates of depression among adults with mild mental handicap, Reiss and Benson (1985) consider two hypotheses. First, depression may be associated with low levels of social support. This hypothesis is suggested by studies of non-handicapped people indicating that low levels of social support may be related to maladjustment and stress (De Araujo, Dudley, & Van Arsdel, 1972; Murphy & Moriarty, 1976; Sandler, 1980; Vaillant, 1977). Depression may result directly from the lack of reinforcement, or may be caused by the stress resulting from reduced access to people who can be of help in solving life problems. Second, depression may result from being labelled as handicapped, resulting in self-perceptions of being treated differently from non-handicapped peers.

Some prior evidence for Hypothesis 1 comes from the study of Schloss (1982). He found that both staff members and peers were less likely to approach depressed individuals with mental handicap than non-depressed people when there was no specific purpose for the interaction. However, there were no comparison groups included in the study, e.g. emotionally disturbed people with mental handicap, which would permit more clear evaluation. This hypothesis was also supported by the results of Reiss and Benson's study: depression was found to be associated with low levels of social support. The relation between perception of stigmatisation and depression was not found to be significant, however. It should be noted, however, that this study looked at people with *mild* mental handicap, and as a consequence was able to employ self-report measures of mood-state and perception of social stigma. Similar studies with more severely handicapped people would prove more difficult in this respect.

2.5.4 Prevalence rates for hospital versus community populations

Jones (1976) highlights the difficulties associated with comparing prevalence rates for people living in institutions and in the community. His study compared prevalence of psychiatric disorder in hospitals and hostels, and found approximately equal levels. He suggests, however, that the diagnostic criteria of "disorder" may have been different for the two populations. Jones comments that it is possible that a higher standard of behaviour is expected in hostels, so that behaviour which would pass unnoticed in hospital is noted and regarded as unusual in the small group setting of the hostel.

Ballinger and Reid (1977) attempted to minimise this effect by using a standardised assessment procedure. Using a modified version of the standardised psychiatric interview (Goldberg *et al.*, 1970), Ballinger and Reid found 31 per cent of the the hospital population to have significant psychiatric disorder. This, they point out, is almost identical to the rate of 32 per cent for behaviour disorder found in the DHSS survey (1972), a fact which is interpreted as indicating that the positive cases in the two surveys are being similarly defined. The notion that behaviour disorder is accounting for a large proportion of cases fits with the fact that a much lower rate (13 per cent) was found in the community group.

Day (1985) found a much higher incidence of neurotic disorders in community admissions (33.3 per cent) than in long-stay residents (3.7 per cent). This, he suggests, adds weight to the growing clinical impression that far from living a relatively stress-free life, people with mild and moderate levels of handicap are subjected not only to the normal range of everyday problems, but also have to cope with the stigma and additional consequences of their handicap, as we shall show in Chapter 5.

2.6 Psychiatric Disorder in Older People with Mental Handicap

Janicki and MacEachron (1984), in a survey of New York residents, state that the use of and need for mental health counselling increases with age from 53 years upwards. This statement looks reasonable at face value, but is difficult to interpret and assess since the criteria of "need" are not made explicit. One thing which is clear, however, is that psychiatric service *take-up* by older community residents, at least in the UK, does not follow this pattern. On the contrary, Ballinger (1979) has found a very low level of psychiatric service take-up by people with mental handicap who are 65+. Over a six year period in a district of about 200,000 people, only *ten* referrals of older people with mental handicap were made. In eight of the ten instances the main reason for referral was behaviour disorder, sometimes associated with a failure in basic self-care. Ballinger also notes that the level of referral is low compared with non-handicapped elderly people.

Day (1985) comes to the same conclusion as Ballinger, i.e. that reduced life expectancy produces a corresponding reduction in age-related psychiatric conditions. Day performed a retrospective study of two groups of people with mental handicap over 40 years of age: (a) A long-stay group of hospital residents, (b) a series of patients admitted from from the community to a psychiatric unit within the same hospital. Data were obtained from case records. Diagnoses were as recorded in the notes, except that where none was recorded Day made a diagnosis on the available evidence. Eighty per cent were aged 40-65, and the sexes were equally represented. There was a progressive fall in the proportion of people with psychiatric disorder as a function of age: 40-49 (48.7 per cent), 50-59 (30.3 per cent), 60-69 (25.2 per cent), 70+ (16.7 per cent). This trend held true for behaviour disorders: 29 per cent, 18.2 per cent, 9.1 per cent and 4.2 per cent respectively. Also for neuroses: 2.3 per cent, 2 per cent, 1 per cent, and 0 per cent. Behaviour disorders were, however, more associated with more severe levels of handicap, and twice as common among males as females. The overall pattern for psychiatric admissions was similar to that of the long stay residents.

Thirty per cent of long-stay residents over 40 years of age were suffering from psychiatric disorder. This is comparable with figures reported in other studies of mental handicap hospitals (Leck *et al.*, 1967; Ballinger & Reid, 1977), but lower than the 46 per cent level reported by Corbett (1979). However, Corbett showed a similar decline in prevalence of psychiatric disorder with age, so that this figure of 46 per cent had dropped to 38 per cent by age 45 years. It appears, therefore, that psychiatric service take-up shows the same decline with age that it does in the general population. However, Day finds that the overall proportion of admissions aged 40 and over is less than half that of non-handicapped people in the same age range. This he attributes to the fact that the substantial increase in admission for dementia and senile psychosis occurs *after* the age of 65. Since non-handicapped people have a greater life expectancy this puts a greater proportion of them at risk for this kind of admission.

Despite the evidence for reduced psychiatric disorder in older clients it does not seem that an interpretation based on reduced life expectancy reducing the number of age-related conditions is the only explanation. A reduced number of clients in the older age ranges would not *directly* affect the age-specific prevalence rates, since these rates are based on proportions rather than absolute frequencies (Corbett, 1987). Rather, Ballinger (1979) and Day (1985) are presumably arguing that older clients are generally in better neurological health since people with severe brain anomalies have a reduced life expectancy. This effect will also have an impact on referrals for severe problem behaviours, since there is a high proportion of people with brain damage who display such problems. Apart from differential mortality, however, there is also clear evidence that severe problem behaviours within individuals become less acute with increasing age (Chapter 4, Table 1). If one takes Day's (1985) figures for overall psychiatric morbidity, and *subtracts* the figures for behaviour disorders, it is interesting to note that the remaining percentage morbidity changes much less over the three age bands: (age 40-49: 19.7 per cent; age 50-59: 12.1 per cent; age 60-69: 16.1 per cent; age

70+: 12.5 per cent). This lends weight to the conclusion that severe problem behaviours are at least partly responsible for the large overall change in psychiatric morbidity with age.

In a more recent study Day (1987) reported that 20 per cent of a hospital population of people with mental handicap suffered from a psychiatric disorder. Of these, 70 per cent had functional disorders and 30 per cent showed organic syndromes. Day gives the following diagnostic breakdown for the twenty patients: Paraphrenia (2), affective psychosis (5), non-specific psychosis (1), dementia (6), behaviour disorder (5), and depression (1).

Carsrud, Carsrud and Standifer (1980) report one of the few studies of the possible causes of psychiatric disorder among older clients. They start with the suggestion that special care facilities often provide the physical care for older clients but pay less attention to emotional and psychological needs. Without effective intervention, feelings of loneliness, uselessness or worthlessness can become a dominant theme for institutionalised people. It is pointed out that behaviour themes which accompany such feelings, disorganisation, disorientation and non-constructive behaviours, often appear similar to those seen in senility. Unlike senility, however, effective intervention could go a long way to ameliorating these conditions.

Their study worked on the assumption that mental health is related to frequency of social interaction. It was specifically hypothesised that positive changes, such as a higher self-concept and engaging in constructive activities, would be related to the quantity of social interactions betweeen clients and staff. A comparison of two dormitories differing in length of client/staff non-interactions showed differences in self-concept, but these differences were not significant. This evidence cannot, therefore, be regarded as unequivocal.

2.6.1 Epilepsy

Epilepsy is common in people with mental handicap, and the prevalence rate increases with severity of brain damage (Corbett *et al.*, 1975). Penrose (1938) found 30 per cent of a hospital population suffered from epilepsy.

Rutter *et al.* (1970a, 1970b) in their survey of the Isle of Wight found a clear association between epilepsy and psychiatric disorder.

There have been few studies of psychiatric aspects of epilepsy in relation to the presence of mental handicap. Veall (1974) has shown that people with Down's syndrome tend to develop epilepsy as they age, a finding which presumably relates to the Alzheimer-type histological changes which have been observed in this group (see next section). In a recent study Lund (1985) observed the relation between epilepsy and psychiatric disorder in 302 adults with mental handicap drawn from the register of the Danish National Services for the Mentally Retarded. Lund found a clear relation between presence of a psychiatric condition and the occurrence of a seizure within the previous 12 months. Fifteen per cent of individuals with a psychiatric disorder had seizures in the past year, compared with 5.5 per cent of the people with no psychiatric condition. As with most surveys of psychiatric disorder in people with mental handicap, Lund included behaviour disorder as a category of psychiatric condition. It should be noted that Lund found epilepsy to be much more strongly correlated with behaviour disorder than with other psychiatric conditions.

In relation to ageing, Lund found that the prevalence of epilepsy *decreased* with age: In the age-range 20-44 years, 10 per cent of people had had a seizure in the previous year. This compares with an equivalent figure of 6 per cent in the age-range 45-64 years, and 4 per cent in the over-65s. This change presumably results from the fact that people with severe brain damage have a reduced life expectancy, so that people with less damage tend to be over-represented in the older groups.

2.6.2 Dementia in people with Down's syndrome

With the increasing longevity of individuals with mental handicap has come the disturbing observation that people with Down's syndrome appear to be considerably more at risk of contracting pre-senile dementia (Alzheimer's disease) than either the non-handicapped population or people with other handicapping conditions. There is now considerable histopathological evidence that the brains of many (or all) Down's syndrome individuals aged 35 and over show the characteristic cerebral changes associated with this particular condition described above, (Ball & Nuttall, 1980; Burger and Vogel, 1973; Crapper *et al.*, 1974; Ellis *et al.*, 1974; Jervis, 1948; Malamud, 1972; Solitaire and Lamarche, 1966). Until recently the commonly accepted medical position was grimly summed up by Ellis *et al.* (1974): "In Down's syndrome, the reward for survival beyond age 40 is presenile dementia" (p 101). A careful reading of the available literature, however, suggests that this extreme position cannot be supported on the basis of the available evidence. Indeed the problems associated with diagnosing Alzheimer's disease are not confined to the mentally handicapped population, but arise from the considerable confusion which results from the medical definition of the syndrome.

In assessing the status of this evidence, an important point to bear in mind is that the relationship between the behavioural symptoms and brain pathology, described above, is not at all clear. While histopathological evidence is considered conclusive, clinical symptoms may not be. It therefore frequently happens that a patient is diagnosed, at post-mortem, as having suffered from Alzheimer's disease, even if there have been no observable clinical symptoms. Also, all three of the major histological signs can be seen in a variety of other conditions, including Pick's disease, Creutzfeld-Jakob disease, Parkinsonism, alcoholism and many more (Solitaire and Lamarche, 1966). Although not occurring so frequently in these other conditions as in Alzheimer's disease, it is clear that the significance of these changes is not fully understood. One might question the status of a syndrome which has no unique distinguishing characteristics, and requires no clinical symptoms to be manifested. As we shall see, this last point is particularly relevant to the research on Down's syndrome individuals.

The notion of an association between Down's syndrome and Alzheimer's disease has been around a long time. Writing only 10 years after Alzheimer first described the syndrome, Fraser and Mitchell (1876) wrote of a sample of 54 Down's syndrome mortalities: "Phthisis caused a large majority of these deaths. In not a few instances, however, death was attributed to nothing more than general decay - a sort of precipitated senility". Jervis (1948) describes the case histories of three Down's syndrome individuals and the histological information resulting from their subsequent post mortems. Ages at death were 47, 42 and 35 years, and in all cases the patients' brains demonstrated the characteristic features of Alzheimer's disease. Jervis was obviously aware of the uncertainty of the brain/behaviour association, in that he raised the question of whether the pathological lesions imply a presence of the morbid processes of dementia, or merely the manifestations of early physiological ageing in individuals of short life span. Given the severity of the lesions in these patients, coupled with the clinical observations, Jervis concluded that diagnoses of Alzheimer's disease were probably appropriate.

It is the detailed presentation of Jervis's cases that makes this paper one of the more useful sources available. It is worth noting some of the observations on the patients' behaviour changes. Case 1 was a woman who died aged 47. Up to 42 years of age: "She was affectionate, even tempered, always cheerful, and interested in her simple manual tasks around the home. An IQ was not determined while at home, but there was sufficient information which makes it possible to estimate retrospectively that her IQ was between 40 and 50. Beginning at the age of 42 years, a slowly progressive mental deterioration was observed. The patient gradually lost interest in her daily tasks, refused to work, became apathetic, showing little emotional reaction toward her mother, whom previously she cherished. At times she was irritable and depressed. While previously she had been very fond of people, she would now spend many hours by herself. Vocabulary became more restricted and was soon limited to a very few words. At 44 years of age she was unable to feed herself, later became untidy and developed tremors of the hand. At 46 years of age, it was noted that she was unsteady on her feet". The other two cases described by Jervis similarly showed marked personality changes and gradual deterioration, occurring at ages 38 and 31 respectively. From Jervis's evidence there seems little doubt that dementia had set in. What we are not told is how this sample of three individuals was selected. Without knowing something about the relative proportion of older Down's syndrome individuals who were not affected it is impossible to draw any conclusions beyond those applicable to the non-handicapped population (ie that individuals suffering from terminal dementia will invariably show the characteristic histopathological signs at autopsy).

Over the last 20 years a number of studies have confirmed the earlier findings of Struwe (1929) and Jervis (1948) that many Down's syndrome people over the age of 35 show pathological lesions similar to those of Alzheimer's disease (Ball and Nuttall, 1980; Burger and Vogel, 1973; Crapper *et al.*, 1974; Ellis *et al.*, 1974; Malamud, 1972; Ohara, 1972; Solitaire and Lamarche, 1966; Wisneiwski *et al.*, 1979). Indeed Malamud (1972) found none of his sample who lived past 40 to be completely devoid of these signs. The possibility that these observed changes in the Down's syndrome brain might be somehow different from those associated with Alzheimer's disease also appears to be ruled out. Modern electron microscope analysis of the processes reveals them to be remarkably similar, both in their dimensions and locations (Ball and Nuttall, 1980; Burger and Vogel, 1973; Ellis *et al.*, 1974).

While the medical findings are impressively consistent it should be noted that the majority of these studies show a conspicuous absence of any detailed evidence of dementing behaviour prior to death. Indeed a number of authors make specific reference to the lack of correlation between clinical symptoms and pathology (Burger and Vogel, 1973; Ellis *et al.*, 1974; Olson and Shaw, 1969; Solitaire and Lamarche, 1966). The observations of Olson and Shaw (1969), one of the few studies to include detailed behavioural information, illustrate this point clearly. They reviewed the cases of 26 Down's syndrome individuals who had subsequently died, and found that the three cases who had lived longer than 35 years all showed the distinct pathological signs of Alzheimer's disease. However, only one of these had a history of dementing behaviour. Obviously the sample size is very small, but it highlights the need for caution in assuming a link between this kind of functional degeneration and Down's syndrome.

2.6.2.1 The prevalence of dementia in people with Down's syndrome. It should be stressed here that we are now talking about dementing behaviour rather than brain pathology. The number of available studies is extremely small, so the conclusions can only be tentative. Owens Dawson and Losin (1971) studied two groups of Down's syndrome residents at a State Hospital in California. One group consisted of residents over 35, the other with ages 20 to 25. Measures were taken of the functioning of the frontal and parietal lobes, and a questionnaire was devised to test memory, orientation, agnosia, and apraxia. Following examination of all members of the older sample it was concluded that none of them could be unequivocally classified as suffering from dementia. There were, however, some significant differences between the two groups. The older individuals demonstrated a higher incidence of difficulty in object identification, frontal lobe dysfunction, and diffuse cerebral dysfunction in general. The authors conclude that "One logical etiologic explanation for this would seem to be Alzheimer changes". On the other hand, it should be pointed out that such minor performance differences would not be acceptable clinical evidence for dementia. Our current techniques for assessment of cognitive degeneration are not sufficiently sensitive to accurately perceive the signs at an early stage.

Reid and Aungle (1974) assessed 155 hospital residents over 45 years of age for clinical evidence of dementia. Eight of these 155 residents had Down's syndrome. The authors found eleven of the group to be suffering from dementia, giving an overall prevalence rate of 7.1 per cent. Of the 155 residents, 22 were aged 65 or over, and three of these 22 were dementing, giving a prevalence rate of 13.6 per cent for this age group. Two of the eight with Down's syndrome were included in the group of 11 suffering from dementia. This represents a prevalence rate of 25 per cent compared with 6 per cent of the people without Down's syndrome. Despite this apparently large differential, it must be borne in mind that the numbers are too small to provide a reliable estimate.

Thase, Liss, Smelzer and Maloon (1982) compared 40 Down's syndrome institutional residents with a similar sized group of institutional controls matched for age, sex, IQ and length of institutionalisation. Measures were taken of orientation, attention span, affect, praxis, matching to sample, delayed visual memory, digit span, object identification, colour naming, and general knowledge. Neurological examinations were also conducted. The authors report an impressive number of measures in which the Down's group performed worse than the controls, and which they tender as evidence for the early onset of degeneration. These include orientation, digit span, object identification, delayed visual memory and apraxia. There is, however, something suspect about these findings. It is stated that the two groups were matched on IQ, (although the criterion is not specified). Three of the significantly discriminating measures, however, are already part of the most common IQ test, the WAIS. This suggests that if the groups have been matched, and the older sample are performing worse on these three sub-tests, that they must actually be scoring better in some other areas. Certainly this kind of problem highlights the need for rigorous attention to the assumptions underlying the various tests used, before making assertions which have such important implications.

Chapter Four

CHANGES IN INTELLIGENCE AND ADAPTIVE BEHAVIOUR

"Mental handicap" is par excellence a condition involving intellectual impairment. In the social sphere we argue elsewhere that ageing people with mental handicap are in double jeopardy from both their handicapping condition and the consequences of ageing. In this chapter we consider a further possible facet of this double jeopardy, namely whether the initial intellectual impairment is exacerbated by further decline in intellectual functioning with age. This question can be broadened to consider the course of change in a range of cognitive functions such as memory, as well as adaptive behaviour. An understanding of such changes is important not only with respect to theories of intellectual function, but also to our expectation regarding people with mental handicap as they get older.

While no one would wish to argue that an understanding of intellectual development in the later years is not both of interest and importance, the value of assessing intellect through standardised tests of intelligence has been questioned. Psychometric tests yielding an intelligence quotient (IQ) have become unfashionable in the field of human services. This partly reflects a theoretical reaction against them (in what sense does such a test measure intelligence?), but also the fact that an assessed IQ or some component of IQ (e.g. verbal ability) has limited value in informing therapy or intervention programmes. Berger and Yule (1986) have recently reviewed the position with respect to intelligence testing and mental handicap, pointing to both the strengths and weaknesses of their use. Schaie (1983a), however, has argued that such tests have good predictive validity in many educational and vocational areas of life and that assessment of intellectual competence is of paramount importance when we reach later life. He goes on: "...I believe that this body of evidence at the present state of the art, provides a reasonable base for making policy recommendations on such diverse issues as determining the age ranges for which adult education may be most profitable or specifying the ages at which workers in industries requiring certain abilities may start to be at a disadvantage. I am fully cognizant that the projections made will be time limited and that new evidence will have to be collected continuously to account for the impact on behavior of our rapidly changing technological environment." (p.129.)

Schaie's (1983a) view rests on the already extensive literature on individuals who are not handicapped. Since this literature raises important questions concerning both the methods by which we explore intellectual change with age and the theory that explains such change, we shall begin by briefly considering these wider issues.

1 INTELLIGENCE

1.1 Concepts and Methods

Botwinick (1977) raises the fundamental question to which so much attention has been directed, namely "Does intelligence decline in old age?" In addition to this question Schaie (1983a) asks whether intelligence changes uniformly or in different ability patterns and what the generational and individual differences in age related to such change are. Both go on to point out that, despite considerable research, controversy remains as to the answer to the question. Part of this controversy is engendered by the fact that there are inconsistencies between studies with respect to what is meant by ageing, the type of tests used, definitions of intelligence, sampling techniques and the research methods used. In the context of mental handicap, we have already discussed the problem of definition with respect to the lower age level to be taken in defining a sample (Chapter 1), and the additional questions obviously have an important bearing on interpretation of the studies that *have* been undertaken with people with mental handicap.

Botwinick contrasts views concerning the nature of intelligence, notably that which emphasises intelligence as an innate, genetically determined attribute of a person, with the view of intelligence as an ability indicative of what a person can do at a given time of testing. The former view implies that while a person's basic potential can be affected by experience and biological change, there is a theoretical limit, or capacity, which is biologically determined. In the latter, there is no view of potential or biological limit and a greater emphasis on the implications of the outcome of an assessment for the individual's role in life. It should be added that we do not need to adopt an either/or position with respect to these two points of view. As Horn and Donaldson (1976) and many others have noted, intelligence is not unitary, and different components may reflect different physiologically-based and experiential influences.

These two positions also lead proponents to adopt differing views of factors that influence performance on a test of intelligence. Thus, fatigue might influence an older person's performance on a test. The view of intelligence as capacity would lead us to argue that the factor of fatigue was extraneous to the assessment of capacity and that the inference that intelligence had declined was not valid. An ability orientated view, however, would argue that fatigue was not extraneous to the assessment of intelligence. Intellectual functioning demands that performance be maintained at a given level if the person is to be effective in an activity. To attempt to remove the effect of fatigue is potentially harmful as it would lead us away from considering how best to arrange tasks and activities for older people. Fatigue is only one possible modifying influence on intelligence. Wider influences, such as education and socioeconomic status, and of special relevance here, institutionalisation, will also substantially influence intelligence.

The research methods employed will also influence the conclusions we draw. Differing patterns of ageing will be observed depending on the criteria used to select the sample. For example, a random sample of people will show age-related decline in a more dramatic fashion than a group selected because its members are of comparable educational level. Again, Botwinick sees this issue as being related to the capacity-ability argument. A capacity view of intelligence would argue for the findings derived from the study of people with matched educational level. The ability position would see random sampling as a more adequate reflection of the real world and therefore a more valid indication of the true state of affairs with respect to changes in intelligence.

The particular findings with respect to age trends will also be closely bound up with whether a cross sectional or longitudinal investigation is undertaken. In the former type of investigation, independent groups at different age levels are tested. For example, in Table 1.3 in Chapter 1, we present the numbers of people in a hospital over 50 years of age in ten-year groups or cohorts, i.e. 50-59, 60-69 and so on. If we then assessed the individuals in these groups taking the average intelligence of each and looked at changes in relation to age, we would have undertaken a cross-sectional study. If, however, we took the 50-59 year old cohort and tested its members at regular intervals for a number of decades, then the study would be longitudinal.

Both methods present difficulties. In the cross sectional study differences between cohorts related specifically to their age may exist. For example, drawing from the field of mental handicap, in the older groups there may be a predominance of people who were placed in the institution many years ago for reasons other than severe mental handicap. In contrast, those so placed more recently may have been specifically because they show severe mental handicap. In this case the average intelligence of the older cohort may be inflated relative to the younger. As Botwinick points out, age and cohort are one, and in the real world cannot be separated. Longitudinal studies also present problems arising from the fact that the samples gradually reduce as people die, and that very often people with certain characteristics die first. We have seen, for example, that people with profound mental handicap die earlier than those who are more able (Lubin and Kiely 1985). Thus, any tendency for intelligence to decline would at least be partially offset by the fact of the higher ability of those individuals surviving. It should be added here that the methodology that has been developed to cope with these fundamental difficulties in research design has become increasingly complex, and the interested reader is referred to Schaie (1983b). Some refinements of cross sectional and longitudinal design in studies of people with mental handicap will be described below.

1.2 Findings in the Non-handicapped Population

The assessment of age-related changes in intelligence has typically been undertaken employing standardised tests of intelligence and its various subcomponents. The Wechsler Adult Intelligence Scales (WAIS) have figured large in studies of non-handicapped individuals. The Scales comprise six subtests concerned with verbal abilities and five concerned with what are known as performance measures. While the verbal subtests assess vocabulary, comprehension and arithmetic, performance subtests cover picture completion and arrangement and object assembly. What has been referred to as the "classic ageing pattern" is well replicated in cross sectional studies in the non-handicapped population employing the WAIS. This consists of a more marked decline in performance scores than in verbal scores, with the sharpest drop in each coming after 70 years of age. Performance measures assess intellectual processes and these tasks reflect ability to deal with manipulation of unfamiliar material in contrast to the verbal tests which involve the manipulation of familiar material, experience of which has been built up over a lifetime. The distinction between these two types of intellectual process accords with the view noted above that intelligence has two components, one "fluid", based on physiological structure and one "crystallised", based on experience and learned abilities.

What, then, can be concluded from these cross sectional studies? Botwinick suggests that when an age related effect is seen it relates more to certain specific functions than to overall intelligence: "A summary...suggests that the age-intelligence relationship tends to be small, with decline not setting in until relatively late in life. When it does, memory, speed of response and perceptual-integrative functions are involved. How crucial even these test abilities are in the daily business of carrying out life's responsibilities is the important question not answered by the investigations carried out to date." (p.589.) Despite a variety of methodological problems connected with longitudinal data collection, Botwinick's review indicates that a similar conclusion can be drawn from such studies. Though the decrements may be less pronounced, similar trends with respect to relatively greater decrements in performance skills relative to verbal abilities are reported. Schaie (1983a) on the basis of his own studies suggests that, before 60, changes are essentially trivial though by 74 all abilities will have shown a reliable decrement. Thus, the studies reviewed by Botwinick point to some late decline in "fluid" intelligence and maintenance of relatively less decline in "crystallised" intelligence. As Horn and Donaldson (1976) are at pains to point out, this formulation in terms of fluid and crystallised intelligence does not predict an inevitable decrement for <u>all</u> individuals. Indeed, Schaie (1983a) argues that even at 81, less than half of all observed individuals showed reliable changes in intelligence in the previous seven years.

Botwinick also reviews studies bearing on the course of development of intelligence in relation to whether a person is bright or dull when young. Do the bright and dull remain so when old? Such a question clearly takes us towards the issue of mental handicap and ageing and we can now consider <u>patterns</u> of change in this population.

1.3 Findings in the population of people with mental handicap

The relatively slow rate of development in people with mental handicap will be reflected in slower growth of the individual's mental age (MA) and possibly in differing periods for which such growth continues. These are shown schematically in Figure 4.1 drawn from Fisher and Zeaman (1970).

In A-1 we can see what they refer to as "the traditional view". Here rate of development is slower but continues to the same age for both people who are and are not mentally handicapped. Thereafter the level

Figure 4.1:

Some alternative patterns of growth of mental age and associated changes in IQ

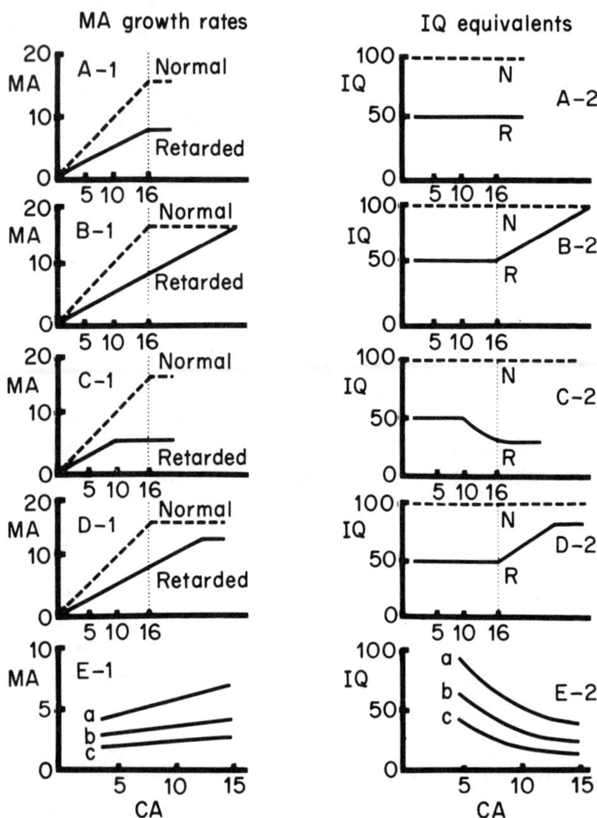

of development remains stable but unequal. In B-1 we again see unequal rates of MA increase, but here the group of people with mental handicap continue to develop beyond the age at which MA stabilises in non-handicapped people eventually catching up with them. In contrast, C-1 shows people with mental handicap ceasing to develop before the growth period for their non-handicapped peers ends, i.e. at 10 years old rather than at 16 in this diagram. Finally, in D-1, initial growth is slower in the mentally handicapped group but continues for longer before finally reaching a plateau. It does not, in contrast to B-1, ever catch up with the MA level for the non-handicapped group.

Concomitant changes in IQ are shown in A-2 to D-2. For A-2, IQ remains constant throughout the life of both groups, though that of the group with mental handicap is clearly lower than for the non-handicapped group. For both B-2 and D-2, IQ continues to increase in the group with mental handicap, reaching the normal level in the former case and levelling off in the latter. Only in the case of C-2 does IQ drop as the result of the short MA growth period.

These patterns of change, Fisher and Zeaman (1970) argue, are all possible and not unreasonable. They note that there had at that time been in the region of three dozen studies of changes in IQ with age. These involved varying age spans (some concerned only with childhood), degrees of retardation and aetiologies. Results varied markedly, from finding no changes in IQ, to decline, and to spontaneous gains, these differing patterns reflecting the very different characteristics of the groups.

This diversity, however, argued for a wider ranging study with groups representing borderline, mild, moderate, severe and profound levels of retardation. The IQ boundaries in their study for these groups were: borderline, IQ 83-68; mild, IQ 67-52; moderate, 51-36; severe, 35-20; profound, 20-0. Ideally, Fisher and Zeaman argued, a longitudinal design should be employed. Across the time course envisaged, virtually birth to death, this was not feasible and they employed a compromise between cross sectional and longitudinal designs that they refer to as "semi-longitudinal". Here two CA levels are selected and a group of individuals tested on the Stanford Binet test at each CA, e.g. 45 and 50 years. The average slope of change in MA is computed. Similar slopes are determined for other age ranges across the full developmental span with other groups. There are thus a series of short term longitudinal curves. These are integrated into a single curve purporting to represent change over the full developmental range. It is also, of course, possible to treat these results cross sectionally by analysing results at each age level.

When such cross sectional analysis was undertaken for all 1000+ individuals in this institutionalised sample, MA continued to rise throughout the 70 years with only slight deceleration. This rise Fisher and Zeaman attribute to the differential death rate, with individuals who were severe and profound dying earlier than those who were more able. Figure 4.2 shows the MA changes for each ability group with the number of people on whom data were collected at the various ages.

Figure 4.2:

Mean semi-longitudinal MA growth functions for the five levels of handicap. Numbers on the curves refer to numbers of subjects measured.

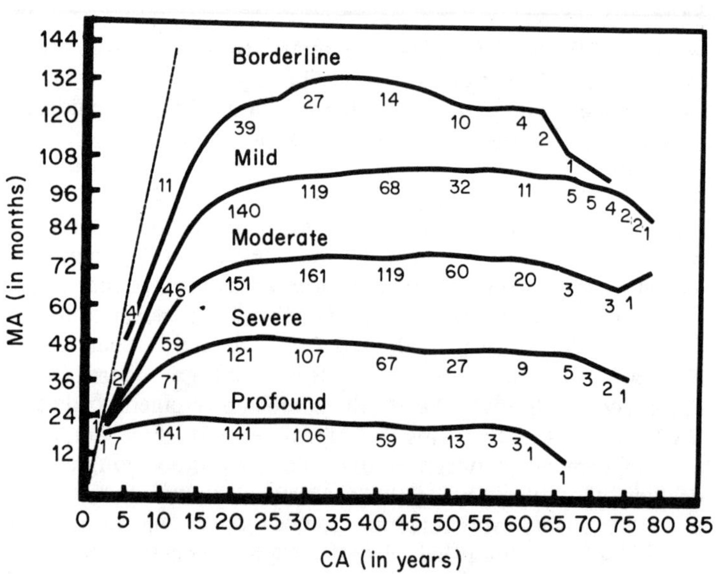

First, all slopes are lower, not unexpectedly, than for non-handicapped individuals, with rate of development of MA directly related to ability group. Second, the higher the ability level the longer the growing season. For the borderline group highest MA is reached around 35 years of age and for the profound group before 15 years. Third, a decline after 60 years is seen in all groups, apparently greater the higher the ability level. Small numbers of individuals at the older levels, however, mean that results at the more advanced ages are possibly unreliable. There is little evidence of sex differences though some suggestion that after 50 males decline more than females. Three diagnostic groups were defined: people with epilepsy; those considered cultural-familial; those with a congenital cerebral defect. No differences between these groups in the pattern of ageing were noted, though a tendency for people with epilepsy to decline more in old age was found. Thus the cause of the mental handicap appears to have little bearing on the course of intellectual change as people age.

Demaine and Silverstein (1978) replicated Fisher and Zeaman's study in a consideration of Down's syndrome vs non-Down's syndrome people with mental handicap living in an institution. They confirmed the earlier studies finding with respect to the growth curve for MA, i.e. that for the non-Down's syndrome group being consistently higher than for their Down's syndrome peers. Their results, however, only cover an age range from CA 4 years to 50, small numbers precluding an upward extension of age.

Fisher and Zeaman used the same semi-longitudinal approach to assess changes in IQ. Figure 4.3 shows that IQ falls from two to sixteen years in all groups. The continued rise in MA in the more able groups results in some increase in IQ. Some decline in IQ is seen in all groups from 50 years onwards, though there is a suggestion that this has begun earlier in the borderline group

Technical considerations limit interpretation of the significance of these changes in IQ, though the authors do not consider that the fact of institutionalisation can account for them. Their own concern is to ensure that the curves can be made to conform to a view of intelligence as a constant, genetically determined aspect of the individual and they go on to transform their results in an attempt mathematically to represent them as reflecting such constancy. Employing the same semi-longitudinal approach, Silverstein (1979) considered again a large group of people with mental handicap living in an institution. Employing the Stanford Binet Intelligence Scale, they confirmed in their essentials Fisher and Zeaman's results. The only discrepancy was that they did not find the longer growing season for more able groups noted above in the 1970 study.

Figure 4.3:

Age changes in IQ for the five levels of handicap computed semi-longitudinally.

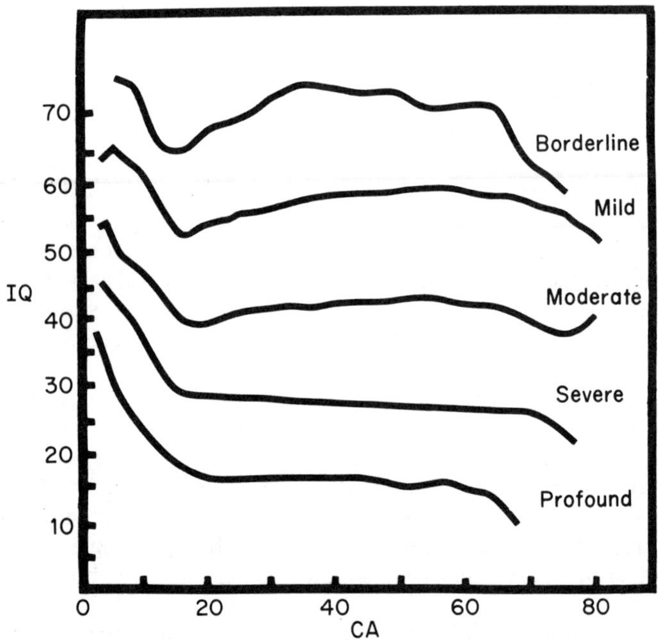

Studies employing the Stanford Binet Scale do not cast light on the Performance-Verbal distinction given such prominence in the literature on non-handicapped people. Rosen, Stallings, Floor and Nowakiwska (1968) explored the reliability of the WAIS over a one to six year period in young adults with mental handicap in an institution. The primary outcome of the study was to demonstrate the satisfactory reliability of the scales and their sub-scales. As defined in this study, a substantial majority of individuals showed no change in Verbal, Performance or Full Scale IQs. For all three Scales increments exceeded decrements, most pronouncedly in the case of Performance IQs. Thus, against a general background of IQ increase in early adulthood, Performance improved significantly more than Verbal IQ, confirming Bell and Zubek's (1960) earlier report. Further confirmation was found in Goodman's (1976) study which covered the age-range 11-44 years and employed both WISC and WAIS with another institutionalised sample. Observations were again taken semi-longitudinally. For this childhood/early adult population there were slight increases in the Full Scale IQ, larger and more consistent for the Performance than for the Verbal Scale. These IQ measures reflect change relative to the normal population, the greater increases in the Performance IQ reflecting the earlier plateauing of the normal population in this area. When an absolute measure of change was taken using the Scales scores, absolute gains were found to be the same for both Verbal and Performance Scales.

Some limitations are placed on the studies employing the Stanford Binet Scales by the fact that (a) the samples are drawn from long-stay hospitals; (b) the studies are not truly longitudinal; (c) numbers of elderly people are quite small. With respect to the studies employing the WAIS, a further limitation can be added, (d) that they did not consider individuals who were over 50 years. Points (b) and (c) are taken into account in a recent study by Hewitt, Fenner and Torphy (1986). In Stoke Park Hospital, Bristol, where psychological assessments had been administered regularly to residents for over 50 years, with 255 (23 per cent) of the 1092 residents being 64 years or over, many of whom were 80+ years. These authors drew on this data bank, specifically 148 of the 255 over 64s who were available for present assessment. (A small number were excluded as functioning below the lower test or limit or having additional impairments that would prevent adequate assessment; in addition, no residents with Down's syndrome were in the sample.) The mean CA of the group was 73.8 years (range 65.0-88.7), average length of stay in the hospital 54.8 years. The repeated measures on the Stanford Binet Intelligence Scale were analysed both cross sectionally and longitudinally. Significant increases in MA were found between 35 and 60 years, and a significant decrease from 60 to 75 years. The longitudinal analysis confirmed this pattern of gradual increase followed by decline. Eighteen people showed significant individual decline, the mean age at which this started being 65.8 years. The authors note that this might be an underestimate of the number showing significant decline because (a) the Stanford Binet is limited in the number of performance items and (b) because some of the less able have been excluded from the sample. They also note that these individuals might represent a pathological sub group within the population. We deal later with the relation of intellectual change to adaptive behaviour as shown in their study.

1.4 Conclusion

Despite varying methodologies, these studies provide a generally consistent picture of intellectual growth and subsequent decline in intellectual functioning as measured by the Stanford Binet Intelligence Scale. Where the WAIS has been employed with young adults, the picture of growth is confirmed, particularly with reference to Performance vs Verbal ability. In some measure the studies support the picture summarised by Botwinick with non-handicapped individuals: where deterioration does occur, it comes relatively late in life and is generally not dramatic. In many respects, however, we have learnt little about this population with respect to the details of intellectual change and ageing. There are four areas that command further consideration:

First, the Stanford Binet Intelligence Scale has generally been employed. This is heavily loaded with respect to language items and poor regarding performance tests. Berger and Yule (1986) have therefore questioned its usefulness with populations of people with mental handicap. In addition, in the light of the findings reported above on the relatively greater decline in performance (fluid) abilities than verbal (crystallised) abilities, the Stanford Binet Scale may well be less sensitive to intellectual change than would be the case if the WAIS were employed. Certainly a replication of the studies with non-handicapped individuals would remedy this shortcoming and tell us more about the nature of intellectual change relative to the rest of the population. What is required is a study extending upwards the age range considered by Rosen *et al.* (1968) and Goodman (1976) described above.

Second, and related to this issue, is the fact that all populations considered were from large institutions. It is argued that these provide relatively consistent environments over time, therefore showing true ageing effects. However, if such consistency does exist, it is also likely to be an impairing consistency, for institutional environments are notoriously handicapping with respect to the very language abilities assessed on the Stanford Binet Scale. Indeed, Hogg (1982) has drawn attention to the fact that relative to fine motor abilities, a clear class of performance behaviour, i.e. language, is much more impaired by the institutional environment. Thus, what we might be seeing in these studies is the rise and decline of one aspect of intelligence in an environment that anyway leads to decrements in this aspect of intellectual development. Paradoxically, in view of Botwinick's review, these studies may have looked at the less likely indicator of intellectual change i.e. verbal rather than performance behaviour. With respect to young adults, Goodman (1976) comments that "In the normal population it is verbal rather than performance abilities which continue to develop through adulthood. If language skills reflect 'crystallized' intelligence, it can be argued that the mental development in the normal population after adolescence is due to learning and practice, not to increased potential. Those without optimal learning opportunities, i.e. the institutionalized mentally retarded, would hardly be expected to 'keep up' in terms of absolute progress with those exposed to a more diversified community life." (p.1004.)

To make full use of information from a test such as the WAIS it is desirable to have an understanding of the test structure when employed with people with mental handicap. This differs from that found in the non-handicapped population. Coolidge, Rakoff, Schwellenbach, Bracken and Walker (1986), for example, show that scatter as reflected in discrepancies between subtest performance (highest subtest-scales score minus lowest subtest-scales score) and verbal-performance discrepancy (Verbal IQ-Performance IQ) are markedly enhanced in adults with mental handicap. In this sample, apparently living in the community and aged 18-66 years, performance IQ was superior to and inferior to Verbal IQ with equal frequency.

Third, the analyses of intellectual change reviewed appear to gravitate to a genetic viewpoint, explicitly so in the case of Fisher and Zeaman's study. By lacking any comparison with alternative environments or between different environments for the same individual, they cast no actual light on the relation between intellectual development and the individual's ecology. Taken together, there would appear to be a need for a study which permits more direct comparison with the wider literature on ageing by assessing both crystallised and fluid intelligence in contrasted environments, ideally in an appropriate longitudinal design.

Fourth, the results presented generally reflect average trends across large groups. At several points in the studies it is clear that not all individuals conform to these trends. Relatively greater improvement, lack of decrements, and alternative patterns are all indicated. Little attention, however, has been given to the issue of individual variability and the prediction and description of differences between people.

From this general picture there are two lines of investigation that must now be considered. First, we can consider broader changes in adaptive behaviour as they occur in the ageing person. Second, we can consider changes in specific psychological processes as assessed through experimental techniques. As we shall see, there are complex links between intellectual, adaptive and process changes that occur with advancing age.

2 ADAPTIVE BEHAVIOUR

The concept of *adaptive behaviour* has become central to the classification of people with mental handicap (Grossman 1973) and in evaluating the impact of the environment on such individuals. Grossman (1973) defines adaptive behaviour as "...the effectiveness or degree with which the individual meets the standards of personal independence and social responsibility expected of his (sic) age and cultural group. Since these expectations vary for different age groups, deficits in adaptive behavior will vary at different ages." (pp. 11-12.) He goes on to list eight areas of interest among which the balance shifts from infancy to adult life:

"1. Sensory-motor skills development
2. Communication skills (including speech and language)
3. Self-help skills
4. Socialization
5. Application of basic academic skills in daily life activities
6. Application of appropriate reasoning and judgement in mastery of the environment
7. Social skills
8. Vocational and social responsibilities and performances"

(p.12).

With respect to classification, the concept of adaptive behaviour was introduced to complement the use of IQ scores in making such a judgement. The main instrument that has evolved to permit direct assessment of adaptive behaviour is the American Association on Mental Deficiency Adaptive Behavior Scale (ABS) (Nihira 1969a, 1969b). Using the ABS, Nihira (1976) produced a parallel study to those concerned with IQ change described above. In this cross-sectional study he examined changes in adaptive behaviour in over 3,300 children and adults of varying degrees of intellectual impairment. As with most of the studies of intelligence, these people lived in large institutions. Though Part 2 of the ABS is concerned with personal and social maladaptive behaviour, the study dealt with the domain of behaviour assessed in Part 1 of the Scales, i.e. *Personal Independence*, a concept comparable to that of *Social Competence.*
Factor Analysis of Part 1 of the ABS identified three major factors which were represented at most of the age-levels studied, i.e. a range from four to 69 years. These Factors were:

I <u>Personal self-sufficiency</u>: defined by abilities in eating, toilet-use, cleanliness, dressing and undressing and motor development

II <u>Community self-sufficiency</u>: defined by abilities in travel (locomotion), general independent functioning, money handling and budgeting, shopping skills, expression, comprehension, social language development, numbers and time, cleaning, kitchen duties and other domestic activities

III <u>Personal-social responsibility</u>: defined by initiative, perseverence, leisure time, responsibility, socialisation, vocational activity, appearance and care of clothing

In a manner analogous to the MA and IQ curves shown above, cross-sectional growth curves for the factor scores on these dimensions were produced (Figures 4.4 to 4.6). It will also be seen that curves for different levels of retardation are shown, i.e. for borderline, mild, moderate, severe and profound retardation.

It can be seen that throughout most of the lives of these individuals adaptive behaviour improves, in that both Personal and Community self-sufficiency continue to develop, as indeed does Personal-social responsibility. There is a slight decrease in adaptive functioning for the more able groups in the age range with which we are concerned, i.e. 50-69 years. This can be seen for all three domains for the borderline groups, for Personal and Community self-sufficiency for the mild and moderate groups, and for the severe group for Personal self-sufficiency. However, less able groups continued to make progress until well into their 60s, notably the profound group on all dimensions and the severe group in Community self-sufficiency and Personal-social responsibility. As with the work on intelligence, it is possible that these trends in adaptive behaviour in people with profound retardation reflect in part selective mortality with the least able dying earlier.

Working with the institutionalised population described above, Hewitt, Fenner and Torphy (1986) considered the further development of abilities

Figure 4.4:

Personal self-sufficiency. Mean factor scores for ten age groups. Each line represents a specific level of measured intelligence.

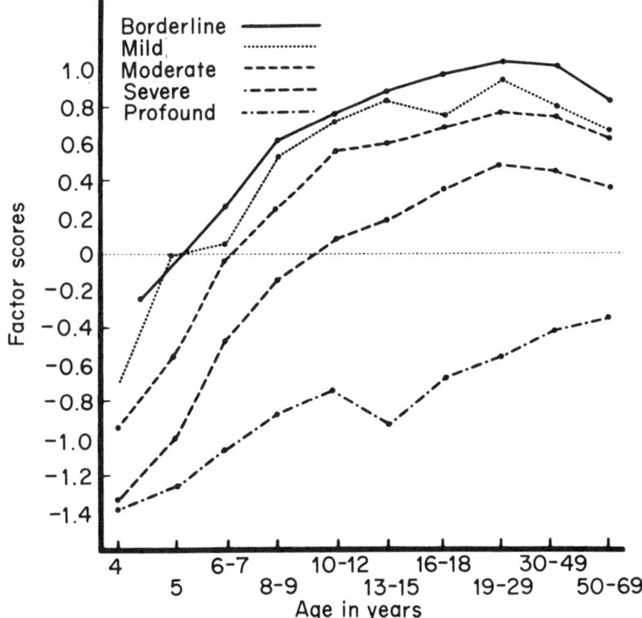

Figure 4.5:

Community self-sufficiency. Mean factor scores for ten age groups. Each line represents a specific level of measured intelligence.

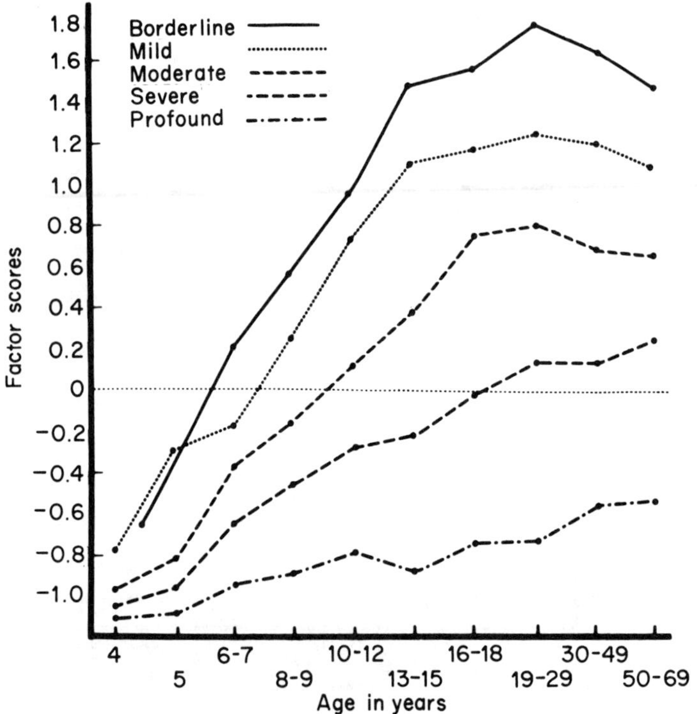

Figure 4.6:

Personal-social responsibility. Mean factor scores for ten age groups. Each line represents a specific level of measured intelligence.

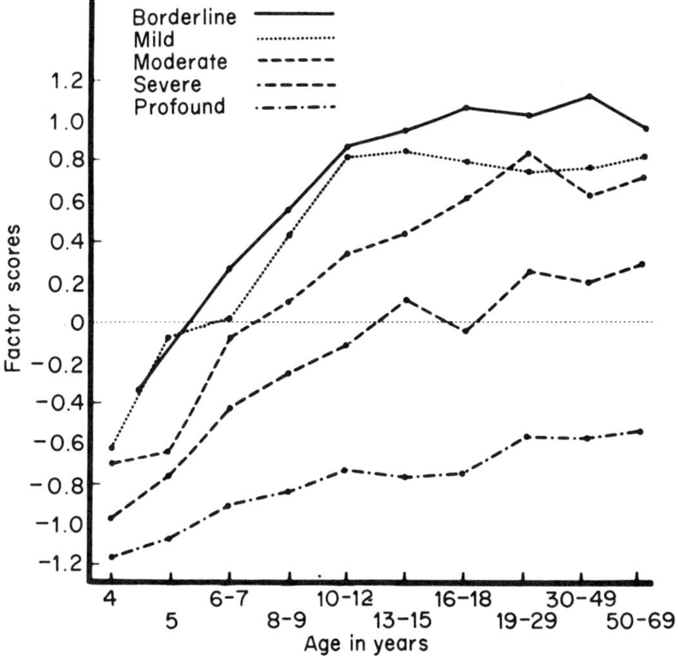

represented on Nihira's Personal self-sufficiency scale, specifically dressing, toileting, washing and feeding skills. The sample were in general of more advanced age than those in Nihira's study, i.e. 65 to 89 years, mean 74 years. On the basis of reports by nursing staff, they indicate that 97 per cent could feed themselves independently, 89 per cent were continent of faeces by day and night, 77 per cent could wash and dry themselves unaided, 75 per cent were continent of urine by day and night and 71 per cent were able to dress themselves without help. Overall, 56 per cent were completely independent in all these areas and only 5 per cent were dependent in two or more areas. Hewitt *et al.* (1986) also considered abilities related to Nihira's Community self-sufficiency, namely orientation with respect to time, place and people. Fifty six per cent of the sample were appropriately orientated in all four areas, 23 per cent for two areas, 16 per cent for one, and only five per cent for none.

Unlike Nihira, Hewitt *et al.* also had nurses rate behaviour disorders which were reported as occurring occasionally or frequently in 41 per cent of the sample. The main categories of problem were violence, stereotyped behaviour, verbal aggression, violence to self and faecal smearing. This result can be compared with information from Calderstones Hospital Register. Taking a slightly wider age range, 60-99 years and classifying behaviour problems in terms of "none", "moderate" or "severe" we find that 22.7 per cent had moderate problems and 4.8 per cent severe, a total of 27.5 per cent. This is somewhat lower than Hewitt *et al.*'s figure, presumably because the category "moderate" implies greater severity than "occasional". As may be seen in Table 4.1, over the years from 50 onwards there is a steady decline in both moderate and severe categories of behaviour in the Calderstones data. This is particularly reliable over the early decades of this period where the sample sizes are large, though from 80 onwards relatively fewer people are available.

Table 4.1:

Percentage of Residents in Calderstones Hospital Showing Moderate and Severe Behaviour Problems

Age Group	Level of Behaviour Problem	
	Moderate	Severe
50-59	28.3	7.8
60-69	26.7	4.8
70-79	20.3	6.3
80-89	16.7	0.0
90-99	0.3	0.0

With respect to these findings on adaptive behaviour, there are three further parallels to be drawn with our observations on the studies of intelligence. First, Nihira (1976) points out that it is important that we do not fall into the trap of regarding adaptive behaviour as a single entity in the same way that the "doctrine of monolithic intelligence" evolved in the past. Both concepts have given way to the view that several distinguishable components are involved in their composition, processes that may be differentially affected by organismic and environmental factors. Second, for a substantial number of the people in Nihira's study, much of their lives must have been spent in institutions (he does not provide specific details on this point). Thus, as with intelligence as psychometrically assessed, gains are seen in adaptive behaviour until well into the 50s or 60s, despite passing the years in what is widely agreed to be a depriving environment. Third, studies of adaptive behaviour as a function of age have also focused on institutionalised populations. We know of no parallel studies undertaken in the community. What we do have recourse to are those studies that have (a) contrasted the lives of people with mental handicap living in different settings, and (b) explicitly considered changes in functioning as people transfer from one environment to another, notably from institution to the community. Both types of study draw attention to the way in which an individual's characteristics and the nature of the environment interact in an interdependent fashion. Such considerations take us into the field of behavioural ecology generally, and that of the ecology of ageing in particular. These issues are discussed in the next chapter (Chapter 5 - Section 2).

Chapter Five

APPROACHES TO INTERVENTION

1 INTRODUCTION

In a recent and comprehensive review of "Aging and Social Care", Cantor and Little (1985) propose that the main objective of supportive services for elderly people is "maintenance of quality of life". The principal components related to the preservation of a positive quality of life for older people, they suggest, include adequate income and health care, suitable housing and environmental conditions, the existence of meaningful roles and relationships, and adequate social supports. This list is readily applicable to all people with disabilities; and, of course, specifically to people with mental handicap. It is the convergence of the changing needs of people who are both ageing and have mental handicaps that is the concern of this book, and such emerging needs must be viewed in relation to Cantor and Little's list of the factors that contribute to the quality of life of people as they age.

It is notable that in framing questions about how these objectives are to be met, several writers have considered the issues arising from the perspective of what Bronfenbrenner (1979) has termed "The Ecology of Human Development". This view emphasises the individual as a part of a complex, wider society. It also draws attention to the changing pattern of interactions as individuals get older, throughout their lifetime.

While this essentially social view of human development is often implicit, rather than explicit, in studies of ageing, it offers an important framework in which to analyse and formulate questions about the lives of older people whether they have or do not have mental handicap. We begin this chapter with a little theoretical background on the ecology of human development in general, and the ecology of ageing specifically.

2 ECOLOGICAL APPROACHES TO HUMAN DEVELOPMENT

Studies of behaviour have increasingly moved away from a concentration on the characteristics of individuals in their own right to an attempt to understand how such characteristics influence and are affected by the environment. In addition, concern with this question has been extended to a consideration of how such interactions change over the course of a person's life. As noted above, Bronfenbrenner (1979) coined the term "The Ecology of Human Development" to describe the way in which such a person develops in interaction with the various settings (e.g. home, neighbourhood and so on) he or she encounters. Bronfenbrenner's definition of the ecology of human development merits quotation:

> "The ecology of human development involves the scientific study of the progressive, mutual accommodation between an active, growing human being and the changing properties of the immediate settings in which the developing person lives, as this process is affected by relations between these settings, and by the larger contexts in which the settings are embedded." (p.21.)

The concept of settings embedded within each other is an important one. In brief, Bronfenbrenner proposes four nested systems which can be thought of as ever widening circles around an individual. The immediate environment, both social and physical, with which a person interacts is referred to as the *microsystem* Thus, the home, a residential setting, a club, would all be considered "microsystems". Since most of us spend our lives in several microsystems, they are linked not only by our presence in each of them, but by other connections such as the participation of other individuals in more than one of these systems. This series of linked microsystems Bronfenbrenner refers to as the *mesosystem.* Of course, the nature of micro and mesosystems is influenced by what happens in a variety of other settings in which the individual does not actually participate. The decision to change a person's place of residence in line with a new policy will be made in an administrative setting far from the present residence itself. Such an outer system that impinges on the individual through indirect influences is referred to as an *exosystem.* At this stage Bronfenbrenner moves to a somewhat different level of analysis. He notes that each society has its own blueprint for its various institutions. Thus, in a given society or segment of society there will be consistencies in both the form and content of an institution. Thus, residential facilities will bear similarities in their organisational structure and the activities that take place within them. Such similarities transcend specific establishments and have been determined by a variety of social, philosophical and political decisions and influences. These consistencies are reflected in the *macrosystem.*

It would be possible at this stage to reconsider in some detail the contents of our description in Chapter 1 of services in Oldham in terms of Bronfenbrenner's system. It will suffice, however, to illustrate the system with some examples from our review. First, we described a number of microsystems. Specifically, the various hostels and ordinary houses constitute such systems and the evaluation of the *Homemaking* scheme illustrates one form of micro-ecological analysis. There, attention was directed to the development of social relations between residents of the ordinary houses. At a physical level we pointed to the constraints placed on the inclusion of people with physical impairments in Wellington Lodge as the result of the nature of the building itself. One assumption underlying placement of people in the community rather than in relatively isolated settings, is that they will have access to a number of different micro-environments. Thus, attendance at clubs drawing a wider pool of participants or local shopping creates a richer network of settings or a more elaborate mesosystem than is possible in a large institution. Indeed, from an ecological perspective, the justification for a life in the community is that the mesosystem will be enriched, increasing the diversity of experiences available and hence the development of a wider range of adaptive behaviour.

Obviously, the very fact that the care in the community policy has been implemented reflects activity in the exosystem. We reviewed the governmental and regional decisions that have occurred leading to the changing pattern of provision. Thus, policies emanating from the North Western RHA are the result of events in the exosystem that determine the very form of the ecology at the micro and ultimately the mesosystem level. In turn, these specific policies reflect philosophical and economic decisions regarding the desirable form of provision for people with mental handicap and with mental illness that have evolved over a period of 30 or more years.

We can give more substance to the ecological model proposed by Bronfenbrenner specifically in relation to ageing by considering a similar model developed by Cantor and summarised by Cantor and Little (1985). Here a schematic model of possible social support systems for elderly people is presented, reproduced here in Figure 5.1

Like Bronfenbrenner, Cantor proposes a nested series of concentric circles which here contain a different type of support element or subsystem.

At the outer reaches of the system are the political and economic institutions that determine a variety of entitlements for older people - including financial benefits, health services and in some areas housing. The social policies and programmes emanating from this outer layer are realised in turn by statutory and voluntary services. We then move into a series of much more immediate networks that become increasingly less formal. "Mediating support elements" operate between formal and informal networks. These might include, in UK society, post office staff giving advice or assistance, religious organisations and churches, or social clubs and groups. We then move through to what has been described as the informal support network, notably friends and neighbours and then family members. As Cantor and Little (1985) note: "Although the model (Figure 5.1) shows each support element as separate and distinct, the subsystems interact considerably, illustrating the dynamic nature of the system." (p.749).

Figure 5.1:

Schematic model of the social support system of the elderly. Arrows indicate interaction between systems.
Note: In this model it is possible to start from the centre and proceed outward or from the outer ring, the macrosystem, inward to the micro level. The direction chosen depends on whether one is concerned with describing the support system of individuals or whether one's interest lies more with the issues of social distance and the impact of macrolevel social policies on individuals and families.

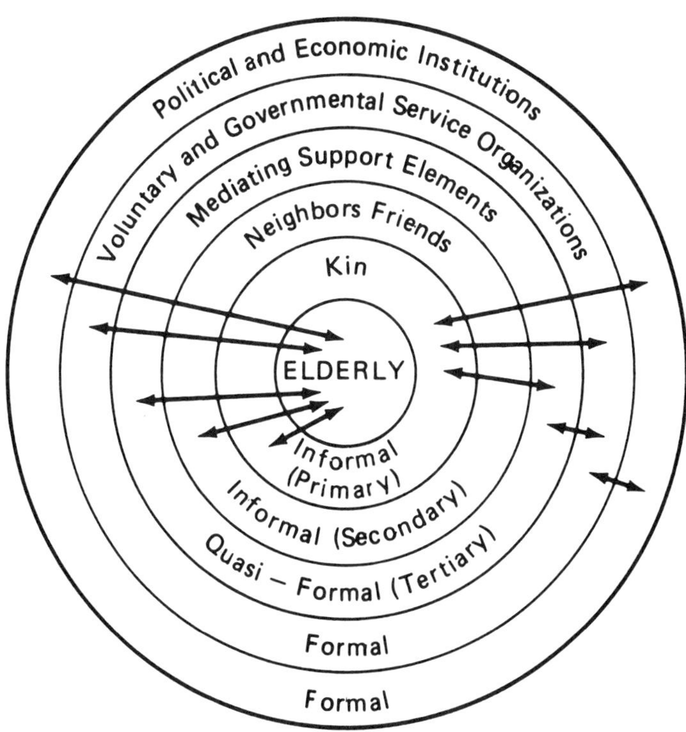

This way of viewing the social support system of elderly people draws attention to two areas that require consideration. (1), the distinction is drawn between two complementary forms of support, formal and informal support networks. (2), a framework is provided in which we can explore anticipated differences in the lives of people with and without mental handicap.

With regard to (1), this chapter explores information relevant to Cantor's entire social support system, with the exception of family support. It deals, therefore, with issues related to both formal and informal support networks, though informal family support is dealt with separately in the following chapter. With respect to (2) we return to the issue of similarities and differences in the ecology of older people with and without mental handicap in our concluding Chapter 9.

Before leaving the issue of the ecology of ageing, we need to draw out a further aspect of this subject central to Bronfenbrenner's account, i.e. the dimension of time. Lawton and Nahemow (1973) note that the ageing process can be seen as one of continual adaptation both to the environment and to changes in internal capabilities and functioning that occur during the span of life. From their point of view the ecology of ageing is defined as a system of continual adaptations in which both the person and the environment change in a non-random way over time. A change in the state of either person or environment can initate a cycle of action in which adaptive behaviour is demanded. Thus, changes in the cognitive processes tapped by intelligence tests will have consequences for adaptive behaviour, as will the altering demands of a changing environment. Many, if not all, the key topic areas in relation to ageing and the ecology that Lawton and Nahemow define will be seen to be equally relevant to people with mental handicap, i.e. institutionalisation and institutional life, relocation and life in the community.

3 INTERVENTION WITH INDIVIDUALS

There is undoubtedly a temptation to initiate programmes of intervention with older people with mental handicap in a reactive and sometimes piecemeal way. Training is seen to be needed, for example, to enable an individual to cope with a major transition, such as relocation to the community, or to acquire a new skill that will enhance adaptive behaviour in a residential setting. In reality, the scope and implementation of intervention should be, and is, far more complicated. As Newcomer, Estes and Freeman (1985) point out, "It is clear that a complex mosaic of political views, values, professional and research interests, funding agencies, and priorities determine the scope and nature of intervention." (p.620). In the field of ageing, they note, three general orientations guide most intervention efforts, orientations towards (a) individual change, (b) social psychological change and (c) social structural levels.

(a) First, intervention with respect to individual change is concerned with an individual's capabilities in functioning in a given environmental setting. Such functioning is dependent on the acquisition of adaptive skills as well as physical and mental health, and can be dependent upon material and social resources. Programmatically, intervention focuses on the individual older person, enhancing skill, emotional well-being or diminishing biological deficits. (b) Second, social psychological change is concerned with modifying the thinking, value or attitudes of a group by providing, for example, information, or the opportunity to participate in social activities. Such programmes can be directed, as well, to professional groups with a view to modifying their attitudes, beliefs and values towards older people. (c) Third, more fundamental intervention aiming at social structural change can also be initiated. Here service and social opportunity structures are modified in specific areas. Such change can affect the form of delivery of services, and in the UK context, the recent Disabled Persons' Act (1986) referred to in Chapter 1 constitutes such a potential, structural change. More extensive structural change is reflected in the process of deinstitutionalisation, where wide-ranging consequences entail broad structural intervention. Comprehensive Regional and State plans will specify the aims and procedures for social structural change, and the North Western Health Authority plan for mental handicap services, described in Chapter 1, exemplifies this approach. The determination of such plans is, of course, ultimately dependent on the philosophical and political climate that prevails in the society.

The movement from individual, to social and structural intervention effectively embraces the nested sequence of ecologies, from the individual to micro-, meso-, and exo-ecologies that we have employed earlier to describe social contexts of the lives of older people with mental handicap. Indeed, many of the programmes of residential provision described there are implicitly interventional in character, though our intention was to approach them descriptively.

In this chapter we will focus more explicitly on the form and content of intervention in the first of Newcomer *et al.*'s (1985) tripartite scheme as it applies to older people with mental handicap, i.e. approaches to individual intervention, though we will also touch on the second area of social-psychological change.

Underlying the development of intervention in ageing and mental handicap, has been a more fundamental change in society's attitude towards groups who in some way are viewed as being disadvantaged in their ability to cope with society's demands. While the concept of social intervention is not new, the institution of systematic programmes of intervention targeted on specific groups is essentially a post-1960 phenomenon. By a short head, intervention in the field of mental handicap evolved in advance of explicit intervention considerations in the field of ageing. In general, this activity in the area of mental handicap focused on children and young people, with a progressive extension over the years to adulthood and eventually to older individuals. The evolving literature on intervention with older people without mental handicap has also shown a progressive increase through the 1970s and 1980s, though it is even now some way behind that generated through work with people with mental handicap. As this chapter will show, where these two streams meet, i.e. in intervention with older people with mental handicap, the extent of published work, though on the increase, is still extremely restricted relative to work with children with mental handicap and indeed, the wider field of ageing.

In the review that follows we have chosen to focus on intervention with older people generally as the backdrop to intervention with older people with mental handicap. At relevant points we introduce studies from the field of work with younger adults with mental handicap into this framework. In this way we hope to ensure that the dimension of ageing remains salient, while acknowledging that much of the work undertaken in the field of mental handicap has profound relevance to work with such people in their later years. It is inconceivable, for example, that we should wish to enhance communication or manage a serious behavioural problem in an older person with mental handicap, without reference to the extensive literature on those topics. However, a *full* consideration of intervention and mental handicap would extend this review to an unacceptable length, and we can do no more than draw the reader's attention to relevant studies.

3.1 Individual Change and Intervention

A useful distinction that has been drawn between classes of approach in individual intervention is between psychological intervention, on the one hand, and educational intervention, on the other. With respect to psychological intervention, we follow Gatz, Popkin, Pino and VandenBos (1985) in viewing such activity as "... planned interpersonal intervention that is intended to have a psychotherapeutic impact of preventative, curative, or palliative nature." (p.755). Intervention of this sort can be viewed as a response to the consequences of a variety of personal difficulties that may be encountered in later life, including the experience of loss, feelings of uselessness and social isolation, as well as conditions arising from organic states. Intervention can also be directed to specifically educational activities which extend the experience and competencies of a lifetime, or which restore abilities lost through factors associated with ageing. Willis (1985), in considering education and ageing, employs the term "education" to refer to lifelong learning, viewing the primary function of such learning as the facilitation of adaptation and optimal development across the life course. Though we are employing the term "individual" in this context, it must be borne in mind that the actual therapeutic or educational context can well involve a group of individuals receiving therapy or education. As we shall see, this extension to group situations is one of some importance in its own right.

It is useful at the outset to say a little about approaches that have been adopted with older members of the non-handicapped populations and the contexts in which such programmes have been developed. Gatz *et al.* (1985) in a review of psychological intervention with older adults provide a valuable framework for approaching this topic, and have analysed many of the issues involved in psychological intervention with ageing people, classifying and describing the various approaches that have been evolved. With respect to the *issues* underlying psychological intervention they consider: (a) the extent to which there is continuity or discontinuity between treatment approaches to younger adults and those who are ageing; (b) the process by which clinical knowledge is created for work with older adults; (c) the types of problems people face; and (d) the principles of therapeutic change common to diverse approaches. Gatz *et al.* also distinguish between intervention with a person in both the individual and the group situation. With respect to the former, they describe several basic approaches emerging from clinical theory and techniques of which the two fundamental methods are: (a) psychotherapeutic strategies; (b) behavioural and cognitive approaches.

3.1.1 Psychotherapy and Related Approaches

The diversity of psychotherapeutic approaches to the problems of ageing people is far too extensive to even list them here. However, it is useful to distinguish between three main classes of problem for the purpose of this review. First, procedures have been developed that enable a person to be helped to come to terms with his or her own life history and unresolved conflicts. Into this group come Life-review therapy and the related approach of Reminiscence therapy discussed below. Second, techniques to ensure that people as they age remain in contact with the realities of the everyday world have been proposed, notably, Reality Orientation Therapy. Third, an emphasis is placed on enabling individuals to cope with loss, both personal and with respect to their status in the community. In the non-handicapped population such losses embrace retirement, diminished economic status, bereavement, decreased social networks, physical illnesses and disabilities and loss of personal dignity, a list which only requires partial revision when we consider the possible psychotherapeutic needs of older people with mental handicap.

Assistance in coming to terms with one's own life and personal history is considered by Butler (1961; 1963) and Lewis and Butler (1974) who describe life-review therapy as a psychotherapeutic approach that derives from the "... universal mental process brought about by the realization of approaching dissolution and death... The life review is characterized by the progressive return to consciousness of past experiences and, particularly, the resurgence of unresolved conflicts." (Lewis and Butler 1974, p.165).

A crucial aspect of life-review therapy is that it is not a process initiated by the therapist. Rather, the therapist "taps in" to on-going self-analysis and participates in it with the older person, making the process more conscious, deliberate and efficient. Lewis and Butler list a variety of methods to elicit memories which can serve as the basis for review, including written or tape recorded autobiographies, pilgrimages through visits or correspondence, reunions, review of genealogy, use of scrapbooks, photo albums, old letters, other memorabilia, reviewing one's life work and where appropriate, one's ethnicity. The use of such procedures in both individual and group settings is described by Lewis and Butler.

Mitchell (1984) emphasises the importance of major life events for older individuals, symbolising change and punctuating the life-cycle as they do. She notes, however, that many older people living in mental handicap hospitals will have experienced few of the significant changes that are typical in the lives of people living in the community, and that significant life events may be restricted to admission to the hospital or movement between such establishments. While such a view is credible, it should be noted in passing that it is based on a number of assumptions regarding the experience of such residents. Against the background of a relatively unvarying life, it is possible that what to us might seem insignificant, may be of considerable importance to a resident, e.g. the loss of a job in the laundry, the day the family letter ceased to come, or the transfer of a friend from the hospital.

Nevertheless, Mitchell rightly argues that the opportunity and encouragement to reminisce about the past could well have a number of beneficial consequences for residents. Specifically, she suggested that such activity may decrease depression, assist in adjustment to new living situations, create a sense of identity throughout life, and enhance communication. Her chosen approach to these ends is through Reminiscence Therapy, which she distinguished from Life-review Therapy with respect to the former making fewer cognitive demands and being less specifically directed to the resolution of past conflicts. Mitchell constituted a small group of six residents of a small mental handicap hospital whose ages ranged from 63 to 76 years. Group leaders encouraged participants to recall past experiences through the use of slides and photographs of the past generally and events in the hospital itself. Residents were able to recall and communicate their memories and in the main appeared and reported that they enjoyed doing so. However, affect was lacking and Mitchell notes that: "It seemed that all of the mentally handicapped people had access to their distant memories and that some could describe these memories in concrete terms, but none had the language available to describe their emotional experiences." (p.23).

Mitchell's study, however, did not attempt to evaluate the more fundamental issues with respect to depression, adjustment, identity and communication that she has raised, and she identifies these as subjects for more systematic evaluation. She notes, too, the need to evolve stimulus material whose content is of specific relevance to members of this group, and to re-frame activities of the kind noted above by Lewis and Butler (1974) in such a way that will most adequately facilitate reminiscence.

The broadly psychotherapeutic techniques noted so far are directed towards enabling the individual to enhance understanding of, and to come to terms with, past and present reality. Where contact with reality has been broken, the need to implement therapy aimed at enabling the older individual to re-establish contact has been proposed, notably by Folsom (1968) who describes the development of Reality Orientation (RO) therapy with older nursing home parents who are confused or disorientated. The technique, developed from work with younger people with brain damage, embraces a variety of approaches that maintain or reintroduce contact between the individual and his or her personal and environmental reality. Thus, an emphasis is placed on the individual using and remembering his or her own name, the date, maintaining continuity in conversations and responding to contact with family members on visits. It is viewed as an around-the-clock approach premised on general principles which include: (a) A calm environment; (b) A set routine; (c) Clarity and consistency of questions; (d) Clarity of speech; (e) Clear directions; and (f) Firmness. This list is developed further in the American Hospitals Association (1976), reproduced by Hanley (1984, p.187). As with other forms of psychotherapy described, reality orientation therapy can in part be conducted through group meetings. Folsom (1968) describes a class-based approach to nursing home residents used in conjunction with individual treatment, though as Green (1984) has pointed out, this procedure must be viewed as supplementary to a 24-hour Reality Orientation programme (24RO).

In a recent appraisal of RO, Hanley (1984) emphasises the potential relevance of the approach to elderly who are dementing (though not excluding the use of RO with other elderly people). With regard to this group, he argues that *reductions* in decline in cognitive and behavioural functioning are the realistic objectives rather than *reversal* of decline. However, any consideration of the utility of RO Therapy with older people with mental handicap should be viewed against a background of recent evaluations of the literature on the use of this approach with elderly people generally. Reviews of both the theoretical basis of RO and its effectiveness have been generally critical. Against the background of such critiques by Burton (1982) and Powell-Proctor and Miller (1982), even a relatively sympathetic account of evaluative studies by Green (1984) concludes "... that within the context of the outcome, measures used in such studies of the effects of

RO are confined to an improvement in orientation with little consistent evidence that it results in any demonstrable cognitive or behavioural change. In the case of the latter, where such change has been found, it has been found to be of a highly specific and circumscribed nature." (p.201).

Hanley (1984) acknowledges the lack of positive evaluation of RO, but argues that it would be premature to abandon a procedure which is premised on a humanitarian concern for the care of elderly people as well as offering highly practical strategies for creating a suitable physical and personal environment. Essentially he advocates that care must be taken to ensure that when an RO programme is initiated, then its implementation by staff is monitored. Negative outcomes can in part result from a failure to execute the relevant strategies. Further, he emphasises the need to develop RO through a more rigorous consideration of its scientific base. It is interesting to note from both Hanley's (1984) and Green's (1984) accounts the extent to which the specificity of the procedures to be employed gravitated to those of applied behaviour analysis. While deriving from the specific recommendations of RO, Hanley's (1984) study, for example, is basically indistinguishable from the behavioural programmes with elderly people that we review later, both with respect to techniques employed and to evaluative methodology. Indeed, Green (1984) explicitly urges this reapproachment when he writes: "... improved orientation *per se* does not lead to behavioural change, rather it acts to elicit or facilitate new behaviours, which must be reinforced in the usual manner as dictated by behavioural principles." (p.204).

Hanley (1984), however, is quite explicit that RO should not be fragmented into a series of discrete programmes but that such programmes should always be conducted against a background of basic guidelines for RO, which direct consistency of cueing and interaction, simplicity of questions and answers etc. The RO ethos, according to Green (1984), at the very least offers a milieu in which formal intervention procedures can be introduced and creates an atmosphere contrary to the nihilism that so often affects staff working with older people. Even critics of RO such as Powell-Proctor and

Miller (1982) acknowledge the usefulness of the facilitating effects of the technique in this regard.

With respect to our preliminary question on the use of RO with people with mental handicap, therefore, the following conclusions may be drawn. First, in establishing a positive milieu in a residential establishment or in relation to a single person, RO could well have a beneficial effect on staff-client interactions. Second, both the attitudinal change by staff and the focus on individual behaviours may open the way to the development of specific programmes directed at selected behaviours or aspects of cognitive functioning. Third, the strategy provides direction in dealing in a positive fashion with people with mental handicap who are dementing, in the absence of any clear statement in the literature on how such people should be dealt with at the psychological level. To date, however, we have traced no formal reports on the use of RO with older people with mental handicap whether in the classroom based format or the more appropriate 24RO.

Psychological intervention with older people has not stopped short with the use of traditional psychotherapeutic techniques or the development of methods enabling such people to cope with past and present reality. A variety of approaches have evolved emerging from and drawing on both the existing values and ecologies of the individuals, on the one hand, and on psychological theory on the other. An example of each situation will suffice.

In Chapter 1 we drew attention to the importance of religious institutions in the lives of some of the individuals with mental handicap living in Oldham. Vayhinger (1980) describes the potential benefit to older people generally of "pastoral psychology" which is based on the trust and rapport between such people and their religious leaders. He noted that involvement of the church with elderly people is a traditional activity, but one only recently recognised by professionals as having a legitimate and effective therapeutic function. Religious leaders have a natural entrèe into the lives of older people who in turn expect them to fulfil a counselling function. However, when occupying such a position, the pastoral counsellor must have a knowledge of, and be able to refer the older person to, the relevant social and health services provided in the community. Sargent (1980) also emphasises the need for therapists not working specifically from a religious standpoint to be aware of the therapeutic potential of the religious component of their client's life.

With respect to therapy deriving directly from psychological theory, Reinhart and Sargent (1980) outline a further non-traditional approach to therapy with older people arising from the theory of self-actualisation which in turn is rooted in humanistic psychology. They describe an extensive programme, SAGE, (Senior Actualization and Growth Explorations) which offers individual and group counselling, as well as a variety of techniques including massage, yoga, sensory awareness, relaxation, meditation, breathing exercises and biofeedback.

What characterises the work described in this brief and admittedly partial summary is not only the diversity of approaches that have been directed to specific problems associated with ageing, but the theoretical heterogenity of techniques that are drawn together under a single rubric. The value of such approaches, however, does not appear to rest in their theoretical coherence or in the demonstration of effectiveness which we still await. Rather they reflect and contribute to a humanitarian view of ageing that stands in marked contrast to earlier nihilism regarding the possibility of positive change in the later years.

Their extension to older people with mental handicap has already begun and is to be justified on these grounds alone. However, their ultimate justification must wait upon adequate evaluation and refinement with respect to a population with reduced intellectual and cognitive competence. With respect to the techniques reviewed, they differ significantly regarding theoretical cohesion and evaluation from the behavioural procedures to which we shortly turn.

As distinct from such individual approaches, group therapy is considered by Gatz *et al.* to be more efficient, yields benefits because it promotes interaction among several people, and enables people to realise that their problems are rarely unique. The form that such group therapy can take is extremely diverse. It embraces community workshops on ageing, groups formed to cope with transitions, such as widowhood, as well as various forms of activity group. Some highly complex programmes have been evolved embracing diverse elements such as relaxation training, meditation, yoga, massage, journal writing, Gestalt techniques and art and dance therapy. In addition to the value of group therapy noted by these authors, several advantages to those working in, and utilising, services for people with mental handicap can be anticipated. Group therapy permits, if properly organised, lower staff-client ratios and the involvement of a variety of professionals for relatively shorter sessions. The diversity of activities permits involvement of people of widely differing abilities including the possibility of fully integrated group activity for some of the components of the programme. Clearly, some aspects of a programme such as SAGE shade into leisure activities. Art or dance therapy may be distinguishable, in the mind of professional therapists, from art and dance as leisure, but in reality may be closely linked in terms of their beneficial effect for the client.

Both individual and group therapy have been conceived very much with respect to therapists working with clients from the defined population, i.e. older people. Gatz *et al.* distinguish this situation from what they refer to as community based approaches. Here, family and marital counselling, including conjoint therapy, is brought to bear on problems arising from interactions between the older person and other family members. Such approaches also embrace friendly visiting services to reduce isolation as well as programmes run by volunteers and paraprofessionals.

The authors draw attention to the diversity of such programmes which have in common the fostering of group participation and success in some activity. They conclude that programmatic studies in this area have demonstrated that problems of anxiety, depression, generalised loneliness, helplessness, and behavioural and family disruption resulting from organic factors have all been alleviated through such community based approaches.

3.1.2 Behavioural Intervention and Ageing

We laid great emphasis at the start of this chapter on the ecological analysis of the lives of older people with mental handicap. There we urged the importance of the setting in which the individual lives and the interaction between behaviour and environment. Behavioural intervention may be regarded as truly ecological whether utilised in the service of individual therapy or education. At both the level of assessment and intervention, an emphasis is placed on understanding the relation between a specified piece of behaviour and the social and physical environmental events that preceded or followed the behaviour. Thus, context is all important, behaviour not being viewed in isolation.

In the field of mental handicap, behavioural intervention has generated several hundred studies bearing on almost every conceivable aspect of intellectual and social behaviour. There are few professionals who have not in some way received formal or informal training in behaviour modification, and many of the adjuncts of behaviour modification programmes, such as assessment checklists and individual programme plans, have taken on a life of their own in services for people with mental handicap. Underlying these developments is the philosophical assumption that competence is not a fixed characteristic of an individual, but can be diminished or enhanced through appropriate adjustment of the interaction between the individual and the environment. In the late 1960s and early 1970s this view began to be invoked with respect to the ageing process in non-mentally handicapped people in their later years, again with profound consequences for how we deal with declining competence that had previously been assumed to be age-related. Indeed, application of the behavioural model to ageing people was seen as a radical alternative to a biomedical model which viewed declining competence as an inevitable outcome of biological deterioration. Even a decade later, it was not thought unreasonable to view behavioural approaches to ageing as "non-traditional" techniques in a volume on this subject (Rosenstein and Swenson, 1980), though Landesman-Dwyer and Knowles (1987) with reference to mental handicap are able to refer to "traditional behaviour modification" (p.26). The introduction of the behavioural model into the field of ageing at that time was particularly pertinent as there was a general reaction against medical deficit models in ageing, leading to a meeting in 1971 concerned specifically with a wide range of alternative, non-medical, approaches (See "Strategies for Psychological Intervention in Old Age: A symposium", Baltes, 1973).

Numerous position papers on behavioural intervention in ageing and the theoretical basis in operant psychology appeared at this time (e.g. Hoyer, 1973; Hoyer, Mishara and Riebel, 1975). Baltes and Barton (1977) review several converging strands of thought that had led to adoption of an operant model in the field of ageing. They note the variability of biological decline with age and the growing evidence that the rate and form of such decline is bound up with a variety of environmental factors. They draw attention, too, to the reversibility of many biological or physiological age decrements. The move away from a view of biologically fixed decline led "... to a behavioral-environmental model which emphasizes the interaction between the organism and its internal and external environments, (requiring) a model for research and intervention conducive to explicit analyses of functional relationships between behavioral and environmental events. Such a theoretical framework then would allow for (a) description of the existing ecosystems for the elderly in the form of maintenance, rehabilitation, or promotion of functioning in the elderly." (p.387).

While emphasising the importance of adverse environmental living conditions for age-performance decrements, Baltes and Barton do not suggest that such interactions provide the whole story. Rather, they see such explanation as taking its place in a wider model of ageing that does take into account other determinants, including biological ones. In the field of ageing the specific application of operant principles within such a wider model has led to the specific discipline of *behavioural gerontology*. At its simplest, this term may be defined as "... the study of how antecedent and consequent environmental events interact with the aging organism to produce behaviour." (Burgio and Burgio 1986, p.321). A more comprehensive analysis will be found in Hussian (1981) and practical realisation of behavioural gerontology described in Hussian and Davis' (1985) book: "*Responsive Care: Behavioral interventions with elderly persons*". While the basic operant model is utilised by Hussian and Davis, their very practical approach to "analyzing and treating behavioral disorders" invariably draws attention to possible medical contributions to deficits. For example, they note the possible contribution to such deficits of drug toxicity, metabolic disease, electrolyte imbalance etc, as well as the contribution of specific psychiatric conditions such as depression. The attempt to restore ambulation, for example, through behavioural means, would only be undertaken if there were no pathological impediment to walking. Behavioural gerontology, then, should be seen as the outcome of the kind of synthesis leading to Baltes and Barton's "multidirectional and multidimensional model of aging", in which medical and psychiatric information would have to be given weight in the development of a specific programme and its implementation. It must be admitted, however, that in the limited published literature of behavioural intervention and ageing, the emphasis has remained primarily on reports of behavioural aspects of the programme rather than any attempt to explore systematically the comprehensive, behavioural gerontology model.

In order to indicate the present scope of behavioural intervention with older people, we review selected studies in a range of areas applicable to both non-handicapped people and those with mental handicap. In each case we will start with studies concerned with the former and will move into the few reports on people with mental handicap, where such exist. Specifically, we will review 3.1.2.1: Social interaction and communication; 3.1.2.2: Self-care with special reference to independence and dependency; 3.1.2.3: Ambulation; 3.1.2.4: Behaviour problems; 3.1.2.5: The design of the physical environment.

A final point should be made regarding the settings in which behavioural interventions have typically taken place. The majority have been conducted in nursing homes of various kinds, with the strong assumption implicit in the theory itself, that such residences have generated many of the problems to be dealt with. Larger institutions have also been considered from the same standpoint. Nevertheless, some consideration has also been given to direct intervention in family settings, approaches that could readily be extrapolated to small group residences.

3.1.2.1 Social interaction and communication. To those who view social disengagement as a natural concomitant of ageing, decreasing social communication and increasing isolation are to be anticipated. However, an ecological view analysed in terms of operant concepts would hypothesise that changes in setting conditions, discriminant stimuli and reinforcing consequences lead to reduced communication and hence that disengagement is an "engineered" rather than a natural concomitant of ageing. Such is the view adopted by Hoyer, Kafer, Simpson and Hoyer (1974) in an early study in this area. Observation on a hospital ward indicated that much communication was non-verbal, particularly during game activities which were successfully accomplished in silence. In the first study four chronic schizophrenics participated, two being reinforced with tokens for the number of words they uttered. Verbalisation increased in both people and, it is suggested, through modelling, in the other two as well. It was number of words rather than frequency that increased, and therefore in a second study four more residents were reinforced for responding to questions about pictures from the Thematic Apperception Test. Here, following reinforcement with chocolates and cigarettes frequency of verbalisation increased. Informal evidence of generalisation beyond the sessions was reported.

Both Berger and Rose (1977) and Lopez, Hoyer, Goldstein and Sprafkin (1980) carried out programmes to enhance interpersonal skills through conversation in elderly people. Lopez *et al.* employed Structured Learning Therapy (Goldstein 1973) a skill training procedure which utilises modelling, role playing, performance feedback and transfer training with small groups of trainees. Lopez *et al.* focused on the initiation of conversation and compared in their experimental design the effect of varying kinds of reinforcement as well as overtraining, i.e. further training beyond the point at which the target behaviour was acquired. All participants acquired the targeted skill and some evidence of transfer of training was observed. However, those *not* receiving additional monetary reinforcement in addition to social reinforcement showed greater transfer than those who did receive such concrete reinforcement. Some indication that overtraining enhanced transfer was also noted.

An important implication of the ecological position, however, is that training for communication should be rooted in specific situations in which such communication has a definite function. In the context of most institutional environments two broad classes of situation in which communication can be anticipated can be identified, (a) those demanding adaptive, self-help behaviour, particularly meal and drink items, and (b) recreational situations. In such contexts both quantitative and qualitative improvements would be desirable. Such improvements were the targets of a study by Cartensen and Erickson (1986) in which communication during periods of refreshment (when fruit juice and biscuits were served) was studied. Here the intervention consisted simply in serving the refreshments for a period each day in contrast to the same period on days on which such refreshments were unavailable. Cartensen and Erickson demonstrated increased attendance and frequency of interaction during refreshment-available periods, but no evidence of any improvement in the quality of interactions. The improvement in vocalisation was mainly in terms of ineffective communications and, indeed, there was a decrease relative to baseline in effective and appropriate communications. These authors urge that attention should be paid to individual communications and techniques taken to shape the qualitative aspects of interactions with special reference to positive and effective vocalisations.

The study of social interaction during periods of recreation also embodies interaction or engagement with the materials available for leisure pursuits (Jenkins, Felce, Lund, and Powell 1977). Hussian and Davis (1985, pp 29-38) provide a detailed discussion of how such provision may increase attendance at group activities. These authors emphasise the importance of environmental variables in establishing ideal conditions for participation, notably the removal of structural and distance barriers to wheelchairs, the use of prompts and cues as to time and availability of leisure pursuits, the arrangement of furniture and suitability of lighting, as well as the content of the activities and materials. Such consideration is complemented by careful assessment of residents' preferences and their psychological and physical ability to engage with the available provision.

The need to programme active intervention to ensure engagement is demonstrated by McClannaham and Risley's (1975) study in which they increased participation in recreational activities in a nursing home. Though the majority of residents were elderly, some were relatively young, i.e. 25 years of age, and it is assumedly these younger people who are described as mentally or physically handicapped. However, no specific report is given on the effect of the intervention on these particular individuals. McClannaham and Risley compared conditions in which leisure pursuit material was not, and was, available. In addition, in the "available" condition they contrasted a situation in which activity leaders prompted engagement with a condition in which engagement was dependent upon free-choice. The central conclusion of the study was that prompting was critical to enhancing engagement, free-choice without prompting not leading to any significant increase in manipulative activities over the baseline condition.

The studies reviewed so far all indicate that with direct intervention, social and recreational participation in nursing homes can be increased. Within these settings and with available procedures, there is the suggestion that constraints exist which inhibit naturally occurring, self-perpetuating interactions. Indeed, perhaps the most appropriate conclusion would be that certain environments are inherently conducive to disengagement and that the resources required to maintain engagement of both high quality and quantity, will tend to be uneconomical. This is not an argument against such approaches, but one which suggests that fundamental change in the size and quality of the living environment should also be introduced in parallel to intervention of the kind described.

Studies of intervention to modify communication and engagement in other settings, particularly the home, are even more limited than those in nursing homes and larger institutions. Linsk, Pinkston and Green's (1982) report on "Home-based Behavioral Social Work with the Elderly" is limited to a single case study. The more recent "Special Section on Behavioural Gerontology" of the *Journal of Applied Behavior Analysis* (1986) includes only one home intervention study (Green, Linsk and Pinkston 1986), with only three further studies referenced since Linsk *et al.*'s 1982 case-study, i.e. Haley (1983); Pinkston and Linsk (1984a; 1984b). It should be added, that, as might be anticipated, these studies focus on various problems in the family setting, in which improved communication is often only an implicit goal.

The two major studies of communication in older people with mental handicap were both carried out in large mental handicap institutions. Kleitsch, Whitman and Santos (1983) worked with four men (CA range 51-57 years; IQ range 39-51) in a group language training programme. All were severely socially isolated, almost never entering into verbal interaction with staff or fellow residents. The procedure entailed use of verbal prompts, modelling and behaviour rehearsal to teach a range of communicative behaviour, notably: self-initiated response to group leader, fellow trainee, and fellow-resident non-trainee; prompted response to group leader, fellow traineee, fellow-resident non-trainee.

The authors employed what they refer to as a "loose training procedure", together with the use of natural contingencies and sufficient exemplars to encourage generalisation of learnt behaviour. This was assessed in two situations, (a) the training setting but in the absence of the trainer, and (b) during an informal break in the kitchen. The procedure was effective in increasing the residents' overall rate of verbalisation, though no increase in mean length of range of verbalisations was observed. The increase was noted in both generalisation situations and was maintained during two follow up observations one and three months later. In addition, verbalisation increased to non-trained peers as well as those in the language training group.

Of particular interest is Kleitsch *et al.*'s observation that one resident, Henry, showed a particularly high increase in verbalisations, and may have acted as a catalyst in enhancing the behaviour of his peers. Selection of individuals with this potential is clearly an important strategy in increasing the effectiveness of interventions of this sort, an approach explicitly adopted by Dy, Strain, Fullerton and Stowitscheck (1981). The setting for this study was an institutional cottage for 30 women with mental handicap (CA range 40-75) from whom two elderly women (CAs 62 and 63 years) were selected, each as models for two of their peers (CAs 59 and 63, and 65 and 69 respectively).

Training took place with interaction around age appropriate material that was nevertheless matched to the residents' competence. The resident-trainer, i.e. "The Confederate", was taught to encourage both gestural and verbal behaviour through demonstration and practice. (A detailed description of the training format is given by Dy *et al.* (1981), in tabular form, p.205.) Direct, but minimal, instruction, role playing and direct prompting were employed in various combinations to teach the confederate, the last two techniques being progressively faded. Generalisation to the confederate and resident-trainee's living room was also assessed.

The procedures adopted were highly successful in inducing the confederate to engage the peers in both motor/gestural and verbal behaviour. Nevertheless, none of the techniques were effective in inducing change in confederates or target peers in the generalisation setting. However, the authors note that "At the very least, the present clinical demonstration suggests that an abundant and competent instructional resource is now under-utilized in mental retardation institutions. If mentally retarded peers can function competently as social behavior change agents, they may also be effective resources for self-help, communication, and many other areas of instructional programming." (p 212).

From an ecological perspective, and in line with the point made earlier by Kleitsch *et al.* (1983), the confederates were selected because they were already engaging in greater social interaction than the socially isolated target peers, and hence were already interacting with their social environment, a situation on which Dy *et al.* attempted to capitalise. The failure of generalisation, they suggest, reflects an environment which is inherently not conducive to social interactions and which perhaps demands "... nothing short of altering the entire social ecology" (p 214). This view is in line with the point made above regarding ecological constraints on change, and one may assume that the term "altering the entire social ecology" is a euphemism for closing down such large institutions.

A further facet of the issue of constraints is the availability of opportunities to exercise a learnt behaviour. Praderas and MacDonald (1986) report a training programme again concerned with communication; appropriate use of the telephone in a nursing home. Here, residents showing significant cognitive impairment, including borderline mental handicap, were involved, and successfully acquired many of the skills requisite to maintaining a telephone conversation. Though such a demonstration may, in itself, be of value, its ecological validity is suspect. The authors note that: "We hoped that increased telephone conversational skilfulness would lead to increased telephone contact with friends or relatives living in the community. However, subjects reported having no calls either to or from friends or family. This finding may be partially explained by the fact that these particular subjects knew almost no one in the community they could call." (p.346). Such a conclusion could have been anticipated if even a relatively superficial analysis had been made of the overall ecological situation with respect to telephone use, and points to the need to undertake such analysis if time is not wasted in irrelevant training of unusable skills.

3.1.2.2 Self-care and independence. The decline in the ability of ageing people to continue caring for themselves is well documented and can reflect physical and physiological decrements. The move away from a biomedical model of ageing, however, has emphasised the extent to which reducing environmental demands can lead to high levels of dependency in older people which leads to the loss of well-established self-care abilities. While this may apply equally to ageing people with mental handicap, many of these individuals will never have acquired certain skills in the first place. As with communication, then, it is necessary to consider the relation between ageing and self-care from the perspective of skills acquired and lost, as well as in relation to the acquisition of new behaviours.

Hussian and Davis (1985) review the general strategies applicable to a range of self-care activities, including urinary continence (pp.42-45), self-grooming skills (pp.45-48), independent eating skills (pp.48-51). The place of medical and behavioural assessment in instituting programmes is carefully specified as is the implementation of the treatment itself. In each of these areas a limited number of specific studies of behavioural intervention have been reported.

Blackman (1977) employed positive reinforcement in conjunction with scheduled visits to the lavatory for urinary continence, while Sanario (1981) employed a modified version of Foxx and Azrin's (1973) toileting method which has been so influential in the area of mental handicap to reduce urinary and fecal incontinence. Atthowe (1972) employed a combination of punishment and of negative and positive reinforcement to decrease nocturnal incontinence. All three programmes noted were carried out in large institutions with people who had been hospitalised for long periods of time.

Hussian and Davis (1985) note the marked contrast between behavioural work with members of the ageing population and the extensive work with people with mental handicap with respect to self-grooming skills. Rinke, Williams and Lloyd (1978) employed physical and verbal prompts with reinforcement to re-establish a variety of facets of self bathing (e.g. soaping, drying etc). In both studies, nursing home residents were the participants in the programmes.

In contrast, Schnelle, Traughber, Morgan, Embry, Binion and Coleman (1983) worked in a geriatric nursing home with individuals incapable of independent toileting. Here a management strategy was introduced in which residents were checked every hour for wetness and received social approval if dry and disapproval if wet. They also prompted the residents to indicate if they wished to use the toilet and toileted her/him if this was responded to in the affirmative. Both affirmative responses to prompting and a spontaneous request for toileting assistance were responded to with social approval. There was a marked improvement in dryness and an increase in requests for assistance over the course of the intervention which was maintained with strong supervisory pressure. However, in one of the two nursing homes, removal of supervisory pressure led to sporadic implementation of the procedure. Burgio,

Engel, McCormick, Hawkins and Scheve (1987) modified and extended Schnelle *et al.*'s (1983) procedure employing a special unit designed for the treatment of urinary incontinence. While the programme did result in substantial increases in dryness, no improvements in independent or appropriate toileting was observed, and all participants actually decreased their rate of self-initiation during training.

The re-establishment of self-feeding was demonstrated by Geiger and Johnson (1974) in residents of a private nursing facility. The target behaviour here was the complete sequence of self-feeding. A simpler technique, readily usable by staff, was employed, in which residents were requested to eat the meal and were reinforced with individually selected gifts. There was an increase from 12 to 84 per cent of meals correctly eaten over the duration of the study. Like Geiger and Johnson (1974), Baltes and Zerbe (1976) employed a reversal design to demonstrate the effect of their training intervention. In contrast, however, Baltes and Zerbe employed immediate reinforcement of self-feeding responses which were broken down into various sub-behaviours, e.g. picking up spoon, taking it to mouth, and so on. Time-out was employed for inappropriate behaviour.

Baltes and Zerbe (1976) interpret the need for intervention in this last study in the framework of an ecological, operant model, in which loss of self-care functions is seen not as an inevitable age-related effect, but as the consequence of an environment that reinforces dependency. Direct demonstrations of the reinforcement of dependency are reported in Baltes, Burgess and Stewart (1980) and Baltes, Honn, Barton, Orzech and Lago (1983). In the first study, the authors reported that during self-care activities (i.e. bathing, dressing, eating, grooming and toileting) independent responses were most likely to be followed by 'no response' on the part of staff members. In contrast, dependent behaviour, i.e. when the resident requests or accepts assistance or refuses to engage in an activity, were almost invariably followed by dependence-supporting behaviour in which the staff member assisted dependent behaviour, reinforced acceptance of help, or actively encouraged dependent behaviour. In the 1983 study, these findings were replicated and extended to consider also positive social behaviour and appropriate engaged behaviour in relation to both staff and to other residents. Even with these extensions to additional categories of independence and to other individuals the basic findings of the first study are maintained. While this conclusion applied to social partners as well as staff with respect to dependency behaviour, one staff-social partner distinction was noted: constructive engagement did receive intermittent support from social partners. Non-engagement, however, produced no response.

Though undertaken in residential settings with people without mental handicap, the concepts underlying these findings on dependency and self-care activities, as well as constructive engagement, are clearly of importance in relation to other settings and to older people with mental handicap on whom we know of no parallel studies. Where an intensive service support is available to such people, and where more able peers are on hand to support dependency, then whatever the environment, learned dependency is a possible outcome of this social ecology. Indeed, for many older residents of mental handicap hospitals this process will already have occurred, leading to an underestimate of adaptive abilities. Such a state of affairs can be perpetuated in a small group home or hostel on transfer from an institution, or in line with the work of Baltes and her colleagues, could diminish competence if a person moves from private or family accommodation to such a residence.

3.1.2.3 Ambulation. Resistance to remaining mobile, whether through walking or use of a wheelchair, despite being physically able to accomplish the requisite movements, is a further impediment to independence. Burgio, Burgio, Engel and Tice (1986) note that impairment to mobility is the most frequently cited of deficits in elderly nursing home residents. These authors and Hussian and Davis (1985) list a variety of consequences of immobility that increase difficulties for both the elderly individual and the staff, notably improper elimination, less efficient functioning of the respiratory system, muscle atrophy, decrease in bone mass, labile blood pressure, depression and insomnia.

Intervention

MacDonald and Butler (1974) dealt with non-ambulation in two nursing home residents who for several months had been moved around in wheelchairs through a sequence of verbal prompts and verbal interaction contingent on walking. Using these relatively simple contingencies these authors demonstrated successful reinstatement of walking. Similarly, Burgio *et al.* (1986) employed MacDonald and Butler's (1974) procedure but also examined cross-setting and cross-subject generalisation, maintenance, and transfer of the technique to nursing home staff. As in the earlier study, the technique was found to be effective and evidence of generalisation across settings was established, though not across subjects, i.e. other residents did not become ambulant through observation of their peers who had received the intervention. Maintenance data were collected for four months showing that ambulation had persisted over this time despite termination of the programme by research staff and its execution by nursing staff.

Burgio *et al.* also raise a general issue of the increased exercise resulting from the programme, though noting that the efficacy of the procedure for health and its psychological impact had not been assessed and awaited further research. The important issue of exercise has received little attention in the literature on behavioural gerontology. Hussian and Davis (1985) make no reference to physical exercise or sport and we are left with a small study by Libb and Clements (1969) in which a small group of "geriatric patients" were reinforced with tokens for increasing their rate of exercise on a stationary bicycle.

While ambulation as a target for people with mental handicap will remain a priority, particularly in the preschool and school years, we do not know how far re-establishment of ambulation is a relevant issue for older residents of large institutions and hostels. Where this is the case the procedures decribed in this section will be of some assistance. It would be hoped, however, that in the new settings in the community, natural engagement with the domestic and neighbourhood environments will ensure that a retreat into immobility is an unlikely and infrequent occurrence.

3.1.2.4 <u>Behaviour problems</u>. In contrast to the behavioural deficits that have been the target of intervention in the preceding sections behavioural excesses may also require attention. Hussian and Davis (1985) give detailed consideration to such behavioural problems that lead to the individual's restriction, seclusion, medication, segregation or avoidance by others. While there is evidence to suggest that behaviour problems are fewer among older people with mental handicap, such problems do exist and can have similar consequences, with segregation here implying that the person continues living in a large institution.

Again, with respect to the definition of a behaviour problem, Hussian and Davis' emphasis on the judgemental nature of the definition also applies to people with mental handicap, i.e. that not only must the context be taken into account, but the values and biases of staff must also be considered. Several possible criteria are listed that would enter into such a judgement: Is the behaviour damaging to the person, others or property?; are the benefits of a programme being diminished for the individual or others?; do the consequences of the behaviour, e.g. seclusion or medication, reduce the person's opportunity to interact with others?; does the behaviour decrease the time available to staff to engage other residents in constructive activities? In addition, damage to staff morale and an increase in staff turnover may result.

With respect to definitions and consequences, similar considerations apply to both elderly people and those with mental handicap. It is clear from Hussian and Davis' (1985) inventory of possible behaviour problems that there will be much comparability in the nature of the problems confronting staff, though there is no study providing comparable prevalence rates of various types of behaviour problem in older populations of people with and without behaviour problems. However, a major point of contrast between the geriatric and mental handicap fields is the dearth of studies on behavioural intervention with behaviour problems in the geriatric population relative to that in the population of people with mental handicap. In their brief review of behavioural gerontology, Burgio and Burgio (1986) only consider this issue in passing though there is now an extensive literature on the subject of mental handicap and behaviour problems.

We have already noted the work of Linsk, Pinkston and Green (1982), Pinkston and Linsk (1984a; 1984b) and Green, Linsk and Pinkston (1986) in dealing with the behaviour problems of older people living at home. Though limited in number, these studies demonstrate how through an appropriate professional, here social workers, family difficulties can be alleviated through assisting family members to analyse and deal with the problem identified. Such approaches are equally applicable to families where an older person with mental handicap is living at home with parents or siblings, and where a behaviour problem is creating such difficulty that maintenance in the family home is ceasing to be feasible.

3.1.2.5 Design of physical environments. We have emphasised above the social aspects of the ageing person's ecology and the way in which it conditions both deficits and improvements through behavioural interactions. Clearly a significant aspect of the environment is physical and this, too, will condition the extent to which productive interactions are possible. Burgio and Burgio (1986) emphasise the importance of devising suitable prosthetic environments for elderly people, and review behavioural analyses of the effect of environmental design on social interaction, personal hygiene, mobility, prevention of wandering, and appropriate toileting. The importance of the increasingly researched area of environmental design and falls in elderly people is noted.

3.2 Psychological Intervention: Some Conclusions

We have approached the question of psychological intervention through a consideration of two broadly defined groups of techniques which we have labelled psychotherapeutic and behavioural. Most of this review has focused on studies and approaches directed to ageing people without mental handicap and less frequently have we been able to cite extension to ageing people with mental handicap. As we argued, the choice of this approach was rooted in the need to take as our starting point intervention with respect to ageing per se. The conclusions drawn from this exercise will, however, lead us into a consideration of the relation between intervention with people with mental handicap generally and intervention with older people in this population. Before considering this issue, however, we will briefly consider Gatz *et al.*'s (1985) conclusions regarding the relation between psychological intervention in younger populations and with older individuals.

It will be recalled that Gatz *et al.* raised four issues for consideration. These were concerned with (a) continuity or discontinuity between treatment approaches to younger adults and those who are ageing; (b) the process by which clinical knowledge is created for work with older adults; (c) the types of problems which people face; (d) the principles of therapeutic change common to diverse reports.

First, Gatz *et al.* consider that continuity characterises the movement towards psychological intervention with older people. Nevertheless, modifications have been made that are specifically related to our knowledge of ageing processes. With respect to the present review, Hussian and Davis' (1985) approach exemplifies the integration of behavioural techniques with gerontological assessment of the individual.

Second, with respect to the creation of clinical knowledge, these authors conclude that "...the evidence to date warrants neither universal pessimism nor resignation to palliative measures ...the aged are being treated psychotherapeutically ... are benefiting from it, and ... there exists a cadre of therapists experienced in the treatment of older adults." (p.774). Gatz *et al.* also caution that there is a need for controlled research. Certainly, outcome studies have been most prevalent in the behavioural field. As a result of such evaluation in behavioural studies the theoretical position stating the ecological nature of behaviour associated with ageing has gained credibility and provides an important scientific platform for continuing these initiatives.

Third, Gatz *et al.* draw attention to the diversity of problems that have been addressed. A persistent dimension that forces itself into consideration throughout their review and the present selective account is that of the context in which intervention has been carried out. While Gatz *et al.* note a number of community based interventions, some of which have been referred to here, there can be little doubt that psychological intervention has most typically been evolved and applied in nursing homes and large institutions. While characteristics of the individual may have contributed to the initial placement in such settings, a persistent strain in the discussion, both theoretical and practical, is the extent to which such ecological circumstances themselves determine behaviour requiring treatment. While community settings may not demand such extensive intervention as that required in larger institutions, it must be acknowledged that there is an imbalance in the extent to which community-related problems have received formal attention and the greater apparent concern with institutional settings.

Fourth, to the principles of therapeutic change there is clearly a lack of systematic information on specific mechanisms in much of the psychotherapeutic work. Gatz *et al.* suggest a variety of mechanisms including the non-specific, such as creating positive expectancies, the importance of therapeutic relationships, catharsis, increased meaning and insight, and enhanced cognition. Some elements of these mechanisms may also be entailed in the implementation of behavioural programmes. It must be emphasised, however, that in behavioural programmes the specific mechanisms of learning inherent in operant theory are demonstrably effective in creating behavioural change. Operant theory does not, however, preclude more diffuse influences of the kind implicated in psychotherapeutic accounts. These are referred to as *setting conditions.* These influence a whole repertoire of responses rather than setting the scene for a specific behaviour. Thus, a good relationship between a member of the care staff and individual might increase the probability of a whole range of responses in the context of a variety of programmes. The possibility of convergence of approaches, psychotherapeutic and behavioural, should also be noted, as with the refinement of Reality Orientation Therapy through behavioural techniques and evaluative procedures.

What we can conclude from Gatz *et al.*'s appraisal is that this is a field which, while progressively evolving, has only limited coherence from the standpoint of psychological theory. These authors suggest that this view of incoherence also extends to wider considerations related to ageing and developmental theory "... the integration of life-span developmental theory and models of change stands as an important challenge to the field of psychological intervention with adults of all ages." (p.777).

This last quote could well be extended to include "... and all degrees of intellectual ability", and takes us to a consideration of the state of the art with respect to ageing and psychological intervention with older people with mental handicap. Here we find ourselves facing two sets of relations, one concerned with intervention in the general ageing literature and the other with respect to intervention strategies and mental handicap.

We must begin, first, with the issues of continuity. With respect to psychotherapeutic approaches, as we noted at the outset, the fundamental concerns with ageing and adjustment to life events will in large measure affect many older people with mental handicap. Nevertheless, differences in intellectual functioning will lead to differing perceptions of age-related experience such as diminishing future life expectancy, death and the experience of isolation. We are only now learning to listen to and communicate with people with mental handicap with respect to their own feelings and aspirations. We note in Chapter 8, for example, the general failure on the part of both families and professionals to take into account the wishes of people with mental handicap in determining their own future. Lack of support following bereavement and relocation were also considered. It is only against a background of an appreciation of these aspects of the experience of a person with mental handicap that we begin to consider suitable psychological support and intervention. It is significant that a number of psychotherapists are increasingly turning their attention to this group and will hopefully contribute to a fuller understanding of the issues.

The extent to which intellectual difficulties in themselves present an obstacle to psychotherapy, and the contribution of a life time of experience in institutions further impairing intellectual and social-emotional development, is a further unassessed influence, but one which is implied in Mitchell's (1984) pioneering study. It might be argued that not only does institutionalisation degrade day to day experience, but that its cumulative effect is distorting the individual's own perspective on his or her life, creating a barrier to the reflective processes that we have suggested occur naturally in people leading their lives in the community. Even here, however, for people with mental handicap living in the community, a variety of normative life-events and transitions may have been denied them, including leaving the parental home, marriage, having children, and retirement.

When we move from the issue of intervention with respect to experiential factors to a consideration of behavioural competence, our review has reported on a number of studies that have effectively enhanced or restored skills in ageing people in institutional settings. There is sufficient information to show that behavioural programmes directed to improving social interaction in older people with and without mental handicap can be effective in enhancing the frequency of such behaviour. It is equally clear that there are major problems in overriding some of the environmental constraints imposed by institutional environments. In the case of people without mental handicap, we are concerned with people who have assumedly once had a normal repertoire of social and verbal behaviour, the loss of which has at least been exacerbated by institutionalisation. While this may be the case for some people with mental handicap, it is more likely that institutionalisation has diminished the very acquisition of such repertoires, and there is hence a more serious difficulty in establishing interactive behaviour. It is important to note that possibly a major resource in such settings is the individual who is already disposed towards interaction and can have a catalytic function. Nevertheless, the case for the use of behavioural techniques to enhance interaction in institutional settings surely takes second place to the closure of such residences as a suitable place for older people, whether mentally handicapped or not. The techniques will almost certainly prove more effective and socially justifiable in normalised settings in the community. As we have noted, little information as yet exists on such application in the general field of ageing, and is entirely absent in the field of mental handicap.

A final point concerns an observation by Burgio and Burgio (1986) regarding the need to extend behavioural training to caregivers in family settings. They cite the work of Pinkston and her colleagues (referenced above) as an example of such an extension, limiting their consideration to assisting families to deal with behaviour problems in elderly relatives. However, no such restriction is in fact required, as families may welcome assistance in developing positive skills. Clearly the receptiveness of parents to such a suggestion will vary, and, for many, such formal structured input will be positively unwelcome, as implied in Cooke's (1987) study reported in Chapter 8. It is possible that siblings looking after an older brother or sister with mental handicap might be more open to such provision though we know of no research evidence to support such a view.

The relation between work on ageing and work on children raises a number of issues, whether or not such work is concerned specifically with mental handicap. At the conceptual level Looft (1973) has considered this relation, drawing attention to the high value placed by society on cognition, and suggesting that it is this that led to such intense intervention in this domain with children. "Why not," he suggests the argument runs, "use intervention strategies to improve or at least maintain the cognitive skills of the aged, much as we have tried to with infants and children?" (p.7). Certainly, in the area of behavioural intervention we have noted above there are examples in which authors have drawn explicitly on material and approaches developed with children and adapted them for adults, e.g. Sanario's (1981) use of Foxx and Azrin's (1973) toileting programme and Green *et al.*'s (1986) use of a behavioural training programme originally devised for parents of children exhibiting behaviour problems.

As strategies of intervention are developed with older people with mental handicap, so we can expect such links to evolve to an even greater extent. Work undertaken with younger people with mental handicap will provide direction for subsequent work with older individuals with respect to both competence in daily skills and in educational matters. It is important at the outset to avoid any suggestion that such an extension is carried out from the bottom up, i.e. the unthinking application of existing techniques developed with children to older people simply because the techniques exist. It is critical that the programme is determined by functional analysis of the older person's specific needs and circumstances and that these are not distorted by use of ready-made programmes developed with the younger population. Following such analysis, the existing literature may be regarded as an invaluable source on which to draw. Critical differences in the lives of older people will, however, affect the way in which the programme is implemented and the nature of the material to be employed. In addition, and in contrast to the prevailing ethos in schools, the exercise of choice will be an important precondition to establishing most programmes, particularly where the person is able to communicate such choice. In the concluding section of this chapter we will consider some of the directions that intervention may take, viewed from the perspective of the acquisition of new competencies, rather than the processes of adjustment and restoration that we have considered above under the rubric of psychological intervention. In other words, we turn to what legitimately should be viewed as the education or training of older people with mental handicap.

3.3 Developing an Educational Strategy

The studies on psychological intervention described above may be distinguished from educational activities in two essential respects. First, they are concerned with the restoration of skills acquired but lost, rather than the acquisition of new experience or skills; or, second, they are concerned with specific transition associated with the experience of ageing, rather than with the progressive development of adaptive skills throughout the life span. Indeed, we have already quoted Willis (1985) who employs the term *education* to refer to lifelong learning as a form of adaptation, the primary function of which is the facilitation of optimal development across the life course. Adaptation, here, may be taken in a broad sense to embrace not only intellectual growth, but as Looft (1973) suggests, aesthetic and emotional experience as well.

Such a view of education stands in contrast to the widely held position that education is essentially a process to be undertaken and completed in the first decades of life. The relevance of this position to people who patently have not acquired the basic skills to cope socially and practically by the latest statutory school leaving age, 19 years in England and Wales, is particulary apparent. We have already described in some detail in Chapter 4 that the psychological basis for continued educational activity with adult people with mental handicap is a firm one, progress being manifest throughout most of the life span even in less favourable environments.

The view that the main focus of educational intervention should be essentially cognitive or focused on adaptive behaviour through structured teaching has, of course, not gone unchallenged. Looft (1973) has raised the question in relation to older non-handicapped people as to whether affective rather than cognitive goals should be set. In the field of mental handicap there is a growing literature offering radical criticism of the structured teaching approaches which emphasises the *special* educational *needs* of people with mental handicap, e.g. Wood and Shears (1986). These authors specifically offer criticisms of curricula for adults based on a hierarchical skill model, citing as an example Whelan, Speake and Strickland's (1984) Copewell Curriculum (Wood and Shears, 1986, pp.14-16) among others. While such critiques merit serious consideration, the nature of educational services for both children and adults will continue to dictate an emphasis on skill orientated training, coupled with the provision of opportunities to enjoy as wide a range of varied experiences as possible.

The form that such educational provision will take with respect to the content and teaching methods that constitute the curriculum will obviously be dependent upon the abilities, characteristics and situation of the individual student. As the teacher will be aware, there are great variations in the degree of mental handicap people display, and the extent of additional handicaps arising from specific sensory and physical impairments. Variation with respect to ability is clearly reflected in the separate graphs for profound, severe, moderate, mild and borderline mental handicap for intelligence and mental age in Figures 4.2 and 4.3 respectively. Similarly variation in personal self-sufficiency, community self-sufficiency, and personal-social responsibility within these ability categories is reflected in Figures 4.4 - 4.7 respectively. While there may be some indication in these figures that, at the higher levels of ability, there is some tendency for the differential in ability between groups to reduce after 50 years of age, it may be seen that the basic distinctions and range of abilities within this population are maintained in the later years, at least in these institutional samples. Clearly, then, the specific competencies of these people (which will in turn condition where they live and with what level of support) will determine widely varying intervention targets and indeed choice of intervention strategies.

A general statement regarding education for older people with mental handicap must therefore begin with the broad, and perhaps obvious statement, that (a) both the objectives and techniques employed will be determined by the particular strengths and weaknesses in competence of a given individual; (b) will be related to enhancing that competence in the specific environments in which the person lives; (c) will have continuity with the curriculum of much younger adults, but will be appropriate to the person's age and dignity. In addition, the educational opportunities offered by the community to older people generally, and not restricted to a skills-orientated educational curriculum, must also be explored as a possible context in which the older person with mental handicap can continue to mature personally and socially.

Given the degree of continuity with the earlier curriculum for adults, it would be beyond the scope of this book to provide a full account of educational assessment and intervention with adults with mental handicap. It is assumed that those coming to this book from the field of mental handicap will have some familiarity with this subject. However, for those who may have come to the volume from a wider background in the field of ageing we will offer a very general background and some illustrations on particular curriculum areas.

For the over-50s who are both profoundly mentally

handicapped and have additional impairments to sensory or physical functioning, assessment will be focused on a number of competencies related to basic motor functions, the pre-requisites of self-help abilities, and early cognitive and communicative abilities. Indeed, though we have seen in Chapter 2 that there is a higher mortality in this population, some *will* survive into the later years having made some, but limited, progress in the early decades. Hogg and Sebba (1986b) describe (Chapter 1) a range of assessment procedures related to these subject areas. They also list (pp.72-81) a number of published curricula relevant to this group. Some of these curricula are directed specifically to adults and would in no way demean older people, while others have been developed for children and would require the nature of the tasks and situations modifying to make them appropriate to the level of competence and the actual age of the student.

It is important to emphasise that with this group, as with children with multiple impairments, apparent profound retardation may be an inaccurate assessment. Adequate exploration of the person's functioning and new opportunities to use communication and computer-based devices sometimes indicate a much higher level of competence than is immediately apparent. It is possible that the over-50s who have not been exposed to the new technology and recent thinking on curriculum development may have been particularly underestimated in these respects, whether living at home or in residential accommodation. One of the exciting prospects of placing such people within the framework of a life-span educational curriculum is that such possibilities might finally be opened up to them.

For people with profound retardation and multiple impairments, the skill model of education is important in permitting us to make tractable the complex job of unpacking the compounding effects of several interacting impairments and establishing clear objectives. However, such an approach should not preclude education through more broadly based experience which include not only suitable leisure activities but also carefully devised situations which will engage them in a productive way when not involved in direct learning. Jones, Blunden, Coles, Evans and Porterfield (1987) have demonstrated how such situations can be established and the benefits to people with profound retardation and multiple impairments.

With progressively higher abilities, so we will move through increasing demands on the competence of older people with respect to the curriculum. With respect to the major areas of everyday life, the Bereweeke Skill-Teaching System (Jenkins, Felce, Mansell, Flight and Dell, 1983) provides one such framework, developed specifically for adults. (For a discussion of this system, see Kiernan, 1987.) Among the areas covered are: "component skills" such as grasping and releasing, fine and gross manipulative, body control and cognitive skills which include imitation, complex sequencing, matching and sorting. Self-care and household competencies embrace eating and drinking, mealtime activities, washing, undressing and dressing, toileting, grooming, clothes care and kitchen and domestic tasks. Language scales cover the functional naming of familiar objects and comprehension of a variety of concepts (colour, number, size/shape, comparisons, prepositions and time), comprehension of simple directions, and use of nouns and verbs. Wider issues of socialisation such as initiating activities are included, and this, together with several other areas embraced in this curriculum will be recognised as covering objectives set in several of the studies noted in this Chapter. The procedures for implementing teaching of these objectives and actual checklists appear in Dell, Felce, Flight, Jenkins and Mansell (1986) and Felce, Jenkins, De Kock and Mansell (1986) respectively.

Although there is no rigid distinction, the progression through most curricula can be seen to reflect increasingly academic skills, or at least functional skills that make progressively greater cognitive demands, such as telling the time. Stroud, Murphy, and Roberts (1984) in a survey of older people with mental handicap in North-Eastern Ohio, draw attention to the educational deprivation underlying the low academic skills in this population. The group of people studied was very varied, some living in a large institution, some now in the community following institutionalisation, others having lived their lives in the community among whom were a small group who had received no services, and spanning the "mild/normal" to profound retardation range. Of these, only 8 per cent read at their mental level while 75 per cent were effectively non-readers, though most could recognise their name or simple signs. Only 32 per cent were able to write their name. Money and telling the time were partially achieved by 59 and 51 per cent respectively. These figures point to marked deficits in the skills required for intellectual adaptive functioning in the community with important, wider, consequences. Edgerton (1967) offered the important insight that any distinction between 'intellectual' and 'social' competence is artificial, since their influence is so pervasive with respect to specific cognitive difficulties that deficits in intellectual abilities in space, time and number invariably lead to incompetence in the social sphere.

While we are well aware that those providing services for older people with mental handicap are engaged in teaching many "academic" subjects, our own search of the literature has confirmed Stroud *et al.*'s (1984) conclusion that "... surprisingly, no studies were found which discussed reading, writing or arithmetic skills in older mentally retarded adults. Nor were there any which investigated functional learning such as use of money and time concepts." (p.4).

A further area of considerable importance identified by Stroud *et al.* (1984) was the need to "... increase conversational skills ... to prepare clients for access to community activities. Small talk and appropriate subjects for conversation need to be understood and practised. Training activities to strengthen conversational skills have been proposed and described by these authors. Parallels clearly exist here with some of the programmes concerned with enhancing social interaction noted in the preceding section on psychological intervention. The contrast between the level of education of older and younger people with mental handicap is noted by Stroud *et al.* and must also prevail in the UK. With the implementation of full-time education for children with mental handicap taking place in 1971 and the general absence of educational integration, it can be expected that very few people with mental handicap over 50 years in the UK will have received an educational grounding in the rudimentary academic skills. Where this has occurred will be in more recent years where adults have been admitted to Colleges of Further Education or where Adult Training Centres have, under their new rubric of Social Education Centres, initiated such teaching. As we noted in Chapter 1, in Oldham, and doubtless elsewhere, a variety of educational schemes both in and out of older clients' residences have been implemented in recent years. A full survey of these initiatives and pooling of the information regarding the over-50s would yield most welcome information.

4 STAFF TRAINING

A central theme running through the preceding review has been the importance of the institutional environment, particularly the influence of staff, in shaping behaviour in older residents. It has been clearly shown, on the one hand, that staff practices can lead to unnecessary dependency, and on the other, that with suitable management practices, staff are a potent force in establishing independent functional behaviour. Burgio and Burgio (1986) draw a direct parallel between the effectiveness of staff training in facilities for people with mental handicap and the need to undertake such training in facilities for older people.

It is important to note at this stage of developing training techniques with both older people generally and those with mental handicap, that there is by now a considerable literature pointing to the ways in which effective staff training can be implemented, and the constraints that exist in maintaining trained skills. (For papers dealing with the spectrum of issues involved in staff training in mental handicap, see Hogg and Mittler 1987.) These issues have been addressed explicitly from the point of view of the ecological analysis of staff training in residential facilities by Landesman-Dwyer and Knowles (1987). They present a strategy for assessing the effectiveness of staff training that takes into account both its direct and indirect effects, its short and long term consequences and the qualitative as well as the quantitative consequences for staff members, residents and the collective social environment. While noting the compatibility between their ecological model and behaviour modification, they emphasise the extent to which their own position urges attention to the total environment and the complexity of the individual and environmental variables. Thus, any simplistic attempt to teach behavioural skills and to make the assumption that they will be applied in a facility where professional or emotional support is lacking, will be doomed to failure. This view has received confirmation specifically in the area of ageing from Davies (1982).

In the studies reviewed, research workers or professionals have determined both the objectives with respect to residents' behaviour and the procedures in which staff themselves engage. A key issue in staff training is to ensure that staff themselves have the requisite skills to determine the goals of training as well as implementing them. Barrowclough and Fleming (1986a) describe the first published attempt to teach direct care staff working with elderly people to goal-plan for this group. Goal planning, a well-established and researched procedure in the field of mental handicap, entails specifying behavioural objectives for clients and devising individual programmes to realise the goals set. It is of interest to note in passing that in Barrowclough and Fleming's study that the selected goals contain, but are broader than, those set in the published behavioural studies reviewed above. While increased mobility was set most frequently, preparing food and drink and self-care domestic skills followed, with subsequent positions occupied by personal hygiene, appropriate medicine and diet use, use of prosthetic aids and shopping. This broadening of priorities clearly reflects the greater diversity and normality of the establishments studied by Barrowclough and Fleming, i.e. day centres, short stay and long stay residential accommodation in contrast to large institutions and nursing homes. This is an important distinction to which we will return later, as it is clear that in the context of present normalisation philosophy, older people with mental handicap will require support across a much broader range of skills than is implied by the literature to date on behavioural gerontology.

We will not review Barrowclough and Fleming's detailed procedure here, but will note two aspects of their conclusion which bear upon the wider ecological issues we have raised in this book. First, these authors endorse the position stated by Landesman-Dwyer and Knowles (1987) regarding the social context in which staff implement learnt skills. They emphasise as crucially important the role of the unit manager, the need for regular weekly meetings to discuss goal plans, the importance of written records and the continuing support of the professionals who initiated the training.

The second point relates to the overlapping ecologies in which older individuals find themselves, and the facilitation of transitions. This issue was of particular relevance in the establishments with which these authors were concerned, as day centre and short term provision obviously entails movement between different settings, in contrast to the facilities which have been explored most in the wider literature of behavioural gerontology. Staff training across settings is therefore advocated, e.g. involving Home Helps, Social Workers, District Nurses who will be assisting the individual in the home. Discussion with the Social Services Department in which the work was undertaken suggested several advantages to such a strategy:

"(a) continuation of goal-orientated work into the community could be seen to have general benefits to interventions of a range of services;
(b) the extension and continuation of goal planning started in the unit would increase the morale of the staff there. Discontinuity and abandonment of goal plans can lead to demoralisation;
(c) the assessments and the monitoring of clients' performance as integral parts of goal planning would constitute a good basis for any multidisciplinary identification of client needs, e.g. Individual Programme Planning;
(d) a more systematic organization, such as in IPPs, of the different services working with elderly clients can only be advantageous." (p.207)

The relevance of Barrowclough and Fleming's programme and observations requires little modification when extended to older people with mental handicap. The utility of behavioural techniques demonstrated in the field of mental handicap generally and the importance of their extension to the older population suggests that the adaptation of Barrowclough and Fleming's programme would be of great value to staff. In addition, their approach facilitates the development of common strategies in different facilities between which people move either once, as in the case of institution to community, or regularly, e.g. ATC to small group home. In addition, extension where appropriate to individuals' own homes can be as relevant as in Barrowclough and Fleming's study. A manual for the training of skills in goal planning with elderly people (Barrowclough and Fleming, 1986b) merits special consideration with respect to its applicability for staff working with older people with mental handicap. More generally, Burgio (1987) reviews the spectrum of staff training and management techniques for use in geriatric, long-term care facilities. Ironically, from the standpoint of this review, he notes not only the dearth of systematic staff training and management research in such facilities, but observes that most of the data he has reviewed has been gleaned from projects conducted in facilities for people with mental handicap, and to a lesser extent, in psychiatric facilities.

The specific concern with dependency in some residential facilities has led to a more focused consideration of staff training with respect to the reduced functional competence of residents. Though not directly involving residents with mental handicap, Sperbeck and Whitbourne (1981) describe a potentially applicable staff training programme aimed at: (a) reducing staff's informational deficits about ageing people; (b) counteracting staff's biases in "blaming" older residents for their functional shortcomings; (c) teaching staff principles and techniques of operant behaviour management. The authors present a set of specific objectives for the staff undertaking the training programme and demonstrate improvement in residents' behaviour during the implementation of the programme.

5 CONCLUSION

In this chapter we have focused on a number of themes, including individual psychological intervention to assist with coping with specific experiences related to ageing;

behavioural techniques for restoring lost functional abilities; education to enhance functional and academic skills. The areas covered in no way offer a comprehensive picture of what is required in providing a service for older people with mental handicap. In the ensuing chapters on work and leisure, residential life, and the role of informal networks, a variety of forms of intervention will be cited, ranging from retirement courses to social work support for the ageing family. In addition, we have touched upon the question of staff training.

In line with the view that behaviour should be considered in a wider ecological framework, thinking in the areas of ageing and mental handicap has undoubtedly converged. Neither generalised decline with age nor static incompetence should be seen as intrinsic to these processes and conditions. There are, indeed, many working in the field of mental handicap who would apply to this condition Sparks' (1973) observation that "... the phenomenon of aging was an artefact of our own philosophical environment and that the goal of humanistic gerontologists in the future should be the elimination of aging and not its compensation." (p.15).

At a practical level the awareness of ecological influences and the operationalisation of this viewpoint through operant psychology must be regarded as having special significance for intervention with older people with mental handicap. However limited the information conveyed in this chapter, the framework for developing satisfactory strategies is clearly available. With the changing demography of ageing and mental handicap described in our opening chapters, there will be ample opportunity to develop and advance our understanding in a way that we trust will be beneficial to older people as well as being in accord with their own aspirations.

Chapter Six

WORK AND RETIREMENT

1 INTRODUCTION

There is very little research relating to the employment of older people with mental handicap, presumably because very few of the group have jobs. Indeed, it is illuminating to note that Chinn, Drew and Logan (1979) in their life-cycle approach to mental retardation, make no reference to either work on retirement in their chapter in "The Aged Retarded". The focus is rather on intellectual decline and lack of family contact. Also, much information on employment relates to people whose level of handicap is only mild. Thus Baller (1936), in a period of severe economic depression, found 20 per cent of the handicapped individuals to be gainfully employed, compared with 50 per cent of the non-handicapped control group. Such figures obviously bear little relation to people whose handicap is severe.

Vocational success has often been listed as a major criterion for community adjustment and as an important ingredient of normalisation (Wolfensberger, 1972). In Edgerton's (1967) study (see Chapter 5), for instance, all the subjects were required to be employed as a criterion for discharge. Changes in this employed status over the years give an interesting insight into the interaction of these people with society-at-large. Six years after discharge, 21 of the 48 remained employed full time, six were unemployed and 21 were married to someone employed full-time. Of the 21 who were married, only three worked, and this was part-time only. In the 1976 follow-up, Edgerton and Berkovici (1976) found only eight of the individuals to be working full-time, with a general overall reduction in socio-economic status. By this time the average age of the group was 47, an age which is not particularly favourable to the unskilled job market. Also, Edgerton and Bercovici noted that a reduction in health-status was a likely contributing factor to this decline in employment. While in generally good health at the time of discharge, by 1976 only 14 of 30 traceable individuals were in good health, nine had disabling ailments, one had a terminal illness and the remainder had died. This finding is, however, at odds with that reported by Stroud *et al.* (1984) who found most older people with mental handicap to be healthy and relatively highly functioning. It is interesting to note that, despite overall life circumstances being rated worse than at discharge, self-rated reports of satisfaction did not agree with this. Twelve people rated themselves as happier, seven were the same and six less happy. It appears that the mere presence or absence of work is not strongly related to community adjustment, any more than it is in the general population. As Chinn, Drew and Logan (1979) suggest: "Happiness may be more a function of being more 'normal', and in periods of high unemployment, many 'normal' individuals may not be working" (p.294).

Since this book is about older people it is inappropriate to enter into a lengthy discussion on the employment of people with mental handicap, since most of this group will be more likely to be contemplating retirement. It is worth noting in passing, however, that the current climate represents a tension between, on the one hand, the new ideas and development of people's potential to the greatest possible degree, and on the other the economic depression which is causing record levels of unemployment. If it were not for this second factor it is probable that more people with mental handicap would be involved in more skilled and fulfilling jobs than ever before. Unfortunately, any discussion of employment opportunities for older people with mental handicap is likely to be unrealistic. In the areas of both ageing and mental handicap, society penalises people particularly strongly in the field of work opportunities. To have both these disadvantages must reduce employment prospects virtually to nil. Indeed, even for younger people with mental handicap, it is sad to note that the industrial training unit described by Pountney (1987) has managed to place only 12 people in open employment over a 6 year period. Similarly, the hoped-for expansion of community involvement of ATCs has failed to materialise. Tinto (1987) reports that Birmingham Social Services foresaw that an average of 3 out of 10 sessions per week would subsequently be occurring in community schemes. So far, they have achieved only 50 of the 1650 needed. MENCAP (1986) have noted additionally that employment legislation, introduced over recent years contributes to the poor employment figures, since employers are aware of the potential difficulties in removing a "difficult" worker, in the belief that a person with mental handicap may be poorly motivated or incompetent. Overall, it is difficult to remain optimistic about employment of people with mental handicap. It is to be hoped that the economic situation in the UK improves in the future, so that current ideas with respect to employment of people with mental handicap can be more fully realised.

2 RETIREMENT

2.1 Sociological Issues in the General Literature

For older non-handicapped people the coming of old age brings the question of how long to continue working, whether to work part-time rather than full-time, or whether to retire fully. The decision to retire is based on a complex interaction between a variety of factors including (a) current financial status and expected financial status following cessation of work; (b) current life-satisfaction and perceived satisfaction in retirement; (c) retirement options available within the particular job situation; and (d) physical health. Retirement involves a disengagement from the work role, a change in status, a possible reduction in income and an increasing focus on leisure activities.

It is a common theme in the literature on retirement that work is an essential part of human life, providing status and a meaningful service role within society. Within this ethos it is traditional to regard retirement as a crisis having profound social and psychological consequences for the lives of older people (Ward, 1984). Robinson, Coberly and Paul (1985) suggest that this negative emphasis reflects an interest among academics and professional gerontologists in solving the injustices and problems of old age. It should be noted, however, that the view of work as a thoroughly positive aspect of life has not always been held. The ancient Greeks and Hebrews saw work as a painful necessity that brutalised the mind (Parker and Smith, 1976). Also, there are indications that the current experience of work is becoming more negative. Gecas (1981) shows evidence of growing alienation and job dissatisfaction at virtually all occupational levels, while Ward (1984) reviews a variety of studies arguing that both manual and white-collar jobs are becoming less intrinsically meaningful, and more alienating and confusing (Braverman, 1974; Sarason, 1974; U.S. Department of Health, Education and Welfare, 1973). Even 30 years ago a study by Dubin (1956) showed that work was not the central concern for three out of four industrial workers, a finding which urges caution in evaluating evidence on the negative aspects of retirement.

Although statutory retirement at 65 years has become the norm for industrialised countries, this rigid age boundary is by no means universal. Ward (1984) states: "Many people have argued that, for better or worse, retirement defines the status of the aged in modern societies and sets off the modern ageing experience from that of non-industrialised countries" (p.132). It is also worth noting that some industrialised countries employ far more elderly workers than the UK and USA. Thus, 30 per cent of males over 65 are employed in Yugoslavia and Portugal, while the corresponding figure for Japan is 50 per cent (Schulz, 1980). Although a number of studies have drawn attention to the negative effect of compulsory retirement (Palmore, 1978), it appears that increasingly few people are actually in the situation of being forced to retire against their will. Streib and Schneider (1971), in a longitudinal study of retirement, made it clear that mandatory retirement is not necessarily unwilling retirement. They found 30 per cent to have been totally willing and made their own choice to retire, 20 per cent made their own decision reluctantly, often because of ill-health, and 20 per cent to have been retired administratively but willingly. This left only 30 per cent who suffered a truly unwilling retirement. Schulz *et al.* (1974) found an even lower level, seven per cent, of workers whose retirement was due entirely to administrative rules, i.e. people who were able to work but unable to find a new job and forced to retire by a mandatory policy. It seems likely that this relatively small number of unwilling retirers is becoming still smaller as people increasingly see the leisurely life of retirement as an attractive alternative to working. Ward (1984) points out that retirement has been increasingly presented as a positive way of life, reflecting a great variety of structural and cultural changes which have taken place in modern societies. Despite the increasing popularity and acceptability of the retired role, there is some evidence that lack of work is associated with low self-esteem and a withdrawal from social interaction (Foner and Schwab, 1981). Viewed from the perspective of a work ethic, not-working is seen as unproductive, lazy and a burden on society. Associated with this view is the notion that retirement is an ambiguous "roleless role" (Donahue *et al.*, 1960; Rosow, 1974) involving few expectations for behaviour and an inevitable disengagement from the valued dynamic aspects of society.

Fortunately, this is not the experience of most people who retire. The majority find retirement a positive experience, describing it in such terms as "active", "involved", "expanding", "busy", "hopeful", "meaningful", "relaxed" and "independent" (Atchley, 1976). Parnes (1981) found that 80 per cent of retirers felt that retirement fulfilled or exceeded their expectations, while 75 per cent said they would retire at the same time or earlier if they had their lives over again. Kimmel *et al.* (1978) found 90 per cent of retirers agreeing that "things are as interesting as they ever were", and 55 per cent that they are "the best years of my life". Few people seem to miss their jobs (Ward, 1984). It appears that a return to work is usually for financial reasons (Foner and Schwab, 1981; George, 1980), while the aspects which are most often missed are not the work itself, but the income, associations and activity levels related to work (National Council on Aging, 1981).

As retirement approaches it is clear that most people undergo some process of adjustment to their coming change of role. Goudy (1981), for example, found that 40 per cent of older workers who did not expect to retire had actually done so within four years. Ward (1984) describes this process as a "loosening of the bonds between a worker and his or her job" (p.157). It is most important to note, however, that a disengagement from the job does not imply a desire to disengage from other aspects of society, or from the desire to maintain an active life. Research shows there is little change in social interaction or community activities, and few differences in the activities of retirers and workers of the same age (Foner and Schwab, 1981; Morse *et al.*, 1983; Mutran & Reitzes, 1981; Streib & Schneider, 1974). As a general policy it does appear, however, that the option of flexible retirement patterns and a gradual decline in hours rather than a sudden cessation favours the maintenance of a high level of life satisfaction (Quinn, 1981). McConnell *et al.* (1980), for instance, found that 50 per cent of all workers would remain employed beyond their planned retirement date if alternatives to the normal working day were available. Part-time work was the most desired of the options.

Much of the work on retirement has been concerned with factors affecting the decision to retire, and ways of predicting the timing of this event. Atchley (1979) points out the need for an adequate definition of retirement, and recommends that research definitions should include: (a) The reduction in hours of employment and weeks employed, (b) income from pensions and retirement plans, and (c) the subjective assessment of retirement status. The choice of definition is important, since it has been shown (Palmore *et al.*, 1982) that determinants of retirement are different for early retirement, late retirement and retirement as defined by the number of hours and weeks worked per year. The strongest predictors of early retirement are self-reported health status and attitudes to retirement, while retirement after the age of 65 is most strongly predicted by financial variables and characteristics of the job. In addition to operationally defining retirement, Atchley (1979) suggests it is important to consider several different <u>types</u> of retirement. His suggested categories are: (a) strong preference for retirement as soon as financially feasible, (b) compulsory retirement and willingness to take it, (c) compulsory retirement and reluctance to take it, (d) retirement following unemployment, (e) retirement due to health problems.

In conceptualising the retirement decision, three elements may be identified: (a) How individuals come to consider retirement, (b) the factors that influence the consideration of the retirement option, and (c) factors that influence the timing of retirement (Atchley, 1979). From a social science perspective the retirement decision is seen as a process of weighing the consequences of continuing to work against the consequences of electing retirement, and thereby exchanging the role and status as a worker for the role and status of a retired person (Robinson, Coberly and Paul, 1985). From an economic point of view, the retirement decision can be viewed as a work-leisure trade-off, involving a conscious choice between these two alternatives according to the individual wealth and the amount of time believed to be important to allocate to the workplace and the home. Atchley (1979) thus suggests there are two basic comparisons made by older people contemplating retirement. First, anticipated financial needs in retirement are compared with the financial resources likely to be available. Second, the person anticipates the likely social situation compared with the current social situation. Personal attitudes to the importance of work versus leisure, and social pressures to retire and make way for younger workers, or keep working and not be a burden on society, all influence this complex tradeoff. Whether the person is active or passive in relation to his or her social environment has an influence on the extent to which the individual is oriented towards planning, which in turn affects the extent to which a rational retirement plan is formulated.

Overall, the two factors found to dominate the decision to retire are health and finance. Older workers in poor health tend to opt for early retirement more often than those in good health. People who expect their retirement income to be sufficient for them to live on show a greater likelihood of retiring early than those who do not expect it to be adequate (Boskin, 1977; Burkhauser and Turner, 1980; Quinn, 1977, 1981). It should be noted, however, that the decision to retire on grounds of ill health is not always left to the individual worker. Standards of health set by employers are sometimes set too high or are irrelevant to the job, needlessly disqualifying older people. In a similar way, educational standards also exclude anyone with a mental handicap. Within the field of industrial gerontology there has been some interest in redressing this problem through the notion of functional age. This entails a close look at the specific functional abilities of an individual worker, which can then be used either to match the person to an existing job, or tailoring a job to fit the needs of the individual. The use of such an approach is a recognition of the fact that neither chronological age nor intellectual level can tell us much about the work capacity and skills of particular individuals.

A person's specific occupation before retirement appears to give little information regarding the subsequent attitude to retirment. Attitude to work is at best a weak prediction of attitude to retirement, even if work had formerly occupied a central position in life (Fillenbaum, 1971; George, 1980; Glamser, 1981; Goudy *et al.*, 1975). Attitudes to retirement seem to be more affected by economic considerations, number of friends, social activities and perceived preparation for the role of retirement (Ward, 1984). In this respect there are found to be social class differences in the level of retirement preparation (Atchley, 1976; Simpson *et al.*, 1966). High status workers tend to be more interested in their job than retirement, and see little need for formal preparation since they are used to making decisions and controlling their world. Low status workers have little access to formal pre-retirement courses, although there is evidence they would be interested in attending such courses (Fillenbaum, 1971). Middle status workers are most likely to be favourably disposed to planning and tend to work in organisations who provide pre-retirement courses. There has been criticism of the relatively low priority given to pre-retirement counselling by many firms (Glamser, 1981; Kalt and Kohn, 1975; Siegel and Rives, 1980), and to the fact that most are geared for literate workers (Atchley, 1976).

There is evidence that pre-retirement counselling can be helpful in enhancing better preparation and more realistic expectations, resulting in less feeling of job deprivation, more involvement in the active process of retirement and better self-rated health (Atchley, 1976). Reviewing a number of studies, however, Ward (1984) concludes that the main effect of pre-retirement courses is to impart information. They appear to have little impact on overall morale or attitudes to retirement. Ward concludes: "It may be unrealistic to expect short-term pre-retirement programs to contribute in a general way to long-term adjustment" (p.172).

2.2 The Changing Role of Leisure in Retirement

One fundamental dimension which is yet to be discussed is the role of leisure within the overall transition from work to retirement. A major difference between work and leisure activities is that leisure involves an independent use of time, and is not ususally required for economic maintenance. On the other hand, it is in a sense somewhat artificial to draw a line between these two domains. Work provides a source of some important components of leisure - stimulation, activity, and friendship, while some leisure pursuits demand very hard work. There is no doubt, however, that most people see a conceptual dividing line between these two domains of life; those who are engaged in boring repetitive jobs would probably draw this line more strongly than those who derive great personal satisfaction from their work. This distinction is often drawn upon in sociological studies, where reference is made to the various 'domains' of life such as work, family, parenthood and leisure.

The place of leisure in the lives of older people has received more attention recently. Palmore's (1979) longitudinal analysis of predictions of successful ageing indicated that later-life adaptation is strongly related to leisure pursuits, particularly to social activity outside the home. Kelly *et al.* (1986) suggest three possible reasons for the way in which leisure occupies this central position. First, leisure may simply fill the time in pre-retirement and retirement in which formerly central roles are becoming less important. Second, leisure may provide opportunities for effectual action in the years when work and family commitments have lessened. Third, leisure may provide a context in which important social relationships are developed and expressed.

Overall, it is probably true that leisure occupies all these positions. It has a dynamic and multidimensional role which is not fixed at some point in time, but has a place in the development of the individual and in coping with the changes required by external events. Kelly *et al.* suggest that definitions of leisure are less important than what people actually do and the personal significance of their actions. In general, leisure may be defined as "activity chosen primarily for its own sake" (Kelly, 1982), highlighting the element of personal choice which distinguishes it from work. On the other hand, this does not mean that leisure has to be some sort of esoteric activity separated from the ongoing and more central contexts of life (Osgood, 1982).

In an attempt to formulate a model of leisure involvement in life, Kelly (1983) has proposed a "core and balance" model. Presenting this approach, Kelly draws attention to the fact that adults have a set of central activities, usually centred in or around the home, which persist throughout life. Such activities include interaction with other household members, reading and watching television, walking and play. Distinct from this 'core' is a balancing set of more specialised activities which tend to shift and change throughout life, as roles, self images and opportunities change. In middle age this may bring a desire for some periods of quiet and solitude as well as for activity and interaction. In old age, a reduction in physical energy is likely, making it more probable that leisure pursuits will be increasingly focused on the home. Kelly *et al.* suggest that this balance is best interpreted within a dialectical perspective which includes both the personal aims and motivations of the individual and their interaction with the expectations, values and opportunities in society.

McCall and Simmons (1978) have extended the core and balance model to an analysis of how people define themselves within their roles ("personal identities"), and how they view themselves as being defined by others ("social identities"). Within society we come to know who we are by interaction with significant others, a process which occurs in all domains of life, including leisure. In this sense, a person's life course can thus be viewed structurally as a sequence of related roles with expected transitions. Whatever the relative weights we ascribe to the various domains of our lives, there will be some carry-over from each one to all others, since there are interactions among the roles based in the domains of family, work and leisure. As with each of the principal domains, leisure has its own particular set of social and personal significances for each individual. It is an area of life which offers a greater degree of freedom than other domains in the opportunity to make choices for immediate experience, self developing activity and social interaction at all levels of social bonding (Gordon *et al.* 1976). A notable dimension of this kind of activity is the communication and intimacy fostered by working with others on a common task. Kelly (1983) and Rapoport and Rapoport (1975) suggest that, for some people, leisure may be the most important domain in life for the development of personal and social identities.

What effect does increasing age have on people's leisure pursuits? One obvious effect is that people can become hampered by ill health, lack of money or simply lack of energy from doing the activities they previously enjoyed. On the other hand, the amount of time available for leisure tends to increase following retirement. The interaction of these various factors, particularly those which constrain rather than facilitate activity, has been explored in a number of studies (Buchanan and Allen, 1983; McAvoy, 1976; Mueller and Gurin 1962; McGuire, 1982; Scott and Zoernick, 1977; Witt and Goodale, 1981). McGuire, Dottavio and O'Leary (1986) used a life-span perspective to investigate shifts in constraint on leisure pursuits as people pass from young adulthood to old age. They make the point that a constraint may take the form of a limitation, i.e. reduced activity, or prohibition, i.e. no activity, and that the relative importance of limitors and prohibitors may vary across the life-span. Overall, lack of time was the most frequent constraint on outdoor recreation. Other frequently listed limiters included: no people to do the activity with, lack of transportation, health reasons and lack of money. Not surprisingly, health emerged as the most common prohibitor to activity.

Lack of leisure companions was found by McGuire *et al.* to exhibit a 'U'-shaped function, with the older and younger respondents apparently finding most difficulty. It is notable, however, that the oldest group

(75 years and older) indicated this to be a less important consideration. This may be because older people have identified a stable group of companions over the years, or alternatively, because older individuals have adjusted to being alone, and are past the point where they might have abandoned the leisure pursuit for this reason.

Interestingly, older people do not, overall, report a greater degree of constraint on leisure activity than younger people. Two reasons are suggested for this finding. First, it is possible that older people have substantially reduced participation in a variety of activities and are hence relatively unaffected by constraints. Second, older people may have developed more adequate coping skills for avoiding or minimising the factors which lead to limitation or prohibition.

Apart from the limits to leisure activity, what changes in the quality of activity can be seen as people get older? Kelly, Steinkamp and Kelly (1986) examined differences in leisure pursuits within four age bands of non-handicapped people: 40-54, 55-64, 65-75, and 75+. Their findings were consistent with a shift toward social integration as being the most important factor for the over 65s, and the availability of family for the over 75s. Later-life leisure was found to demonstrate considerable continuity over the life-span, despite these predictable changes, this continuity being represented by the "core" of accessible day-to-day activities. Increasing age showed no reduction in overall level of activity, but rather a shift from organised and resource-based activity requiring considerable exertion and effort. Health and physical ability, rather than age itself, was shown to be crucial in dictating a reduction in later-life activity, although there was a cohort effect in that older people tend to have less expectation of continuing activity in later life. Although there was generally no change in activity levels with age, the oldest group (75+) were found to have a considerable constriction of leisure pursuits, both in social context and geographical range. For people in this age group, interaction and social support becomes the most important dimension of leisure. Indeed, this general trend could be seen in the younger age-groups of the study. Later-life leisure (i.e. over 40) is not so much recreational in the sense of organised activity, so much as maintaining or developing important relationships, filling time, escaping from problems and an expression of the self.

The development of an individual's personal leisure style can be viewed from various perspectives. From one of these perspectives, leisure styles respond to age-related role expectation and the immediate contexts of peoples' lives. Major life events or turning points in a person's life may therefore produce abrupt changes in the leisure domain. On the other hand, "Leisure is for the most part integrated into overall life patterns that differ only in detail from those common to other persons in the same social stratum and life period" (Kelly *et al.*, 1986, p.536). From another perspective, leisure activities and the development of a leisure style can be seen as a response to the availability of resources. Geographical location, community facilities, educational and occupational status, culture and family variables interact with personal variables to determine the range of available options. Within this interaction, changes in leisure resources can influence the choice of activity, which in turn can affect the person's orientation to leisure.

From the results of their study, Kelly *et al.* concluded that most people manage to retain the core and balance of leisure throughout their lives. They point out, however, that Palmore (1979) found that organised community and physical activity is associated with the highest levels of retirement satisfaction. It is precisely these two areas which, in Kelly *et al.*'s sample, showed the lowest rates of participation. How could leisure participation at this level be increased? Very few elderly people receive effective pre-retirement counselling, so it seems likely that the most promising approach is for environmental planners to pay attention to the importance of providing easy access to stimulating social environments, with careful attention to location, scheduling and social support. In this respect, Kelly *et al.* point out that "Most people prefer to be with their peers - those whom they find congenial and supportive - in contexts that foster interaction" (p.537).

Summarising the general literature, one concludes that most people successfully retire and find the experience a positive one. If anything, the transition has been made easier by the fact that society has moved away from the negative view of retirement as lazy, unproductive and worthless, to a much more positive view of increasing opportunities for leisure and self development. It is also clear, however, that the maintenance of prior activity levels is crucial to the successful adjustment of the individual in retirement. Pre-retirement counselling has become popular as a way to aid this transition, and to ensure that activity levels are maintained through the development of interests which can replace those which were provided through work. The efficacy of such counselling is, however, probably limited mainly to the short-term imparting of information.

The changing role of leisure is central to the transition from work to retirement. Leisure provides not merely a way of filling in time which was previously occupied by work, but is an important context in which social relationships are formed. Particular attention is drawn to (a) the opportunities that leisure activities afford, and (b) the fact that, for older people, social interaction becomes one of the most important dimensions of leisure. From the sociological perspective of the "core and balance" model, it is important to ensure the continuity of the core activities throughout the life course.

2.3 Issues in the Retirement of People with Mental Handicap

The way in which these various fundamental dimensions of retirement can be interpreted from the perspective of people with mental handicap depends partly on the life history of the particular individual under consideration. Different experiences of working, or non-working, will have their own particular impact on the nature of the retirement decision. For people who have experienced a more or less conventional working life in open employment, this decision involves many of the same factors as for non-handicapped individuals. Indeed this also applies to more able individuals who have not necessarily worked in open employment. An appraisal of the financial outcome of retirement, possible loss of satisfaction and anticipated benefits with respect to leisure undoubtedly influence decision making. For most individuals, assistance in making such an appraisal will be of value, a state of affairs that is equally applicable to more able people who also require supportive couselling in reflecting on such an important decision. There is a growing concern that people with mental handicap have the opportunity to state their own preferences and that assumptions should not be made regarding their inability to communicate in some way their needs and expectations (e.g. Cooke 1987; Flynn and Saleem 1986). Where ill-health has become a factor in continuing work or day-service attendance, discussion is equally applicable as enforced retirement without understanding might be highly detrimental to an individual's self-esteem.

The counselling involved in enabling an individual with mental handicap to weight the various factors in arriving at a decision regarding retirement must also be informed by a wider appraisal of the person's capacity to continue work and possible changes in this activity. We noted above the development of procedures in the field of industrial gerontology in which consideration is given to matching changing functional abilities to available jobs or activities.

People with mental handicap who are in the fortunate position of being able to retire from a job are more likely to find that general pre-retirement courses are relevant to their needs than people who have never worked in open employment. Age Concern, for instance, runs a number of such courses. Suitable efforts from staff from Mental Handicap Services should make it possible to integrate working clients into appropriate groups if they wish to attend. The individual may also benefit from help in making contact with other groups and clubs in the community which cater for the leisure and social needs of older people. There is no simple prescription in this respect, beyond the fact that it is important for mental handicap services to have good contact with all groups and agencies which may be of interest to older clients. From the basis of a high level of community involvement it should be possible to help working clients make the transition to an increased focus on leisure and social interaction in the same way as their non-handicapped peers. The two assessment instruments developed by the ACCESS project in Ohio (see p. 224) may be of help in determining (a) the appropriateness of various community facilities for older people with mental handicap, and (b) the choice of activities which best match the individual's wishes, needs and abilities.

2.4 Day Services for Older Adults

Regrettably, few people with severe mental handicap are fortunate enough to have a job, particularly in the present economic climate. For most of these people, work has been limited to attendance at an ATC/SEC. For these people the decision to retire, if available as an option at all, is far less complex. There is no delicate tradeoff to be made between income before and after retirement, since people working in ATCs are not permitted to earn more than a few pounds a week. Even if engaged in commercial contract work, income remains at the level of Social Security payments. On the other hand, current service philosophy is moving towards the view that *some* form of alternative retirement option should be made available. In a recent report on Day Services, MENCAP (1986) made the following statement:

> "In moving towards an effective series of Day Service facilities, practitioners and facilitators must understand the part they are playing in a continuum of service provision covering infancy, childhood, adolescence adulthood and old age ... There must be a sensible and sensitive realisation that the appropriate training and socialisation programme at a particular developmental stage needs to be related to the type of service provision which has preceded it, and the current training programme to what may follow it. This continuum must be maintained" (p.12).

In the USA these concerns are increasingly being incorporated into federal and state legislation. The Older Americans Act, for instance, states specifically that services shall be available to people over 60, and that priority is to be afforded to those in the greatest social or economic need. The most recent amendments to the OAA make specific reference to people with mental handicap as a special population to be served (Sutton,

1987). Similarly, the Ohio Department of Mental Retardation and Developmental Disabilities adopted the following policy: "Although no mandatory retirement is required, adults of 55 who no longer desire a program emphasizing work skills training and employment shall have available to them a retirement program emphasizing leisure time, nutrition and health, exercise, community integration, and other training components" (Ohio Revised Code 5128: 2-2-06).

These policy statements pose the question of how to provide an appropriate continuum for old age. In the UK, as in Ohio, many Local Authorities operate the policy of no formal retirement age for ATC attendance. People attend as long as their health permits and their desire to attend remains. This approach is based on the philosophy that maintenance of activity is as important in old age as in the rest of life, and that activity needs of older people are not fundamentally different from those of younger individuals. We have learned of other schemes which operate a formal retirement policy, sometimes involving a run-down of attendance over a period of time. Such a run-down may, for instance, involve attendance 4 days a week for three months, then 3 days a week for a similar period, and so on. This avoidance of an abrupt cessation of work has been shown in the general literature to be beneficial. It will also be remembered, however, that this same literature stresses the importance of maintaining similar levels of activity in retirement. Any policy of retirement from ATCs should therefore be operated in conjunction with a scheme for transfer to appropriate replacement Day Service provision. Indeed, it is notable that the older people themselves will often express this preference if given the opportunity. In the ACCESS study (Sutton, 1986) clients were asked if they liked what they were doing and whether they wished they could retire. Several replied that it would not be a good idea to retire from the workshop because "a person ought not just to sit at home and watch television" (Sutton, 1987, p 2). There was a general feeling that people needed to be around others and to keep active. Many people noted that their main interest in the Day Service was the opportunity for friendship and social interaction.

In response to current thinking, two notable

developments have taken place. First, some Mental Handicap services have set up pre-retirement courses for older clients, and second, a number of Local Authorities are now running Day Centres for older people with mental handicap. Details of these initiatives are reported below.

2.5 Pre-retirement Courses

For non-handicapped people, the sometimes abrupt shift in emphasis caused by a total cessation of work has led to the introduction of pre-retirement courses designed to aid the individual in making this transition. Evidence from the American literature suggests that many older workers would be keen for their employers to set up programmes of this kind. People want to plan effectively for retirement but feel they need help in doing so (Fillenbaum, 1971; Pyron and Manion, 1970). Modelled on this approach, some mental handicap services are now providing pre-retirement courses for older clients. Haines (1986) for instance, has reported on the development of a Workers' Educational Association course in the Salisbury area. She points out that there are difficulties in deciding on priorities and areas of interest, since courses of this kind are so new that there is no available blueprint from which to work. Haines therefore started from a consideration of the ways in which old people might occupy themselves at home, other than watching television - ways of remaining active and involved in the community. There were ten people in the group, which met for 30 sessions over 30 weeks. Among the activities provided, Haines mentions the following:

- A visit to an old people's home
- A visit from a dietician
- A visit from a dental hygienist
- Discussion of facilities for elderly people at the local library
- Introduction to Age Concern information
- Trips to the theatre
- Making music at home
- Meals on wheels
- Church involvement

- Luncheon club
- Gardening
- Walking
- A talk from a physiotherapist
- Keeping pets
- Birdwatching

Haines makes the point that the group members responded very variably. Some have developed new, absorbing interests, while others have remained passive. She concludes: "I look at my group and wonder about the future. I see Mary happily in her home village enjoying the cats, the garden and making tea for the ladies' afternoon meeting. I see John listening to his music, going to concerts, attending church, alive with his involvement as an Oblate of the Benedictine Order. I see Ivy in her village, just managing to look after herself, with the help of neighbours who she is wily enough to call on at mealtimes! I see Nora as the searching, questioning one who wants more than life is offering at the moment.

But what of Norman, Maurice, Richard, Ted, George and Francis? They seem placidly content to accept life as it is. The reality is - the quality of their life in retirement is going to be a reflection of the quality of all their previous life".

The article by Haines demonstrates the energy and dedication of the course organiser in arranging a stimulating course of events. The list of activities fits well with the kinds of needs that old people are traditionally expected to have. In considering the needs of older people with mental handicap, however, we need to explore these issues a little more closely, to look below the surface of the "face validity" of courses modelled on those provided for non-handicapped individuals - courses designed to help the transition from regular work to a golden old age of gardening, luncheon clubs and meals on wheels. This does not imply any criticism of courses providing activities of the sort described by Haines. On the contrary, the stimulation and companionship which these activities potentially provide can only be beneficial. On the other hand, these needs are not <u>specific</u> to older clients, and indeed the majority of the activities provided in this course would be of enjoyment to people of all ages. Retirement planning for non-handicapped people generally posesses the two main components of (a) finance and (b) ways to re-structure one's time - two components which alter drastically with the cessation of work. For people with mental handicap these two components are much less relevant, (although an obligatory retirement from ATC attendance may produce a similar change in time structure if no alternative Day Services are provided at a similar frequency of attendance).

Are there any specific needs of older clients which we should therefore be addressing in a pre-retirement course? Cheseldine (1987) has found that a crucial component arising in discussion with older clients is a lack of happy memories to look back on, and an inability for clients to locate themselves in the immediate history of their local area. (See Chapter 1, p. 36) for details of Cheseldine's "Step Forward" pre-retirement group in Oldham, and Chapter 5 for a fuller discussion of approaches to intervention involving life-review and reminiscence therapy.)

2.6 Day Centres for Older People

It should be noted from the outset that the initial provision of these facilities has not always stemmed from changes in the philosophy of care, but rather from administrative decisions. We visited two Day Centres for older clients which are described shortly. In both cases we were told that the initial need for the new provision developed from the fact that local ATCs were becoming overcrowded. With a policy of no retirement, clients were staying on into their 60s and 70s, with the result that there was no space for young school leavers. The idea of "hiving off" the older clients was a neat solution for solving the overcrowding problem. On visiting these two centres it was most interesting to see how each developed its own philosophy and *raison d'etre*. The fact that the centres were initially set up for administrative reasons had left open the possibility of becoming a "dumping ground" for old people - a possibility which appears to have become a reality in the first of the centres to be described.

Day Centre A

Day Centre A is a day centre for people with mental handicap over the age of 55 years. It was originally set up as a collaborative project between the voluntary sector and Social Services, although it is now staffed exclusively by Social Services. The centre was set up as a solution to the overcrowding in the four local ATCs resulting from the fact that the majority of clients at these centres continue to attend as long as they are physically capable. The basic idea of Day Centre A was therefore to provide a retirement day centre to which the ATC attenders move when they attain the age of 55. Unlike ATCs, Day Centre A does not provide a structured programme of activities or specific training, but rather allows people to engage in whatever pursuits they wish, or to put their feet up and relax. We were told that the age criterion of 55 is not rigidly applied. A 'young' 55 year old may stay longer at the ATC while, conversely, a younger person who is showing signs of slowing up or being unable to cope with the regime of the ATC may move to Day Centre A before 55.

The building is a modern purpose-built construction having basically one large room which is extensively glazed. The fact that it is surrounded by a tarmac car park lends the impression of being in a school classroom. There was very little evidence of activity among the residents - most seemed to be taking the option of "putting their feet up". A few were talking, while one or two were knitting or making rugs. Neither the physical environment nor the available resources appeared to offer much in the way of stimulation to the people attending. Watching the elderly people sitting inactive around the edge of the room lent the impression that the clients were very much older than they really were.

Talking to the immediate care staff it become apparent that staffing shortages were a major problem. With only three professional staff and volunteers it was quite impossible to provide the degree of input necessary to maintain a good level of stimulating activity. In addition, it was felt that, although there is a place for a facility offering a relaxing atmosphere to clients who are finding it difficult to maintain a full day's work, it is essential that this should be part of an integrated service with other facilities. In particular, it was suggested that there should be strong and regular links with the various clubs for elderly non-handicapped people in the surrounding area.

Without this additional input the carestaff agreed that Day Centre A is little more than a dumping ground for older people with mental handicap. Although it does seem to be a potentially valuable facility, there is a need to review the policy on admission, activity, training and involvement with other services, while there is an urgent need to increase the staffing ratio. This last aspect should shortly be improved by the addition of two extra full-time staff.

The age criterion for transfer from ATC to Day Centre A, although being stated as having some degree of flexibility, nevertheless appears to take insufficient account of adaptive and physical status. The oldest attender, for example, a man of 74, was also said to be the <u>most</u> active. Among his pursuits he goes swimming every day. The integration of this facility with a range of other services would help to maintain functioning, rather than allowing it to degenerate. In the present context there was clear evidence that such degeneration <u>was</u> occurring. We were given the example of a woman who, before coming to Day Centre A, had been active and independent, attending clubs regularly and going to the cinema by herself. Following her transfer to Day Centre A she became extremely lethargic; doing almost nothing. A great improvement occurred when she started attending keep-fit classes run by the care assistant. This staff member felt that more of this type of activity should be organised, although she was conscious of the fact that it would be preferable for properly qualified staff to run these sessions. This again points to the importance of increased staffing and service integration. A further quoted case was that of a woman whose main hobby is creative writing. She is visited by a teacher from the nearby Adult Education College. It was suggested to us that, although this service input is desirable, it would be much better if the client were provided with the necessary support and transport to enable her to attend herself.

Day Centre B

The second of the facilities we visited was not housed in purpose built premises, but operated on the ground floor of a very large semi-detached house, the rest of which was a 27-bedded hostel for people with mental handicap. The instructor told us that he felt this situation was far from ideal - he would prefer to see people having to make their own way to another place as part of the maintenance of functional skills. Of the 26 members in this elderly day group, eight lived independently in the community, three were in sheltered accommodation, one was in another hostel for older clients, one lived with a sister and three lived in group homes. The remaining 18 lived on the premises. This naturally implied that the hostel has a clear age bias towards older residents. When questioned on this, the instructor told us he knew of no specific policy in this respect, although many of the clients have been relocated from hospitals through a Health Authority joint funding scheme. The age bias evident in hospital populations, mentioned frequently in this book, would obviously account for the large proportion of elderly clients living on the premises. Despite the absence of a specific age-placement policy, the instructor felt it was unlikely that the relocation of a 23-year old to this particular hostel would be considered appropriate.

Their elderly group had been running for three and a half years at the time of our visit. The instructor told us that, as with Day Centre A, the group was mainly formed, not for the members' sole needs, but to enable younger school leavers to have more opportunity to attend ATC, i.e. to reduce the waiting list. At its original inception there was a fixed age criterion of 55-60 years for transfer from ATC to elderly group. Now, however, the policy is to pay very close attention to the needs and wishes of individual clients. Some people prefer to stay on at the ATC because they like the nature of the activities. We were given an example of one man who started in the elderly group but did not get on well and expressed a desire to return to the ATC. As the client himself said: "That lot are all soft! They do no work". Conversely, some people fit well in the elderly group at a much younger age than originally conceived. One man of 42, for instance was completely misplaced in the ATC because of his total lack of motivation to work. On joining the elderly group, however, his interest in life and level of activity has blossomed. Thus, one can see that a flexible approach to group membership takes account of widely varying individual needs. Overall, the activities of the older group are more likely, on average, to suit older clients, while younger people usually fit in at the ATC. There is a recognition, however, that individual needs are so variable that age can only be taken as a rough criterion.

On entering Day Centre B we were struck immediately by the feeling of being in a hive of activity, quite unlike the first centre we visited. Most people were engaged in activities of various sorts, constructional, reading etc., and many were working in groups round tables. Some people were sitting alone and inactive, but even these people were attending to things going on around them, or listening to the record player and chatting to people as they went past. Most surprising of all is that this level of activity was achieved with a staffing ratio no better than Day Centre A. How was this remarkable effect achieved? The answer lay, quite simply, in the highly unusual management structure, and in the energy and dedication of the instructor in setting it up and making it work. Management was conducted, almost totally, by the clients themselves. The following description was written by the instructor himself:

> "When the group came from the ATC to its present base the philosophy changed also. The group was originally described as a pre-retirement group. The main aim of the group was to useful hobbies, skills etc. - to hopefully keep them from stagnating during retirement. The thought of so many elderly people with a mental handicap sitting around in the 'traditional' manner filled me with horror.
>
> Since moving to the present premises the group took on a different look when 'acquiring' new members who were already past retirement. With the aid of the 'non-active' approach the group has become an able and self-seeking unit. I see my function as that of 'enabler' - helping mainly in an

organisational capacity. With minimum stimulus they are very vocal and active - determining their day-to-day involvement and indeed non-involvement.

The group has a natural committee which calls meetings only when problems arise. They take a very direct line of action and they do have 'real' power. Recently they asked for, and received, the removal of one of their members who refused to conform to their 'norm'. In a series of meetings he was 'warned', then 'fined' (by having his allowance stopped) and finally removed from the group.

A management committee was formed almost twelve months ago and two of the group members are on this committee. They do in fact have quite a say within the committee and have been directly responsible for major pieces of equipment purchased. Members of the group also take part in staff interviews and, it is hoped, a way can be found to write it into the Authority's Policy Document in the future."

Apart from this radical departure in management structure, Day Centre B also maintains a full programme of structured activities planned on a week-by-week basis. Apart from activities within the Centre, clients make regular visits to shops, parks etc. A specimen time-table appears in Figure 6.1.

<u>Falmouth MENCAP Day Centre</u>

The MENCAP day centre for older adults has been described in the report of a recent MENCAP conference (Carr, 1986). This Day Centre, unlike either of the two described above, is staffed entirely by volunteers, with the exception of the co-ordinator. As with Centres A and B, the idea was to provide a day centre for older people with mental handicap, many of whom have been retired from the workshops of the local hospital, Trelawney House. Setting up of the project was a collaboration between various agencies, funding being provided by the Mental Health Foundation, Social Services, the Area Health Authority and the MENCAP City Foundation. It opened in 1985.

ELDERLY GROUP (Staffing and Activities)

MONDAY	TUESDAY	WEDNESDAY	THURSDAY	FRIDAY
A.M. - M.S.C. (1 F/T) - TEMP. INSTRUCTOR - CARE ASSISTANT Activities Talks/Discussions on Weekend Activities Stone Cross (12) Arts & Crafts Gardening/Handyman/ Maintenance (3-4)	- M.S.C. (1 F/T) - TEMP. INSTRUCTOR - CARE ASSISTANT - M.S.C. (1 P/T) Activities Morning Tea and Toast (Group of 5-6) Singing/Acting etc. (Sue McDonald) Gardening etc.	- M.S.C. (1 F/T) - INSTRUCTOR - CARE ASSISTANT - M.S.C. (2 P/T) Activities Friar Park Shopping Skills Arts & Crafts Gardening etc.	- M.S.C. (2 F/T) - INSTRUCTOR (2 H/T) - CARE ASSISTANT - M.S.C. (1 P/T) Activities Morning Teas & Toast Film Show (Training) Arts and Crafts Gardening etc.	- M.S.C. (1 F/T) - INSTRUCTOR - CARE ASSISTANT - M.S.C. (2 P/T) Activities Windmill Centre Shopping Skills
P.M. - M.S.C. (1 F/T) - TEMP. INSTRUCTOR - CARE ASSISTANT Activities Personal Interviews & Recordings Introduction to Cooking/ Living Skills Arts & Crafts Gardening etc.	- M.S.C. (2 F/T) - TEMP. INSTRUCTOR - CARE ASSISTANT - M.S.C. (1 P/T) Activities Bingo Session Craft Sessions Introduction to various Crafts Personal Interviews & Recordings Gardening etc.	- M.S.C. (1 F/T) - INSTRUCTOR - CARE ASSISTANT - M.S.C. (2 P/T) Activities Film Show (Training) Activities related to Films Gardening etc.	- M.S.C. (2 F/T) - INSTRUCTOR (H.TOP) - CARE ASSISTANT - M.S.C. (1 P/T) Activities Craft Activities Keep Fit Session Personal Interviews & Recordings Gardening etc.	- M.S.C. (1 F/T) - INSTRUCTOR - CARE ASSITANT - M.S.C. (2 P/T) Activities Bingo Session Free Choice Session Talks/Discussions on coming Weekend Film Show (Fun) Stone Cross

Figure 6.1: Specimen timetable for the activities of Day Centre B

Carr's (1986) report describes the daily activities as following: "a very relaxed pattern. There are activities running through every day - sewing, knitting, painting, cooking, music and dancing; we have recently introduced skittles and basketball. There is no pressure to join in any activities, but most clients do willingly. There is always that friendly ear to talk to and to listen to problems, and the chats have proved a great part of the centre" (p.59). It is clear that there is a dynamic approach to the development of new ideas. Carr reports several ideas which have been suggested and instigated by the clients themselves. Such schemes include a football sweep, crossword, tuck shop and raffle. In her conclusions, Carr suggests that: "There is a need for this type of centre for elderly mentally handicapped people who after all have missed out on all the services that we now take for granted for the young ..." (p.61).

Case studies are presented for ten people attending the Centre, of whom five live at home and five in hospital. Retirement policies from hospital workshops and ATC is not spelled out, but the age range (51-75 years) suggests a flexible approach. Carr suggests that the oldest person has probably benefitted most from the Centre. His case study symbolises the traditional view of what retirement is all about: "Hugh is a quiet old fashioned gentleman, very happy and contented. He arrived at the Centre a little bewildered and confused. After a very short time he settled well and enjoys mostly having conversations with his volunteer friends. They discuss Plymouth docks which seems to be Hugh's favourite subject. He has been involved in crossword puzzle work and preparing Christmas items; but on the whole he likes to sit and observe all that is going on around him. I feel that he has benefited most from the Centre in that it is a place where he knows he can choose activities in peace ..." (p.62).

In Ohio, USA, the provision of Day Services for older people with mental handicap has been developed at the University of Akron, through funding provided by Ohio State. As a result of this endeavour, service planners have clearly been encouraged to focus resources on the specific needs resulting from ageing. It is notable, for instance, that the County Board Program permits older people to continue part time working if they wish, while also participating in structured activities in the Day Centre and in the community. The County Board provides staff who are specially trained in dealing with age-related changes in the biological, psychological and social spheres. The stated aim of this approach is to improve the planning of age-appropriate activities.

The paper by Sutton (1987) provides a detailed report of the way in which access to community facilities can be improved for older people with mental handicap. Most of this information is fairly obvious to anyone who is working professionally with clients in the community, although the detailed breakdown of issues is probably a useful guide to service providers who wish to plan a programme of integration into community facilities. Sections deal with (a) ways in which the client can be taught to integrate more easily into community settings, and (b) the various steps which group leaders can follow to "prepare the ground" before attempting to integrate clients into a new setting. Many, if not all, of these points are not age specific, but relate to adults of all ages.

Within the ACCESS project, two assessment instruments have been developed. These deal with (a) appropriateness of specific community facilities, and (b) the needs of the specific client. The first of these two instruments is a straightforward checklist which offers a guide to the evaluation of the characteristics of a particular community activity. It includes items on (i) Accessibility and safety, e.g. "Are there elevators?", "Are there any possible safety hazards?" (ii) Social climate and expectations, e.g. "Are there printed rules and regulations?", "Will the others who are there be open and receptive to these handicapped participants?", (iii) Programme characteristics, e.g. "Is it age-appropriate for older people?", "Is it a place or event which will be in any way familiar to the participants? Have they had a similar experience at an earlier time?"

The second has been developed as a result of the ACCESS project's firm belief in the importance of matching retirement activities to client characterisitcs and wishes. Physical health, self care, social skills, personality (shyness, aggressiveness, outgoingness), leisure skills and conversational ability are evaluated, along with strengths and weaknesses in specific skills and personal interests. The aim is subsequently to coach individuals in weak areas so that their skills can be increased to make a greater choice of activities available. One part of the schedule is an interest survey to be completed in an interview with the client. The other section is completed by staff. As with the first schedule, the instrument is not designed to be a formal test with scoring criteria. Rather, it is an aid to obtaining a full profile of information before planning services for an individual client.

It is clear from the descriptions of these various services that much thought and dedication is now being put into the Day Service needs of older people with mental handicap. Visiting some of these facilities there is little doubt that some have managed to provide a more stimulating environment than others - variations of this kind can be seen in any service provision. From a research point of view it is perhaps time to pay some attention to the relation between the different kinds of activities provided by the ATCs/SECs and by groups and centres catering specifically for older people. What range of activities should we be providing for the later years? Should it be more of the same, or programmed to fit with the traditional view of a retirement affording less formal structure to the day? Has the distinction in activities between ATC and elderly groups become so small as to be meaningless, given the move away from repetitive contract work towards the social education role which ATCs are increasingly undergoing? Should we, instead, be providing a unitary service for all age ranges, embodying the flexibility necessary to cope with the individual needs of all clients?

2.7 Leisure Activities in Later Life

Generally speaking, people with mental handicap have more available leisure time since they are only rarely parents or family bread-winners. Rather than time limitations, the main limitors to leisure activity are money, transport, lack of facilities and lack of knowledge of the available options. Also, the shift in emphasis of ATCs from work involvement to social training has somewhat blurred the already unclear distinction between work and leisure domains. On the other hand, the fundamental qualities of leisure compared with other domains of life remain the same for people with mental handicap, and in this respect there are clear lessons to be learned from the wider literature.

Leisure is, first and foremost, the domain which is identified by the element of personal choice. It is through the exercise of this choice that leisure aids the development of the individual and the ability to respond flexibly to changing external events. The "core" of central activities, mainly centred on the home, provides the continuity, while changing specific activities respond to the changing life roles and expectations as well as to changes in available facilities. One point which emerges clearly from this literature is that core activity, although representing a large portion of total leisure time, should not necessarily be interpreted as gaining its significance from either the specific activities engaged in or the level of activity demonstrated. This is a most important point concerning the evaluation of leisure as pursued by people with mental handicap. The gerontological literature has too often adopted an over-simplified "activity" model of leisure. This perspective focuses on the element of intentioned activity and its achievement, activity in gerontological terms being associated with well being, relationships with significant others and positive affect (Kelly *et al.*, 1986). Over-simplification of this model has resulted in counting frequency or number of activities as a measure of effective leisure, rather than seeing activity as a resource for coping with change. Almost all people say that the leisure they value involves interaction with others, or the investment of effort to achieve mastery. "They may spend more time watching television, but they define themselves by and invest themselves in more intensive enjoyment" (Kelly *et al.*, 1986, p.532).

Relating this to a practical example, one can envisage two very different day centres, one in which the individuals watch television because they are bored and unstimulated, and one in which television is a "catalytic" activity, part of the core of activities through which people maintain and foster their interactions with others. Obviously, the difference between these two functions of the same activity arises not from the activity itself, but from the overall pattern of activities and social interaction within the centre. Taking this one stage further, it can be seen from Kelly *et al.*'s findings that frequency of activity is only one of a number of considerations. The element of personal choice is also crucial. This suggests that a structured day, heavily programmed with leisure activities, will only provide the qualities present in non-handicapped people's leisure pursuits if the activities correspond to those that the client wishes. Flexibility in choice of activities is of paramount importance.

A number of other points which arise from the wider literature also bear on the leisure activities of people with mental handicap. The importance of leisure in the development of personal and social identities highlights the need to attend very carefully both to the activities available and to the opportunities for meaningful social interaction within the various pursuits. The client group-management structure of Day Centre B, decribed above, represents a remarkable example of the extent to which older clients are able to make their own choices and operate within a group structure. Having seen the group in operation there is no doubt that this has fostered a climate of involvement of the kind which older non-handicapped people value so highly in the later-life leisure. The need for communication and the intimacy which arises from working on a common task are also nourished by this approach.

The need for continuity of activity over the life-span, stressed by Kelly *et al.* (1986) obviously extends to all other domains of life. Dramatic life events such as the loss of a spouse, or relocation of a person with mental handicap, can have traumatic and long-lasting effects. The need to re-forge links and to retain whatever continuity is possible is as true for leisure activity, particularly the components of intimacy and friendship, as it is for any other life domain.

The lack of companions with which to pursue leisure activities in later life is unlikely to be a problem for people living in hostels, or hospitals. On the other hand, people living alone, or even in group homes if they have no one available who shares their interest, may have more of a problem. Kelly *et al.* suggest that people prefer to be with their peers, people who have shared some similarity of experience in life. This contention is, however, lacking the kind of evidence which would permit clear conclusions. Certainly, it seems likely that some people with mental handicap will prefer to be with members of their own age group for some leisure activities. Such opportunities should be available for those who want them.

The final point to be made from the literature on non-handicapped people is that later-life adaptation is strongly related to the development of leisure activities. The need to provide a stimulating environment, a wide range of options and easy access is as great for people with mental handicap as for their non-handicapped peers.

This is an inappropriate context within which to discuss the ever-growing range of leisure opportunities and schemes available for people with mental handicap. These topics have been fully discussed elsewhere (eg MENCAP, 1986). Generally speaking, there is no reason why any of these opportunities should be denied to older clients, unless on the basis of physical health or stamina. In closing, however, it is interesting to note that the National Federation of Gateway Clubs, the foremost organiser of leisure activities for people with mental handicap, is beginning to develop in the direction of "age appropriate" activities for older members. Sheffield Gateway Club, for instance, have set aside Tuesday afternoon for older clients, while other clubs are considering the setting up of Darby and Joan clubs. Interestingly, the response of older members to the idea of such schemes, while thoroughly positive, has always been accompanied by concern that this should not imply a reduction in participation on regular club days (Oliver, 1987). Thus, the need for continuity and involvement, so clearly evident in the work of Kelly *et al.* (1986), is just as evident in people with mental handicap. The Federation is, at the time of writing, twenty years old. Many of the members have been enrolled from the beginning, a fact which obviously indicates a sizeable proportion of older people in the membership. At the time of writing there were 20 per cent of the members over 40 years of age. It seems likely, however, that the older membership lobby will grow stronger as the proportion increases. It should not be thought, however, that older Club members' needs will be met exclusively through the provision of Darby and Joan clubs. We were told, for instance, of one 67 year old man in Lytham St Annes who is still the regular goal-keeper for the Club's football team!

Chapter Seven

THE ECOLOGY OF AGEING: RESIDENTIAL ACCOMMODATION AND COMMUNITY ADJUSTMENT

1 ECOLOGY OF RESIDENTIAL PROVISION

The issues concerning residential provision for people with mental handicap have been the subject of a great number of experimental studies, legislative measures, and assertions of the rights of individuals to live a community life which approximates as nearly as possible to that of non-handicapped people. At the same time, the residential needs of elderly non-handicapped people have also been the focus of concern by researchers and service planners. One might conclude from this that there is likely to be a substantial body of literature relating to the needs of those people who are members of both groups - i.e. older people with mental handicap. This is not, however, the case. To give an idea of the lack of overlap between the two literatures, McCarver and Craig (1974) cite 150 references in their review of community residential alternatives for people with mental handicap, while Lawton (1985) provides 181 citations relating to living environments for elderly non-handicapped individuals. Not one of these references is common to both bibliographies. At the time this chapter was written, Medical Abstracts included 382 citations back to 1966 with the key words "residence characteristics" and "aged". Of these, five were concerned with people with mental handicap. The need for further well designed studies is therefore clear.

Within the following sections, three broad questions will be asked in relation to residential provision for older people with mental handicap. First, do older people have a greater chance of suffering traumatic effects when being relocated to a new living situation?; second, does the age of a person with mental handicap affect the extent to which satisfactory adjustment can be expected when moving from an institution to a community residence?; third, does the age of a person with mental handicap affect the nature of the residential choice for relocation to the community following deinstitutionalisation? Each of these questions has important implications for service planning. The likelihood of a major traumatic effect, for instance, may lead to a conclusion that the decision to relocate should be considered cautiously in the case of an older client. On the other hand, a finding that most people benefit from relocation, even if the initial effects are traumatic, might lead to a conclusion that greater support should be given to older people at the time of relocation, in preference to the conclusion that they should not move at all. The third question, effect of age on relocation choice, should give an indication of the extent to which older people with mental handicap are currently being placed in appropriate situations. Are older people with mental handicap being given different residential placements from younger people? Do such differences reflect genuine differences in the functional abilities of older versus younger clients? We then consider the work of Edgerton and his colleagues which offers the only truly longitudinal study of ageing in people with mental handicap living in the community. His conclusions on adapting in the community then lead us into a consideration of the methodological issues involved in predicting such adjustment.

1.1 The Effects of Relocation

Apart from the general concerns of matching environment to individual, there have been some suggestions that the relocation of older clients may have undesirable consequences for health and subsequent adjustment. Evidence from the literature on relocation suggests that it is a process which can be highly disruptive, can lead to the breakdown of established social patterns, and may even reduce life expectancy. The process of moving leads almost inevitably to a loss of existing friends (Wells and McDonald, 1981), while

Stuckey and Newbrough (1981) point out that deinstitutionalisation has not prompted the kind of change in neighbourhood settings which might stimulate the easy development of new contacts. The potential traumatic effects of moving are obviously of relevance to people of any age, with or without handicap. In the present context, however, the question of particular interest is: "Does the fact of being elderly introduce considerations over and above those applicable to people with mental handicap in general?".

Within this context it is likely that the starting and finishing place for relocation will change as a function of age. For elderly *non*-handicapped people, the most likely move is *from* a community setting *to* an institution, e.g. hospital or nursing home, or at least to a congregate-care setting such as old people's flats. There is no doubt that older people with mental handicap will, and do, have to make similar transitions in the face of increasing infirmity. On the other hand this book has chosen a lower limit of 50 years for a definition of older clients. With regard to issues of relocation it is clear that there is a lack of comparability between the population of older people with mental handicap thus defined and people in the general population considered to be 'aged'. People with mental handicap over 50 years of age are being asked to undertake relocation in the *opposite* direction, i.e. from institution to community, at a relatively late stage in their lives. In these cases the move is being made because the resident is (hopefully) *increasing* in community skills rather than becoming incapacitated due to age-related infirmity. For this reason it is important to bear in mind that research on the effects of relocation in elderly non-handicapped people may not generalise to the situation in which many older people with mental handicap currently find themselves. On the other hand, two reasons suggest that it is important to consider the literature on normal ageing in the present context. First, the literature on relocation of non-handicapped elderly people is a good starting point for estimating the negative and positive effects of the major disruption caused by a change in residential situation. In particular, the relative impacts of voluntary versus involuntary moves have been studied in some detail, making it possible to appraise effectively the importance of this factor. Second, it is clear that relocation for some older clients *will* be in the direction of community to institution. This will apply particularly to very aged clients and those who have become infirm at an earlier period in their lives than would be expected in the absence of a handicapping condition. For this client group it is reasonable to assume a good generality from findings in the field of ordinary ageing.

1.1.1 Relocation Trauma in Non-handicapped Elderly People

Change of residence is one of a number of major life-events which are considered to have a deleterious effect on individual well-being. With regard to elderly people, a number of studies have attempted to estimate the magnitude of effect by measuring post-transfer mortality rates. Although this index is simple and easy to apply, it suffers from the fact that no meaningful comparisons can be made unless very careful control is kept on factors relating to the nature of the move. Such factors include prior physical health, prior living situation, characteristics of the new environment and the extent to which the move was voluntary. Also, Seltzer, Sherwood Seltzer and Sherwood (1981) have pointed out that successful relocation does not *necessarily* result in improved adaptation or health status. It must be demonstrated that changes in behaviour or health were caused by the relocation. Some changes in behaviour will occur naturally over time, while health status may be changing dramatically in a case where relocation is being necessitated on health grounds. A central methodological issue is therefore to determine what would have happened if the client had remained in the previous location. A situation could be envisaged, for instance, in which relocation had the *positive* effect of *reducing* the rate at which a client's health was deteriorating. Clients who deteriorate less are evidence of a positive effect of relocation.

A further consideration is that mortality rate is a very simple and limited measure of relocation trauma. It hardly seems an adequate measure of the range of experience and emotions, both negative and positive, which people are likely to experience as a result of the move. Measurements of *quality of life* and health status present greater problems than using mortality rates, but are obviously essential in any serious study of relocation.

A number of gerontological studies documenting increased mortality rates following relocation (Aldrich and Mendhoff, 1963; Aleksandrowicz, 1961; Bourestom and Tars, 1974) have been cited by critics of institutional moves for elderly people. Thus, Bourestom and Tars (1974), studying non-mentally handicapped individuals, concluded that residents involved in radical change, i.e. new location, new staff, new programmes and patients, experienced higher mortality, poorer behaviour and greater pessimism about health. On the other hand, Heller (1985) points out that there are at least as many studies showing no increase or even a decrease in mortality rates following transfer (Borup *et al* 1979; Brand and Smith, 1974; Coffman, 1981; Kowalski, 1978; Lawton and Yaffe, 1970; Strandt & Wittels, 1975).

Ferraro (1983) suggests two factors which may contribute to these inconsistent findings. First, full account is often not taken of the characteristics of the residential environment. Ferraro's own work concentrates on research relating to moves which may be classified as 'home to home', although he points out that most studies of elderly non-handicapped people are more concerned with 'home to institution' relocation. With this particular focus, Ferraro demonstrates that there is a danger of classifying two residences as a 'home' when in fact the differences between them are so great that the move from one to another may be comparable to that of moving from home to an institution. Schulz and Brenner (1977), for example, consider relocation from home to an old people's housing project to be 'home to home'. Ferraro suggests, however, that the age-segregated nature of some housing for elderly people is so different from a family home that the adjustment required, while probably being less than that involved in permanent hospitalisation, is nevertheless considerable. Ferraro's second point is that these varied outcomes may depend partly on the extent to which the relocation was *voluntary*. Thus, Beaver (1979) found that the desire to move clearly affects personal adjustment. Kasteler *et al.* (1968) studied the personal adjustment of a sample of older people who had been involuntarily relocated to make way for road building and found negative effects on attitudes to health. In his own study of a group of low income and disabled people, however, Ferraro (1983) failed to demonstrate that the level of 'voluntarism' significantly affected health status. It appears, therefore, that the contribution of this variable is unclear. Even without clear-cut findings, however, humanitarian grounds alone should be sufficient reason for minimising involuntary relocation except on strong medical grounds or in the face of severely reduced functional skills.

It appears, therefore, that a great many factors probably have to be taken into account before clear conclusions can emerge from this type of research. In general, the evidence suggests that such moves do not normally pose great threats to health; indeed the positive consequences appear to be at least as great. Carp's (1966, 1967) research on new residents of Victoria Plaza, an apartment building for elderly people, showed increases in self-ratings of health following the move. Sherwood *et al.* (1981) observed the effect of moving older people into a medically oriented apartment complex and generally found a consequent improvement in health.

1.1.2 Relocation Trauma in older People with Mental Handicap

In general, studies of deinstitutionalisation among people with mental handicap have not shown consequent increases in mortality (Heller, 1985). One exception, however, was Miller's (1975) study of residents with profound handicap moving from Pacific State Hospital to convalescent institutions. In this case a two-fold increase in mortality was noted. The fact that this work focused on profound handicap is probably highly significant. The result fits with a hypothesis of Lazarus (1966) that environmental change would be more stressful and have more drastic consequences for people lacking adequate resources, supports and coping mechanisms. People with profound handicap may come within this category. Similarly, there is evidence both from people with mental handicap (Heller, 1982) and elderly non-handicapped people (Goldfarb, Shahinian and Burr, 1972; Killian, 1970; Marlowe, 1976) that individuals whose health is already poor are exposed to the greatest health hazard during relocation.

Much has been written of the double jeopardy of being elderly and mentally handicapped (Sweeney and Wilson, 1979) so it is not surprising that this group is considered to be particularly at risk (Heller, 1985). What *is* surprising, however, is that the evidence does not seem to support such a conclusion. In an observational study of 147 residents moved from an old institution into remodelled units (Landesman-Dwyer, 1982), older residents did not differ from younger residents in their behavioural reactions to transfer, except that they slept more. Braddock, Heller and Zashin (1984) investigated the effects of age on behavioural adaptation of 185 residents who were being transferred from a large institution which was being sub-divided into four smaller units. Prior to transfer, the group of residents over 50 years of age showed no significant differences in any of the nine behavioural categories which were measured: object interaction, positive affect, negative affect, social interaction, staff attention, abnormal, antisocial, other non-social and inactive. Following transfer, some small differences were observed, the elderly people showing a greater drop in smiling and laughing and an increase in object interaction behaviour. Heller (1985) suggests that this may be due to the staff at receiving facilities focussing more on the younger residents than the older ones, in comparison with the previous residence where staff/resident relationships were well established and thus less influenced by the client's age. Heller (1985) re-analysed data from an earlier study of closure (Heller and Berkson, 1982), looking for age effects in resident adaptation during transfer from a large institution to one of 132 smaller residences. Six months following transfer there was no indication of significantly worse transfer effects for the group over 50 years old. Thirty months later, the older and younger clients showed similar behavioural adaptation to the community.

With such a paucity of evidence it is difficult to draw firm conclusions regarding the potentially hazardous effects of relocating older clients. Evidence from the non-handicapped literature does suggest, however, that it is important (a) to minimise the magnitude of the environmental transition, and (b) to involve the resident as far as possible in the process of choosing to move, and in the choice of residential location. In her summary of research on ageing and relocation, Heller (1985) concludes that increased *short-term* trauma amongst older clients is not the aspect causing most concern. Rather, the effects tend to be manifested in the long term, demonstrated by older residents experiencing more health problems compared with younger clients.

1.2 Community Adjustment

With the change in focus from institutional to community residential provision has come an increasing emphasis on the fact that people's satisfaction with life, motivation and communication are deeply affected by the characteristics of the place in which they live. As Mechanic (1974) has pointed out, an individual's ability to cope is modified by the degree of fit between personal characteristics and the physical and social environment. Ideally, people should be able to meet the environmental demands, while at the same time achieving satisfaction of their own needs (Stuckey and Newbrough, 1981). A central consideration in providing appropriate residential alternatives is therefore the need to maintain a balance between maximising motivation for independence while not overstepping the client's tolerance for stress (Heller, 1985). This relation between environmental demands and individual characteristics has been formalised in Lawton and Nahemow's (1973) theory of "ecological press". They suggest that negative outcomes will result when the environmental demands are either too low, resulting in understimulation, or too high, resulting in stress. An environment whose demands are slightly beyond the individual's current abilities will be ideally stimulating, while demands which are slightly below the current level of functioning will result in a highly supportive situation. Working from Lawton and Nahemow's model, one would predict that clients who are highly competent and independent would derive less benefit from a highly programmed environment than more handicapped individuals.

Virtually all the published work relating to community adjustment has been from the point of view of deinstitutionalisation. There appear to be few studies looking at the relocation of clients from one residence to another *within* the community. Such studies tend to be restricted to the non-handicapped population. McCarver and Craig (1974) review the literature on age at release and its relation to successful placement. The authors cite 11 references providing evidence that older clients are more successful than younger clients, five indicating the reverse, and ten showing no conclusive difference. Thus Appel *et al.* (1963) found the mean age of successful dischargees to be 39 years, compared with 23 years for the unsuccessful group, while Hamlett and Engle (1950) found mean ages of 37 and 22 years in a similar study. One of the studies providing evidence for the greater success of older clients in relocation found the mean age of the successful group to be 19 years, compared with 18 years for the unsuccessful group (Jackson and Butler, 1963). In general, however, the majority of studies reviewed by McCarver and Craig were concerned with school children or young adults. None were concerned specifically with older clients.

The main study which has focused on the relative community adjustment of older and younger clients is that of Seltzer, Seltzer and Sherwood (1982). They observed the effects of deinstitutionalisation on two groups of clients, aged 18-54 years and 55+ years old. The 153 subjects had been released from a State institution in Massachussetts, and represented 82 per cent of all the residents who underwent community relocation during a three year period. Community adjustment was measured using Seltzer and Seltzer's (1976) Community Adjustment Scale, which asks questions relating to (a) adaptive behaviour in the areas of personal care, housekeeping, communication, social skills, time, transport use, finance and use of services; (b) the extent to which the client actually performed these skills regularly and independently; (c) characteristics of the residential environment; (d) the client's motivation to perform community living skills. Results of the study indicated that the older group functioned significantly lower in the number of adaptive skills they mastered, the extent to which they performed these skills on a regular basis, and their motivation for independent performance.

Seltzer *et al.* suggest that one explanation for these

findings is that complications associated with advancing age contributed to the lower overall functioning of the older group. This may be true, although it would not be possible to state this conclusively without independent evidence that the older group do indeed have more complications, and that these complications are related to individual adjustment. The authors present no information of this kind. In addition, one of the observations made in this study implies that conclusions would be difficult to reach. Seltzer *et al.* found that older clients were likely to be initially relocated to a more restrictive residential alternative than younger clients of the same functional level, a point which is discussed in greater detail in the next section. It should be noted here, however, that the measurement of environmental adjustment is bound to be affected by the nature of the residence in which the measurement is being taken. Staff in a restrictive environment designed to cope with difficult problems may be less aware of certain problems, simply because they are managed more effectively. Without presenting elaborate detail on the interaction of the measuring instrument with the setting it is impossible to estimate the importance of this factor. Certainly, any research dealing with the complexity of residence/client interactions is bound to have some shortcomings. The main problem in drawing conclusions regarding the significance of age as a factor is that this is the *only* study of central relevance.

1.3 Current residential provision

Within the United Kingdom there is currently no available published work which has surveyed residential alternatives which are specifically for older people with mental handicap. Indeed, it is unlikely that there are sufficient facilities of this kind to draw any clear conclusions concerning their characteristics. In the USA the situation is somewhat different. A much larger proportion of clients are housed in private-sector accommodation, with the result that there is a wide diversity in the philosophies of care, criteria by which a resident is accepted, and length of time a resident is expected to stay.

Table 7.1:

Percentages of Developmentally Disabled Persons Aged 45 and over in the Province of Alberta, living in various Residential Environments

(From Badry *et al.*, 1986)

Characteristics	Mean or Percentage
Active Treatment Hospital	0.5 %
Adult Foster Care	0.1 %
Approved Home	3.6 %
Auxiliary Hospital	2.6 %
Cooperative Living	0.3 %
Extended Care Centre	3.8 %
Group Home	8.0 %
Group Residence at Institution	5.3 %
Independent Living	4.2 %
Institution for the Handicapped	56.5 %
Living with Parents/Relatives	3.2 %
Minimally Supervised Apartment	0.4 %
Nursing Home	9.3 %
Lodge	0.9 %
Other	0.8 %

N of Cases = 742

Two major surveys (Baker, Seltzer and Seltzer, 1977; Willer and Intagliata, 1984) provide the main information on residential alternatives for older adults. In addition, the National Profile of Projects and Studies on Aging/Aged Persons with Mental Handicap (Hawkins,

Garza and Eklund, 1987) lists four further ongoing epidemiological surveys which include information on residential characteristics. The state of Alberta, Canada, has also recently completed a similar survey (Badry *et al.*, 1986a). Table 7.1 gives Badry *et al.*'s figures for the breakdown of percentages of clients over 45 years of age living in various kinds of residential provision.

From a global postal survey of 518 community residences, Baker *et al.* (1977) derived the following 10 categories of facility, based on size, type of resident and model of care:

1. Small group homes, serving 10 or fewer adults with mental handicap
2. Medium group homes, serving 10-20 adults with mental handicap
3. Large group homes, serving 21-40 adults with mental handicap
4. Mini-institutions, serving 41-80 adults with mental handicap
5. Mixed group homes, housing adults with mental handicap and former mental hospital patients in the same residence
6. Group homes for older adults, whose residents are specifically older people with mental handicap, and sometimes including non-handicapped older people as well
7. Foster family care, serving five or fewer adults with mental handicap in a family's own home
8. Sheltered villages, providing a segregated, self contained community for retarded adults and live-in staff in a cluster of buildings usually located in a rural setting
9. Workshop dormitories, serving adults with mental handicap, where the living unit and workshop training program are associated administratively and sometimes physically
10. Semi-independent units, providing less than 24-hour supervision of adult residents with mental handicap

Comparisons between these various models were made on the basis of (a) level of handicap, (b) autonomy afforded to the residents, (c) responsibility for routine household tasks, (d) work, (e) clients turn-over rate, and (f) a compound measure reflecting the number of ex-residents relocated from this particular model and the quality of destination placement in terms of independence achieved. Fig 7.1 reproduces the results of these comparisons, from which it can be seen that the *Older Adults* category was strikingly different along most of the six dimensions.

Given the greater age of the clients compared with other models, it might be expected that aspects related to work will score relatively low. The *work* scores shown on the graph were derived by Baker *et al.* by an unspecified formula from the amount of time spent by residents in open employment, sheltered employment, Training Centres and work at the residence itself. Retirement from any of these activities would naturally lower the score. Scores relating to autonomy, however, cannot be so easily explained. Baker *et al.* suggest that the comparatively low levels of autonomy afforded to residents in this kind of facility, and the *very* low levels of responsibilities undertaken, were unlikely to have been a direct reflection of the clients' functional levels.

On visiting these facilities, Baker *et al.* concluded that these low levels of responsibility resulted largely from the philosophies of the institutions themselves: "... most of these facilities are protected settings; much is done for the residents, and they are closely bound to the house, having limited contact with the outside community. The residences seem to be safe and comfortable, albeit not very stimulating. Their "low-key" programs are perhaps justified for some elderly persons, but may prevent more capable residents from leading a fuller life" (p. 85).

The average facility was found to be staffed by one operator or houseparent, who often owned the facility. There was generally a low priority placed on training for the future or development of community living skills, reflected in the low responsibility score for this model. Residents were rarely involved in cooking, cleaning, shopping etc, although Baker *et al.* found *no evidence* that they were unable to perform these activities. Very significantly, those facilities in which handicapped and non-handicapped residents were mixed showed marked differences in attitude to the two groups on this dimension. The non-handicapped people were generally expected to continue performing these functions unless incapacitated.

Figure 7.1:

Characteristics of various residential settings as measured on six different scales by Baker *et al.* (1977). Columns in black represent group homes for older adults.

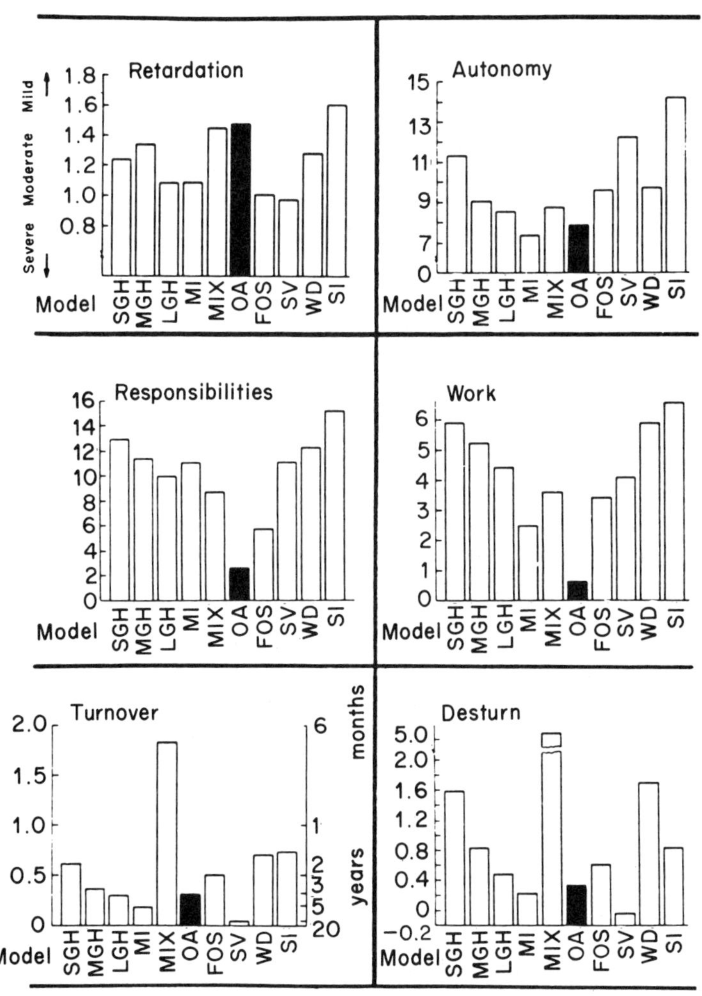

With regard to the low level of autonomy afforded to residents, every one of the group homes for older adults provided 24-hour supervision, and most placed restrictions on visits from people of the opposite sex. This, coupled with the fact there is less probability of having single-toilet bathrooms, single bedrooms and own keys, results in an environment which affords less privacy and personal control than other group homes. Baker *et al.*'s description of a typical day gives a clear impression of the lifestyle:

> "Residents generally awaken at 7:00 am, although they remain in their rooms until called to breakfast. Miss B. prepares all the meals; residents are not permitted to participate in meal preparation, we were told, because a state regulation 'prohibits their using or being near stoves'. Menus are posted several weeks in advance, also in supposed compliance with state regulations.
>
> After breakfast, the women clean their bedrooms and spend the rest of the morning involved in activities such as sitting outside, playing cards, drawing, sewing, or watching television. Lunch is served at noon, and the afternoon hours are spent much the same as the morning ones. After supper, served at 5:30 pm, residents are again free to do as they like until bedtime, which is at 9:00pm. Deviations from this typical schedule are infrequent. On occasion, the women go on picnics, give birthday parties, or have guest entertainers. The weekends are indistinguishable from the weekdays except for Sunday mornings, when the women dress up in their best clothes and watch church services on television." (p.91.)

Willer and Intagliata (1984) provided the other major account (which is currently available) of residential care settings for older people with mental handicap. They found, in general, that residences specifically for this group were more likely to be generic than specifically for people with mental handicap. This, they argue, is due to the fact that the process of growing old reduces the functional abilities of some non-handicapped people so that the distinction between elderly handicapped and non-handicapped becomes blurred. In addition, the loss of income and a valued social role means that many non-handicapped older people struggle with the same constraints as their handicapped peers.

Within the USA, the term "Domiciliary Care" is used to cover a wide variety of community residential alternatives which are designed primarily for older people. The accent is on shelter and protection, rather than training for future relocation to a less restrictive alternative. There are thus, in theory at any rate, two classes of person who would be appropriately placed in such facilities: (a) people whose level of functioning and community skills are already sufficiently advanced that they need no further training, and (b) people who for reasons of increasing infirmity cannot be expected to benefit from such training. In general, Willer and Intagliata found the following features to distinguish domiciliary care facilities from other community residences for people with mental handicap:

1. They are mainly in the private sector
2. They are generally larger and house a greater number of residents
3. Most domiciliary facilities were originally opened to serve a population of non-handicapped people, such as people who are elderly, mentally ill or socially disadvantaged. Although some facilities are specifically for people with mental handicap, most serve them as a minority population
4. The vast majority of residents with mental handicap are over 50 years of age.

Within the general category of domiciliary care, Willer and Intagliata identified two broad classes of facility: (a) Those whose primary purpose is to provide a residential setting, and (b) those which provide some form of nursing or health care. The first of these includes boarding homes, board and care homes and adult homes. Generally, these facilities offer a room and meals to their residents, and some also provide a degree of supervision. The second category includes convalescent homes, nursing homes, skilled nursing facilities and other health-related facilities.

Institutions within the first of these categories were found hard to classify because of the wide variation between them. Fifteen per cent were unlicenced, and the size ranged from 1 to 500 beds, with a mean of 28 beds. Health care facilities are more homogeneous. All are licenced and operate through Medicare or Medicaid.

In New York State, Willer and Intagliata found the most commonly used facility in the first of these categories to be the Private Propriatory Home for Adults (PPHA). This type of facility corresponds to the type discussed above (Baker *et al.*, 1977). The PPHA is a profit making facility of 5-200 adults, and was widely used for relocating adults when deinstitutionalisation reached a high level. It was in facilities of this type that the Mental Health system was accused of "dumping" people with mental illness (Bassuk and Gerson, 1978). Approximately 10 per cent of adults with mental handicap in New York State reside in PPHAs.

In the available studies of quality of care in PPHAs there are few which could be described as positive. Christenfeld and Haveliwala (1978) described the PPHAs in their study as being "mini-institutions", the residents having no expectation of moving to a less restrictive setting in the future. Edgerton (1975) found that residents were often not informed by the management of their right to move, since the economic necessity of maintaining a full house was a paramount consideration. Edgerton states "The little institutions appear to be no better than the large ones from which they came, and some are manifestly worse." (p.131.)

With regard to Health Care Facilities (HCFs), Willer and Intagliata present figures indicating that between 18 and 26 per cent of people released from public institutions enter this kind of setting. Relocation to nursing homes has attracted considerable criticism, since over 50 per cent of such facilities have more than 200 beds. Brown and Guard (1979) have shown that, consistent with the findings of Baker *et al.* (1977), the levels of autonomy and activity in HCFs is low. Indeed, Brown and Guard's findings indicate that the levels are actually *lower* than in the institutions from which they came.

Willer and Intagliata's own study looked at 464 people of various ages who had been discharged from a

New York State institution between 1973 and 1976. Of these, 12.5 per cent entered PPHAs and 5.0 per cent were placed in HCFs. The age bias in placement to these kinds of facility is demonstrated by the fact that the median age of placement in PPHAs was 63 years, and for HCFs was 69 years. (This is presumably much higher than mean ages of clients located in other types of facility, although Willer and Intagliata do not provide these figures.) As Willer and Intagliata point out, this age bias is consistent with Baker *et al.*'s (1977) finding of a mean age of 59 years for placement in Group Homes for Older Adults.

Despite the apparent age bias in entry to HCFs, it should be noted that Willer and Intagliata's figures do not give a totally representative picture. They point out, for instance, that one of the HCFs took three individuals from the sample of 464, the mean age being only 25. In general, HCFs tend to take a wide age range, including many younger residents with ambulation and behaviour problems. In comparison, there is much less variation in the intake of PPHAs. Only five of the 58 people in Willer and Intagliata's sample who entered this kind of facility were under 50, and all were over 45 years of age.

Using a similar technique to that of Baker *et al.* (1977), Willer and Intagliata characterised the residential environments of a number of PPHAs and HCFs. Their main conclusion was that, in comparison to group homes, these facilities place less emphasis on imparting skills which would prepare residents for a future move to a less restrictive alternative. The impression of PPHAs is of an unstructured environment with little attention paid to individual needs. HCFs on the other hand, tend to provide a highly structured environment in which the activities of the residents are planned and controlled by the staff.

Confirming the findings of Baker *et al.* (1977), Willer and Intagliata found the daily routines in HCFs and PPHAs to be generally of a poor standard. Thus, only 65 per cent of PPHA and 19 per cent of HCF residents were involved in structured daytime programming. This compares with a figure of 90 per cent for residents living in either family care or group homes.

A recent national survey in the USA (Wyngaarden *et al.*, 1986) reports on residential services catering for older clients. Of the 332 residential programmes which were surveyed, the authors report that approximately 53 per cent (n=176) had "evolved" due to the fact that the majority of clients had reached old age, and 47 per cent (n=156) had been created specifically to cater for older clients. The peak years for setting up these new services were 1981-2. Wyngaarden *et al.* give information on staffing, licencing, costs and services provided in six types of facility: 1. Foster homes, 2. Group homes, 3. Group homes with a resident nurse, 4. Intermediate care facility, 5. Sheltered housing, 6. Mixed residential (i.e. serving multiple target populations such as mentally ill or elderly non-handicapped).

Overall, the survey gives important information on the extent to which the various types of residential service have adapted to the needs of older clients. Wyngaarden *et al.* conclude: "Foster homes were the least professionalised, provided the fewest services, and had a high percentage of residents remaining in the home during the day. Group homes, the most prevalent type of residence in the National Survey, had the second highest staff to resident ratio and served a diverse population in terms of level of retardation. These programs, the most deeply rooted of the community based residential models, have further shown an ability to modify their staffing structure with the inclusion of of a program nurse as one mechanism for meeting the needs of a specific target group. ICFs/MR were the most specialized program model, with a high percentage of created programs, and a service and staff-rich program structure. Apartment programs and Mixed Residential Programs served less impaired elderly mentally retarded persons and provided fewer services to them. The elasticity of the residential care system for mentally retarded persons, as illustrated by the ways in which service delivery and staffing patterns have been modified, is quite remarkable." (p 9).

The surveys of Baker *et al.* (1977) and Willer and Intagliata (1984) serve to demonstrate a most important point, namely, that the lack of involvement in daily activities for elderly residents of PPHAs and HCFs *cannot simply be attributable to age.* Older, non-handicapped residents living alongside people with mental handicap are subject to a different set of expectations. These clients are expected to fulfil domestic responsibilities as long as they are physically and mentally capable, while people with mental handicap are denied these opportunites to demonstrate competence.

Given this conclusion, it can be seen that the opportunity for a subsequent move to a genuine community alternative becomes severely curtailed if one's initial placement is to a facility of this kind. Willer and Intagliata's observations on the mean age of placement indicate that older people are much more likely to be relocated to PPHAs and HCFs than younger people, even if their level of functioning would permit a less restricted alternative, a finding which is confirmed by others (Benz and Halpern, 1982; Seltzer, Seltzer and Sherwood, 1982). In this way, the "double jeopardy" of mental handicap and old age is firmly established.

It should be noted, however, that the tendency for older people to remain in institutions cannot always be ascribed to a bias in the relocation service. There is a clear generational effect of attitude, in that many older clients have lived in their institution for so long that they make an active choice to remain in the place they feel to be their home. This expression of choice is likely to be related to functional level. Paradoxically, therefore, it is sometimes found that the *most able* residents are the ones who are most reluctant to leave. Stroud *et al.* (1984) report a striking example of this effect. They present data on clients from three settings: Institutionalised, Deinstitutionalised and Community (i.e. never having lived in an institution). It was found that all individuals having a level of cognitive development in the Normal/Mild range lived in the *institution*. These people had mostly refused offers of community relocation, even when the move would be to a location close to their place of origin.

It may be argued that the studies reviewed above point to the impact of a non-normalised environment, and that people with mental handicap are maintained, or maintain themselves, in the community in the belief that life in a normalised environment is beneficial to them as individuals and the quality of their lives is enhanced. A finer level of analysis is therefore to consider how the deficit of normalisation in a given residence affects social development. Eyman, Demaine and Lei (1979) used the three domains of the Adaptive Behavior Scale described more fully in Chapter 4 to evaluate the impact of normalisation on residents of family-care and board and care homes over a three year period. Each environment was characterised with Wolfensberger and Glenn's (1975) Program Analysis of Service Systems (PASS 3) and related to changes in (a) Personal Self-sufficiency, (b) Community Self-sufficiency, and (c) Personal-Social Responsibility (For fuller descriptions see Chapter 4, pp. 141-142). From the perspective of this review, Eyman *et al.*'s division of "younger and older" is regrettably limited, creating as it does the under-18s as one group and the over 18s as another. We will therefore only summarise briefly the outcome of the study and the specific observations on the influence of age.

First, with respect to Personal Self-sufficiency, three aspects were enhanced by facilities' higher scores on PASS 3. Adaptive behaviour in this area was enhanced by environmental blending of the facility with the neighbourhood, location and proximity of services, and the comfort and appearance of the facility. Older residents benefited specifically from positive ratings of location and proximity, though comfort and appearance of the facility was related to enhanced self-help skills regardless of age. Second, Community Self-sufficiency was related to positive scores on PASS 3 with respect to administrative policies directed specifically towards normalisation, location and proximity of services and comfort and appearance. Older individuals benefited particularly from good ratings of administrative policy, while those who were also mildly retarded benefited from good location and proximity ratings. Third, with respect to Personal-Social Responsibility, a high score on location and proximity led to enhancement in this area, though improvement was restricted to individuals who were older and mildly mentally handicapped. One other factor from PASS 3 was related to Personal-Social Responsibility, namely comfort and appearance.

From the above it can be inferred that PASS 3 ratings concerned with comfort and deployment of staff, facility openness blending with the neighbourhood and proximity of services enhance adaptive behaviour. Eyman *et al.* also suggest that older individuals and those who are less handicapped show greater improvement and are less sensitive than younger and less retarded people to these influences, i.e. will improve in social adaptation "regardless of where they resided" (p.336). This analysis is truly ecological in that it explores the interaction of personal characteristics (i.e. age, IQ) in relation to factors operating in the mesosystem. Extension of such analysis to older individuals in the 50+ range would be illuminating.

2 METHODOLOGICAL CONSIDERATIONS

In experimental terms the relation between client and the residential and wider community environment has been looked at in two basic ways. First, there have been numerous empirical studies attempting to determine the interaction between residential setting and client characteristics, following relocation from an institution. The term "Community Adjustment" is often used to describe the success of subsequent adaptation. Second, some efforts have been made to characterise the social and physical environment in terms of the extent to which it fulfils the principle of normalisation (Eyman, Demaine and Lei, 1979).

This principle has not tended to be applied to residential environments in relation to the specific needs of older clients. There have not, for instance, been any formal comparisons of residential settings for older clients compared with their non-handicapped peers. It is worth noting in passing, however, some of the main implications that the principle of normalisation has for the residential environment. Janicki (1981) points out that there are two important integration considerations which apply to the design of a residential setting: physical and social integration. Physical integration into the community is essential if the aims of community involvement are to be met. Location, context, accessibility and size are four factors which Janicki suggests are critical in this respect. The second of these concerns, social integration, relates to the actual interaction of residents with members of the surrounding community. Janicki points out the importance of encouraging this process in a two-way fashion. Individuals living in the residence should be encouraged to become members of the wider community, while members of the general public should be encouraged not to regard their handicapped neighbours as being transient neighbours.

With regard to the measurement of community adjustment, there have been numerous articles which have attempted to isolate specific aspects of adaptive behaviour as determinants of subsequent placement success (eg Aninger and Bolinsky, 1977; Rosen, Floor and Baxter, 1972; Taylor, 1976; Theil, 1981). Failure to adjust to a new residence can be examined in various ways, one of the most frequently utilised being subsequent return to the previous institution. Among the factors found to predict failure in these terms have been IQ, adaptive behaviour failures, physical disabilities (Eyman, O'Connor, Tarjan and Justice, 1972) and disruptive behaviour (Wolf and Whitehead, 1975). A general conclusion to be drawn from these studies, however, is that there is little consistency regarding the prediction of successful placement (Cotten, Purzycki, Cowart and Merritt, 1983). Thus, Gollay (1976) concludes that there are no clear determinants of 'successful' adjustment, nor are there clear measures of 'success'. The very mixed findings of the initial report on success of placement in Oldham Borough's "Homemaking Scheme", described in Chapter 1, despite intensive assessment and preparation, support this general conclusion.

The failure to draw firm conclusions regarding the effects of residence on adjustment is undoubtedly due partly to the complexity of human beings and their interaction with the world. Apart from this, however, there are some factors which can be seen either to be shortcomings in experimental design, or problems resulting from the fact that research has been conducted in the context of existing service provision. Notable among these problems is the fact that different kinds of clients are often assigned to different kinds of residence (Heal, Sigelman and Switzky, 1978), with the result that it is rarely possible to rule out the effects of preselected individual characteristics. Heal *et al.* provide a number of examples of conflicting experimental findings which they attribute to this cause (p.238). For example, Eagle (1967) concluded that foster home placements were no more likely to result in premature return to an institution than were home leaves or vocational leaves. This finding is in direct contradiction to several studies which have shown *high* rates of failure for this type of placement (Adams, 1975; Gollay, 1976; Keys, Boroskin, and Ross, 1973).

With regard to experimental designs, it has been noted by Seltzer, (1981) that until 1970 most researchers used the simplest criterion of community adjustment, namely, remaining in the community versus return to the institution (eg Jackson and Butler, 1963; Krishef, 1959; Madison, 1964). Freedman (1976) has noted that this simple success-failure dichotomy has been used to operationalise what is certainly a more complex phenomenon. In addition, McCarver and Craig (1974) identified four methodological problems which make it difficult to compare results from specific studies of community adjustment following relocation: 1. Use of varying criteria of success 2. Sample attrition and the difficulty of determining how "lost" subjects might influence results 3. Varying methods of data collection, particularly in regard to follow-up techniques 4. Variations between studies in the length of time clients had been in the community at the point of measurement, particularly in view of the fact that return to the institution is most likely to occur soon after placement (Heal *et al.*, 1978).

From the point of view of the clients themselves it is also evident that the rate of adjustment following a change of residence is a crucial consideration in formulating an adequate research design. Thus, Cotten *et al.* (1983) support Edgerton and Berkovici's (1976) conclusion: "... it is important to recognise the possibility, even the probability, that social adjustment, particularly among mentally retarded persons, may sometimes fluctuate markedly, not only from year to year, but from month to month or even week to week. Therefore, investigators doing prognostic research are likely to produce illusory results unless they provide sufficient continuity of measurement over time to permit assessment of microshifts in adaptation of a short term, emergent nature." (p.1).

Related to this conclusion is the comment by Seltzer, Sherwood, Seltzer and Sherwood (1981) that the impact of relocation should be regarded as the difference between how the clients fare in their new residence and how they would have fared at the same point in time if they had remained in the original residence. In other words, changes over time, even when measured prospectively, are not synonymous with the impact of relocation. To prove the effect has been due to relocation one would have to demonstrate that the change would not have taken place without the client's moving. Taken together, the points raised by Cotten *et al.* and Seltzer *et al.* suggest that (a) Longitudinal designs are essential for a reliable measure of relocation adjustment, and (b) adequate controlled comparisons need to be incorporated if valid conclusions are to be reached. More generally, Seltzer *et al.* (1981) have suggested that it is inappropriate to use "normal" functioning as the standard against which to assess the adaptation of people with mental handicap. On this basis the majority of clients moving from hospital to community would be considered as having failed to adapt satisfactorily. As an alternative, Seltzer *et al.* (1981) have suggested the conceptualisation of community adaptation as improved functioning. Thus, it is not the absolute level of a person's performance at any point in time which should be of interest, but rather the extent to which a person shows improvements over time.

Seltzer (1981) has incorporated this point into his study investigating the relation between residential environment and adjustment. He points out that the high correlation between IQ and adaptive behaviour measures means that clients labelled as severely of profoundly retarded are unlikely to be considered satisfactorily adjusted when skill mastery is used as the measure of adjustment. In order to reduce the redundancy between measures of skill mastery and IQ, Seltzer developed a Performance Index designed to measure the extent to which clients *use* the skills they have mastered, irrespective of absolute level of mastery. This ensures that "... all subjects, regardless of their level of retardation, have the potential of being considered adjusted..." (p 629).

Overall, the methodological points discussed above have been presented to give an impression of the complexity of factors involved in residential adjustment and its measurement. They should be borne in mind when drawing conclusions from the small number of studies concerned with age as a factor in placement choice and placement success. Heal *et al.* (1978) provide a salutary conclusion to their review of placement success. They point out that Gollay's (1976) comprehensive study of deinstitutionalisation, based on individual characteristics, institutional experiences, institutional characteristics and community characteristics accounted for only 9.5 to 34.3 per cent of the variance in outcome measures, and only 21.4 per cent of the variance in predicting return to the institution. Though not bearing specifically on the relative contribution of these variables, recent work on a further class of residential provision, adult family placements, points towards several significant factors that influence community involvement.

3 ADULT FAMILY PLACEMENT

A significant alternative to the residential options described so far is that of adult, or foster, family care. This model of provision, in which an adult with mental handicap lives, on a long or short term basis, with a family other than his or her own, is not new. Such placements for people with mental and physical disabilities have been employed since medieval times, and Scheerenberger (1983) describes both the initiation of one of the best known programmes evolved in Gheel in Belgium at that time which is still in effect. He notes, however, that later commentators were critical of many aspects of such provision and adoption of the model in Germany, Scotland, Switzerland, France, Ireland and England did not take place until late in the nineteenth century.

The first programme in the United States for people with mental handicap was implemented by Charles Vaux during the 1930s. Significantly those participating in 1932 embraced a wide range of abilities (IQ 19-84) and ranged in age up to 65 years. Some were multiply handicapped though this does not appear to have led to any insurmountable difficulties. Scheerenberger quotes Vaux' summary of his experiences: "(the residents) can enjoy a happier, more normal kind of life with more liberty; the majority of families will take a greater personal interest in the welfare of the patient than their contract implies; that many patients will improve and some sufficiently to raise their economic status; that schools in neighbouring villages will accept our younger patients without question; that many children of school age will attain a good social adaptation; and that the total average per capita cost is less than for institutional residents." (Quoted by Scheerenberger 1983; p.201.) It is salutary to note that these very contemporary observations were made over half a century ago in 1936.

The development of adult placement models has continued in the USA and in Europe. The benefits described by Charles Vaux have remained a central *raison d'etre* for this residential model and have been the subject of an increasing body of research. Here we shall draw attention to a report of particular relevance by Newman, Sherman and Frenkel (1985) as their work considers the influence of age on the success of the placement. These authors comment that adult placement or foster care involves a complex of variables and that the outcome for realising normalisation goals is highly variable. Such goals relate, of course, not only to integration within the placement family, but with the community in which that family itself lives. Two distinguishable facets of community integration are defined, acceptance by the community, and participation in community life. With respect to the latter, use of community resources, socialisation and sharing in community activities can be further distinguished.

All people with mental handicap in Newman, Sherman and Frenkel's study were over 45 years of age with the oldest being 92. Ability ranged from profound retardation to borderline intellectual functioning. Interaction by the resident within the family was found to be high and carers typically viewed the relationship with the person with mental handicap as family-like. A variety of measures of community integration were taken with neighbour acceptance the first measure, and participation being measured by the extent of use of community resources, socialisation with carer, socialisation without carer, activities with carer and activities without carer. In general, neighbour acceptance was high but in content reflected only a casual level of acquaintance. Use of community resources was typically high with respect to contact with doctors (and hairdressers/barbers) (over 90 per cent had had contact) and use of shops (60 per cent and over). Socialising with neighbours with carers present occurred in over 75 per cent of placements, this figure dropping appreciably for independent socialising to just over half this percentage of contacts. A similar picture emerged for engaging in activities such as frequenting meeting places, retaurants, parties, religious services, plays and concerts. For example, accompanied visits to meeting places with the carer was 93 per cent in contrast to the highest unaccompanied attendance, 39 per cent at religious services. There is a strong suggestion in these data of an "independence factor" with individuals showing relatively high levels of community integration across a number of these variables.

An attempt was made to establish predictors of community integration, of which the most significant were carer characteristics. The carers' own level of socialising and engagement in outside activities was related to several aspects of the resident's level of integration. With respect to residents' characteristics, these were most predictive of activities without the carer. Specifically, younger and more able residents showed more independent activity than their old and less able peers. However, age was not related to engaging in activities with the carer.

Newman, Sherman and Frenkel (1985) conclude that: "...family care not only provides the residents with encouragement to use the community but that the care providers actually serve as facilitators of the participation. This is particularly important for elderly residents who tend not to participate as much in activities <u>without</u> the provider." (p.375.) They suggest that this facilitatory role could be enhanced through training. The fact that age does not affect engagment in activities with the carer, however, emphasises how beneficial involvement with an active family can be. Thus encouragement of the family's involvement in the community can also enhance integration of the older person with mental handicap.

The study reviewed provides a powerful argument for the development of adult placement generally and for such placement for older people in particular. From the perspective of an ecological model, Newman, Sherman and Frenkel's findings are consistent with the predictions that might be made regarding successful community integration. Despite this, it must be noted that the scale of this residential option is much lower in the UK than in the USA. Cooper (1987) has drawn attention to this contrast but has noted a number of recent developments of adult placement schemes in England.

Among these is the Hampshire Social Services Adult Placement Scheme introduced in 1979 for people with mental handicap but extended in 1981 to those with other disabiities and elderly individuals as well. In line with the evaluative criteria outlined by Newman, Sherman and Frenkel (1985), Hampshire Social Services (1984) note among the key aims of the scheme provision of a vital component of community care giving scope for direct and individual contributions by members of the wider community. A full management and administrative structure is also described. It is important to note the term "component" in the above statement. An adult residential placement takes its place along side suitable day service provision, holiday or programmed relief and training opportunities as part of a total service. In addition, the developed model pays close attention to the characteristics of the family as critical determinants of the placement's success.

One highly significant feature of the HSS Adult Placement Scheme is the success with which older individuals are varying disabilities and needs have been incorporated. In 1985, while the largest single age group was 18 to 30 years, 48 per cent of all clients were over 50 years, while five per cent were over 80 years.

It is clear from Cooper's (1987) review that adult placement is an increasingly used option in making residential provision for adults with mental handicap, including those who are over 50. A national survey of these developments and some formal evaluation of these initiatives would make an important contribution to the evolution of this form of provision.

4 CONCLUDING COMMENT

While there is a growing literature on the factors influencing successful residential provision, there is as yet no coherent account that would enable accurate predictions of placement success to be made. Nevertheless, much of the available evidence is compatible with an ecological account of the determinants of residents' adjustment. In broad terms positive findings are consistent with the view espoused by advocates of normalisation, though available results must caution against any simplistic view of normalisation as a unitary or prescriptive concept. Within this broad framework the role of ageing has only been briefly touched upon and should be incorporated as a key variable in all future studies undertaken on factors influencing the success of residential placement.

Chapter Eight

INFORMAL SUPPORT NETWORKS: NEIGHBOURS, FRIENDS AND FAMILIES

1 INTRODUCTION

We described in Chapter 1 the process by which individuals from long stay hospitals, hostels and, indeed, their own family homes were progressively moving into settings demanding either a relatively high level of independent functioning or some necessary support. These ranged from their own flat or house, through warden controlled accommodation, to staffed, small group homes. In addition, we should remind ourselves that several individuals lived with older parents or with their siblings. In this chapter we will review the available information on how friends and neighbours support individuals with mental handicap and their families, and also how families cope with a member with mental handicap as they age, considering too, the long term pattern of adaptation as people get older.

In Chapter 5, we presented Cantor's model of Social Support Systems for elderly people, and noted the three 'nests' of informal support: primary (family); secondary (neighbours and friends); and tertiary (mediating support elements). Cantor and Little (1985) list six elements that go to make up the primary and secondary informal systems, i.e. spouse, children, siblings and other relatives on the one hand, and friends and neighbours on the other.

It is, of course, notable that in terms of our definition of "ageing people with mental handicap" as 50+ years, a major element is usually omitted with respect to people with mental handicap, namely, the individual's parents who are likely to have died. Other distinctions must also be drawn. As Seltzer (1985) points out, most ageing people with mental handicap do not have children or a spouse so support from these sources is therefore lacking. This effectively leaves siblings or siblings' children. As Seltzer notes, little is known about their relationship with the person with mental handicap in later life. This she identifies as "...an important issue in need of research ... (i.e.) ... the extent to which aging siblings maintain relationships and provide support to their also-aging retarded members." (p.261). We will return to this subject later. In this Chapter, we have chosen to lower our age criterion somewhat. Many parents reach old age long before their child is 50 years old. We therefore judged it would be unhelpful in a review of this sort to limit ourselves solely to the scanty information available on over-50s who still live at home with parents.

2 SUPPORT FROM FRIENDS AND NEIGHBOURS

In reviewing the wider literature on secondary informal networks and ageing non-handicapped people, Cantor and Little (1985) report only a limited number of studies, drawing the following conclusions. Friends and neighbours are important where healthy or only mildly disabled older people lack real support from their family. With respect to long-term support of frail elderly people, friends and neighbours cannot be counted upon to the same degree and become increasingly unavailable as disabilities become more severe. However, friends and neighbours do act in a compensatory way where family support is not available, often preparing the ground for such support well in advance. Cantor and Little (1985) draw attention to the fact that as life-styles change, (e.g. increase in divorce, or non-marriage), so the need for support for ageing people from friends and neighbours will increase.

These limited conclusions do have implications for older people with mental handicap. First, as we have seen, only restricted family support for them is likely to be available and in some cases will be totally unavailable. They constitute, therefore, a group more like the "familyless elderly" than the typical ageing person for whom spouse or children constitute the main informal supports. Second, the extent to which secondary support will be forthcoming will also be related to their degree of disability. More able people with mental handicap will have a better chance of enlisting support for friends and neighbours than those who have severe or profound disabilities. This observation should be viewed against the background of Janicki's (1986) report on the considerably greater degree of disability in the older institutionalised population than in those older people already in the community. Those coming from the institutions to the community will be less likely to, and less able to, enlist secondary informal network support. In addition, we might surmise that many will have fewer family resources at their disposal. Third, the notion of "anticipatory socialisation" by which an ageing person prepares the ground for future support will not be a strategy available to many people with mental handicap through lack of social competence.

That some people with mental handicap also form friendships is a matter of common observation, and is confirmed by Seltzer's (1985) review of the limited literature on the topic. Landesman-Dwyer, Berkson and Romer (1979), for example, observed friendship patterns in 18 group homes. They found that people with less disability have more intense friendships, while larger friendship groups were associated with larger residences. Overall, Landesman-Dwyer *et al.* found that residential variables, rather than individual characteristics, were the significant predictors of affiliation. While acknowledging that it is likely that emotional support is derived from these relationships, she concludes that: "The extent to which aging retarded persons provide and receive informal support to and from their friends is unknown." (p.262).

To people with mild mental handicap, however, the role of friends, neighbours and other social contacts in helping them to maintain themselves in the community has been documented in a series of studies by Edgerton and his colleagues that initially did not set out to consider ageing per se. As we shall see, however, they draw together a variety of themes with which this and earlier chapters are concerned, ranging through informal support networks, the place of work and health, and indeed, the self perceptions of the people studied.

In 1967 Edgerton published *"The Cloak of Competence: Stigma in the lives of the mentally retarded"*, an ethnographic study of 48 residents of a large institution who were discharged into the community. Of relatively high IQ (mean=64), these men and women showed broadly successful adaptation to their new life, though Edgerton's research drew attention to the fact that this successful adjustment owed a great deal to secondary informal network support in the form of non-handicapped benefactors rather than to any specific level of skill, attitude or training. He also describes the strategies by which these people attempted to present themselves to the world as "normal", strategies which often did not actually reflect true competence in that they essentially found ways round problematical situations rather than actually coping with the difficulty.

The situation just described pertained in 1960-1961 after the individuals had spent six years in the community. Edgerton and Berkovici (1976) report on a follow up of traceable people some twelve years later in 1972-1973, while Edgerton, Bollonger and Herr (1984) report a further investigation in 1982. In the early 70s those who could be located were in their mid 40s (men, CA=44.4 years, IQ=65.9; women CA=46.9, IQ=64.3). In 1982, the comparable mean CA was 56 years and IQ=61.7.

As with the first study, interviews and participant observation were employed to investigate the quality of the residential environment, employment, sex, marriage and reproduction, use of leisure time, reliance on benefactors and concern with passing for normal (including the avoidance of stigma). In addition, they were asked to compare their lives at the time of the earlier and later studies.

Social competence and independence were judged through a variety of observer ratings such as economic security, relative independence, social participation, absence of antisocial behaviour, employment and leisure, sexual-marital adjustment, feelings of stigma. The life circumstances in eight individuals were, overall, considered better, in the 1976 study, 12 the same, 10 as worse, relative to the 1967 study. There was great diversity in the lives of people *within* each of these groups. One man had indeed initially been among the most competent in the group and had gone from strength to strength, while one woman, "formerly cloistered, timid, dependent" had begun to venture into the world and assert herself. Nora had initially earned her living as a headless lady at an amusement park, engaging in passing affairs and living partially off welfare. By the earlier 70s she was married with three children, working with her husband in a factory and with a pleasant stable home life.

Similar diversity would be found among those who had not successfully adjusted. Robert, of average independence in the original study, was initially employed and sharing an apartment with a homosexual man. In 1972-3 he was "penniless and hungry with no place to sleep and was apparently an alcoholic as well", surviving by selling his blood. Dorothy was dependent on her first husband in 1960-1, but in her next marriage after his death, was not only dependent, but subject to difficulties linked to heroin and her husband's increasing age, with few resources and little hope for the future.

In Edgerton's (1967) study the high dependence on benefactors and concern with stigma that we noted above were critical concerns in the social thinking of the individuals studied. By 1972/73, however, dependence on benefactors and concern with stigma appeared to play a less important part, although the reasons for this change are not clear. It may be that 12 years of experience reduced the need for support, while belief in personal stigma declined. Certainly, these trends continued throughout the subsequent decade (Edgerton, Bollonger and Herr, 1984).

Before beginning the 1972-3 study, Edgerton predicted, on the basis of the earlier information, which individuals would adapt successfully in the community. These predictions proved correct in less than half of the cases, and even where they were correct, this was often for the wrong reason. It is interesting to recall in Chapter 1 the care that was given to selecting people to live together for the Oldham Home Making scheme and yet the apparent failings in predicting adjustment within the homes. Bear in mind, too, that Edgerton's predictions were made following a period of six years of community adaptation. While some predictions of failure were regarded as relatively easy, others went very far off the mark; e.g an explosive and violent man whom it was assumed would get into trouble and not stay in work, but was holding down the same job in 1972-3 as he had in the early sixties. Edgerton's judgement is that these failures are in line with the larger literature "... in which it is reported that the best available prognostic variables, whether measures of attitude, personality, status, or life circumstances, have failed to be accurate predictors of community adjustment" (p.489).

Edgerton and Berkovici (1976) argue that the lives of people with mental handicap may be inherently unstable because of the very nature of the ecology in which they live. They lack job security, have few marketable skills, and lack a network of reliable friends or relatives. Loss of a job or partner can totally destabilise what adaptation has been achieved while restoration can suddenly result in a higher level of adaption.

In 1984 Edgerton, Bollonger and Herr extended the period of study of this group to 20 years of community living, noting that their concern was now explicitly with the process of ageing. The mean age of the 15 people on whom it was possible to collect information was 56 years, with mean IQ=61.7. Again, change in the lives of the individuals was a central concern and ratings indicated that over the past decade one person's life was in continuous flux, while the lives of five were stable. For four people, life had deteriorated, while for three it had improved. For two, the complexity was so great that they defied categorisation. Edgerton *et al.* see the major factors in influencing them to be related to the social and personal resources available to the individuals. With respect to the four people whose lives had worsened, a major loss had been sustained while none had a strong benefactor, support network or service support.

Decline in health was found in ten individuals, both in the 1972-3 and 1982 studies. Of the 30 individuals in the former study one was terminally ill and nine had disabling ailments. No one showed improvements in health since 1960-1. By 1982 ten of the sample of 15 had declined further, all of whom realised that this was related to age. While some used their condition strategically others refused "to give in".

Recent work by Flynn (1987; 1988) has examined the perception of informal networks from the perspective of the clients themselves and of their Social Workers. These 88 people, ranging in age from 22 to 79 years, all lived independently in the community, the majority with a life history in a hospital or hostel. Of these, 26 lived alone, 37 with one other person, and 25 with two or more other people. Of the 37, 13 lived with friends and 18 (nine couples), with a marriage partner or cohabitee. This situation, Flynn (1987) urges, is not static, but subject to change through a variety of pressures. Flynn (1987) presents five detailed case studies, some of which we drew on in Chapter 1 to illustrate the position of people living independently in Oldham.

With respect to social networks, we will describe the situation vis-a-vis families in a later section. With respect to non-family members, social workers estimated that 38 people had regular contact with neighbours, 32, intermittent contact, and seven no contact (missing data, 11 people) (Flynn 1988). The overall picture reported is that people in her sample have friendly relations with neighbours. However, unwelcome interference by neighbours and placement in flats for elderly people were both reported as sources of dissatisfaction, while 23 people complained about their neighbours and 12 recollected complaints that had been made. Flynn makes the important point that the quality of the neighbourhood itself will condition the quality of social networks to some degree. Twenty-two of her sample lived in 'hard to let' tenancies and 14 talked of their fear of neighbours and young children. Nine people indicated that they would like to leave the area in which they lived in order to have different neighbours.

Although the distinction between friends and neighbours is not a rigid one, Flynn also noted that 62 people had regular contact with friends, both mentally handicapped and non-handicapped, while 11 had intermittent contact. Only four had no contact (no information being available for the rest of the sample). During the interviews, 59 people were non-commital in their comments on their contact with others, while 20 'appeared' positive and only five expressed dissatisfaction.

As Flynn noted, from an analysis of this sort it is not possible to determine how age, experience of institutionalisation, contact with services and family, influence contact with individuals described as 'friends'.

Edgerton *et al.* describe the resilience with which most individuals cope with the social and health changes that accompanied ageing, in contrast to the dependency reported by Baker, Seltzer and Seltzer (1977) and Seltzer, Seltzer and Sherwood (1982), and the difficulties reported by Flynn (1987) (see Chapter 1). They emphasise the indomitability of these people:

> "There is a central theme to their lives, whether those lives have worsened, improved, or remained very much the same; the theme is hope. With the exception of one woman who was quite depressed, all the rest had an unshakeable optimism; they still had hope that life would be rewarding, or more rewarding than it had been, and they believed that their own actions could help to bring this outcome to pass." (p.350).

Edgerton's studies offer a unique insight into the process of ageing in more able people with mental handicap, although the findings do not necessarily generalise to other people with mental handicap who live in differing social and cultural settings, or who are less able. Using ethnographic techniques rather than quantitative or semi-quantitative techniques, however, Edgerton and his co-workers have illustrated the impact of Bronfenbrenner's (1979) micro- and meso-systems on these individuals and the way in which processes reflecting ageing influence and contribute to community adjustment. The presence in the individual's ecology of benefactors and the opportunity for care, for example, will both have a profound effect on the individual's ability to adjust. Similarly, positive changes in social competence will enhance adjustment while ill health will markedly, and often progressively, impair the ability to cope. We have already seen in our brief review that Flynn's work, too, demonstrates something of the complexity of the way in which individual and environmental factors interact to influence quality of life.

Viewed from an ecological perspective, Edgerton's

and Flynn's work point to the complexity of the community situation to which people with mental handicap have to adjust, and the way in which the passage of time with its concomitant ageing plays positive and negative roles in this process. In their conclusion to the 1972-3 study, Edgerton and Berkovici (1976) point out that "the lives of these 30 persons are demonstratively complex, heterogeneous and changeable" (p.495) and go on to consider the implication of this state of affairs for development of prognostic criteria for successful social adjustment. First, from a methodological point of view they emphasise the need to monitor short term fluctuations in adjustment in such a way that there is continuity of measurement. Single outcome measures are not appropriate to this. Second, they emphasise the need to consider prognosis in a truly ecological framework emphasising all levels of Bronfenbrenner's formulation of nested ecologies:

> "Researchers have attempted to predict social adjustment largely by relying on variables that relate to the persons who are doing the adjusting. The various environments to which these persons must adjust are seldom considered in comparable detail. Since shifts in these environments involving such matters as public attitudes, welfare legislation, or employment opportunties, can in principle, have profound effects on social adjustment, as can differences in residential environments, it is imperative that prognostic researchers attend as carefully to environmental variables as to personal ones." (p.495).

Flynn (1988) confirms this view when she concludes: "What is clear is that the social integration of people who are mentally handicapped and living in their own homes cannot be assumed". In a study also involving people with mild mental handicap who left an institution for the community, Wolfson (1955; 1970) had reached a similar conclusion. Here, by 1970, these people ranged in age from 26 to 77 years with a mean age of 42 years. Wolfson (1970) surmised that "Perhaps we are reaching another milestone in this field; instead of talking of a collective group of mildly mentally retarded, we should begin to consider them as individuals with varied personalities and capacities for self-determination, who are prone to various levels of adjustment." (p.22.)

It will already have been appreciated that in considering the omnibus concept of social adjustment in relation to mental handicap, we must also integrate information of prediction of successful ageing. The literature on this topic is restricted to non-handicapped individuals but points towards issues and situations that would have to be taken into account in the kind of analysis envisaged by Edgerton and Berkovici. Palmore (1979) reviews some of the numerous studies on predictors of successful ageing and draws on the First Duke Longitudinal Study of ageing in which 18 predictor variables were employed. (Siegler, 1983, provides a review on the relevance to the psychology of adult development and ageing of both the First and the Second Duke Longitudinal Studies.) It is worthwhile noting the way in which these predictions have been brought together in this predictive study, as many of them have received some attention already in this volume. The variables include:

> "Age, sex, marital status, physical-function rating, happiness rating, cigarette smoking, intelligence (WAIS verbal and performance), activities ratings (primary group, secondary group, physical, and solitary), attitude scales (usefulness, work satisfaction, and emotional security), and socioeconomic status (education, financial status, and prestige rating)." (p.428).

Successful ageing was defined in terms of survival to age 75; less than 20 per cent disability; and rating indicating general contentedness. Predictions were made approximately from the mid to late 60s to post 75 years. The two strongest predictors for men and women were the physical functioning rating and happiness rating, based on a scale ranging from "unhappy, discontented, worried, fearful, frustrated" to "very happy, exultant, great contentment". Thus the best predictors of successful ageing are those indicative of this status at the start of the study. Of more interest were other significant predictors, of which the single best predictor was involvement in secondary group activity, defined at the successful extreme as "time filled with many groups, much reading, always on the go or occupied with reading etc". This variable was followed by involvement in physical activities for women and work satisfaction for men (this including non-paid work). Neither verbal nor performance IQ nor years of education predicted successful ageing, nor did involvement in primary group activities defined at the positive extreme as "daily contacts closely incorporated into group life". Nevertheless, it will be recalled that in Chapter 3 we noted that older, non-handicapped, people living alone and currently isolated were not actually at any greater risk for psychopathological conditions, including depression, than their less isolated peers.

Any extrapolation of results of this sort to people with mental handicap has to be undertaken with great caution. We might expect declining health in the 60s to predict poor health in the 70s with a concomitant decline in successful ageing. On the other hand, with an IQ range of, say, 30 to 75 we might expect both verbal and performance IQ to have an important influence on adaptation. Similarly, in the light of Edgerton's work we would anticipate both primary and secondary group activity would have a role to play in successful ageing.

In the last analysis it is, of course, likely that the complexity of this situation will preclude anything approaching complete accuracy of prediction and, as in most areas of human life and experience, we will have to live with considerable uncertainty.

3 THE AGEING FAMILY

3.1 Background

For many families with a son or daughter with mental handicap, "community care" means care by the family as far as their child is concerned. In all the discussion about living in the community, it is easy to forget that the single largest group of adults with mental handicap are those living with their parents. Estimates of the number of people in this situation vary from around 60,000 adults (DHSS, 1971) to between 40-60 per cent of all adults with mental handicap (Campaign for People with Mental Handicap, 1984; Sanctuary, 1984). One recent article suggested that 10,000 adults with mental handicap live at home with parents aged 70+ years (Morris 1985). Grant (1985) points out that elderly people represent the single largest carer group for adults with mental handicap living at home, and as demographic trends have shown a shift towards longevity, these numbers can only increase.

The awareness of those providing services of the growing demand created by this situation has also been documented. A survey conducted in 1978 by Devon County Council examined 689 people with mental handicap who were living at home. Thirty seven per cent of them were aged over 25 years. In order to assess the likely future demand for services the researchers looked at the age and health of the carers. Out of a total of 432 adults they found that 143 people with mental handicap were with parents/carers aged over 65, ie. approximately one third of all the people surveyed. Forty six of the 432 adults were living in a "very high risk" category due to the age and fraility of the carers, and would almost certainly need a different carer during the next ten years. A further 67 adults were considered to be "high risk". A similar picture was found by Somerset Social Services Department (1976), Lambeth Social Services Department (1979) and for the Department of Mental Health at Bristol University (Inckelen, 1980).

The White Paper, "Better Services for the Mentally Handicapped" (DHSS, 1971), stated that each individual should live with his/her own family as long as this does not impose a burden on either themselves or their family, and he/she and his/her family should receive advice and support. The assumption behind this document was therefore that adults with mental handicap would remain at home with their families unless this situation proved problematic. Decisions to leave home are therefore based on negative reasons rather than for the positive good of the adult and/or parent. However, the Jay Report, which was published in 1979 (DHSS, 1979) took a rather different line. It suggested that every young person with mental handicap should have the chance to leave home and live independently of his or her parents as virtually every other person does. In July 1980 the Government responded to the Jay Report, expressing some doubts about the applicability of the Report's recommendations to adults with more profound handicaps, though broadly accepting the principles underlying the recommendations. At the end of 1980 the Government produced its review of progress since the 1971 White Paper (DHSS, 1980), reaffirming the White Paper's principles. The Department would therefore appear to be embracing two conflicting ideologies. In accordance with the Jay committee's model of care, adults ought to have the choice of of leaving home. The Department *also*, however, maintains the White Paper position that adults should stay at home unless insurmountable problems arise.

3.2 Life at Home

In both the statutory and voluntary sectors concern is now being expressed regarding the family situation where an older person with mental handicap is living at home. *Age Concern* has commented: "Bearing in mind that it was recently estimated that 25,000 mentally handicapped people live in the community with parents over 60, this is an important subject about which we have insufficient knowledge." (p.40) (Greengross, 1986). Fairbrother (1986), a parent of a woman who has mental handicap and who was herself a vice-chairman of Mencap is more explicit about what is needed, noting that many elderly mentally handicapped people are living with people who are more elderly themselves, including their parents and that support and advice are required. This will embrace information on claiming benefits, on drawing up a will and on respite care, both for the benefit and relief of the carers, but also preparation of the mentally handicapped person for residential independence from his or her carers (Fairbrother, 1986).

There is now an extensive literature on the effects on a family of a member with mental handicap, and the impact of that person on the family itself. (See Byrne and Cunningham, 1985 for a thorough discussion of this research.) Allusion to older people with mental handicap and their families is typically only made in passing, usually with reference to crisis situations occurring on the death or illness of a parent. In a recent book titled "Families of Handicapped Children - Needs and Supports Across the Lifespan" (Fewell and Vadasy, 1986), no real discussion of anyone over 20 is attempted. Nevertheless, there is an emerging literature on which we can draw for this review.

Grant's studies considered both a dependency group and a cluster of supporters whom he characterised as entering the twilight of their lives and who provided a unique chance to study older people as care givers rather than as care-receivers. The studies involved interviewing 103 carers of adults with mental handicap aged 20-49 who, with the exception of one, were all living with their parents. Grant wished to explore the nature of informal care for this group and to probe the factors which might affect its scope and functioning. He therefore looked not only at *who* helped the carers, but *why*, and what adaptations carers are capable of making in the face of changing needs and obligations. Demographically, there was a considerable age range and variations in material and social care resources. About 60 per cent were lone carers, many lived in council accommodation, and few had access to a car in the household. He pointed out that, although these were only outward features which have come to be associated with elderly people living in the community, they take on a different appearance when the elderly people in question are viewed as primary care givers with the obligations and responsibilties that this role brings.

Wertheimer (1981) suggests how their earlier experiences may have shaped their approach to their roles as carers in later years. None of the thirteen families in her study had received any useful or sustained help and support in the "early and difficult years". The lack of support and professional pessimism (which sometimes included the suggestion that the child should be put away) led many families to the idea that the best option was to cope alone with their child. She contrasts this with the experience of many families today who find support and services more readily available. Tyne (PSCC 1978) noted that the improvements seen in services made many older parents feel they could "manage now". They had become self-reliant and made only modest demands on services.

The lifelong care of people with mental handicap has been almost exclusively the responsibility of women. Grant (1986), suggests that even as mothers grow older, there is little escape from the responsibilities of looking after their handicapped adult offspring. His data mirror the findings of studies of young children with handicaps, for example those by Wilkin (1979) and Ayer and Alaszewski (1984). Grant found that 87 per cent of the main carers in his study were women, and that personal care, such as bathing and dressing, was the primary responsibility of women, and mothers in particular, no matter what the age of the carers. While fathers had traditionally been faced with employment obligations which gave them little time for caring, Grant found that even when retired from work and "available" as full-time carers, routines into which families have become socialised continued to determine the performance of tasks. He noted that it often appeared to be easier and less disruptive to the handicapped person to carry on existing practices rather than re-socialising everyone into new roles in later life.

In Cooke's (1987) study of twenty-six older families, no fathers were sole carers, 50 per cent of carers were widows and 69 per cent said they had only fair or poor health. There were two cases where both parents were still alive but illness of the mother had resulted in a re-socialising of roles. In both cases the father had experienced great difficulties in being accepted in his new role by his son or daughter. Fathers were most often described in terms such as "a great help" to mothers; their main domain as carer was usually the financial side of life at home.

It can be argued that the probable major factor underpinning this gender breakdown is unequal job opportunities and the consequence of women being "relegated" to the roles of carer and homemaker. (See Finch and Groves, 1980, for a fuller discussion of this point.) These self-regulating routines of care have also been discussed by Bayley (1973). Grant (1985) suggests that where personal care was needed, regularity, reliability and intimacy were required. These requirements could easily be met by people living with the person with a handicap. He also discusses how attitudes especially those of parents might perpetuate this situation of self-sufficiency and independence. Most responsibilities connected to the person with mental handicap were <u>not</u> likely to be passed on to others, as caring for one's adult child was seen as needing a special sort of knowledge that could not be easily imparted to others. Grant summarises the reasons why for many older parents only they and very close relatives are seen as necessary for the role of carers:

a) Parents want to maintain their own independence.
b) "The problem is not a problem". Grant found that in many instances, the middle-aged and older carers in this study had developed long-established routines for managing the dependency needs of their handicapped children. He also found examples of families who would find ways and means of "structuring surveillance" so that potential problems could be avoided. He concludes this section with the statement: "It would most certainly be wrong to assume however, that the existence of a mentally handicapped person at home is equivalent to saying that there is a problem. A good number of parents refute this and reject the idea that caring is unduly intrusive in their lives". (Grant, 1986; p.15.)
c) Parents want to avoid unsympathetic attitudes.
d) The role of carer would require "special" knowledge .
e) Instrumental vs. expressive support. Grant found that for many parents the perceived role of friends and neighbours was to "care about" rather than "care for". Families wanted moral support rather than involvement with personal and household care. However, while families were often self-contained units, they seemed to need the acceptance of the person who was mentally handicapped by friends and neighbours to know that they were being supported. "This type of expressive support could be given by friends and neighbours because it could be provided non-intrusively" says Grant. It also enabled family carers to be the "arbiters of when to invoke neighbourly help". (Grant, 1986; p.18.)
f) Chronicity vs. acuteness of need. Help from friends and neighbours was not expected to be regular, as caring for someone with mental handicap at home is a long-term commitment for many families. Grant takes up Bayley's point about the "chronic indebtedness" some families felt towards friends and neighbours especially

when they could not reciprocate. Some families in Grant's study attempted to lessen their dependency on friends and neighbours by only asking for short-term help.

3.3 Support for the family: Relatives, friends and neighbours

A further part of Grant's (1985) study looked at available support systems <u>outside</u> as well as within households. Other relatives *were* involved with the lives of people in Grant's study. These more distant sources of support helped with shopping, "minding" and other tasks which did not require the intimacy of personal care. Grant concluded that there was reassuring evidence that roughly the same number of kin are available to younger and <u>older</u> carers alike. However, he felt the numbers concealed three factors:

a) Not all kin were equally available or accessible so the care provided varied greatly.
b) Even when kin were available <u>and</u> accessible, main carers did not always seek their assistance.
c) There was also much variation within the age-groups he studied. For example the mode for the number of kin who were contributing to care varied from six for the 55-64 age group to four for the 65+ age group.

He also found that in households of older carers there appeared to be significantly fewer household members available to assume caring roles, leading to restricted networks for the older carers.

Drawing on these findings, Grant suggests that it would be foolish to assume that the *size* of a network equals its *strength.* He found other examples of situations where one or two supporters were sometimes all that the main carer needed to sustain them. Grantovetter (1973) has also illustrated the strengths of diffuse networks which consist of many unconnected strands in situations where irregular help is required. As previously mentioned, Grant found that many parents preferred to keep the caring private and restricted to very close relatives, therefore the type of support offered by diffuse networks may well be suitable for some families. Wertheimer's study (1981) of older parents with a person with mental handicap living at home examined the level of support from the extended family. She also pointed out, like Grant (1985), that the potential amount of support depended on the accessibility of the extended family, if such support was available at all. In addition, two out of the thirteen families questioned, reported how attitudes within the family had prevented parents receiving support. One father said, "You never get accepted...the family just keeps away." (p.18). In another family, Wertheimer talks of how "It seems that the rest of Mrs H's family think that she should have had Paul "put away" and it is probably her refusal to do so which has caused the rift in the family" (p.18).

Grant's study mentions the possibility that involvement of relatives outside the household is also dependent upon socio-economic class in addition to geographic proximity. Socially mobile families were likely to live long distances from other relatives making close involvement difficult. However, he believed that these typically middle-class families were often reluctant to cause interference in the careers or the marriages of sons and daughters who had moved away from home. Several parents mentioned that the lives of their other non-handicapped sons and daughters had been disrupted or affected during childhood and there was no wish to see this continued. With respect to non-handicapped siblings from lower socio-economic groups, Grant also found "impressive examples of the lengths to which this group (of siblings) will go to 'see Mam and Dad right'", especially among siblings in manual occupations. These people were more likely to be living locally so they were more immediately accessible. Overall, Grant (1986) notes that siblings' contributions to the personal care of their brothers and sisters are even more marginal than those of many fathers. He attributes this finding to the family or work obligations of the adult sibling.

Seltzer (1984) observes that no research had been conducted on changes in the quality of sibling relationships throughout the full life cycle in families with a retarded child, identifying this as an important issue in need of research to establish the extent to which ageing siblings maintain relationships and provide support to their also-ageing brothers and sisters with handicap.

A paper on the attitudes and life commitments of older siblings by Cleveland and Miller (1977) reported a positive adaption to the siblings with handicap that they studied. The study suggested that a sibling with mental handicap is *not* seen as having effects on life commitments by the non-handicapped siblings in the large majority of the cases. However, Cleveland and Miller found a striking difference between male and female siblings. The female sibling generally had a closer relationship to the sibling with handicaps, not only in childhood, but also in later years. It appeared likely that she was assigned more parent-surrogate responsibilities, therefore her adult life commitments were more likely to be affected. Another more recent American study on the relationships between adults with a mental handicap and their siblings (Zetlin, 1986), re-affirmed these findings. Sisters were found to play a greater role than did brothers in providing support to their siblings. However, all subjects were no longer living with parents, so only the the relationship of the non-handicapped siblings to the adult with mental handicap who was living independently was discussed. Most people viewed their siblings as sources of future help, and these siblings were often current providers of occasional and supplementary help. Some people had already started to rely on siblings as primary resources while a few thought to turn to siblings in times of crisis only.

In eight of the twenty-six families studied by Cooke (1987), siblings were still living at home and involved to varying degrees with caring for their brother or sister. Among siblings supporting the family from outside the family home, the sexual differences outlined by the American studies were the same i.e. predominantly female input. However, of the eight siblings still living at home, there were two cases where the male siblings were adamant that they would assume the role of carer once their parents died.

We have already considered the role of friends and neighbours in the independent lives of adults with mental handicap. What of their role for family carers? From both Wertheimer's (1981) and Grant's (1985; 1986) studies, it would appear that many older carers do not rely on their friends and neighbours for support. Grant found that 51 per cent of carers aged over 65 in his study had few friends or neighbours in their care network, compared with 33 per cent of younger carers and 34 per cent of pre-retirement carers. He cites three possible reasons for these figures:

a) natural attrition through death or migration of peers of older carers,
b) loss of ties maintained by one's spouse who may now be deceased,
c) increased incapacity and immobility among older carers and their friends and neighbours, making contact more difficult to sustain.

He describes the contribution offered by friends and relatives, when judged in terms of day to day routines of care, as very small, but help provided by friends and neighbours was valued very highly.

Grant also discusses how friends and neighbours are often involved with the handicapped person <u>through</u> the main carer. The result is that these friends and neighbours are often the same gender and in the same age-group as the principal carer. "The handicapped person's friends and neighbours, not infrequently, are therefore other mentally handicapped people whom they meet at the ATC or Gateway Club, or else a group of people in the neighbourhood who are a generation older." (Grant, 1985, p.15).

As mentioned previously, he also found that contributions from neighbours were often not expected. Therefore, for many of the families, a "good neighbour" would be someone who kept a polite distance. Examples were also found of families who wished to avoid indebtedness to friends and neighbours. Grant felt that many families would not be in a good position to return help that might be offered by friends and neighbours. In addition, some families were unsure of the responses to requests for help from friends or relatives. Therefore, uncertainties and/or the possibilities of unsympathetic attitudes were sometimes strong enough deterrents to requests for help. Carers also seemed very conscious of the obligation of friends and neighbours and would not lightly ask them for help if this was likely to prove burdensome to them.

In conclusion, Grant stresses that while care by friends and neighbours was definitely secondary to care by the family, this does not mean that communities are uncaring, and the impression he gained was that much latent goodwill existed in communities.

Wertheimer (1981) also found that very few of the older families she studied felt they had friends and neighbours on whom they could rely for help, support and friendship. She noted that neighbourly contact did depend to a certain extent, on the type of area and whether it had a stable or a transient population. Her study also revealed that as Grant observed, for most of the older parents, their most regular support comes from other parents of handicapped people in the neighbourhood, particularly those parents of their own age group, who also have a son or daughter living at home. Wertheimer comments on the isolation from other families that she found, and questions whether it results from choice by the family or rejection by the ouside world. She points to the segregation from non-handicapped children at an early age that a separate educational system ensures for children with mental handicap, though for many of these adults there had been no educational involvement. The problem of feelings of isolation is exacerbated when parents become aware of the differences which occur in the lives of their handicapped child and the non-handicapped children of friends. "As one parent described it - 'You see other people's children growing up, going out with boys and getting married and having children... and that my daughter can't do.' This parent has decided that the only way to cope with this is to cut herself off from those friends with 'normal' children so that she doesn't have to face these comparisons." (Wertheimer, 1981; p.19).

3.4 Statutory and Voluntary Support

The range of services available to families today did not exist for many families when their sons or daughters were born. Such families brought up their children with little or no help from statutory services, so it is perhaps not surprising that parents are often reluctant or suspicious of services which are now being more freely offered. Wertheimer (1981) describes older parents as still tending to be relatively modest consumers of specialist health and social services.

Grant (1985) found that for the families interviewed in his study, general practitioners and social workers were the most frequent visitors, few other professions being remembered by the families. The majority of the 103 families he interviewed *were* seen by visiting professionals on at least a six-monthly basis. However, that contact with the professionals did not automatically mean that carers turned to the individuals concerned when help was required. By asking families whom they count on to provide help it turned out that only 46 per cent of carers aged up to 55 looked to professionals; but for those aged 55 to 64 the figure dropped to 23 per cent; while for those aged 65 or over it was 34 per cent.

It appeared that for many families the "homeostatic" nature of caregiving in the informal care system meant that direct support from social workers, community nurses and other professionals was not expected. There had to be a "problem" or a "disequilibrium in the informal care system" before families even thought of asking the statutory services for help. Consequently, by the time this had happened, the situation was often at crisis point. Grant found some examples where losses in the care network caused, for example, by ill-health of carers, had generated difficulties with the attendant risks of premature admissions to residential care.

Some families seemed to regard the involvement of a professional worker as a "kind of insurance policy", especially if the carer was older and more likely to suffer sudden changes in health. There were a "small but highly demanding group" of cases in his sample where professionals were in constant demand from certain families. Grant reports that these families usually had a long history of involvement with the helping agencies which was not always a happy one. The professionals involved were left feeling frustrated as they were both unable to modify "unrealistic demands" by clients and also unable to break through the bureaucracy of existing services to find more customised packages of care for their clientele.

Wertheimer's study draws a similar picture of little

contact between older parents and statutory services. Only two of the thirteen families studied were receiving more or less regular visits from social workers. She believes the reason lies in the "low priority" status given by services to older parents with adult sons or daughters who are mentally handicapped. These families only rank as "high priority" when a crisis occurs, usually when the parent becomes ill or dies, thus precipitating a request for some form of alternative home for the adult. However, she also noted that, in her sample, most families used the general community services available, such as GPs, if the handicapped son or daughter had no serious additional problems or illnesses. The families in Cooke's (1987) study talked of a general low level of involvement with statutory services. One mother in her seventies who had never had a social worker spoke of her need for one as she got older.

Several studies report on older parents' views of the day services their offspring require. The main service used by most families is the Adult Training Centre. Wertheimer (1981) found most of the families studied to be dissatisfied with the Centres. The lack of liasion between families and the centres over sharing of information and shared planning about the person with mental handicap was apparent. Parents also complained about "mixed" centres which also catered for people with physical disabilities and ex-psychiatric patients. These parents felt that their children were given the worst jobs. Several of the parents mentioned the importance of the educational component in ATC activities, although some felt this was a very neglected area in the centres their sons or daughters attended. Transport to and from the Centre was also mentioned as a problem. Parents often have to go out and wait with their offspring for the bus to the centre, if they feel they could not wait on their own. Obviously, as parents get older, increasing frailty and poor health make this arrangement more difficult to maintain.

The lack of contact between parents and day Centre staff was also highlighted by the older parents. An obvious consequence of this factor was that "it seems unlikely that trainers are aware of what behaviours they may be nurturing or extinguishing and whether these are appropriate to the needs of the handicapped person in the home context" (Grant, 1986; p.12). Card (1983) examined attitudes towards ATCs and found that while parents were enthusiastic about social skills and independence training at the Centres, it was unusual for this training to be utilised or continued at home. On a more positive note, Grant (1986), reported that most families were generously appreciative of the relief from full-time caring that day services provided for them.

The involvement of voluntary services in the lives of older parents and their sons and daughters was also examined by both Wertheimer and Grant. Twelve out of the thirteen parents Wertheimer studied were members of their local Mencap society, many were founder members of their local group and had been active in these groups for over 20 years. For most parents, involvement with a voluntary organisation seemed to mean that their (parental) contribution in the forms of fund raising or organising social events or social clubs (e.g. Gateway Clubs), was often greater than the contribution made by the organisation to their lives. However, many parents spoke of the obvious benefits and support they gained from their involvement and Wertheimer stresses that "for some families their local Mencap group provides the central focus of their social life, a place where they can all go in the evenings and where parents can enjoy a quiet drink while someone else "keeps an eye" on their son or daughter." (p.21). She maintains that these social occasions also give people an opportunity to socialise in an atmosphere where there is tolerance and acceptance of mental handicap and where no-one feels stigmatised.

Some of the older parents in her study mentioned that their local Mencap group consists of mainly older parents. While some felt regret at what was thought of as a missed opportunity for both age groups to learn from one another, others felt bitter at what they felt was the complacency of younger parents who had had "it all handed to them on a plate". Many older parents had obviously had to fight for many years to get services established, including social clubs, and felt younger parents just accepted these better services without further campaigning. One woman pointed out however, that although services for younger people and children with mental handicap are much better than when their children were young, parents need to be made aware of the fact that services for adults are still very under-developed in many areas. Several of the parents in Cooke's study also expressed bitterness towards the non-involvement of younger parents in voluntary organisations. One mother was also critical of Mencap because of what she felt its "southern emphasis" and its limited access to people with little money.

Grant's study reported that local voluntary organisations, again predominantly Mencap groups, provided important contacts for many of the carers studied. However, again it appeared that involvement by and for these groups, decreased as the carers grew older. The findings indicated that the pensionable-age carers were visited less by these groups than the younger carers. Grant believes that to some extent this probably reflects lower levels of voluntary group membership by older carers and he found that membership of Mencap groups was inversely related to the carer's age: for those aged up to 55, membership comprised 46 per cent; for those aged 55 to 64 it dropped to 34 per cent, and for older carers it fell to 27 per cent. "Low levels of car ownership, carer frailty and the inability to obtain minding services appear to be plausible reasons why membership tails off with advancing age." (Grant, 1985; p.18).

It is interesting to note that in Grant's study visitors from the local churches or chapels were one of the few categories of visitor that actually increased as carers got older. Grant debates whether this is just a product of the local culture (a rural North Wales area), or whether, as it appeared, this involvement was often triggered by major family crisis such as bereavement. In only a few cases, however, did this appear to extend to more intensive forms of pastoral work with the families concerned. As we noted in Chapter 1, there is a visible level of church involvement with similar families in Oldham. In contrast to Grant's findings, however, this was a continuing involvement, in a non-rural setting. Recent studies from the USA also emphasise the importance of support from church and religious groups in the lives of older people with mental handicap e.g. Cotton *et al.* (1986); Stroud *et al.* (1984).

3.5 Rewards and Stresses of Caring at Home

Richardson and Ritchie (1987), writing about parents caring for their adult children with mental handicap, stress that there are two complex sets of emotional responses among parents. On the one hand, there is a very positive side arising from a strong parental bond and the pleasure in having a loved child at home. On the other, there is a negative side, arising from the stress placed on a family by a handicapped member. They argue that the strengths of these two conflicting responses depend largely on the nature of the son's or daughter's handicap and the amount of support parents receive and suggest that both love and stress are present to some degree.

Dobrof (1985) suggests that older parents may have difficulties resulting from a failure to "come to terms with the reality of the disability of their children and unresolved feelings of guilt and anger and self-blame may be a blight on the old person's declining years." (p.206). She notes that the psychological separation of child from parent may not have been achieved and the ideal relationship between adult child and parent, the relationship of "filial maturity" may not be possible.

According to Grant (1985), the stresses and rewards of caring for adults with mental handicap at home were not difficult to identify. "There were anxieties about the future stemming from the anticipated deterioration in the health or mobility of the carer, the lack of statutory services, the desire to avoid obligating relatives or friends and neighbours to assume responsibility for care and, in short, the inability to control what the outcome might be." (p.22).

Wertheimer's study of the views and circumstances of older parents found a largely positive picture of caring at home. Only one out of the 13 parents expressed any resentment about continually having their son or daughter around. One parent reported how she longed to get away from her son sometimes and have a "normal" conversation. She quickly followed this up with wondering whether this was wrong, although as she said, "I need a break; I like to get away from it all." She particularly missed "normal conversation" since her husband's sudden death two years ago.

For some of the other parents, caring at home for their children gave them a great deal of "personal happiness and satisfaction" even when this required great demands on their time and energy. Wertheimer finds the mutual bond of affection between parent and handicapped person refreshing when set against the common stereotype of the person with mental handicap as a burden on others. However, she cautions about the long-term implications of this closeness, as it raises the question of how the handicapped person will cope when the parents are no longer alive and a move to unfamiliar surroundings is necessitated.

Whittick (1985) examined attitudes to care-giving, including the attitudes of mothers with handicapped sons or daughters living at home. Although not a study specifically focused on older parents, her study raises questions about the role of carers. She discusses how some research on the lives of families with a child with mental handicap emphasises repeated family traumas at various stages throughout the life of the person with mental handicap, especially at stages when developmental milestones fail to be met. Other researchers suggest that a state of stable acceptance can be reached within these families and that they are not necessarily pathological. Her study examined the attitudes of three groups of carers, i) the daughters of dementing older parents, ii) mothers of children with mental handicap aged 5-8 years, iii) mothers of adults with mental handicap less than 25 years old. She found that the daughters of dementing parents reported greater stress than either group of mothers and suggested that the attitudes of mothers do not change as they and their child with mental handicap grow older. In an investigation of their attitudes to caring, mothers were more likely to hold attitudes of "love" and less of "stress". She found that the most stressful combination of attitudes was to hold strong negative attitudes of "conflict" and weak attitudes of "love".

Whittick concluded by asking, if attitudes do determine stress, should professionals be attempting to change those attitudes about the care-giving situation? "If holding attitudes of love and fulfilment are least stressful perhaps we should be acknowledging more the value of the carers' roles or at least dissipating negative attitudes." (p.18). However, she warns that "if we change attitudes regarding care in the community, are we perhaps then just supporting government policy regarding transfer of care to the community in the absence of adequate services and resources?" (p.18).

3.6 Issues of Independence and Dependencies

One of the major stereotypes held about parents of people with mental handicap is that they are "over-protective" towards their children. This stereotype is commonly applied to older parents whose adult sons and daughters still live at home with them, one assumption being that parents would have encouraged their children to leave home earlier if they wanted to see them becoming more independent. There are a few studies which explore the issues surrounding parental attitudes towards independence by asking parents themselves. These and other studies will now be discussed.

Evidence from as yet unpublished research by Richardson and Ritchie gives some explanations by parents themselves of reasons why a tendency to protectiveness can occur in *some* families with a member who is mentally handicapped. Some families suggested that this tendency developed from the "usual" practice of protecting children when they are young and vulnerable. As some parents still thought of their adult offspring as children, they continued to protect their adult sons and daughters as if they were much younger. Other parents mentioned how negative comments from people outside the family (eg. "She's better off dead") had made them keep their children "close to home" where they would not be exposed to such hurtful attitudes. Guilt was apparent in some parents who were aware that they were over-protective but could not modify their worries; others talked of much unwanted outside pressure from staff and others to let their children become more independent. Another reason given by parents who "did more" for their adult offspring was their wish to compensate their children for the fact that they were handicapped. Richardson and Ritchie suggest that the wish to protect is sometimes a result of real experience of accidents involving their children. There are also mixed feelings for parents who are told that their children are more skilled and independent <u>outside</u> the home, for example at the Adult Training Centre. While expressing happiness at this, they sometimes feel a sense of failure at the fact of this comparison. Richardson and Ritchie describe the issue of "protectiveness" as a vicious circle; the child with mental handicap is not taught skills so does not learn them, the child becomes more defenceless and, with increasing age, parents become protective as an inability to cope becomes more apparent.

Card's (1983) study of families caring for adults with mental handicap at home considers these issues in detail. He stresses that parents' ability to "let go" and allow greater independence depends on a number of factors. "The extent to which parents of mentally handicapped people should have an influence over their offspring's lives is a complex question, involving beliefs as to the nature and status of the handicapped person both in society and within the family" (p.20). He proffers suggestions for explaining the stereotype of "over-protection" among parents. "Commonly, guilt and social pressure, together with inadequate early counselling, is given as an explanation for over-protectiveness among parents of mentally handicapped people. This, however, does not seem to be an adequate explanation for the large proportion of my sample wishing to care for their son or daughter until age or ill-health makes this impossible. Perhaps the positive aspects of the parents' position need further examination so that we may understand the very real feelings of loss or potential loss experienced by parents when the question of independence or their offspring leaving home is raised" (p.21).

Card believes that for parents with a son or daughter with mental handicap the usual loss of status or role as parent or provider through adolescent rejection of parental protection does not often occur. "Parents of mentally handicapped adults perceive themselves as needed, indeed essential, to the wellbeing of their adult offspring. The process whereby adolescents become independent from their parents is one in which the onus is on the child. Frequently the child will have to exert considerable force in order to break away from the parents' protective behaviour. Without this rejection parents of mentally handicapped people can find that they are unable to regard their offspring as adult or look to their future independence" (p.21). He found that with respect to future residential accommodation, parents wanted somewhere which provided a similar degree of supervision to that of home. As regards independence training offered by ATCs, Card found that there was much evidence of enthusiasm for it, but little in the way of parental encouragement to continue at home. Parents often praised the staff for their efforts with their children, while at the same time emphasising their offspring's weaknesses and the dangers of increased independence. "In reality parents are often unwilling to allow the exercise of new independence within the home since this may result in friction within the family and loss of status for them as carers and providers" (p.9). Grant (1985) therefore questions the validity of a training model which emphasises increasing independence for people who get little chance to practise new skills at home. "If training is to continue on a large scale, should the emphasis on training for independence give way in some degree to training for inter-dependence? If training was more customised to the living environment from which the mentally handicapped person came, would this provide added scope for these dependents to make a greater contribution to the support of their own families?" (p.22). Grant also suggests that parental feelings of protectiveness towards their sons and daughters may be caused by "external factors" such as the lack of residential options open to carers.

Returning to the importance of independence for people with mental handicap for their future life, a group of parents led by social workers in Lancashire (Slater, Fitzpatrick and Carrins, 1981) looked into the questions surrounding these issues. Initially the group focused, in the light of the current economic climate, on the need for more resources to provide "total care" for their children. As the group progressed, however, parents began to see that by trying to develop their offspring's abilities, "...this resource would be less necessary and their view of the future become more positive... They also realised the difficulty their offspring would face in adjusting abruptly to change and this led on to parents considering the concept of preparation for change" (p.14).

The concept of inter-dependence between older parents and their sons and daughters is an important and often neglected area (Grant, 1985; Greengross, 1986). Card (1983) found examples of sons and daughters who acted as babysitters, general domestic assistants and two women who were withdrawn from their ATC whenever a member of the family became ill. "These women had acquired a sort of maiden-aunt role within the extended family and were seen as essential to the continued welfare of the family group" (p.21). While the merits and potential disadvantages of this type of relationship for the sons and daughters themselves has been commented on, Fryers (1986) points to the importance of the mutual relationship for parents. "As older parents (often mothers alone) become more frail, they may become increasingly dependent upon their son or daughter. This symbiosis must be understood and accepted, and never broken up crudely without proper preparation." (p.50).

3.7 Transition and Future Planning

Many individuals with mental handicap eventually face the double trauma of parental death <u>and</u> moving to a new home. Several factors have been suggested as leading to such a critical and unprepared transition. Sweeney and Wilson (1979), for example, believe that frustration, distrust and avoidance of the system account for parents' unwillingness to see their children become more independent and leave home. They proposed that "re-education" of parents was necessary. Richardson and Ritchie (1986) suggest that the complicated feelings surrounding this issue for parents are not unrelated; rather they might often serve to reinforce each other. For example, as parents become increasingly used to their situation over the years, so they may be loath to change it as they become increasingly dependent themselves.

The rewards and stresses of caring for a son or daughter with mental handicap have already been discussed in an earlier section of this chapter. However, as Richardson and Ritchie point out, many parents' views about the move from home are influenced by the very positive side to caring at home. "The ordinary activities of caring are commonly carried out in the context of family warmth; there is the companionship, common interests, shared humour and general intimacy which can occur within any family. On a deeper level, the positive side is hard to describe without recourse to the overused but overriding sentiment of "love". For these families, it appeared that the parent-child bond became strengthened over time, deepened by the many years of constant care and attention and by the added vulnerability arising from a handicap" (p.34, 1986). Some parents also reported that having their sons and daughters around kept them feeling younger. Many parents have a strong sense of responsibility towards their child, something which has often been emphasised by others, usually "outsiders" such as doctors. Richardson and Ritchie (1986) found that many parents in their study had been told that caring was their responsibility "which they should not try to impose on others" (p.43). Parents who continued to care at home were led to believe that "they were the 'good' ones, willing to devote their lives to a son or daughter with a mental handicap, compared to others who 'put them away' " (p.43).

Other inhibitors to moving included the reasoning that there was no natural breaking point, a time when it would seem "normal" for the son or daughter to leave home; also the parents had had many years to adjust their lives to living with someone with mental handicap so that any restrictions he or she imposed would by now have been largely taken for granted. Richardson and Ritchie point out that these older families are to some extent "self-selected" in that many of them would have taken action earlier if the burden of caring at home had become too great. Some parents in their study talked of their feelings that their home was the right and proper place for their adult children. There were those who were concerned about whether the children would be happy living anywhere else, and also parents who felt that their son or daughter might be happier living away from home. Card's (1983) study is one of the few that actually asked the sons and daughters themselves whether they wanted to move <u>now</u> as opposed to the inevitable move later. Two women he interviewed at home with their parents present, expressed a wish to remain at home. However, when interviewed alone at the ATC, they both declared their desire to leave their family home and live in a local authority flat.

Warren and Mulcahey (1984) in a US study, concluded that the concerns of ageing parents with home-living handicapped dependants were quite substantial. All 80 parents in their sample identified their number one concern as what would happen to their son/daughter when they were no longer able to care for him/her. It was something that many of them literally worried about every day. There is every reason to believe that the situation is comparable to that of parents in the United Kingdom. Bayley (1973), in one of the first in-depth studies of parents' views in this country reported that anxiety about the future pervaded the lives of most of the families with home-living dependants he studied. Three central issues demand consideration: (a) What plans, if any, do parents make for their sons and daughters? What sort of residential provision do they want for them? What do they think of existing provision? (b) How do parents think their offspring will react to these plans, now and in the future? (c) Have parents made the necessary legal arrangements for their sons' and daughters' future?

3.7.1 What Future Plans have been considered?

Evidence from unpublished research by Richardson and Ritchie suggested that there are three main attitudes parents hold about making future plans, avoidance, ambivalence and actively seeking a move for their children. The findings of their study indicated that older parents tended to hold attitudes of avoidance and ambivalence. Those making preparatory plans were in a minority. Bayley (1973) also found that, while the necessity for future planning was a major preoccupation, the number of parents who had any clear ideas about what would happen to their son or daughter when they could not look after them were few. These parents often did not want their sons and daughters to leave home, at least while they were still alive. Card discovered feelings of ambivalence among the parents he interviewed. They knew that they would have to make plans at some time, but they did not want to see that time come. He found that in spite of an apparently great demand for residential accommodation, when parents were consulted concerning their offspring leaving home, they rejected the idea.

3.7.2 With whom have Future Plans been discussed?

Parents' discussion of the future care of their sons and daughters appears to remain largely a family matter. Grant (1985) found that close relatives were the ones most often used as sounding boards. "It would often be the same people who were consulted when important decisions had to be made about the future care of the handicapped member" (p.13). When both parents were still alive it was usually the spouse who was the confidant, but with widowed parents, a son or daughter was usually the first to be consulted. Findings from the unpublished work by Richardson and Ritchie showed that parents expressed difficulty about discussing their problems with people outside the home. Older parents expecially, would often regret their lack of discussion about future plans with others which could have helped them before a crisis situation occured. Most parents were quite adamant that they could not talk about the future with the very people for whom they were planning it, their sons and daughters themselves. Parents felt that either they would not understand or else they would get upset (See section 3.7.6 for the attitudes of sons and daughters to future plans). Only Cooke's (1987) study reported parents as having discussed future plans with service personnel. Ten out of the twenty-two families who had social workers said they had considered future plans with them. Of the remaining twelve, one parent felt her social worker was reluctant to bring up the subject of the future for fear of upsetting her. She, herself, was quite desperate to talk about her worries for her son's future but wanted her social worker to initiate the conversation.

3.7.3 What Options have been considered?

Discussion of parents' wishes with respect to the future homes of their offspring can only be considered against a background of the residential alternatives from which they must make their choice. With the move to community care, the option of long stay hospitals for people with mental handicap is ceasing to be available. Under the Housing (Homeless Persons) Act 1977, priority groups were named. People with physical and mental handicap who are are homeless or threatened with homelessness are given such priority and Local Authorities must make provision for them. Residential provision by the Local Authority falls broadly into the following categories: (a) Hostels, (b) Group Homes, (c) Fostering, (d) Boarding out. For a full description of their typical features, see Malin, Race and Jones (1980). Private sector and voluntary organisations offer various other alternatives. For example, Mencap offers their Homes Foundation scheme which enables parents to leave their house to Mencap who will attempt to ensure that their son or daughter can, with the support of Mencap staff, then remain in their own home after their parents have died. Where this is not feasible, the scheme can also involve Mencap selling the property and moving the son/daughter to another house. While there might seem to be some variety in this provision to parents who have cared for their son or daughter for a lifetime, there are some parents for whom none of these alternatives to home care is necessarily acceptable. One mother's comment in Bayley's study exemplifies this point: "Only definite plan I have, it sounds terrible but I do have it, if I came to be ill and I knew I was really ill and I knew I couldn't get better, I'd give him a bottle of tablets."

Cooke (1987) asked the twenty-six parents in her study what decisions had been made regarding future residential provision for their children. The highest number of parents had made no decision at the time of interview, while the second highest figure was for those wanting continued family care. Hostels were the third most popular option. Bayley (1973) reports on the plans of a group of 53 parents between 40 and 70+ years. Thirty-four had no plans, while 12 were looking to permanent care but had made no definite plan. One family <u>expected</u> relatives to take over, while one <u>hoped</u> this would be the case. Two refused to think about the problem and only three families had placed their son or daughter on a waiting list. Grant (1985) found a relatively higher expectation with regard to anticipated family support that increased with parental age (33 per cent, under 54 years; 35 per cent, 55-64 years; 59 per cent, 65+ years). Acceptance of the need for statutory help now or in future declined through these age groups, 49, 43 and 37 per cent. This lack of definite preparation was confirmed by Wertheimer (1981).

While a large number of the British studies showed that continued family care was a favoured future option for many older parents, there appeared to have been little investigation of this choice. Grant (1985) suggests that younger parents were more likely to pursue help from statutory services as they had had less negative dealings with them compared with older parents. Over 60 per cent of the parents in Cooke's study said they had considered continued family care at some stage. When questioned further, it appeared that only 16 per cent of these were making real plans in this direction and had discussed these plans with the family. For some parents, saying they were considering continued family care appeared to be another way of deferring a concrete decision. One father said that this option allowed him to give this difficult decision-making to his other children to sort out when he was dead.

Grant also found a marked effect of socio-economic group. Families in professional occupations were almost three times as likely as other families to have made a definite decision to give responsibility for care to local health or social services authorities. Those families in non-professional occupations were almost twice as likely to be looking to their own family resources. He believes these figures were "less than accidental given the greater availability of family members to this group and the existence of values stressing interdependence between family members" (Grant 1986, p.8).

In the US, Warren and Mulcahey (1984) found that 70 per cent of the families had no formal long-term residential planning. There were, however, substantial differences between urban and rural families in this respect. Twenty per cent of urban families had their child on a waiting list for residential placement while none of the rural families did so. On the other hand,

25 per cent of the rural families had made specific arrangements with siblings to care for the dependent person in the long-term, versus 13 per cent of the urban sample. They believe possible explanations lie in the fact that rural families tended to be larger and that more residential alternatives were available in the urban settings. They also found a correlation between age of parents and the existence of some kind of plan. Those parents aged under 65 tended not to have made any type of plan. Parents aged 65+ had done so, perhaps because 65 is regarded by many people as a milestone, a point at which one puts affairs in order.

Other US studies allude to preference by parents for future family support. Schatz (1983) found when interviewing 235 parents about the future prospects of their handicapped offspring that at least a quarter of them were hopeful that a sibling would provide a home for them at some stage. Zetlin's (1986) study went a stage further and asked siblings their opinion of these parental wishes and expectations. She found a wide variation in sibling reactions and sibling relationships. In some cases, parents expected that, after their death, siblings would carry on in their place. Evidence that siblings were accepting this responsibility was shown by their increasing involvement in their handicapped siblings' lives. There were other families, however, where there was no such involvement and no expectations. Zetlin also discovered examples of parents who, despite the realisation that their non-handicapped siblings did not want to be burdened, continued to hope that when the time came, they would do the "decent" thing by keeping in touch and possibly becoming a "caretaker" for their siblings. She proposes that, while the age of non-handicapped siblings may affect the relationship, middle-aged siblings were generally regarded as the closest and most reliable of supporters. Other factors can, however, have major effects on this general conclusion. For example, a marriage to someone who discouraged the sibling's role as benefactor may easily create a reduction in willingness to act as a caretaker.

3.7.4 Parents' Knowledge and Opinions of the Alternatives to Home

Clearly, parents' knowledge of residential options, and their attitude to such provision, will have an important influence on their ease or difficulty in making future plans. Some parents might welcome a place with mixed accommodation, while others might be vehemently opposed to it. Sanctuary (1984) believes that the lack of options open to parents looking for a future home for their offspring is a major reason for many parents' reluctance to "let go".

Evidence from work by Richardson and Ritchie (unpublished) suggests that an understanding of parental opinions must take account both of the options available and of their knowledge of these options. They point out that, while parents may have strong views on alternatives, the extent to which they or their offspring have actually experienced them varies considerably. Some parents may form their opinions from direct experience, i.e. their daughter might have used a local hostel for regular short breaks from home, while others rely on the experiences of friends or others. Card (1983) examined the opinions of parents on residential alternatives and found that, "Criticism of low standards of supervision and poor standards of cleanliness and dress tend to be the most common complaint. Comments concerning absence of stimulation or curtailment of freedom through institutional living are less frequent" (p.20). His experiences of working with parents led him to the conclusion that many parents want to find a form of accommodation that will "duplicate the protection that they have provided over the years" (p.21). He found it somewhat surprising, then, that so few parents will consider the less institutional types of accommodation such as boarding out with families. However, he feels that this can be partly explained by the parents' wish for permanence of accommodation. Many parents want to see their son or daughter settled for life and a hostel seems in some ways to represent a form of permanence that parents find reassuring. Boarding out, however, can seem to them fraught with uncertainties and concerns regarding the motivation and nature of the family who takes the mentally handicapped person in.

Richardson and Ritchie found the most important residential quality demanded by parents to be "homeliness", a quality including love and affection, a capacity to meet individual needs and give a sense of belonging. Many parents thought permanence of the home an essential feature. Size was also important, parents wanting the residence to be small rather than large, with the potential benefits of individual attention and family-like atmosphere. It should also look like a home. The staff ratio and personal qualities of the staff were more important to many parents than professional qualifications. Other studies confirm this finding (e.g. McCormack, 1979).

Potential differences in attitude among parents included whether the residences should be mixed or single-sex and whether their sons and daughters should be encouraged to develop independence skills in their new homes or not. McCormack (1979), however, concluded that only a few parents really cared about these seemingly contentious issues. "Simplistic as it may be, but they find it hard to understand why the bureaucrats and professionals spend so much time talking, instead of putting the needs of the handicapped first and getting on with the caring" (p.200). She points to the apparently homogeneous way of looking at the residential needs of people with mental handicap, "Nobody queries the integrity and sense of a non-handicapped person who chooses to live in a remote village against someone who prefers life in a city flat. So why should there be only one route to perfect residential care for the mentally handicapped? People are infinitely varied, the mentally handicapped even more so. Conformity is not the answer. They and their families need choice" (p.201). McCormack believes that currently parents get little choice because most parents opt for a similar type of a care and there is not enough to go round. "There are, in fact, not enough places of any kind, and the current trend towards encouraging families to keep their children at home overestimates the percentage who will manage to do so" (p.201).

Wertheimer's study (1981) of older parents looked at the current use of local residential services by people with mental handicap living with their parents. Wertheimer found that very few of the sons and daughters regularly stayed away from home in Local Authority or Health Service accommodation, although this would seem to be a useful experience in preparing for the future. She found that the general reluctance to use short-term residential facilities is partly due to parents' suspicions that the standards in hostels do not match up to those in their own homes, and partly to a reluctance to be separated from their offspring.

Again, Wertheimer draws the conclusion that it is the unacceptability of what residential provision is on offer that makes many families desist from planning for the future. Criticisms of hostels included their usual size (too big), the lack of discrimination in the types of people who lived in the hostels, the lack of supervision and the fact that they could not provide the sort of home comforts their offspring were used to. While Wertheimer felt that a group home might well offer the possibility of somewhere with more homelike qualities, parents tended to feel that they offered inadequate supervision. The concern about the "types" of people who lived in hostels manifested itself in comments such as "ignorant rough people", "some very difficult people there". Wertheimer suggests that while parents disliked hostel provision, their knowledge of them is often based on hearsay alone. Attempts to explain and give parents direct experience of hostels appeared to be almost non-existent in the area studied.

(Slater, Fitzpatrick and Carrins, 1981) report on the preferences expressed by a group of middle aged parents. There was unanimous agreement on the need for adequate preparation so that their children would know what to expect from their new home. The idea of "family placements" was introduced to the group and met with a favourable response.

Rudie and Riedl (1984) examined the attitudes of parents of people with mental handicap who had previously lived in state hospitals but who were now living in community facilities. They found that the vast majority of parents interviewed indicated that they were satisfied with their offspring's community placement. Their conclusion, based on this and two previous studies, was that parents prefer that their sons and daughters remain in their *current* placement, whether in the community or in a state hospital, i.e. they wished to maintain the *status quo*. Cooke (1987) found the idea of group homes as a future alternative very unpopular among parents. The main reason seemed to derive from the inadequate knowledge the majority of parents had of this alternative. Many parents believed that *all* group homes were unstaffed, no matter what the level of handicap was of the people living in them.

There is little evidence readily available on parents' views of private and voluntary residential provision except in letters to journals such as Mencap's house journal "Parents Voice". One parent wrote in support of village communities, where she felt people with mental handicap would feel "happier and more relaxed in their own community, where they are not being forced to 'keep up' with normal neighbours" (Wells, 1983). She proposed that the enthusiasm for smaller units is probably based on economic reasons. Other parents in Wertheimer's study (1981) felt very strongly that their sons and daughters should not have to leave the area they had lived in all their life when they left home.

In conclusion, parents show a wide variation in both positive and negative opinions about the various alternatives. The consistent finding is that hopes for their childrens' residential future are incompatible with the options currently available. Direct knowledge of alternatives is, however, quite patchy.

3.7.5 Legal Issues concerning Future Plans

Legal preparation is a critical part of future planning. The whole area has been described as "a jungle, with traps for the unwary, and with the paths hard to find" (Sanctuary, 1984, p.10). He makes the point that professionals such as lawyers and social workers are often unaware of the ways in which the general law and the various statutory regulations operate with regard to people with mental handicap. Examples are given of cases where erroneous advice has been given to parents, or where the law has changed, making it necessary for people to alter their wills. It is beyond the scope of the chapter to review the legal issues arising from making future provision. The reader is directed to Sanctuary's (1984) lucid exposition and his related Mencap Information Sheet (Sanctuary, 1983).

Warren and Mulcahey (1984) in the US surveyed parents of people with mental handicap, service providers and attorneys to assess knowledge and extent of legal planning. Seventy-five per cent had not made legal arrangements or had made a faulty will. Service providers generally lacked sufficient knowledge to provide appropriate advice to parents. Warren and Mulcahey found them to be "particularly unknowledgeable about various fundamental legal issues and estate planning and were aware of their lack of knowledge in these areas (they specifically requested further information)" (p.10). The interviews with members of the legal profession also highlighted the fact that at least some lawyers who plan estates had insufficient and erroneous knowledge. The 26 older parents in Cooke's (1987) study were asked if they had made legal arrangements. Only eight parents had made plans, only two of these eight having made arrangements under the guidance of a solicitor. Parents gave lack of money and the painfulness of future planning as the main reasons for not making arrangements. Lack of legal knowledge caused anxiety in several families.

3.7.6 Attitudes to, and of, the Son or Daughter

Some parents have said that a concern not to upset their son or daughter has been a major inhibitor to future planning. Other parents say they do not discuss plans with them (e.g. about their own preferences, discussions about death) because they do not understand such subjects. Professionals caring for the son or daughter who has been bereaved and has had to move to a new home have been described as holding insensitive attitudes towards that person's natural reactions of grief and loss.

Out of the thirteen families in Wertheimer's study, five people had lost a parent and yet in only one instance had the bereavement been explained to that person. One mother excused her silence on the matter by saying "Life's hard enough for them anyway... and I don't like to see children at funerals". Her son was 31 when his father died. People were told that the deceased parent had "gone to work a long way away", or "gone to sleep". Oswin's (1983) paper on bereavement and people with mental handicap underlines the additional "sad things" that may happen to an adult on top of a major bereavement. "The research is showing that after a widowed parent dies some mentally handicapped people have as many as three moves to different residential settings in the first twelve months after the death occurs" (p.36). People may lose their parents, their home, friends and a life with its routines that they have been used to for many years. Oswin stresses that professionals must realise that people with mental handicap, no matter how handicapped, are just as capable as non-handicapped people of feeling grief and this must be respected and acted upon. Although we have argued in Chapter 7 that the relocation syndrome is far from invariably observed, Clegg (1986) suggests ways of avoiding stress that can be the outcome of relocation. This can be attained if the individual "has choice over the move, if the new environment is familiar and predictable, and if the move leads to the individual having increased control over their lives" (p.22). It would seem reasonable to expect that the same suggestions might help many adults with mental handicap who face a similar situation.

In the research reviewed so far, there is little reference to the opinions of the adults with handicaps. In Grant's (1985) study of older carers, he questioned this lack of consultation with the "other" consumer: "What indeed are the views of mentally handicapped people...their voice is heard all too infrequently and suggests perhaps priority should be given to self-advocacy and advocacy services before too many services are fashioned without proper consultation" (p.21).

It is only in recent years that adults who are mentally handicapped have been encouraged to be primary informants about their own lives. One particularly significant mechanism which has helped this has been the development of the advocacy movement. In a general sense, advocacy means to plead the cause of another and to take "action in support of one's belief and in a cause" (Lourie and Lourie, 1972). But advocacy also involves self-advocacy, ie. efforts made by individuals to reach their highest possible level of independence, speak for themselves, take action on their own behalf, and act upon decisions and situations which affect their life. As Saleem (1985) says, in one of the few studies on the views of adults living at home, "Only mentally handicapped people themselves can speak from the daily experience of their own lives, and of the attitudes and behaviours of others towards them. Only they know what they are talking about from personal experience" (p.15).

These recent endeavours, however, have tended to concentrate on people living either in hospital or more commonly people who have been de-institutionalised and are now living in the community, as in the work of Edgerton and his colleagues described above. Studies in Britain have included interviewing people living in Social Services Group Homes and Hostels (Atkinson, 1984; Malin, 1980). The foci of the interviews varied from what support people were receiving to their typical activities during the week and at weekends.

However, it appears that little effort has been made to record the impressions of people with mental handicap still living with their parents. In the studies on older parents' views, some judgements are made by parents about the lives and views of people with mental handicap, but there are no opportunities given to the sons and daughters themselves to express their views about their current circumstances or their futures. Saleem describes the situation as one in which the desires, wishes and opinions of these people are very rarely taken into consideration. A secondary source such as the person's caretaker, schoolteacher or other informed person's opinion is rarely sought. It is possible that living with their older parents may give people less opportunity to speak for themselves for a number of reasons:

a) As noted earlier, older parents and their families have been neglected by service and research personnel. Therefore considering the lack of research on the views of people with a mental handicap generally, people living even more "invisibly", are more likely to be forgotten;

b) There is a growing consensus that this extended parenting to which adults are subjected, "fails to acknowledge their adulthood ... and they are exposed to constraints and rules that non-handicapped adults will not tolerate" (Flynn and Saleem 1986, p.2).

Referring to the situation that adults living at home will eventually experience, that of the "double

trauma" of their parents dying and having to move to often totally new circumstances, Saleem (1985) believes there are two facets to the issue of people with a mental handicap who live at home with their parents:
a) they are not given the opportunity to move away from home to live independently;
b) they remain at home until it is no longer possible, quite often facing the loss of a parent and the loss of a home they have known all their lives at one and the same time.

Saleem believes it is therefore all the more important that people with mental handicap are given the opportunity to decide for themselves the way in which they wish to run their lives.

In some of the few studies available that examine the views of people with mental handicap, their attitudes to living at home with their older parents have been elicited. Although Cooke's (1987) study concentrated on parental views, she was anxious to document the opinions of the sons and daughters living at home where possible. A small sample of nine people were interviewed. Main findings were that two out of the nine people interviewed expressed uncertainty about staying at home until a move was necessary. A few others enunciated awareness of their parents' anxiety towards their increased independence and the possibility of them leaving home. Some people were also aware of their responsibilities to their "carers" and there was evidence of the inter-dependency that Grant (1985; 1986) talks about. A few people expressed an interest in alternatives to the ATC as they grew older. Two thirds of the people interviewed expressed their awareness of future plans, including the death of their parents and the need for a new home. A criticism of the potential future homes for many people, the hostels, was the lack of choice and freedom people felt from their short-term stays in them. Several people said they preferred home for these reasons. In the report on the "workshop for ideas and hopes and plans and people" held by the Campaign for People with Mental Handicap, reference is made to the views of five people who lived at home: "For delegates who still lived at home, this was the best place to be; none of them would choose to live in hospital or a hostel instead. For them, relationships were good; those with jobs paid a certain amount of money to their mother and were pleased to help the family budget; mothers and daughters and fathers and sons shared shopping expeditions; parents often gave their children luxury items; sometimes the family went on holiday together" (CMH, 1973, p.3).

Saleem's (1985) study explored the perceptions of adults with a mental handicap living with their parents concerning their lives. When asked about living at home and the possibility of living elsewhere independent of their parents, the responses were varied. Nine of the twelve people interviewed expressed a wish to live independently, either in a flat by themselves or sharing accommodation with friends; three people did not wish to leave home; and four people made statements regarding the fact that their parents would not like them to leave home. All those who expressed a wish to live independently of their parents felt that they would manage on their own. However the pressures from family members to remain in the family home were perceived as quite considerable.

The study by Card (1983), discussed earlier, also involved some interviews with the adult offspring of older parents. He discovered that some adults interviewed in the presence of their families offered contrasting views when interviewed in private. When interviewed at home, they said they were happy to stay living at home with their parents, but when interviewed at the ATC they expressed a desire to move out as many other people of their own age would have done.

Flynn and Saleem (1986) also found that the adults had few opportunities to use the skills taught in the ATC at home. They found that "it is unusual for training to be continued or utilised in the parental home. While it is possible that some adults are unable to participate in household tasks because of their daily absence at the ATC, it is clear that some adults experience frustration at the few opportunities to employ their skills in the home" (p.21). For example, while all interviewees said they were being taught to cook at their ATC, nine people remarked that if they cook at home they are always supervised. Likewise in shopping, cleaning and laundry, there were many examples of restricted opportunities.

Parental preference was also obvious in respect to work and the ATC. "Two people stated that their families will not let them have jobs. It is noteworthy that seven people expressed a wish to have a job, particularly in view of the fact that in a survey of ATCs only 4.2 per cent stressed the importance of "training for employment" (Whelan and Speake, 1977). Arguably, almost ten years later with national unemployment in excess of three million, fewer ATCs would be as committed to this aim" (Flynn and Saleem, 1986, p.15).

CMH (1973) also reports that, compared to the people living in residential units, those living at home had <u>more</u> choice, especially in the area of leisure. "People who lived at home had chances to chose a hobby that really fulfilled them that people in residential units seemed to lack. One man who lived with his family spent his Saturday mornings in record shops and went to jazz clubs in the evenings; he played the drums himself: "miles away, nothing in the world, just behind there bashing away. It's how it gets you, you know" (p.15). Saleem, however, found that almost all her subjects had home-based interests and that five people pursued their interests with a family member. The interviews also discovered that three people expressed some measure of dissatisfaction in this area and three people expressed a desire to change. When asked about friendships, <u>no</u> interviewees said they had any friends who were not mentally handicapped.

While parents of people with mental handicap may view the future with trepidation, Flynn and Saleem believe that their study "demonstrates that parents do not have the monopoly in being anxious about the future" (p.15). Their interviews with the sons and daughters showed that many of them *do* have thoughts and worries about what will happen to them when their parents die; yet parents and services still continue to deny these feelings to people with mental handicap and to take them seriously. "It is evident that this anxiety has not been adequately addressed by services, particularly for the man whose social worker's response to his request for a flat was 'I don't know' followed by no subsequent reference to this request. The tension perceived by these people merits particular acknowledgement. They appreciate that their endeavour to live independently of their parents or siblings is attended by doubts and concerns regarding their ability to manage" (p.14).

CMH (1973) reports views of people who had already been forced to leave the family home on the death of their parents. "For many delegates who had left home, this seemed entirely natural, part of the way life developed as parents died and brothers and sisters married and had their own life. For some, however, their life now didn't compensate for the loss of their parents or being forced to leave their family homes" (p.14). Some delegates talked of their grief; two had been particularly crushed by the death of their mother and found no relationship that could take the place of this one. "I miss her a lot", said one man; "she cooked nice meals, not like the hostel; she looked after me; she was a nice lady; I miss her all the time" (p.13). The feeling from these people was that "their life at the moment lacked a very important element; neither the people who they lived with nor the staff who looked after them had enabled them to get over their loss and find new relationships to take its place" (p.14).

3.7.7 Conclusions

Some people with mental handicap are going to outlive their parents by as much as thirty or forty years. Parents appear to be generally dissatisfied with the services and alternatives to home that are available to their sons and daughters. Wertheimer (1981) concludes that "...parents see the future, in so far as it is contemplated at all, with pessimism, fear and some anger that the services cannot provide what they want. They rarely see themselves as having any part to play in planning the mentally handicapped person's future; nor does there seem to be any move to involve the mentally handicapped people themselves. Parents seem only able to "live for the present"; the future of the mentally handicapped without them is ignored, perhaps because it is too painful to contemplate" (p.33).

With regard to their sons and daughters, people with a mental handicap do have ideas about their present and future lives and service planners should take note before any further developments. Likewise, the paucity of research which asks people living with their parents to be the primary informants about their own lives needs to be remedied. As Flynn and Saleem (1986) conclude from their study "Preparation for independent living and employment or 'significant living without employment' are major areas of concern for services. Residence in hostels, sheltered accommodation, group homes and minimum support units following residence in the family home, concerns parents and families. We know now that these concerns are shared by adults who are mentally handicapped" (p.15).

Chapter Nine

REVIEW AND CONCLUSIONS

1 INTRODUCTION

We have tried in the preceding chapters to approach the subject of ageing and mental handicap by considering the individuals with whom we are concerned as having much in common with their non-handicapped peers. A great deal of the material we have reviewed has, therefore, dealt with information from the wider ageing population. Against this background we have considered the impact of mental handicap on the ageing process and on the wider ecology in which the person ages. Thus, we have seen that there are parallels in changing intellectual function with age between individuals with and without mental handicap (Chapter 4), but have also noted the influence of such handicaps on the likelihood of being employed (Chapter 6) and on family functioning (Chapter 8), where substantial divergence from the norm can be discerned. While there is as yet no thoroughly worked out theoretical picture of the impact of mental handicap on the processes and experience of ageing, it is clear that there is a substantial advantage to viewing this population within the wider context of ageing in society, in the same way that critical benefits have accrued to our understanding of development in younger children with handicaps through a consideration of their growth in the wider framework of child development theory.

There is, however, a second context implicit in this view which we briefly described in Chapter 1, i.e. that ageing in people with mental handicap must be considered with respect to the wider policies through which society deals with such people. In that chapter we reviewed the development of the community care policy with respect to people with mental handicap and described some of the realities of its implementation. Since we cannot divorce the situation of older people with mental handicap from the impact of such policies, our reflections on the material in this book must be related to this wider framework. It is beyond the scope of this venture to cover in any detailed fashion the many issues arising from the care in the community policy which have been ably discussed in a variety of documents in the past few years (Audit Commission, 1985; 1986). However, some reference to the relevance of community care policies to the lives of older people with mental handicap is called for at this stage. In addition, the wider situation of older and elderly people without mental handicap must at least be be noted.

We will begin by considering what is the meaning of the word "policy" when we speak of "the policy of community care". Binstock, Levin and Weatherley (1985) demonstrate that there is a very real problem in defining what we mean by the very term "policy". They note that "Neither scholarly definitions nor popular conceptions of the term are adequate, since they imply that policies are relatively clear, authoritative expressions of public goals that provide a fundamental context within which other governmental decisions and activities can be viewed and interpreted. The implication is unrealistic because any attempt to reify "policy" disintegrates when political behavior is examined. The language of a legislative act (and 'the intent' behind it) is no more or less a policy than the decisions made by the bureaucrats who implement it (and their intentions in doing so).....one cannot work with a definition of policy that excludes implementation" (p.590). These authors go on to draw a distinction between policy adoption and policy implementation. For present purposes the former embraces governmental legislation and directives, while the latter is concerned with the activities set in motion primarily at regional and local levels.

The significance of this distinction is fully exemplified in the recent report: "Making a Reality of Community Care" (Audit Commission 1986). Here the interaction between policy adoption and implementation as it is conditioned by financial, structural and administrative factors is reviewed in some detail as it affects the development of the care in the community initiatives for people with mental handicap, mental illness, physical handicap, and those who are elderly. We will note some of the specific observations made in this report as we consider particular areas of concern below. Here we will simply draw attention to the overall conclusions of the report as the situation described is one which will almost totally condition the lives of older individuals with mental handicap, whether living at present in the community or moving into it from the larger institutions.

The report draws three classes of conclusion. First, and overall, they consider the extent to which the adopted policy has been realised, and conclude: "There are serious grounds for concerns about the lack of progress in shifting the balance of services towards community care. Progress has been slow and uneven across the country; and the near-term prospects are not promising. In short, the community care policy is in danger of failing to achieve its potential." (p.13). Second, there are major underlying problems to be tackled related to the pattern of distribution of finance, with local authorities being penalised through loss of grant when community care services are initiated. In addition, there is organisational fragmentation and confusion with responsibility being divided between a number of organisations whose funding is from different sources and who often fail to co-operate. They note, third, that radical change will be necessary if we are to avoid missing the opportunity **now** to establish appropriate services. There is a danger that a new pattern of services will emerge and become entrenched that is neither effective as community based provision nor cost effective either. Against this somewhat pessimistic background, however, they emphasise that progress has been made and that examples of good practice can be observed. We would refer the reader again to our own Chapter 1 where provision within Oldham falls well within the descriptions of good practice that the Audit Commission offers.

The conclusions of the Audit Commission are equally applicable to elderly individuals with whom the report is also concerned as to people with mental handicap. For the majority of older people without a mental handicap, an independent life in the community or a life supported by relatives is a reality. Of those over 65 years, only two per cent are in residential care while 13 per cent live with support from statutory services in the community (Audit Commission 1985). Nevertheless, the picture drawn by the British Medical Society (1986) in their report: "All Our Tomorrows: Growing old in Britain" is a depressing one with respect to the quality of the lives of elderly people. We have reviewed elsewhere the information in this report (Hogg 1986) and will here note that with respect to housing, finance, medical care and quality of life as reflected in part in leisure and educational activities, a highly unsatisfactory picture emerges of the status of, and value placed on, elderly people. They conclude that elderly people are neither second-class citizens nor a race apart from society at large. "They are equal and ordinary members of the community and have the right to participate fully in the life of the community. Their tastes, wishes and needs should be treated with the same consideration and respect as is afforded other groups." (p.53). It will not have escaped the reader that nothing in this statement would require changing, other than the generic term, to make it equally applicable to people with mental handicap.

Against this wider background of policy and existing provision, then, we will consider the implication of the material reviewed in this book. In the following sections we essentially follow the chapter sequence of the book. We will return to more general considerations of policy and philosophy at the end of the chapter.

2 EPIDEMIOLOGY AND MORTALITY

The studies reviewed in Chapter 2 have shown clearly that Mental Handicap Services are having to plan for the needs of a population of older people whose numbers are projected to increase well in to the next century. It was shown that this increase is not simply attributable to improvements in medical care but also reflects the underlying trend of the general population. Two major booms in the birth rate, one in the immediate post-war years and the other in the 1960s, will increase the number of people aged 50-55 from 2.7 million in 1981 to 4.5 million in 2010. Thus, services for people with age-related needs will have to expand by 67 per cent if current levels are to be maintained.

As a result of these pressures, considerable effort in the field of mental handicap has gone into attempting to make accurate estimates of likely client numbers in different age groups, and to give some projections of population characteristics. Health status, residential characteristics and services received represent three of the most commonly sought areas of information, although the level of detail and sophistication of measuring instruments employed has varied greatly from study to study. In the early 1980s, most of this work appeared to have been carried out in the United States, the major survey of Janicki and MacEachron (1984) in New York being a notable example. Very recently, however, we have learned of a number of Local Authorities in the UK who are conducting their own surveys of needs and services to older clients. The increasing number of such surveys suggests that Local Authorities and District Health Authorities are now making their own population projections, rather than relying on information collected by someone else in a different geographical location. This approach is well founded, although it must be stressed that accurate information will only result from well designed studies.

The review of studies in Chapter 2 indicates some of the pitfalls evident in existing work, and which need close attention in the future. Most notable among these problems is the method of defining the population to be surveyed. This single consideration involves some difficult decisions: (a) the choice of an agency or household survey, (b) the location of people who are unknown to Mental Handicap Services, (c) the criteria for including or excluding people from the sample, (if selection is not simply on administrative grounds), and (d) which people to include of those who are currently living in institutions both inside and outside the administrative area. The answers to these questions are not self-evident. Indeed it will be remembered that Conley (1973) reported two studies whose estimates of prevalence differed by a factor of 46 times.

Overall, any study which results only in a

statement of numbers is of little use to service planners. Rather, what is required is information on the *implications* of having an older population of a particular size. This requires a much more detailed study yielding information on a whole range of client characteristics, service variables and informal care networks. However, it is important to bear in mind that even detailed information of this kind remains of little use to planners if it is presented simply in terms of categories and frequencies. It is of little use to know that X per cent are suffering from dementia, Y per cent have no living relatives and Z per cent live in a particular form of accommodation. What is needed is an understanding of the ways in which these various factors *interact*. What combinations of client characteristics and family variables are predictive of a change in service needs? How responsive is the overall service to the needs of the client? Does the age of the client affect the provision of services, irrespective of functional level? It is these kinds of questions which future surveys should be addressing. Simply to assess the characteristics of individuals without reference to the social and service context in which they live is to ignore essential dimensions of the total situation which are critical to an understanding of the process of ageing.

3 HEALTH AND PSYCHIATRIC ISSUES

The considerable scope of Chapter 3 is partly a reflection of the importance of physical and mental health to the quality of life of older people, and of the significance of these factors to service provision. In addition, the complexity of the issues relating the general literature to people with mental handicap required thorough discussion. One of the main conclusions to be drawn from the reviews of both physical and mental health is the need for carefully designed studies which would allow accurate comparisons to be made between the needs of elderly people with and without mental handicap. At the present time, the only way to make comparisons is to draw on evidence from various studies which have often employed different criteria for case inclusion, and have relied on retrospective information from medical records. There are at least two types of problem inherent in the use of retrospective information. First, it may not be safe to assume that records are accurate and complete. Second, the actual treatment received by an individual in the past may not give a complete picture of medical or psychiatric status at that time, since there may have been other conditions which went undetected and untreated. The only effective way to get round this problem is to avoid the use of records altogether, relying instead on current assessments carried out under standardised conditions. There are currently no such comparative studies of the physical or mental health of elderly people with and without mental handicap.

An important consideration for future work in these areas is the excessive emphasis which has in the past been given to institutional populations. The temptation to rely on such information is obvious. The population is captive, records are readily available, and referral and diagnosis procedures are roughly equivalent for all residents. On the other hand, the physical and mental health status of people living outside institutions may be very different. Also, one must not forget those people who may have mental handicap but are *unknown* to service providers. How does *their* medical status compare to non-handicapped people, and to people with mental handicap who *are* known to mental handicap services? These important questions can only be answered by surveys which sample the whole range of individuals, not simply those from one residential setting.

Within the field of physical health, the problems inherent in devising appropriate surveys are probably less than those relating to mental health. Diagnostic procedures and criteria for physical conditions are generally well defined, and show a high level of agreement between individual practitioners. On the other hand, psychiatric diagnosis among people with mental handicap presents enormous problems. These difficulties arise partly from the reliance on language for diagnoses, partly from the social definition of mental illness and the fact that people with mental handicap often live very different lives from their non-handicapped peers, and partly because of the ill-defined interaction between behaviour disorders and psychiatric conditions. When considering *older* people with mental handicap, there is the added complication that medical health care systems have tended to give preference to younger people and the treatment of acute rather than chronic conditions. There is obviously a great deal of work to be done in this area; indeed the complexity of these factors suggests it will be many years before clear conclusions will be forthcoming.

3.1 Physical Medicine

Although the amount of hard data relating to the physical medical status of older people with mental handicap is very small there is no shortage of sweeping statements which have appeared in the literature. These either refer to the "special" needs of the older client group, or alternatively suggest that their needs are "no different" from those of the general population. The review presented in Chapter 3 shows quite clearly that current information is insufficient to determine the truth or falseness of either of these views. Even the largest of the available surveys (Janicki and MacEachron, 1984) presents no details of the way in which the information was collected, or of the criteria used for establishing diagnoses. Without this detailed information, tables of frequencies for different types of disorder become impossible to interpret. Indeed, it is salutary to note the widely varying estimates in general surveys with respect to certain disease categories such as musculoskeletal disorders. If any conclusion *can* be stated, it is the tentative statement that there probably are few differences between the physical health status of older people with and without mental handicap. McDonald (1985), however, draws attention to some important exceptions of which carers should be aware. She points out that attention to posture and appropriate exercise, with a general focus on prevention rather than cure, could reduce the high level of orthopaedic problems among those people who are immobile or bed-ridden. Apart from the improved quality of life for the individuals themselves, McDonald shows that the increased level of functioning following appropriate orthopaedic rehabilitation can significantly reduce the cost of caring.

The other group of problems mentioned by McDonald are those relating to respiratory and middle-ear infections. It is clear that every effort should be made to avoid such problems being contracted by people with mental handicap. The very high level of mortality from these causes (see Chapter 2) attests to the importance of doing everything possible to minimise the risk. McDonald suggests that the use of correct posture for feeding and greater assistance from staff where appropriate, could have a significant impact on the level of these problems. The importance of avoiding respiratory infection suggests that urgent attention should be paid to this aspect of management in high-risk groups.

Apart from these two groups of problems, which relate particularly to people with additional physical handicaps, poor mobility and profound handicap, the general conclusion regarding physical health is that there is no marked difference between people with and without mental handicap. In the absence of a specific medical problem there is no reason why an older person with mental handicap should not lead a full and active life. There should certainly be no restriction of activity based on the assumption that physical health may otherwise be impaired.

For future work on the morbidity of older people with mental handicap, there is urgent need to direct efforts not simply to the major disease categories, but also to the major *handicapping* conditions of old age, such as stroke, Parkinson's disease and arthritis. While this has long been of concern in the general population, no survey data exist in relation to people with mental handicap. This obviously partly reflects the small amount of work which has so far been conducted in this area but may also indicate the fact that *additional* handicaps in people with mental handicap have attracted little attention in the past. It seems likely that the increasing independence of people with mental handicap will alter this perception. An older person will, like anyone else, be able to maintain independent living as long as the *combination* of circumstances and problems can be successfully overcome by the combined efforts of the individual and relevant supports.

The presence or absence of age-related infirmity is

obviously a crucial factor in determining the capacity for independence. This suggests two fundamental questions which need to be answered: (a) Do people with mental handicap tend to be equally, or more, susceptible to age-related handicapping conditions than the general population? and (b) how does the ability to cope with the presence of such conditions interact with functional level? In other words, are people with mental handicap more likely to be robbed of their independence in old age than their non-handicapped peers? Again, one is led to the conclusion that the collection of demographic and epidemiological data should be directed not simply to the collection of statistics showing the proportions of people in various categories, but should be attempting to develop models which can highlight the *interactions* between these various factors. How much more useful it will be if we are able to predict, from a knowledge of individual characteristics, available services and informal support networks, the extent to which a person living independently in the community can cope with, for instance, severe arthritis.

3.2 Mental health

Mental health disorders represent one of the greatest burdens in old age, frequently being the precipitating factor which leads to hospitalisation. Unlike physical disorders, the criteria used for the general population and for people with mental handicap are not necessarily the same. Mental illness, apart from conditions whose origin is clearly organic, is essentially socially defined, with the result that factors relating to the individual's environment and to the "pathway" by which professional care is gained, become very important. As a result, the comparison of psychiatric problems in elderly people with and without mental handicap is made difficult by the very different life styles of these two groups.

Elderly non-handicapped people appear to suffer from at least as many psychiatric disorders as younger individuals, but receive fewer services. This is possibly because older people are reluctant to seek help, although this reluctance may partly result from the feeling that medical service staff are less interested in the problems of ageing. Dementia and depression, the two main age-related conditions, are likely to go undetected, with the result that random surveys of mental illness show far higher rates than surveys based on treatment episodes. Depressive symptoms are found in about 20 per cent of elderly people, often relating to specific life events such as loss of spouse, failing health and loss of independence. Dementia, a condition often leading to eventual hospitalisation, is found at a clinical level in up to 5.8 per cent of people over 65 years of age.

Elderly people with mental handicap show even lower referral rates than non-handicapped individuals. This is no doubt related partly to factors which are unrelated to ageing. These include the perception and expectation of psychiatric disorder by caregivers, the containment of problem behaviours in institutional settings, and the lack of peer group advice to seek treatment. The fact that this reduction in referral rates with age mirrors that found in the general population may be spurious. In older non-handicapped people there is probably a cohort effect, in that people brought up in the earlier part of the century sometimes have a pride which prevents then seeking advice from a physician. In addition, there may be a reluctance to accept that one's health and independence are failing, or a fear that one may be stigmatised for having a mental disorder. In people with mental handicap, the evidence presented in Chapter 3 suggests that a reducing level of severe problem behaviours with age is partly responsible for the reduction in observed prevalence. This serves as a reminder of Goldberg and Huxley's (1980) finding that disorders having a high "nuisance" value are more likely to be detected, while disorders such as dementia and depression are more likely to go unnoticed.

As with any ageing population, people with mental handicap show an increasing prevalence of dementia. Despite the vast literature on the relation between Down's syndrome and Alzheimer's disease, however, it is certainly not the case that all people over the age of 40 with the former condition will start to dement. Indeed, the information relating to the prevalence of *clinical* symptoms is very sparse. This is an area which certainly demands detailed examination in the future.

From a diagnostic point of view, dementia is easier to detect than many other conditions in people with mental handicap, due to the fact that a cognitive *decline* over a period of time can be measured in people whose original cognitive level was already quite low. In one sense, a positive diagnosis of dementia is of no comfort to anyone, since the condition is incurable. Also, planning future service needs is not made a great deal easier by the knowledge, since the time course of the disease is unpredictable. On the other hand, if the person turns out to be suffering from a condition which is *not* dementia, a condition which may actually respond to treatment, then it is important to establish this fact as early as possible. Drug toxicity effects, for instance, can sometimes produce a confusional state which is not unlike that seen in dementia.

Depression, the other main mental affliction of old age, is less reliably detected in people with mental handicap. This is a condition in which environmental and social factors play a large part. Loss of friends or spouse, and failing health are all contributory factors which increase the likelihood of a depressive episode. The evidence presented in Chapter 3 indicates that a great many older people suffer from pervasive depression, particularly if they have lost some of their independence. For many people with mental handicap, some of these contributory factors, particularly those relating to loss of social role, are not related to age in the same way as the general population. Many of these people have suffered these disadvantages *all* their lives, not just in old age. What is not clear, however, is whether this fact increases the chances of depression in the earlier years among people with mental handicap, or whether it is the *sudden* change of circumstances in old age which is liable to trigger a depressive episode. In either event, it is important to remain vigilant to the possibility of depression occurring in people with mental handicap.

In general terms, the main implication for professional carers and families is the importance of considering the *possibility* of a psychiatric disorder in a person with mental handicap. As with any individual, it is a *change* in the established personality or day-to-day functioning which is usually the first sign. It is for this reason that individuals who know the person closely, family, friends or immediate professional carers, who are usually the first to notice the problem. When in doubt, it is wise to seek professional advice. Research on the complex pathway to psychiatric care suggests that many people with mental handicap may never be referred for genuine psychiatric conditions. The main way in which this situation will be improved is to increase general awareness of the possibility of mental illness in people with mental handicap. Appropriate training of GPs, direct care staff, social workers and psychologists is particularly important in this respect. There is also a need to provide adequate training of psychiatrists in the field of mental handicap. Some posts have now been set up to provide a psychiatric service specific to this client group, an approach which tends to be supported by the Royal College of Psychiatrists (Reid, 1982). This ensures a clear focus on the particular needs of people with mental handicap, although it could be argued that this is contrary to the philosophy of treating these individuals as far as possible within normal service provision. Such issues will no doubt become clearer as our knowledge of the area becomes more comprehensive.

4 INTELLIGENCE AND ADAPTIVE BEHAVIOUR

The assessment of intelligence in people with mental handicap has become increasingly unfashionable in recent years. The rejection of such assessment has reflected a wider concern with the abuse of classificatory procedures and with labelling based on classification. (See Hogg and Mittler 1980 for a brief review of this critical position.) Criticism of intelligence testing, classification and labelling jointly reflect two possible outcomes of these procedures that are deemed not in the interest of the person with mental handicap. First, the classification of individuals on the basis of an intelligence quotient has been employed prescriptively, i.e. has been used to allot individuals to particular forms of service provision. The global nature of an IQ assessment is inappropriate for such a prescriptive purpose, failing as it does to differentiate strengths and weakness in competence or predict future performance with any accuracy. Second, the IQ score arising has tended to suggest some invariant property of the person assessed, failing to take into account the fact that an individual's behaviour, as we argued in Chapter 5, reflects ecological determinants in interaction with that person's competence.

Nevertheless, acceptance of these arguments does not mean that the assessment of IQ in the field of mental handicap is valueless, only that caution must be exercised in the use we make of this information. Berger and Yule (1987) have argued that such tests have an important part to play in contributing to the diagnosis of mental handicap in conjunction with other information on social adjustment and developmental history. Detterman (1987) has recently noted that 100 years ago it was not possible to differentiate people with mental handicap from those with mental illness, and that the possibility of reliably classifying people with mental handicap has been a major achievement of psychometrics. They also have an important scientific function with respect to defining population for the purposes of epidemiological and demographic research, as we have seen. As Detterman notes, "No phenomenon can be scientifically studied unless it can be reliably indentified." (p.2).

To these uses, then, we can add the part that such assessment can play in scientific studies of the nature of intelligence in people with mental handicap generally, and more specifically the processes of ageing in people in this population. In our review of the limited literature on this latter topic in Chapter 4, we noted that our knowledge was limited relative to the wider literature on ageing. An over emphasis on institutional populations and on the use of Stanford-Binet test has failed to yield a comparable body of literature to that developed on the population at large. This should not suprise us, as even in the relatively well-researched area of development of children with mental handicap the literature is small compared to published studies of development in non-handicapped children. However, we concur with Detterman (1987) that there is a need for a scientifically valid general theory of intellectual functioning in mental handicap, and we would argue that is an essential prerequisite to a theory of intellectual ageing in this population. Indeed, through the study of age-related changes in older people with mental handicap some contribution to this understanding could be made. Such an undertaking would guide choice of measurement instruments which would embrace appropriate tests permitting different components of intelligence to be distinguished and choice of experimental assessments focusing on specific processes. It has come as something of a suprise to us to find that there are virtually no well designed experimental studies of this population concerned with learning, memory and information processing.

We concluded in Chapter 4 that existing evidence on changes in intelligence in ageing people with mental handicap was generally a cause for optimism. Intellectual functioning advances through a substantial proportion of the life-span and, in the absence of organic conditions, should show decrements only relatively late in life. In so far as the evidence permits the conclusion, the picture is similar to that found in the wider population. In Chapter 5 we observed that such a state of affairs makes continued life-span education as viable a possibility for people with mental handicap as for their non-handicapped peers.

The development of objective measures of adaptive behaviour in part reflected the need for assessment instruments related to observable competence in everyday tasks rather than the more abstract processes of which the IQ is a reflection. As with intelligence tests, however, the use of adaptive behaviour assessment instruments should also be used in conjunction with other forms of assessment (Raynes 1987). Such assessment bears directly on a variety of practical concerns with respect to the social competence of individuals with mental handicap, though the scientific usefulness of the concepts of adaptation and competence have recently received some critical comment (Zigler, Balla and Hodapp (1984). From the point of view of our present purpose, however, such instruments have shown, even in institutionalised populations, that throughout most of the life-course competence in a variety of key areas defined by the dimensions of personal self-sufficiency, community self-sufficiency and personal-social responsibility continues to advance. As with progressive increases in IQ, such a state of affairs bodes well for the extent to which older people with mental handicap can benefit from intervention and adjust to life in the community. Such adjustment is likely to be enhanced by the decreasing prevalence of behaviour problems as people with mental handicap age. Against this optimistic picture we can now turn to specific interventions in their own right (Section 5) and the wider ecological issues raised by day services (Section 6) and residential services (Section 7) which constitute wider intervention contexts.

5 PSYCHOTHERAPEUTIC AND EDUCATIONAL INTERVENTION

We have emphasised in this book an ecological perspective on the processes of ageing in people with mental handicap, noting with Gatz *et al.* (1985), that there is as yet no coherent theory integrating life-span developmental theory and models of psychological and behavioural change. An ecological view implies that provision in any area of a person's life is in some sense interventional in character. Thus, making appropriate day and residential services available will condition in a very direct way a person's view of his or her own life and the kind of behaviour engaged in. In Chapter 5, however, we focused more directly on what might be termed programmatic intervention of a psychotherapeutic and behavioural sort.

It is significant that in emphasising the extent to which care in the community involves a total change in approach to service delivery, the Audit Commission (1986) draws attention to the importance of possibly the most significant factor i.e. improvement in the techniques through which the basic skills of daily living are taught. In considering such intervention, we noted that information would be drawn from both the field of ageing and that of work with people with mental handicap in the younger (under 50) age-range. Both these lines of research emphasise an optimistic view with respect to the possibility of change. In the former case, ageing is not seen as an inevitable process of decline, while the possibility of behavioural, affective and cognitive growth throughout the life-span is seen as the consequence of providing beneficial environments and suitable programmes of intervention for people with mental handicap. Such views, of course, are in large measure confirmed by the psychometric and adaptive behaviour literature reviewed in Chapter 4. Commentators on these perspectives contrast the optimism generated by this interventional stance with the pessimism of a purely biomedical view of growth and decline and the nihilism of staff attitudes associated with this view.

Our review showed, however, that the psychotherapeutic literature concerned with ageing was relatively underdeveloped theoretically and despite recent interest little applied in the area of ageing and mental handicap. It also showed that there was very little intersection between the growing literature of behavioural gerontology and the extensive body of behavioural studies in the field of mental handicap. There is then, considerable scope for both the provider of services and the research worker to advance this intersection by drawing on both fields in the context of older people with mental handicap.

Certain caveats were noted, however. The larger proportion of work in the field of behavioural gerontology has focused on remediating the adverse consequences of congregate care through the re-establishment of contact with the environment and lost behavioural competencies. While in some instances the institutionalisation of people with mental handicap will have resulted in loss of existing skills, we surmise that the major consequence has been that the development of competence has been inhibited by the social and physical deprivation of the setting. Rather than utilising the specific techniques described there is a more important lesson to be learnt from the field of behavioural gerontology. This is the extent to which even apparently benign environments can, because of their social and physical structure, be detrimental to a person's development. The work of Baltes, Hussian and other innovators in this area demonstrate the importance of viewing intervention in relation to a close analysis of the ecology of the person. There is little point in teaching skills that will not be maintained by natural contingencies in the environment, while an excess of support can unwittingly increase dependency. A further caveat concerned the extrapolation of approaches from younger people with mental handicap, particularly children, to the over 50s. We argued that information from such work was critical for people working with this older group, but that all techniques should be viewed in relation to the differences in circumstances and characteristics of such people. With respect to circumstances we emphasised the need to ensure that choice was exercised by the client wherever possible with respect to participation and also that gerontologically relevant information should be incorporated in the programme. Hussian and Davis' (1985) book gives much information on this synthesis, and we will deal with its relevance to staff training below.

With respect to psychotherapeutic work, we noted possible differences in the lives of some older mentally handicapped people and their non-handicapped peers. For the former, particularly those who have spent many years in institutions, the past may not have been defined and punctuated with salient events as is the case for most of us. Assisting such people to achieve such a history is potentially a worthwhile goal, and one which some professionals are now attempting to achieve. However, there is clearly a need for theoretical and methodological analysis if such aims are to be achieved retrospectively. We also noted that professionals should show some caution in assuming that clients have *not* achieved *some* concept of the course of their own lives. Prospectively, a more normalised life in the community should be sufficient remediation for this situation, though this can be enhanced through encouraging the collection of photographs, memorabilia and the writing of diaries (e.g. Blom-Cooper 1985).

Limited though the information is on psychological intervention with older people with mental handicap, the dearth of studies on education for this group is still greater. For this part of the review we drew on Willis' (1985) definition of education as refering to lifelong learning as form of adaptation, a definition highly relevant to the population with which this book is concerned. We also followed Looft (1973) in emphasising that such learning could be not only intellectual, but also aesthetic and emotional. Our own review of the literature on education, ageing and mental handicap confirmed the finding of Stroud *et al.* (1984)

that there are no studies on the acquisition of basic academic skills such as reading, writing and arithmetic in this population, nor have we found any curricula developed with specific awareness of the gerontological and age-related factors that are relevant to this group. We did point out, however, that there would be continuity with the educational curricula developed for younger adults. The starting point for education and the sources to be drawn on would, however, also be conditioned by the level and pattern of disability and examples of different curriculum sources were suggested.

We would like to suggest that, building on existing curriculum models, educators and those responsible for community provision address the issues of: (a) how such models may be modified to meet the educational needs of people with mental handicap as they age; (b) that the appropriateness of the materials involved should be analysed; commendable though it may be that an older person is, for the first time learning to read, the use of primary school readers cannot be regarded as the most acceptable way of acquiring this skill; (c) how far specifically gerontological factors influence the form and content of education; (d) the use of community resources with respect to further education (e.g. Adult Education Colleges, Community Colleges; (e) the use of volunteers to act as teachers; (f) to what extent such education can be undertaken in contexts in which there is no age and/or ability segregation.

Within such an educational model the weight given to these factors in interaction with differing levels of ability and additional impairments would have to be determined. We concluded Section 3 of Chapter 5 by noting that a full survey of the initiatives that are undoubtedly being developed would yield information that would be of considerable value in providing a basis for this exercise.

The Audit Commission's (1986) report has emphasised that staff are the key resource for community care, and that for them effective training is essential. While a variety of specialists will be involved in both individual psychotherapy, behavioural programmes and education, we considered in Chapter 5 the issue of staff training for other professions concerned with the day to day delivery of services. Here, the ecological model is of prime importance, as no one should any longer be under the illusion that staff-training in the form of teaching limited skills will inevitably lead to behaviour change by the trainee. To illustrate the complexity of the determinants of effective staff behaviour we cited Landesman-Dwyer and Knowles (1987) recent discussion on this topic. This position is acknowledged in an important paper by Barrowclough and Fleming (1986a) concerned with teaching staff goal-planning for older people in a variety of community settings. We outlined a number of critical factors they identified with respect to successful implementation of learned skills, specifically with regard to continuity of intervention across different settings and assessment and monitoring as the basis of multidisciplinary collaboration. We noted that the relevance of Barrowclough and Fleming's staff training programme to people working with older individuals with mental handicap was clear, and the adaptation of their approach would be a welcome move forward with respect to staff training for those working with this client group. We noted, somewhat ironically, that in a recent review of staff training in the area of gerontology by Burgio (1987), most of the evidence he found to draw on actually came from the mental handicap rather than gerontological field.

As in the wider area of gerontology, however, it is important at this stage of service development for older people with mental handicap to note that staff training must go well beyond the teaching of specific intervention skills. Cotten, Britt and Moreland (1986) have a substantially more all-embracing view of what should be involved in staff training in providing services for older people with mental handicap. Here, the findings of a task force established to develop services for elderly people with mental handicap living in Mississippi are reported. Among the recommendations offered are:

(a) For those involved in making specialised provision training in normal ageing and mental health should be available;

(b) Joint training of those providing mental handicap services and mental health services should be undertaken. Clear areas of concern would be those of depression and

dementia;
(c) Training for those providing generic services (i.e. not mental handicap specialists) in the nature and special difficulties entailed in the process and consequences of ageing for a person with mental handicap;
(d) Training in use of functional assessments and utilisation of the information in programme planning;
(e) Training in effective treatment plans, an approach that clearly would draw upon the kind of emerging information we have described in this chapter;
(f) Broadly philosophical training to counteract the myths associated with ageing and mental handicap and the stereotyping of people in both groups;
(g) Information on medication, particularly with respect to monitoring its effects and the abuse of polypharmacy;
(h) Sensitivity training in order to recognise and cope with concerns and conflicts in the lives of older people with mental handicap;
(i) Training in the utilisation of statutory and voluntary services and resources in the community.

It is interesting to note that, in line with our own observations on the role of the church in Oldham (Chapter 1), a similar emphasis is placed on its importance in Cotten *et al.*'s report on Mississippi and Stroud *et al.*'s (1984) on North-Eastern Ohio. Indeed, much of the literature from the USA refers to the pastoral role of churches in providing a focus for and support to older people with mental handicap.

This summary is by no means exhaustive. It does however point to the breadth of training that staff will require, either as individuals or in teams, to provide a full and effective service for older people with mental handicap, and to the sources through which the development of training will proceed. Within the framework of services in England and Wales, Mittler (1987) has described a variety of strategies with respect to training staff working with people with mental handicap. It is beyond the scope of this review to relate the wide range of professional groups covered by Mittler to the various training needs identified above. However, certain broad service contexts should be noted in which appropriate staff training with respect to this specific population should be offered.

First, we have seen that a substantial number of

older people with mental handicap reside in long-stay hospitals though many will be making the move to the community in the coming years. To meet the need for new learning a number of key professions working in the National Health Service are to be given update training, the Health 'PICK-UP' scheme developed by the National Health Service Training Authority (NHSTA) in collaboration with the Department of Education and Science. The training will be modular and it is to be hoped that a module dealing specifically with the special needs of older people with mental handicap will be incorporated.

With the change in role implied by the move from Adult Training Centres to Social Education Centres we would hope that initiatives will be taken by staff and advisors in these Centres to enhance the knowledge of staff with respect to this client group and how its needs can best be met. Particular consideration needs to be given to the wider ecology of community living and its implications for course content. A specific issue of some importance has been raised by Grant (1985) who asks whether the content of training and teaching in these establishments is relevant to the needs of middle-aged and older people with mental handicap who are living at home. He asks whether training for independence should make some room for training for *inter*dependence, and whether this would give people more opportunities to contribute to their families' livelihood and accord them a more valued role.

Attendance at an ATC/SEC can be complemented by involvement in appropriate educational courses elsewhere. At present, the development of a curriculum is taking place in the Further Education and Community Colleges who are catering for adults with mental handicap. Again, staff would benefit from gaining a clearer picture of the life-span development of people with mental handicap and the consequences of ageing in later life.

The recent success of the Open University's *"Patterns of Living"* course also suggests that distance learning can play a part in enhancing the knowledge of professional staff, unqualified helpers, volunteers and family members. Consideration is at present being given to a second phase of this course in which specific consideration would be given to the topic of ageing and mental handicap.

The Audit Commission (1986) report emphasises the extent to which cost-effective and flexible services can be evolved by collaboration between statutory services and voluntary organisations. Age Concern, the principal voluntary organisation concerned with older people generally, is at present taking the first steps to develop a training programme for its own volunteers dealing with older people with mental handicap. It is to be hoped that the content and framework developed are used widely to inform both voluntary and statutory staff on how best to meet the needs of older people with mental handicap.

It will be apparent that our consideration of staff training has broadened considerably beyond the immediate issues raised in our review of psychological and educational intervention. This, however, is essential if we are to convey the scope of staff training needs in the various environments in which older people with mental handicap spend their later years. It should be borne in mind in the following sections on day and residential services and on the support of families in the home that staff training in a full spectrum of skills and tasks is called for.

6 DAY SERVICES

The sociological literature relating to retirement has examined in considerable detail the factors affecting the decision to retire, notably health, social interaction and economics. Chapter 6 attempted to map the findings from this work on to the needs of people with mental handicap, a task which is made difficult by the fact that, for many of these people, the relative contributions of these various factors will be considerably different from those in the lives of most people. It was suggested, however, that for those people retiring from open employment the general literature is more directly applicable. If the person's employment has been confined to ATC/SEC then the financial component of the decision becomes relatively insignificant. Naturally, a mandatory retirement policy on the part of Social

Services may, as with members of the population working in open employment, force an unwilling decision to retire on the individual.

Each of the three main factors influencing the decision to retire has a major impact on quality of life after retirement. Health, as noted above, is, for most older people with mental handicap similar to that of the general population. Finance, where a private income is not available, is restricted to statutory benefits and cannot, therefore, be enhanced significantly by service providers, whether statutory or voluntary. In addition, where Supplementary Benefit is available, means testing will result in deductions against accommodation charges when the individual's savings are in excess of £3000. This leaves the area of social interaction, and indeed leisure in general, as the chief area to which retirement services have been directed. Such efforts have taken three basic forms. First, increasing access to services already available on a general basis to elderly people is one way of enhancing leisure and social opportunities for people with mental handicap at relatively little cost. Ohio University's ACCESS project is a highly developed example of this kind of project. Second, a number of mental handicap services are offering pre-retirement courses. Third, a number of Day Centres have been set up to cater specifically for the needs of older clients. There seems no reason to take issue with the first of these approaches. Increasing contact with general services can only be of benefit to people with mental handicap, both by ensuring meetings between people with mental handicap and their non-handicapped peers, and by widening the range of available leisure options. The approach is consistent with integration within the community and offers the most normalised approach to service provision for older people. It does seem, however, that the other two approaches need some further examination. The existence of a well thought out retirement policy must be of benefit to clients, and it does appear at face value that the provision of pre-retirement courses and Older Day Centres is an expression of such a policy. On the other hand, it is important to evaluate the true impact of these efforts, rather than simply to measure the extent to which they conform to a model of good service provision. Such evaluation is made difficult by the fact that ongoing philosophies of care tend to hold great sway, independently of information concerning their effectiveness. Nevertheless, the synthesis of information from the general literature and from the mental handicap field does indicate that a number of tentative conclusions may be drawn.

6.1 Pre-retirement Courses

Research from the general literature suggests that the impact of such courses is probably confined to the short-term imparting of information. This point needs to be borne in mind when planning courses for older people with mental handicap. It is perhaps profitable to use such an approach as a way to introduce the client to activities and social opportunities in the wider community. This was the approach adopted by Haines (1986), in which she organised activities involved with the Church, Local Library and Luncheon Club. Cheseldine (1987), however, is hoping that the impact of her pre-retirement course will extend beyond this level of imparting information. She hopes to demonstrate, in addition, a measured increase in the level of social interaction between the group members. To evaluate the extent to which this aim is achieved, she intends to monitor interaction via the use of videotapes throughout the period of a complete course, and subsequently to analyse the data for significant changes. We look forward to the results of this research.

One general problem in providing pre-retirement courses to people with mental handicap is the difficulty in presenting the course in such a way that it is distinguishable from other aspects of training which constitute part of general day service provision. This problem may arise because so many clients have received day services all their lives that they are unaccustomed to the idea that the course is designed partly to *increase independence* as preparation for the future. As a result of this confusion, it is sometimes difficult to wean people off the course once they have started. Cheseldine (1987), for instance, described her attempts to make the group self-functioning. After a number of meetings it was agreed that the group would meet alternately at the

Centre and at the flat of one group member. The plan was for the private meetings eventually to take over completely. In the event this did not work out, partly due to the fact that the women were reluctant to go to a man's flat without a chaperone, and subsequently because the man who owned the flat suffered a bereavement. It was shortly after this that the group broke up completely.

Overall, the evidence for the benefits of pre-retirement courses is equivocal. Future research in this area needs to demonstrate clearly that this is a profitable direction in which to develop services.

6.2 Day Centres for Older Adults

As with the conclusion regarding the usefulness of pre-retirement courses, there is a need for research to demonstrate that Day Centres for Older Adults represent a good direction for service developments to proceed. A number of fundamental questions need to be asked: (a) Are there clear distinctions between the activities preferred by older and younger clients, (b) if so, are these better provided in separate Centres, (c) is there a sufficiently large number of people who would rather attend an age-segregated facility?

In our visits to segregated day facilities it was notable that the kinds of activities were not really distinguishable from those in an ATC/SEC, apart from the chronic *lack* of activity in *one* Day Centre described. The fact that there is no difference may partly reflect the fact that these centres were set up for administrative reasons, rather than being based on a specific philosphy guiding the form provision takes. There is a need for these issues to be clearly defined as a prerequisite to the development of segregated Day Provision. In addition, there is a need to evaluate the impact of such Centres on client functioning and the extent to which they reflect the wishes of those people who attend them. Is segregated provision the best approach? What activities should be provided? What about those people who prefer to attend an ATC? Wolfensberger (1985) suggests a similar set of questions to address in order to avoid the devaluation to which the lives of older people with mental handicap are so often subjected.

7 RESIDENTIAL ENVIRONMENTS

Characteristics of the residential environment are central to the individual's ecology, and must therefore be a crucial consideration in service planning. The work reviewed in Chapter 7 shows how strong can be the effect of the environment on the individual. Placement of a person in an appropriate setting can have a beneficial effect, leading to improved functioning and a possible move towards further independence. Inappropriate placement can restrict stimulation to an excessive degree for the person's functional level, with a resulting demoralisation and consequent reduction in adaptive behaviour.

The available information relating specifically to older people with mental handicap is mainly survey data. These studies indicate the proportions of people living in various types of setting and the characteristics of the treatment regime. Such information is useful in giving an overall view of the current situation, but gives little help in directing the planning of improved residential services for the future. In this respect there is a need for an objective appraisal of the policies responsible for the placement of older people in specific types of residential provision. Such an appraisal needs to be developed along two fundamental axes: first, the age-related changes which have inescapable consequences for planners in terms of increased need for service support, including changes in physical and mental health (reviewed in Chapter 3) and IQ and adaptive functioning (reviewed in Chapter 4), and second, the whole range of factors which, certainly in the general population, makes most older people desire *different* residential characteristics than younger individuals.

The first of these axes has direct and theoretically predictable consequences for staffing levels. Some people with mental handicap will, as they age, become more reliant on service support, and may eventually need to move to a more intensively staffed environment. Naturally, services must be able to respond to such needs, although it has been stressed that it is important to maintain a balance between the need for support and the need for stimulation. The right balance will help to enhance functioning, rather than allowing it to decline.

The second of these axes is more difficult to appraise in terms of changes in level of support, although it does seem likely that a greater focus on the personal choices of older people will have resource implications.

In general, most elderly people do not live with a group of young adults, but tend to live alone, with a spouse, with their family, or in a congregate care setting with people of a similar age. Maybe older people *would* live with young adults if this were a common option in society, although there is little indication that many people would take up such an option if available.

In contrast, many older people with mental handicap *do* live with younger individuals to whom they are not related. This sometimes comes about through the implementation of a specific policy on age integration. It may also occur because the choice of companions, following relocation from a hospital, is limited. Such limitations come about for a variety of reasons, including (a) a requirement that each resident must return to the District of origin, (b) the fact that there are few combinations of people who can live successfully together in a close residential situation.

There is certainly no clear evidence that age-integrated residential settings are harmful or even undesired. On the other hand, there is no evidence that this is what older people with mental handicap would necessarily choose. A real increase in the level of choice available to older people is therefore an important consideration in planning future services. There are two fundamental avenues along which this effort should be directed. First, a wide range of residential options should be made available. These options should extend not just to the type of accommodation, e.g house, flat, group home, hostel etc., but should permit choice concerning the age range of the other residents. Some people may, for instance, prefer to live in a hostel specifically for older people, rather than in a fully age-integrated residence.

The second of these avenues is to increase the clients's *genuine* influence on the overall choice of location, within the general principles of self advocacy. In this respect, it is particularly important not to adhere to policies such as "houses are good, hostels are bad".

There is nothing sacrosanct about the house as a living unit. Some people may actually prefer the support and community feel of a hostel, while other will welcome the challenge of a greater degree of independence. Overall, we have a long way to go towards genuine self advocacy for people with mental handicap. The development of such self expression may, in the future, give a much clearer lead to the planners of residential accommodation for older people with mental handicap than is currently available.

Any comparison between the literature on relocation of older people with and without mental handicap is made difficult by the fact that the wider literature is mainly concerned with the moving of very elderly or infirm people to accommodation offering greater support e.g. independent living to sheltered housing, or independent living to hospital. There is no doubt that, for people with mental handicap who have failing health or functioning, such a move may also be called for and lessons from the wider literature can be drawn. Specifically, there is some evidence of increased mortality and pessimism about health in cases where change is radical and involuntary. Sometimes, of course, change of this sort is necessary due to the individual's failing abilities to maintain an independent life. In such cases it is important to ensure as much continuity as possible from the old environment to the new, a difficult objective if the old person is moving to congregate care or hospital after a lifetime of independence. In such cases the emphasis must be upon smoothing the transition through counselling and support.

Most studies of relocation in people with mental handicap, in contrast to the general literature, have concentrated on resettlement in the community following hospital closure. Here, the client age is usually much lower than in the studies discussed above, and the relocation is more related to a change in the philosophy of care, rather than as a direct result of changes in individual needs. In these studies the evidence is fairly clear that age has little relation to subsequent adjustment. Those negative effects which *have* been observed indicate an interaction between health and level of handicap. People in poor health and with a profound level of handicap do appear to be at some risk during relocation, a finding which confirms the suggestion of Lazarus (1966) that people with the lowest level of resources to cope are in greatest danger. Staff on Oldham's relocation programme (see Chapter 1), for instance, told us of one individual whose epilepsy recurred following relocation from hospital to community, although he had previously been free from fits for many years. People in this at-risk category should have extra care taken in preparation for relocation, and in the subsequent support given after the move.

Findings from studies of adjustment following community relocation are very mixed. McCarver and Craig (1974) reviewed a series of studies, and reported 11 to have demonstrated improved adjustment following relocation, 5 showing a deterioration and 10 showing no difference. Interpretation of such studies is made difficult by the evidence that the choice of relocation residence suffers from an age bias, at least in the USA where the main studies have been carried out. This again points to the need for an equivalent UK survey.

Ideally, services should respond appropriately to the needs of the client alone in determining the appropriate residential choice. Age *per se* should play no part in this choice. An age bias in this respect is particularly pernicious in that it can rob the person of independence unnecessarily, and hence lead to a loss of functional skills rather than a gain. The fact that many non-handicapped older people are put in this position is no reason to adopt it as a model of good practice. In such cases, Wolfensberger (1985) suggests that we should be "Valorising" the person's role, rather than "Normalising" it, i.e. raising it *above* the current expectations for the general population rather than simply matching them. Of all the service planning issues which have been raised in this book, this is one which should be relatively easy to redress. Suitable research on client characteristics and residential choice will expose any age bias, which can subsequently be rectified.

8 INFORMAL NETWORKS AND FAMILY LIFE

In Chapter 8, we noted that, with respect to informal social networks involving people other than relatives, many adults with mental handicap fare somewhat poorly. Where friendships are formed, these appear to be related more to the characteristics of environments rather than individuals, though people with relatively less disability tend to form more intense friendships than their more disabled peers (Landesman-Dwyer, Berkson and Romer (1979). Similarly, Flynn (1988) makes the point that the quality of the neighbourhood will in some measure influence the quality of social relations. Indeed, her own work exposed some individuals living in extreme isolation and with very unsatisfactory relations with their neighbours. The work of Edgerton clearly shows how critical the role of other, non-family members, is in enabling adults with mental handicap to cope with life in the community. When we bear in mind Seltzer's (1985) point that most older people with mental handicap will not have their own adult children to depend on, the potential for isolation with its debilitating consequences cannot be underestimated.

We noted that many people as they approach their later years engage in anticipatory socialisation in which they prepare the social ground for the future. Lack of cognitive and social competence can preclude any such preparation by people with mental handicap, resulting in a decreasing support network as circumstances, e.g. retirement from work or ATC, change.

From the points of view of both statutory and voluntary provision there are clearly two ways forward to ensure that informal networks develop and are maintained. First, much of the provision we have described in Chapters 5, 6 and 7 will offer natural contexts in which friendships can be formed. The more integrated such provision is, the greater the probability of forming relationships with peers of a similar age, whether mentally handicapped or not. Indeed, age-level has been urged in the wider literature on ageing (e.g. Looft 1973) and would also enhance the possibility of younger non-handicapped people befriending older people with mental handicap. Second, having established a natural ecology in which relationships can form spontaneously, more direct intervention can be initiated to strengthen these relationships either through devising situations that have this outcome or through appropriate programmes. We described in Chapter 5 one extreme of this continuum of intervention with respect to programmes devised to enhance interaction (Section 3.2.2.1). The creation of these conditions represents a particularly important challenge to service providers, given the number of factors which come together to preclude the maintenance of informal social networks for older people with mental handicap.

With respect to family support, it will be recalled that in Chapter 8 we loosened our criterion for inclusion in this review by considering individuals who in the main were under 50, and still living in the family home. We would justify this by arguing first, that any consideration of ageing in the population of people with mental handicap would be incomplete without taking into account the wider family as it, too, ages, and second, that so far as the future is concerned, it is this group who will increasingly be presenting itself to service providers in the community.

Generalisations regarding recommendations with respect to this group should, however, only be made with considerable caution. As one of the parents in Cooke's (1987) study said when asked for recommendations for helping older families, it obviously depends on the individual needs and circumstances of the parents and sons and daughters involved; heterogeneity of families must be acknowledged both with respect to the current home lives of older families and with regard to their future plans. What can be said, then, first of home life with an older member with mental handicap, and second with respect to future plans?

8.1 Home Life

It is clear from several studies that many older families *are* coping at home, and in many respects, coping successfully. Two major suggestions arising from the studies reviewed in Chapter 8 may assist service providers to enhance such coping still further. First, more information should be offered to parents. This should be done, however, in a non-intrusive fashion leaving the parents to utilise the information in whatever way they choose and to whatever extent they choose. In this way threat to, or disturbance of, the coping system will be avoided. Information on availability of services, benefits, aids and adaptations to the house, and availability of short term care, are areas identified as being of particular significance. Further information on the possible effects of ageing on people with mental handicap would be of value in many instances. The concern expressed by parents of sons or daughters with Down's syndrome regarding the possibility of Alzheimer's disease is one specific area where information would be valued. Any misapprehension that this disease will inevitably be contracted should be disabused. Clearly, this will entail professionals themselves ensuring that they are appropriately briefed on this condition.

Second, we must address the role of the family in relation to other, secondary, informal social networks. We noted in Chapter 8 that the increasing age of the parents can have a limiting effect on the social life of some of the sons and daughters, a situation that will be exacerbated the more insular and isolated the family is. In a real sense the benefits of having successfully maintained their son or daughter in the community will be offset by such isolation. If friendships and supportive networks for sons and daughters are to be built up before their parents die, then those working with the families will have not only to encourage parents to allow their sons and daughters to become involved in activities where social encounters can take place, but will also have to ensure that provision acceptable to parents and their offspring is available. Ideally we are looking to the establishment of secondary networks that will complement the professional input when parents are no longer able to cope.

8.2 Future Plans

While it is obvious that individual families must make the decisions about future plans, service providers need to know how they can help parents and sons and daughters plan and prepare for the move from home. Richardson and Ritchie (1986) suggest that there are two main areas of intervention, one related to the nature of available provision, the other to the help which might be given to families to ease the process of transition.

The literature suggests that both parental age and socio-economic class influence parents' approach to preparation for the future. There is a need for intervention with middle-aged parents in this area long before the issue of ageing becomes too salient. Young adults with mental handicap living at home today are growing up with more scope for independence and choice, e.g. attendance at college in preference to an ATC, more opportunities for leisure and increased availability of short term care. There is more encouragement to leave home before a crisis occurs, and leaving home is more likely to be seen as a "natural" progression through which most young adults go. With their increased contact with services, younger parents are also more likely to accept a professional input on these issues than those who are older. Therefore, intervention with younger parents about future planning can start early and be conducted consistently.

Research suggests that it is unlikely that most older parents will want their sons and daughters to move from the family home before they die. It is also difficult to know how far parents can make plans in the present climate of cutbacks and change. However, there are two main areas in which they can be given help: planning and information. A possible medium for the former is "parent groups" for older parents, the content varying according to the needs of the group. Visiting speakers could give information on a variety of topics including that of coping with old age. Cooke (1987) found evidence that parents obtained much support and encouragement from other parents also in their own situation. It is possible that having members of the group who had made difficult decisions about the future, possibly even seeing their offspring leave home and settle into a new residence, might help others to engage in planning. A disadvantage of the groups, however, might be that some parents would find that they had issues forced on them, in which case some degree of mediation by a professional participant would be of value.

Richardson and Ritchie (1986) suggest that, as with information about caring at home, any guidance offered regarding future planning should be both accessible and be given to parents over a long period of time. Parents sometimes feel guilty about even approaching the issues, let alone acting on them. Evidence from Cooke's (1987) study suggests that parents want to be asked about their plans. A number of people had not talked about important future planning with their social worker, yet when asked in the context of a research interview were prepared to talk at great length on the subject. With respect to future arrangements, information and support should be given on all aspects of planning, i.e. legal, financial and residential. It should present parents with the range of available service and residential options and help them to assess the alternatives. Wolverhampton Social Services Department (1982) has prepared such a guide for parents detailing all these issues.

With respect to legal advice, which is of course intimately bound up with the issue of future financial provision, it is essential that this is offered to parents in an informed and intelligible way. As our review made clear, in studies in both the USA (e.g. Warren and Mulcahey 1984) and the UK (e.g. Cooke 1987), a substantial proportion of parents have little knowledge in this area and have as yet made no legal provision for their son or daughter. It is essential that professionals familiarise themselves with legal issues and can put families in touch with members of the legal profession who are knowledgeable with resect to disability and law. Though now requiring some revision, we would suggest that all those concerned with families with a member with mental handicap should study Sanctuary's (1984) excellent book on this subject. In addition, it should be noted that the Royal Society for Mentally Handicapped Children and Adults (MENCAP) provides advice through its legal department while the British Institute of Mental Handicap has produced a reading list on the subject. The issue of legal provision for older people with mental handicap requires systematic study, and is being addressed in an ongoing demographic survey being conducted by the authors.

Regarding the nature of future residential provision, many parents wish to see a more "open-door" policy to the various alternatives to the family home. Knowledge on the features of these alternatives, other than hostels, tends to be very poor. Parents are often unaware of the diversity of residential provision and often have misconceptions regarding those of which they do have knowledge. For example, group houses are often seen as places with inadequate supervision.

Conclusions

Although an open door policy would be difficult to maintain in residences which are already other individuals' homes, services need to address themselves to this problem.

We have emphasised the desirability of involving the son and daughter in any decision making regarding his or her *own* future. This should apply not only to the choice of where the future residence might be, but also to preparation for the inevitable transition, bereavement and its likely consequence with respect to leaving the family home. Oswin (1982) has emphasised how important it is that professionals learn to understand how people with mental handicap communicate grief, and their difficulty in coping with the experience of bereavement. Several articles by parents have described both the severity and long duration of grieving in the their own sons and daughters (e.g. Bradford, 1984; Ray, Payne and Stryker 1978). When it is borne in mind that bereavement and enforced departure from the family home frequently go hand in hand, then the extent of trauma can in some measure be envisaged. Minimisation of the double trauma can be effected by maintaining the person with mental handicap in the family home following the death of the parents. In both the statutory and voluntary sectors (e.g. the Mencap Homes Foundation), innovatory schemes are being introduced to make this possible.

While a greater emphasis on self-advocacy is called for, problems can be identified with respect to implementing such an approach. Card (1983) raises the question of what happens when a son or daughter wants to leave home before a crisis, but a parent resists the move. Service providers in such situations have to decide, conditional on the individual circumstances, for *whom* they are working, the parent, the son or daughter or both. The conflict engendered by such a situation emphasises the need to address the issue of future placement well in advance of a move enforced by a crisis situation.

Consideration of the competence of the person with mental handicap to cope with demands in the future must also be made. Cooke (1987) showed that for some parents the useful skill areas, such as cooking, can be quite threatening leading them to discourage their offspring from increasing their skills in such areas. Parents need to be helped to realise how beneficial these skills are for their children in the future. These skills can also help maintain the current home situation as parents become increasingly less active themselves. Richardson and Ritchie (1986) suggest that, if money were spent on making people more independent, many would be able to live with much less support than at present, reducing the current heavy demand for accommodation.

Underlying many of the recommendations made above regarding *approaches* to older families with a son or daughter at home is the issue of resources and services. As Ritchie and Richardson point out, there is little point in helping parents and sons and daughters to plan if there is no suitable provision. Evidence from Cooke (1987) and other studies suggests that many parents find existing accommodation inadequate for their children. Part of the preparation for the future should therefore be preparation of the residential services themselves. We must view problems that parents experience in coming to terms with the future not as a purely personal difficulty, but as society's failure to create conditions that are conducive to making transitions acceptable.

We cited above the recent Audit Commission (1986) report which places considerable emphasis on the problems of developing co-ordinated services in a situation in which, nationally and locally, there is considerable fragmentation in service delivery. Grant (1985) emphasises the need to develop more integrated and comprehensive services for ageing carers and their families. This will propagate heavy demands on the collaborative resolve of health and social service authorities and voluntary bodies. Much reorganisation of services would need to occur, though as the Audit Commission report emphasises, there are sufficient examples of where this has occurred to show that such reorganisation *is* feasible.

We also reviewed work on the use of adult placements for people with mental handicap, and drew attention to research by Newman, Sherman and Frenkel (1985). The critical aspect of foster family provision of this sort is that it sets the scene for optimal natural integration into a locality, since the person with mental handicap is drawn into naturally occurring interactions in which the families themselves are engaging. It has been suggested that such integration is more likely to be enhanced than is possible when professional carers are involved, though it was noted that not all individuals benefited equally, older people with mental handicap showing somewhat less integration than their younger, adult peers. In the UK, as in the USA, the development of such provision is offering an important complement to the family home and other forms of residential provision.

Finally, research is needed in several areas related to the issues discussed in this section. Evaluation of the initiatives already developing in this area is essential, including the viability and effectiveness of parent groups and factors influencing the success in making transitions from the family home. Special consideration needs to be given to the issue of self-advocacy at both the level of service provision, i.e. how is information on the person with mental handicap's own perceptions utilised, and technique, i.e. the development of increasingly effective interview techniques. A start *has* been made on siblings perceptions of their own role with respect to family needs and future provision but this area merits extensive exploration. In addition, the factors influencing community integration in different forms of provision need to be clarified. A study comparing the family home, adult placement and small group houses could be illuminating in determining the constraints and facilitators of involvement in the community.

In contrast to the wider ageing literature, we have come across no *formal* studies on ethnicity and primary support networks in relation to ageing and mental handicap. Contact with service providers, however, clearly reveals interest and concern with respect to cultural differences that determine family attitudes towards support of family members with mental handicap. In the multicultural societies of the industrialised world research into this subject is urgently needed.

9 CONCLUSION

Theoretically, this book has drawn on a variety of sources, though a central theme has been concerned with the ecological analysis of the development of people with mental handicap as they age. From the point of view of social policy, we have emphasised that the care in the community initiative is as applicable to this older group as to it is to younger individuals. This policy, however, embodies more than simply residential relocation. It emphasises the creation of a context in which the range of choice and services available to the person with mental handicap is comparable to that of her or his non-handicapped peers. Wolfensberger (1985) has observed, however, that there are several difficulties involved in applying the concept of normalisation to older people with mental handicap. As we have noted in this review, for many non-mentally handicapped elderly people society makes poor provision in virtually all areas of their life. Second, the earlier life of many adults without mental handicap differs in important respects with regard to work and the development of family and other informal support networks. Thus, Wolfensberger argues, any direct application of the principle of normalisation would lead to a devaluing of the older person with mental handicap and social and material deprivation in his or her later years.

Instead of pursuit of "normalisation", Wolfensberger proposes the principle of "social role valorisation", briefly defined as "...the use of culturally valued means in order to enable, establish, and/or maintain valued social roles for people." (p.61). He applies the concept to both people with mental handicap and those who are elderly, and of course, to those who are both mentally handicapped and elderly. We would like to suggest that the introduction of the concept of social role valorisation at the present juncture in implementation of care in the community for a variety of groups (mentally handicapped, elderly, mentally ill and physically handicapped) has some value in drawing our attention to the way in which people in these groups can and have been devalued. The introduction of the concept of social role valorisation also must be viewed as an acknowledgement of some of the inherent ambiguities in the concept of normalisation. Analyses from a variety of sources which are critical of present services acknowledge that what is normative for substantial segments of these populations is unacceptable both in terms of intended policy realisation and broader assumptions regarding the quality of peoples' lives. The problems entailed in reducing the gap between intention and implementation are extensive, involving limitations on the availability of public funds, the processes by which these resources are allocated at national and local levels, and the need to change a variety of facets of the social and physical ecology. Thus, while the concept of social role valorisation may reconfirm values already implicit in intended policy, it offers little by way of specific direction in dealing with these problems and operationalisation of the concept is less clear at this juncture than is the case for some aspects of normalisation.

The progressive development and improvement of services for all groups requiring special consideration with regard to care in the community is at present a central concern of social policy. Such development is called for in all areas identified in this book, ranging from the provision of adequate generic and specialist services through to scientific research in a variety of areas of health, psychological and social functioning. While older people with mental handicap will always constitute a relatively small, if growing, group relative to the wider populations of elderly people and of individuals with mental handicap, we believe there is value in focusing on their special situation. Hopefully this review will make some contribution to gaining a clearer picture of a hitherto neglected and at times invisible group of people.

REFERENCES

Acheson, R.M., & Acheson, E.D. (1958) 'Coronary and other heart disease in a group of Irish males aged 65-85', *British Journal of Preventative and Social Medicine*, *12*, 147-153

Adams, M. (1972) 'Social aspects of medical care for the mentally retarded', *New England Journal of Medicine*, *286*, 635-638

Adams, M. (1975) 'Foster family care for the intellectually disadvantaged child' in M. Begab and S.A. Richardson (eds.), *The mentally retarded and society: A social perspective*, University Park Press, Baltimore, MD

Aldrich, C., & Mendhoff, E. (1963) 'Relocation of the aged and disabled: A mortality study', *Journal of the American Geriatric Society*, *11*, 185-194

Aleksandrowicz, D. (1961) 'Fire and its aftermath on a geriatric ward', *Bulletin of the Menninger Clinic*, *25*, 23-32

Allardice, M.S., & Crowthers, V.L. (1975) 'The role of the practitioner in serving the elderly mentally retarded' in J.M. Hamilton & R.M. Segal (eds.), *A consultation-conference on the gerontological aspects of mental retardation: Proceedings*, University of Michigan, ISMRRD, Ann Arbor, MI

American Hospitals Association (1976) *The way to reality - A guide for developing a reality orientation program*, AHA, Chicago, IL

American Psychiatric Association (1980) *Diagnostic and statistical manual of mental disorders*, American Psychiatric Association, Washington, DC

Aninger, M., & Bolinsky, K. (1977) 'Levels of independent functioning of retarded adults in apartments', *Mental Retardation*, *15*, 12-13

Anthony, J.C., LeResche, L., & Niaz, U., von Korff, M.R., & Folstein, M.F. (1982) 'Limits of the 'Mini Mental State' as a screening test for dementia and delirium among hospital patients', *Psychological Medicine*, *12*, 397-408

Appell, M.J., Williams, C.M., & Fishell, K.N. (1963) 'A residence program for retarded males in a community setting', *American Journal of Mental Deficiency*, *68*, 104-108

Arie, T. (1973) 'Dementia in the elderly: Diagnosis and assessment', *British Medical Journal*, *4*, 540-543

Atchley, R.C. (1976) *The sociology of retirement*, Schenkman, New York

Atchley, R.C. (1979) 'Issues in retirement research', *The Gerontologist*, *19*, 44-54

Atkinson, D. (1984) *Steps toward integration*, Unpublished PhD thesis, Univ. of Southampton,

Atthowe, J.M. (1972) 'Controlling nocturnal eneuresis in severely disabled/chronic patients', *Behaviour therapy*, *3*, 232-239

Audit Commission (1985) *Managing social services for the elderly more effectively*, HMSO, London

Audit Commission (1986) *Making a Reality of Community Care*, HMSO, London

Ayer, S., & Alaszewski, A. (1984) *Community care and mental handicap services for mothers of mentally handicapped children*, Croom Helm, London

Badry, D.E., Vrbancic, M.I., Groeneweg, G., McDonald, L., & Hornick, J. (1986a) *An examination of the service needs of older developmentally disabled persons in the province of Alberta*, Faculty of Social Welfare, University of Calgory, Calgory, Alberta

Badry, D.E., Vrbancic, M.I., McDonald, L., Groeneweg, G., & Hornick, J. (1986b) *A demographic and needs analysis of older developmentally disabled persons in the province of Alberta*, Report No.1: Michener Centre, Faculty of Social Welfare, University of Calgary, Calgary, Alberta

Badry, D.E., Vrbancic, M.I., McDonald, L., Groeneweg, G., & Hornick, J. (1986c) 'Report No.2: A comparison of community based and congregate care populations' in *A demographic and needs analysis of disabled persons in the province of Alberta*, Faculty of Social Welfare, University of Calgary, Calgary, Alberta

Baker, B., Seltzer, G.B., & Seltzer, M.M. (1977) *As close as possible: Community residences for retarded adults*, Little, Brown, and Co., Boston, MA

Balakrishnan, T.R., & Wolf, L.C. (1976) 'Life expectancy of mentally retarded persons in Canadian institutions', *American Journal of Mental Deficiency*, *80*, 650-662

Ball M.J., & Nuttall, K. (1980) ' Neurofibrillary tangles, granulovascular degeneration and neuron loss in Down's syndrome: Qualitative comparison with Alzheimer dementia', *Annals of Neurology*, *7*, 462-465

Baller, W.R. (1936) 'A study of the present social status of a group of adults who, when they were in elementary schools, were classified as mentally deficient', *Genetic Psychology Monographs*, *18*, 165-244

Ballinger, B.R. (1978) 'The elderly in a mental subnormality hospital: A comparison with the elderly psychiatric patient', *Social Psychiatry*, *13*, 37-40

Ballinger, B.R. (1979) 'The elderly mentally handicapped in the community and a psychiatric service', *Apex: Journal of the British Institute of Mental Handicap*, *7*, 40-41

Ballinger, B.R., & Reid, A.H. (1977) 'Psychiatric disorder in an adult training centre and a hospital for the mentally handicapped', *Psychological Medicine*, *7*, 525-528

Baltes, M., Honn, S., Barton, E.M., Orzech, M., & Lago, D. (1983) 'On the social ecology of dependence and independence in elderly nursing home residents: A replication and extension', *Journal of Gerontology*, *38*, 556-564

Baltes, M.M., & Barton, E.M. (1977) 'New approaches toward aging: A case for the operant model', *Educational Gerontology*, *2*, 383-405

Baltes, M.M., & Zerbe, M.B. (1976) 'Independence training in nursing-home residents', *Gerontologist*, *16*, 428-432

Baltes, M.M., Burgess, R.L., & Stewart, R.B. (1980) 'Independence and dependence in self-care behaviour in nursing home residents: An operant-observational study', *International Journal of Behavioural Development*, *3*, 489-500

Baltes, P.B. (1973) 'Strategies for psychological intervention in old age', *The Gerontologist*, *13*, 4-6

Barrowclough, C., & Fleming, I. (1986a) 'Training direct care staff in goal planning with elderly people', *Behavioural Psychotherapy*, *14*, 192-209

Barrowclough, C., & Fleming, I. (1986b) *Goal Planning with Elderly People*, Manchester University Press, Manchester

Bassuk, E.L., and Gerson, S. (1978) 'Deinstitutionalization and mental health services', *Scientific American*, *238*, 46-53

Bayley, M. (1973) *Mental handicap and community care: A study of mentally handicapped people in Sheffield*, Routledge and Kegan Paul, London

Beaver, M.L. (1979) 'The decision-making process and its relationship to relocation adjustment in old people', *The Gerontologist*, *19*, 567-574

Bell, A., & Zubek, J. (1960) 'The effect of age on the intellectual performance of mental defectives', *Journal of Gerontology*, *15*, 285-295

Benz, A., and Halpern, A.S. (1982) *Rehabilitation of elderly mentally retarded persons: Service needs and obstacles*, Paper presented at 110th meeting of the American Public Health Association, Montreal, Canada

Berger, M., & Yule, W. (1986) 'Psychometric approaches' in J. Hogg & N.V. Raynes (eds.), *Assessment in mental handicap: A guide to tests, batteries and checklists*, Croom Helm, London

Berger, R.M., & Rose, S.D. (1977) 'Interpersonal skill training with institutionalized elderly patients', *Journal of Gerontology*, *32*, 346-353

Bergmann, K. (1978) 'Neurosis and personality disorder in old age' in A.D. Issacs (ed.), *Studies in geriatric psychiatry*, Wiley, Chichester

Bingley, W., & Mitchell, P. (1986) *Disabled persons Services, Consultation and Representation Act 1986: Handbook for voluntary organisers*, RADAR and MIND, London

Binstock, R.H., & Shanas, E. (eds.) (1985) *Handbook of aging and the social sciences, second edition,* Van Nostrand Reinhold, New York

Binstock, R.H., Levin, M.A., & Weatherley, A. (1985) 'Political dilemmas of social intervention' in R.H. Binstock and E. Shanas (eds.), *Handbook of aging and the social sciences, second edition*, Van Nostrand Reinhold, New York

Black, D.A.K., & Pole, J.D. (1975) 'Priorities in biochemical research: Indices of burden', *British Journal of Preventative and Social Medicine*, *29*, 222-227

Blackman, D.K. (1977) *Control of urinary incontinence among the institutionalized elderly*, Paper presented at the meeting of the Association for the Advancement of Behavior Therapy, Atlanta, GA

Blackwell, M.W. (1979) *Care of the mentally retarded*, Little Brown, Boston, MA

Blake, R. (1981) 'Disabled older persons: A demographic analysis', *Journal of Rehabilitation*, *47*, 19-27

Blom-Cooper, J. (1985) 'Jeremy's Silver Award', *Parents Voice*, *Spring*, 12

Borup, J.H., Gallego, D.T., & Heffernan, P.G. (1979) 'Relocation and its effects on mortality', *The Gerontologist*, *19*, 135-140

Boskin, M. (1977) 'Social security and the retirement decision', *Economic Enquiry*, *15*, 1-25

Botwinick, J. (1977) 'Intellectual abilities' in J.E. Birren & K.W. Schaie (eds.), *Handbook of the Psychology of Aging*, Van Nostrand Reinhold, New York

Bourestom, N.C., & Tars, S. (1974) 'Alterations in life patterns following nursing home relocation', *The Gerontologist*, *14*, 506-510

Bourliere, F., & Vallery-Masson, J. (1985) 'Epidemiology and ecology of aging' in J.C. Brocklehurst (ed.), *Textbook of geriatric medicine and gerontology*, Churchill Livingstone, Edinburgh

Bracco, L, & Amaducci, L. (1980) 'Dementia: Clinical aspects' in G. Barbagallo and A.N. Exton-Smith (eds.), *The aging brain: Neurological and mental disturbances*, Plenum Press, New York

Braddock, D., Heller, T., & Zashin, E. (1984) *The closure of the Dixon Developmental Center:A study of the implementation and consequences of a public policy*, Institute for the Study of Developmental Disabilities, University of Illinois at Chicago, Chicago, IL

Bradford, J. (1984) 'Life after death', *Parents Voice, May*, 6-7

Braverman, H. (1974) *Labour and Monopoly Capital: The Degradation of Work in the Twentieth Century*, Monthly Review Press, New York

Bremer, J. (1951) 'A social psychiatric investigation of a small community in Northern Norway', *Acta Psychiatrica Neurologica* (Kbh), Supp. 62

British Medical Society (1986) *All our tomorrows: Growing old in Britain*, BMS, London

Bronfenbrenner, U. (1979) *The ecology of human development*, Harvard University Press, Harvard, MA

Brown, F.W. (1963) 'Orthopedic surgery in the mentally retarded', *Journal of Bone and Joint Surgery*, *45*, 841-855

Brown, J.S., & Guard, K.A. (1979) 'The treatment environment for retarded persons in nursing homes', *Mental Retardation*, *17*, 77-83

Bruininks, R.H., Meyers, C.E., Sigford, B.B., and Lakin, K.C. (eds.) (1981) *Deinstitutionalization and community adjustment of mentally retarded people*, American Association on Mental Deficiency, Washington, DC

Buchanan, T., & Allen, L. (1983) *Barriers to participation among the urban elderly*, Paper presented at the 1983 Society of Park and Recreation Educators' Leisure Research Symposium, Kansas

Burger, P.C. and Vogel, F.S. (1973) 'The development of pathologic changes of Alzheimer's disease and senile dementia in patients with Down's syndrome', *American Journal of Pathology*, *73*, 457-468

Burgio, L.D. (1987) 'Behavioral staff training and management in geriatric long-term care facilities' in P. Wisocki (ed.), *Clinical Behavior Therapy for the Elderly*, Plenum Press, New York

Burgio, L.D., & Burgio, K.L. (1986) 'Behavioral gerontology: Application of behavioral methods to the problems of older adults', *Journal of Applied Behavior Analysis*, *19*, 319-328

Burgio, L.D., Burgio, K.L., Engel, B.T., & Tice, L.M. (1986) 'Increasing distance and independence of ambulation in elderly nursing home residents', *Journal of Applied Behavior Analysis*, *19*, 357-366

Burgio, L.D., Engel, B.T., McCormick, K., & Hawkins, A. (1987) 'Behavioral treatment for urinary incontinence in elderly inpatients: Initial attempts to modify prompting and toileting procedures', *Behavior Therapy*, In press

Burkhauser, R.V., & Turner, J.A. (1980) 'The effects of pension policy through life' in R.L. Clark (ed.), *Retirement policy in an aging society*, Duke University Press, Durham, NC

Burton, M. (1982) 'Reality orientation for the elderly: A critique', *Journal of Advances in Nursing*, *7*, 427-33

Busse, E.W. (1973) 'Mental disorders in later life - organic brain syndromes' in E.W. Busse & E. Pfeiffer (eds.), *Mental illness in later life*, American Psychiatric Association, Washington, DC

Butler, R.N. (1961) 'Reawakening interest', *Nursing Homes*, *10*, 8-19

Butler, R.N. (1963) 'The life-review: An interpretation of reminiscence in the aged', *Psychiatry*, *26*, 65-76

Byrne, E.A., & Cunningham, C.C. (1985) 'The effects of mentally handicapped children on families-a conceptual review', *Journal of Child Psychiatry*, *26*, 847-864

Campaign for People with Mental Handicap (1973) *Listen: Conference report written By Ann Shearer*, CMH, London

Campaign for People with Mental Handicap (1984) *Hope for the future?* (CMH's evidence to the Social Services Committe on Community Care), CMH, London

Cantor, M., & Little, V. (1985) 'Aging and social care' in R.H. Binstock & E. Shanas (eds.), *Handbook of Aging and the Social Sciences, second edition*, Van Nostrand Reinhold, New York

Card, H. (1983) 'What will happen when we've gone?', *Community Care*, *28*, 20-21

Carp, F.M.A. (1967) 'The impact of environment on old people', *The Gerontologist*, *7*, 106-108

Carp, F.M.A. (1966) *A future for the aged*, University of Texas Press, Austin

Carr, P. (1986) 'Setting up a day centre for elderly mentally handicapped people' in A. Wynn-Jones (ed.), *Elderly people with mental handicap*, MENCAP, Taunton

Carsrud, A.L., Carsrud, K.B., & Standifer, J. (1980) 'Social variables affecting mental health in geriatric mentally retarded individuals: An exploratory study', *Mental Retardation*, *18*, 88-90

Cartensen, L.L., & Erikson, R.J. (1986) 'Enhancing the social environments of elderly nursing home residents: Are high rates of interaction enough?', *Journal of Applied Behavior Analysis*, *19*, 349-355

Carter, C.O. (1958) 'A life-table for mongols with the causes of death', *Journal of Mental Deficiency Research*, *2*, 64-74

Carter, G., & Jancar, J. (1983) 'Mortality in the mentally handicapped: A 50-year survey at the Stoke Park group of hospitals (1930-1980)', *Journal of Mental Deficiency Research*, *27*, 143-156

Chaney, R.H., Eyman, R.K., & Miller, C.R. (1979) 'Comparison of respiratory mortality in the profoundly mentally retarded and in the less retarded', *Journal of Mental Deficiency Research*, *23*, 1-7

Cheseldine, S. (1985) Personal communication

Cheseldine, S. (1987) Personal communication

Chinn, P.C., Drew, C.J., & Logan, D.R. (1979) 'The aged retarded' in P.C. Chinn, C.J. Drew & D.R. Logan (eds.), *Mental retardation: A life cycle approach*, The C.V. Mosby Company, St Louis, MO

Christenfeld, R., & Haveliwala, Y.A. (1978) 'Patients' views of placement facilities: A participant-observer study', *American Journal of Psychiatry*, *135*, 329-332

Clegg, J. (1986) 'Review of research information' in A. Wynn-Jones (ed.), *Elderly people with mental handicap*, MENCAP, Taunton

Cleveland, D.W. & Miller N. (1977) 'Attitudes and life commitments of older siblings of mentally retarded adults: An exploratory study', *Mental Retardation*, *15*(June), 38-41

Coffman, T.L (1981) 'Relocation and survival of institutionalized aged: A re-examination of the evidence', *The Gerontologist*, *21*, 483-500

Collmann, R.D., & Stoller, A. (1963) 'A life table for mongols in Victoria, Australia', *Journal of Mental Deficiency Research*, *7*, 53-59

Commission on Professional and Hospital Activities (1978) *International classification of diseases, clinical modification: ICD-9-CM* (9th ed.), Edwards Brothers, Ann Arbor, MI

Conley, R.W. (1973) *The economics of mental retardation*, Johns Hopkins, Baltimore, MD

Cooke, D.J. (1987) *Older parents and their adult sons and daughters with mental handicap: Home lives and future plans*, Unpublished MSc thesis, University of Manchester, Manchester

Cooper, S.J., (1987) *Foster care for mentally handicapped adults*, Unpublished dissertation for Advanced Certificate in Mental Handicap, West Midlands College of Higher Education, Walsall

Coolidge, F.L., Rakoff, R.J., Schwellenbach, L.D., Bracken, P.D., & Walker, S.H. (1986) 'WAIS profiles in mentally retarded adults', *Journal of Mental Deficiency Research*, *30*, 15-17

Corbett, J.A. (1979) 'Psychiatric morbidity and mental retardation' in F.E. James & R.P. Snaith (eds.), *Psychiatric illness and mental handicap*, Gaskell Press, London

Corbett, J.A. (1987) *Personal communication*

Corbett, J.A., Harris, R., & Robinson, R.G. (1975) 'Epilepsy' in J. Wortis (ed.), *Mental retardation and developmental disabilities* (Vol 7), Brunner Mazel, New York

Cotten, P.D., Britt, C.R., & Moreland, A. (1986) *Services for Elderly Mentally Handicapped Mississipians: A coordinated plan*, Mississippi Department of Health and Boswell Retardation Center, Sanatorium, Mississippi, MS

Cotten, P.D., Purzycki, E., Cowart, C., & Merritt, F. (1983) 'Changes in adaptive behavior of elderly mentally retarded as a function of community placement', Mississippi Department of Health and Boswell Retardation Center, Sanatorium, Mississippi, MS

Craft, M. (1971) 'A North Wales experiment in subnormality care', *British Journal of Psychiaty*, *118*, 199-206

Crapper, D.R., Dalton, A.J., Skopitz, P., Scott, J.W., & Hachinski, V.C. (1975) 'Alzheimer degeneration in Down's syndrome', *Archives of Neurology*, *32*, 618-623

Crisp, A. (1985) 'Personal communication'

Crisp, A.H. (1976) 'Depression' in S. Krauss (ed.), *Encyclopaedic handbook of medical psychology*, Butterworth, London

Daniels, P.J. (1979) *Gerontological aspects of developmental disabilities: The state of the art*, The University of Nebraska at Omaha, NE Gerontology Program, Omaha, NE

Davies, A.D.M. (1982) 'Research with elderly people in long-term care: Some social and organisational factors affecting psychological interventions', *Ageing and Society*, *2*, 285-298

Davies, B.H. (1985) 'The respiratory system' in M.S.J. Pathy (ed.), *Principles and practice of geriatric medicine*, Wiley, Chichester

Day, K. (1985) 'Psychiatric disorder in the middle-aged and elderly mentally handicapped', *British Journal of Psychiatry*, *147*, 660-667

Day, K. (1987) 'The elderly mentally handicapped in hospital: A clinical study', *Journal of Mental Deficiency Research*, In Press

Dayton, N.A., Doering, C.R., Hilferty, M.M., Maher, H.C., & Dolan, H.H. (1932) 'Mortality and expectation of life in mental deficiency in Massachusetts: Analysis of the fourteen year period 1917-1930', *New England Journal of Medicine*, *206*, 555-570

De Araujo, G., Dudley, D.L, & Van Arsdel, F.P. (1972) 'Psychosocial assets and severity of chronic asthma', *Journal of Allergy and Clinical Immunology*, *50*, 257-263

Deaton, J.G. (1973) 'The mortality rate and causes of death among institutionalized mongols in Texas', *Journal of Mental Deficiency Research*, *17*, 117-122

Dell, D., Felce, D., Flight, C., Jenkins, J., & Mansell, J. (1986) *The Bereweeke Skill-Teaching System: Handbook, Revised Edition*, NFER-Nelson, Windsor

Demaine, G.C., & Silverstein, A.B. (1978) 'MA changes in institutionalized Down's syndrome persons: A semi-longitudinal approach', *American Journal of Mental Deficiency*, *82*, 429-432

Deniker, P. (1976) *Advances in drug therapy and mental illness*, World Health Organisation, Geneva

Department of Health and Social Security (DHSS) (1971) *Better services for the Mentally Handicapped*, HMSO, London

Department of Health and Social Security (DHSS) (1972) *Census of mentally handicapped patients in hospital in England and Wales at the end of 1970*, HMSO, London

Department of Health and Social Security (DHSS) (1979) *Report of the committee of enquiry into mental handicap nursing* (Cmnd 7468-1), HMSO, London

Department of Health and Social Security (DHSS) (1980) *Progress, problems and priorities: A review of mental handicap services since 1971*, HMSO, London

Department of Health and Social Security (DHSS) (1981a) *Care in action: A handbook of policies and priorities for the health and social services in England*, HMSO, London

Department of Health and Social Security (DHSS) (1981b) *Growing older*, HMSO, London

Deshayes, I.L. (1979) *Senility - A stereotype curse*, Paper presented at a symposium on the 'Gerontological aspects of developmental disabilities', Omaha, NE

Detterman, D.K. (1987) 'Theoretical notions of intelligence and mental retardation', *American Journal of Mental Deficiency*, *92*, 2-11

Dickerson, J., Hamilton, J., Huber, R., & Segal, R. (1979) 'The aged mentally retarded: The invisible client: A challenge to the community' in D.P. Sweeny and T.Y. Wilson (eds.), *Double jeopardy: The plight of aging and aged developmentally disabled persons in Mid-America*, Exceptional Child Center, Utah State University, Logan, UT

Dobrof, R. (1985) 'Some observations from the field of aging' in M.P. Janicki and H.M. Wisniewski (eds.), *Aging and developmental disabilities: Issues and trends*, Paul Brookes, Baltimore, MD

Donahue, W., Orbach, H., & Pollack, O. (1960) 'Retirement: The emerging social pattern' in C. Tibbitts (ed.), *Handbook of Social Gerontology: Societal Aspects of Aging*, University of Chicago Press, Chicago, IL

Donges, G.S. (1982) *Policymaking for the mentally handicapped*, Gower, Aldershot

Droller, H., & Pemberton, J. (1977) 'Cardiovascular disease in a random sample of elderly people', *British Heart Journal*, *15*, 199-204

Dubin, R. (1956) 'Industrial workers' worlds', *Social Problems*, *3*, 131-142

Duncan, A.G. (1936) 'Mental deficiency and manic-depressive insanity', *Journal of Mental Science*, *82*, 635-47

Dupont, A. (1981) 'Medical results from registration of Danish mentally retarded persons' in P. Mittler (ed.), *Frontiers of knowledge in mental retardation*, University Park Press, Baltimore, MD

Durow, L., & Pierson, J. (1975) 'Design and use of the workbook' in J. Hamilton & R. Segal (eds.), *Consultation-conference on the gerontological aspects of mental retardation*, Institute for the Study of Mental Retardation and Related Disabilities, University of Michigan, Ann Arbor, MI

Dy, E.B., Strain, P.S., Fullerton, A., & Stowitschek, J. (1981) 'Training institutionalized, elderly mentally retarded persons as intervention agents for socially isolated peers', *Analysis and Intervention in Developmental Disabilities*, *1*, 199-215

Eagle, E. (1967) 'Prognosis and outcome of community placement of institutionalized retarded', *American Journal of Mental Deficiency*, *72*, 232-243

Eaton, L.F., & Menolascino, F.J. (1982) 'Psychiatric disorders in the mentally retarded: Types, problems, and challenges', *American Journal of Psychiatry*, *139*, 1297-1303

Edgerton, R.B. (1967) *The cloak of competence: Stigma in the lives of the mentally retarded*, University of California Press, Berkeley, CA

Edgerton, R.B. (1975) 'Issues related to the quality of life among mentally retarded persons' in M.J. Begab and S.A. Richardson (eds.), *The mentally retarded and society: A social science perspective*, University Park Press, Baltimore, MD

Edgerton, R.B., & Berkovici, S.M. (1976) 'The cloak of competence: Years later', *American Journal of Mental Deficiency*, *80*, 485-497

Edgerton, R.B., Bollonger, M., & Herr, B. (1984) 'The cloak of competence: After two decades', *American Journal of Mental Deficiency*, *88*, 345-351

Ellis, W.G., McCulloch J.R., & Corley C.L. (1974) 'Presenile dementia in Down's syndrome', *Neurology*, *24*, 101-106

Eyman, R.K., Demaine, G.C., & Lei, T. (1979) 'Relationship between community environments and resident changes in adaptive behavior: A Path model', *American Journal of Mental Deficiency*, *83*, 330-338

Eyman, R.K., O'Connor, G., Tarjan, G., & Justice, R.S. (1972) 'Factors determining residential placement of mentally retarded children', *American Journal of Mental Deficiency*, *76*, 692-698

Fairbrother, P. (1986) 'MENCAP's Minimum Standards for elderly mentally handicapped people' in A. Wynn-Jones (ed.), *Elderly people with mental handicap*, MENCAP, Taunton

Fancolly, J.K., & Clute, W.T. (1975) *The social environment of the aging mentally retarded: Implications for the aging process and service delivery*, Paper presented at the 28th meeting of the Gerontological Society of America

Felce, D., Jenkins, J., deKock, U., & Mansell, J. (1986) 'The Bereweeke Skill-Teaching System: Goal setting checklist for adults', NFER, Windsor

Fennel, G., Phillipson, C., & Wenger, C. (1983) 'The process of ageing: Social aspects' in DHSS (ed.), *Elderly people in the community, their service needs*, HMSO, London

Ferraro, K.F. (1983) 'The health consequence of relocation among the aged in the community', *Journal of Gerontology*, *38*, 90-96

Fewell, R.R., & Vadasy, P.F. (1986) *Families of handicapped children: Needs and supports across the life span*, PRO-ED, Austin, TX

Fillenbaum, G. (1971) 'On the relation between attitude to work and attitude to retirement', *Journal of Gerontology*, *26*, 244-248

Finch J., & Groves, D. (1980) 'Community care and the family: A case for equal opportunities', *Journal of Social Policy*, *9*, 487-511

Fisher, M.A., & Zeaman, D. (1970) 'Growth and decline of retardate intelligence' in N.R. Ellis (ed.), *International review of research in mental retardation* (vol. 4), Academic Press, New York

Flynn, M. (1986) Personal communication

Flynn, M. (1987) 'Independent living arrangements for adults who are mentally handicapped' in N. Malin (ed.), *Reassessing Community Care*, Croom Helm, London

Flynn, M.C. (1988) 'The social environment of adults living in their own homes' in M.C. Flynn (ed.), *A Place of Me Own: Independent living for adults who are mentally handicapped*, Cassell, London

Flynn, M.C., & Saleem, J.K. (1986) 'Adults who are mentally handicapped and living with their parents: Satisfaction and perception regarding their lives and circumstances', *Journal of Mental Deficiency Research*, *30*, 379-387

Folsom, J.C. (1968) 'Reality orientation for the elderly mental patient', *Journal of Geriatric Psychiatry*, *1*, 291-307

Foner, A., & Schwab, K. (1981) *Aging and retirement*, Brooks/Cole, Monterey, CA

Forrest, A.D, & Ogunremi, O.O (1974) 'The prevalence of psychiatric illness in a hospital for the mentally handicapped', *Health Bulletin* (Edinburgh), *32*, 199-202

Forssman, H., & Akesson, H.O. (1965) 'Mortality in patients with Down's syndrome', *Journal of Mental Deficiency Research*, *9*, 146-149

Forssman, H., & Akesson, H.O. (1970) 'Mortality of the mentally deficient: A study of 12,903 institutionalised subjects', *Journal of Mental Deficiency Research*, *14*, 276-294

Foxx, R.M., & Azrin, N.H. (1973) *Toilet training the Retarded: A rapid program for day and nightime independent toileting*, Research Press, Champaign, IL

Fraser, J., & Mitchell, A. (1876) 'Kalmuc idiocy: Report of a case with a autopsy; with notes on sixty-two cases', *Journal of Mental Science*, *22*, 169-179

Freedman, R. (1976) *Approaches to defining and measuring the community adjustment of mentally retarded persons: A literature review.*, Abt Associates, Cambridge, MA

Friis, H., & Manniche, E. (1961) *Old people in a low-income area in Copenhagen*, Technisk Forlag, Kobenhavn

Fryers, T. (1984) *The epidemiology of severe intellectual impairment: The dynamics of prevalence*, Academic Press, New York

Fryers, T. (1986) 'Providing for the needs of ageing mentally handicapped people' in A. Wynn-Jones (ed.), *Elderly people with mental handicap*, MENCAP, Taunton

Gallagher, D., Thompson, L.W., & Levy, S.W. (1980) 'Clinical psychological assessment of older adults' in L.W. Poon (ed.), *Aging in the 1980s*, American Psychological Association, Washington, DC

Gardner, W.I. (1967) 'Occurence of severe depressive reactions in the mentally retarded', *American Journal of Psychiatry*, *40*, 61-67

Gatz, M., Popkin, S.J., Pino, C.D., & VandenBos, G.R. (1985) 'Psychological interventions with older adults' in J.E. Birren & K.W. Schaie (eds.), *Handbook of the Psychology of Aging, second edition*, Van Nostrand Reinhold, New York

Gecas, V. (1981) 'Contexts of socialization' in M. Rosenberg & R. Turner (eds.), *Social psychology: Sociological perspectives*, Basic Books, New York

Geiger, O.G., & Johnson, L.A. (1974) 'Positive education for elderly persons: Correct eating through reinforcement', *The Gerontologist*, *14*, 432-436

George, L. (1980) *Role transition in later life*, Brooks/Cole, Monterey, CA

Gianturko, D.T., & Busse, E.W. (1978) 'Psychiatric problems encountered during a long-term study of normal ageing volunteers' in A.D. Issacs (ed.), *Studies in geriatric psychiatry*, Wiley, Chichester

Glamser, F. (1981) 'The impact of preretirement programs on the retirement experience', *Journal of Gerontology*, *36*, 244-250

Goldberg, D.P., & Huxley, P. (1980) *Mental illness in the community*, Tavistock Publications, London

Goldberg, D.P., Cooper, B., & Eastwood, M.R. (1970) 'A standardised psychiatric interview for use in community surveys', *British Journal of Social and Preventative Medicine*, *24*, 18-23

Goldberg, E.M., Mortimer, A., & Williams, B.T. (1970) *Helping the aged: A field experiment in social work*, George, Allen and Unwin, London

Goldfarb, A.I., Shahinian, S.P., & Burr, H.I. (1972) 'Death rate of relocated residents' in D.P. Kent, R. Kastenbaum and S. Sherwood (eds.), *Research planning and action for the elderly*, Behavioral Publications, New York

Goldstein, A.P. (1973) *Structured Learning Therapy: Towards a psychotherapy for the poor*, Academic Press, New York

Gollay, E. (1976) 'An analysis of the factors associated with community adjustment' in *A study of the community adjustment of deinstitutionalized mentally retarded persons* (Vol 5), Abt Associates, Cambridge, MA

Goodman, J.F. (1976) 'Aging and IQ change in institutionalized mentally retarded', *Psychological Reports*, *39*, 999-1006

Gordon, A. (1918) 'Psychoses in mental defects', *American Journal of Insanity*, *75*, 489-499

Gordon, C., Gaitz, C., & Scott, J. (1976) 'Personal expressivity across the life cycle' in R. Binstock and E. Shanas (eds.), *Handbook of aging and the social sciences, second edition*, Van Nostrand Reinhold, New York

Gostason, R. (1985) 'Psychiatric illness among the mentally retarded. A Swedish population study', *Acta Psychiatrica Scandinavica* (Suppl), 318, 1-117

Goudy, W.J. (1981) 'Changing work expectations: Findings from the Retirement History Study', *The Gerontologist*, *21*, 644-649

Goudy, W.J., Powers, E.A., & Keith, P. (1975) 'Work and retirement: A test of attitudinal relationships', *Journal of Gerontology*, *30*, 193-198

Grant, G. (1985) *Older carers, interdependence and the care of mentally handicapped adults*, University College of North Wales, Bangor, Gwynedd

Grant, G. (1986) *Working Paper no.41*, Social Policy and Development Centre, University College of North Wales, Bangor, Gwynedd

Grantovetter, M. (1973) 'The strength of weak ties', *American Journal of Sociology*, *78*, 1360-1380

Green, G.R., Linsk, N.L., & Pinkston, E.M. (1986) 'Modification of verbal behavior of the mentally impaired elderly by their spouses', *Journal of Applied Behavior Analysis*, *19*, 329-336

Green, J.G. (1984) 'The evaluation of reality orientation' in I. Hanley & J. Hodge (eds.), *Psychological Approaches to the Care of the Elderly*, Croom Helm, London

Greengross, S. (1986) 'A view from Age Concern' in A. Wynn-Jones (ed.), *Elderly people with mental handicap*, MENCAP, Taunton

Gress, L.D. (1979) *Medical needs of the aging/aged developmentally disabled and possible service delivery systems*, Paper presented as part of symposium on the 'Gerontological aspects of developmental disabilities', Omaha, NE

Grossman, H.J. (1973) *Manual on terminology and classification in mental retardation*, AAMD, Washington, DC

Gurland, B.J., Copeland, J.R.M., Kuriansky, J., Kelleher, M.J., Sharpe, L., & Dean, L.L. (1983) *The mind and mood of aging: Mental health problems of the community elderly in New York and London*, Haworth Press, London

Haines, C. (1986) 'Preparation for retirement' in A. Wynn-Jones (ed.), *Elderly people with mental handicap*, MENCAP, Taunton

Haley, W.E. (1983) 'Behavioral self-management: Application to a case of agitation in an elderly chronic psychiatric patient', *Clinical Gerontologist*, *1*, 45-52

Hall, B. (1964) 'Mongolism in newborns. A clinical and cytogenic study', *Acta Paediatrica* (Stockholm) Supplement 154,

Hamilton, J.C. & Segal, R.M. (eds.) (1975) *Proceedings: A consultation conference on the gerontological aspects of mental retardation*, Institute for Study of Mental Retardation and related disabilities, Ann Arbor, MI

Hamlett, I.C., & Engle, T.L. (1950) 'Mental health analysis of furlough patients', *American Journal of Mental Deficiency*, *55*, 257-263

Hampshire Social Services Department (1984) *Adult Placement Scheme*, HSSD, Winchester

Hanley, I.G. (1984) 'Theoretical and practical considerations in reality orientation therapy with the elderly' in I. Hanley & J. Hodge (eds.), *Psychological Approaches to the Care of the Elderly*, Croom Helm, London

Hawkins, B.A., Garza, J., & Eklund, S.J. (1987) *A national profile of projects and studies on aging/aged persons with devlopmental disablities*, Indiana University Developmental Training Center, Bloomington, IN

Heal, L.W., Sigelman, C., & Switzky, H. (1978) 'Research on community residential alternatives for the mentally retarded' in N. Ellis (ed.), *International review of research in mental retardation* (Vol 9), Academic Press, New York

Heaton-Ward, A. (1977) 'Psychosis in mental handicap', *British Journal of Psychiatry*, *130*, 525-533

Hecht, H.M. (1980) 'Psychogeriatric assessment of dementia', *South African Medical Journal*, *58*, 697-698

Heller, T. (1982) 'The effects of involuntary residential relocation: A review', *American Journal of Community Psychology*, *10*, 471-492

Heller, T. (1985) 'Residential relocation and reactions of elderly mentally retarded persons' in M.P. Janicki & H.M. Wisniewski (eds.), *Aging and developmental disabilities: Issues and trends*, Paul Brookes, Baltimore, MD

Heller, T., & Berkson, G. (1982) *Friendship and residential relocation*, Paper presented at the Gatlinburg Conference on research in mental retardation, Gatlinburg, TN

Hendricks, J., & Hendricks, C.D. (1978) 'Ageing in advanced industrialized societies' in V. Carver & P. Liddiard (eds.), *An ageing population*, Hodder and Stoughton Educational, Sevenoaks

Heron, C. (1983) 'Focus on the elderly: Communication problems', *Nursing Mirror*, *157*, ix-xi

Herskovitz, H.H., & Plesset, M.R. (1941) 'Psychoses in adult mental defectives', *Psychiatric Quarterly*, *15*, 574-588

Hewitt, K.E., Fenner, M.E., & Torphy, D. (1986) 'Cognitive and behavioural profiles of the elderly mentally handicapped', *Journal of Mental Deficiency Research*, *30*, 217-225

Hoffer, M.M. (1981) 'Symposium on orthopedic surgery on the mentally retarded', *Orthopedic Clinics of North America*, *12*, 1-203

Hogg, J. (1982) 'Motor development and performance of severely mentally handicapped people', *Developmental Medicine and Child Neurology*, *24*, 188-193

Hogg, J. (1986) 'What future?' in A. Wynn-Jones (ed.), *Elderly people with mental handicap*, MENCAP, Taunton

Hogg, J., & Mittler, P. (eds.) (1980) 'Recent research in mental handicap: Issues and perspectives' in J. Hogg and P. Mittler (eds.), *Advances in mental handicap research* (Vol 1), Wiley, Chichester

Hogg, J., & Mittler, P. (eds.) (1987) *Staff training in mental handicap*, Croom Helm, London

Hogg, J., & Sebba, J. (1986a) *Profound retardation and multiple impairment: Volume 1. Development and learning*, Croom Helm, London

Hogg, J., & Sebba, J. (1986b) *Profound retardation and multiple impairment: Volume 2. Education and therapy*, Croom Helm, London

Hollender, M.H. (1977) 'Personal communication' in C.E. Wells (ed.), *Dementia* (Contemporary Neurology Series), F.A. Davis, PA

Horn, J.L., & Donaldson, G. (1976) 'On the myth of intellectual decline in adulthood', *American Psychologist*, *31*, 701-719

Hoyer, W.J. (1973) 'Application of operant techniques to the modification of elderly behavior', *The Gerontologist*, *13*, 18-22

Hoyer, W.J., Kafer, R.A., Simpson, S.C., & Hoyer, F.W. (1974) 'Reinstatement of verbal behavior in elderly mental patients using operant procedures', *The Gerontologist*, *14*, 149-152

Hoyer, W.J., Mishara, B.L., & Riebel, G. (1975) 'Problem behaviors as operants: Applications with elderly individuals', *The Gerontologist*, *15*, 452-456

Huber, A.M. (1985) 'Nutrition, aging and developmental disabilities' in M.P. Janicki, & H.M. Wisniewski (eds.), *Aging and developmental disabilities: Issues and trends*, Paul Brookes, Baltimore, MD

Hucker, S.J., Day, K.A., & George S. (1979) 'Psychosis in mentally handicapped adults' in F.E. James and R.P. Snaith (eds.), *Psychiatric illness and mental handicap*, Gaskell Press, London

Hurd, H.M. (1888) 'Imbecility with insanity', *American Journal of Insanity*, *45*, 261-269

Hurst, J.W., & Logue, R.B. (1970) *The heart*, McGraw Hill, New York

Hussian, R.A. (1981) *Geriatric psychiatry: A behavioral perspective*, Van Nostrand Reinhold, New York

Hussian, R.A., & Davis, R.L. (1985) *Responsive care: Behavioral interventions with elderly persons*, Research Press, Champaign, IL

Inckelen, B. (1980) 'Mental Handicap and family needs. l', *Research Report no.5 Department of Mental Health*, Bristol University, Bristol

Ireland, W.W. (1898) *The mental affections of children: Idiocy, imbecility and insanity*, Churchill, London

Isaacs, B., & Akhtar, A.J. (1972) 'The Set Test', *Age and Ageing*, *1*, 222-226

Isaacs, B., & Kennie, A.T. (1973) 'The Set Test as an aid to the detection of dementia in old people', *British Journal of Psychiatry*, *123*, 467-470

Jackson, S., & Butler, A. (1963) 'Prediction of successful community placement of institutionalized retardates', *American Journal of Mental Deficiency*, *68*, 211-216

Jacobson, J.W. (1982a) 'Problem behavior and psychiatric impairment within a developmentally disabled population: I. Behaviors and frequency', *Applied Research in Mental Retardation*, *3*, 121-139

Jacobson, J.W. (1982b) 'Problem behavior and psychiatric impairment within a developmentally disabled population: II. Behavioral severity', *Applied Research in Mental Retardation*, *3*, 369-381

Jacobson, J.W., Sutton, M.S., & Janicki, M.P. (1985a) 'Demography and characteristics of aging and aged mentally retarded persons' in M.P. Janicki & H.M. Wisniewski (eds.), *Aging and developmental disabilities: Issues and approaches*, Paul Brookes, Baltimore, MD

Jacobson, J.W., Sutton, M.S., & Janicki, M.P. (1985b) 'Planning services for an older developmentally disabled population' in M.P. Janicki & H.M. Wisniewski (eds.), *Aging and developmental disabilities: Issues and approaches*, Paul Brookes, Baltimore, MD

Janicki, M.P. (1981) 'Personal growth and community living environments: A review' in H.C. Haywood & J.R. Newbrough (eds.), *Living environments for developmentally disabled persons*, University Park Press, Baltimore, MD

Janicki, M.P. (1984) *Comparisons of older mentally handicapped persons residing at home and institutions*, Paper prepared for a Roundtable Discussion 'At home & institutional care', 11th Int. Conf. Geront., Rome

Janicki, M.P. (1986) 'Older mentally handicapped persons residing at home and institutions', *British Journal of Mental Subnormality*, *32*, 30-36

Janicki, M.P., & Jacobson, J.W. (1982) 'The character of developmental disabilities in New York State: Preliminary observations', *International Journal of Rehabilitation Research*, *5*, 191-202

Janicki, M.P., & MacEachron, A.E. (1984) 'Residential, health, and social service needs of elderly developmentally disabled persons', *The Gerontologist*, *24*, 128-137

Janicki, M.P., & Wisniewski, H.M. (eds.) (1985) *Aging and developmental disabilities: Issues and approaches*, Paul Brookes, Baltimore, MD

Janicki, M.P., Ackerman, L., & Jacobson, J.W. (1984) *Survey of State developmental disabilities and aging plans relative to States' older developmentally disabled population*, NY Office of Mental Retardation & Developmental Disabilities, Albany, NY

Janicki, M.P., Otis, J.P., Puccio, P.S., Rettig, J.H., & Jacobson, J.W. (1985) 'Service needs among older developmentally disabled persons' in M.P. Janicki, & H.M. Wisniewski (eds.), *Aging and developmental disabilities: Issues and trends*, Paul Brookes, Baltimore, MD

Jenkins, J., Felce, D., Lund, B., & Powell, L. (1977) 'Increasing engagement in activity of residents in old people's homes by providing recreational materials', *Behaviour Research and Therapy*, *15*, 429-434

Jenkins, J., Felce, D., Mansell, J., Flight, L., & Dell, D. (1983) *The Bereweeke Skill-teaching System*, NFER-Nelson, Windsor

Jervis, G.A. (1948) 'Early senile dementia in mongoloid idiocy', *American Journal of Psychiatry*, *105*, 102-106

Jones, A.A., Blunden, R., Coles, E., Evans, G., & Porterfield, J. (1987) 'Evaluating the impact of training, supervisor feedback, self-monitoring and collaborative goal setting on staff and client behaviour' in J. Hogg & P. Mittler (eds.), *Staff training in mental handicap*, Croom Helm, London

Jones, K. (1976) *Opening the door: A study of new policies for the mentally handicapped*, Routledge and Kegan Paul, London

Kalt, N.C., & Kohn, M.H. (1975) 'Pre-retirement counseling: Characteristics of programs and preferences of retirees', *The Gerontologist*, *15*, 179-181

Kasteler, J.M., Gray, R.M., & Carruth, M.L. (1968) 'Involuntary relocation of the elderly', *The Gerontologist*, *8*, 276-279

Kay, D.W.K., & Bergmann, K. (1966) 'Physical disability and mental health in old age: A follow-up of a random sample of elderly people seen at home. Session 1 - Psychiatric and somatic disorders in old age', *Journal of Psychosomatic Medicine*, *10*, 3-12

Kay, D.W.K., Beamish, P., & Roth, M. (1964) 'Old age mental disorders in Newcastle-upon-Tyne. Part I: A study of prevalence', *British Journal of Psychiatry*, *110*, 146-158

Kay, D.W.K., Foster, E.M., & Bergmann, K. (1973) *Indications for domicilary services*, Paper presented to the World Psychiatric Assn., Psychogeriatric Section, Institute of Psychiatry, London

Kelly, J.R. (1982) *Leisure*, Prentice-Hall, Englewood Cliffs, NJ

Kelly, J.R. (1983) *Leisure identities and interactions*, Allen and Unwin, London

Kelly, J.R., Steinkamp, M.W., & Kelly, J.R. (1986) 'Later life leisure: How they play in Peoria', *The Gerontologist*, *26*, 531-537

Kennedy, R.D., Andrews, G.R., & Caird, F.I. (1977) 'Ischaemic heart disease in the elderly', *British Heart Journal*, *39*, 1121-1127

Keys, V., Boroskin, A., & Ross, R. (1973) 'The relvolving door in a MR hospital: A study of returns from leave', *Mental Retardation*, *11*, 55-56

Kiernan, C. (1987) 'Criterion-referenced tests' in J. Hogg & N.V. Raynes (eds.), *Assessment in Mental Handicap: A guide to assessments, practices, tests and checklists*, Croom Helm, London

Killian, E. (1970) 'Effects of geriatric transfers on mortality rates', *Social Work*, *15*, 19-26

Kimmel, D., Price, K., & Walker, J. (1978) 'Retirement choice and retirement satisfaction', *Journal of Gerontology*, *33*, 575-585

Kirman, B.H. (1979) 'Mental illness and mental handicap: Reflections on diagnostic problems and prevalence' in F.E. James & R.P. Snaith (eds.), *Psychiatric illness and mental handicap*, Gaskell, London

Kitchin, A.H., Lowther, C.P., & Milne, J.S. (1973) 'Prevalence of clinical and electrocardiographic evidence of ischaemic heart disease in the older population', *British Heart Journal*, *35*, 946-953

Kleitsch, E.C., Whitman, T.L., & Santos, J. (1983) 'Increasing verbal interaction among elderly socially isolated mentally retarded adults: A group language training procedure', *Journal of Applied Behavior Analysis*, *16*, 217-233

Korman, N., & Glennerster, H. (1984) *The Darenth Park Project: A narrative of a hospital closure*, London School of Economics, London

Kowalski, N.C. (1978) 'Fire at a home for the aged: A study of short-term mortality following dislocation of elderly residents', *Journal of Gerontology*, *33*, 601-602

Kriger, S.F. (1975) 'On aging and mental retardation' in J.C. Segal & R.M. Hamilton (eds.), *Proceedings of a consultation-conference on the gerontological aspects of mental retardation*, The University of Michigan, Ann Arbor, MI

Krishef, C.H. (1959) 'The influence of rural-urban environment upon the adjustment of dischargees from the Owatonna State School', *American Journal of Mental Deficiency*, *63*, 860-865

Kushlick, A. (1961) 'Subnormality in Salford' in M.W. Susser & A. Kushlick (eds.), *A report on the mental health services of the city of Salford for the year 1960*, Salford Health Department, Salford

Kushlick, A. (1964) *The prevalence of recognised mental subnormality of I.Q. under 50 among children in the south of England, with reference to the demand for places for residential care*, Paper read at the International Copenhagen Conference for the Scientific Study of Mental Retardation

Kushlick, A., & Blunden, R. (1975) 'The epidemiology of mental subnormality' in A.M. Clarke & A.D.B. Clarke (eds.), *Mental Deficiency: The changing outlook*, Methuen, London

Lambeth Social Services Department (1979) *Mentally handicapped people living at home* (Research Section report, 102), LSSD, London

Landesman-Dwyer, S. (1982) *The changing structure and function of institutions: A search for optimal group care environments*, Paper presented at Lake Wilderness conference on Impact of Residential Environments on Retarded persons

Landesman-Dwyer, S., & Knowles, M. (1987) 'Ecological analysis of staff training in residential settings' in J. Hogg & P. Mittler (eds.), *Staff Training in Mental Handicap*, Croom Helm, London

Landesman-Dwyer, S., Berkson, G., & Romer, D. (1979) 'Affiliation and friendship of mentally retarded residents in group homes', *American Journal of Mental Deficiency*, *83*, 571-580

Lawton, M.P. (1985) 'Activities and leisure', *Annual Review of Gerontology and Geriatrics*, *5*, 127-64

Lawton, M.P., & Nahemow, L. (1973) 'Ecology and the aging process' in C. Eisdorfer & M.P. Lawton (eds.), *Psychology of adult development and aging*, American Psychological Association, Washington DC

Lawton, M.P., & Yaffe, S. (1970) 'Mortality, morbidity and voluntary change of residence by older people', *Journal of the American Geriatrics Society*, *18*, 823-31

Lazarus, R.S. (1966) *Psychological stress and the coping process*, McGraw-Hill, New York

Leck, I., Gordon, W.L., & McKeown, T. (1967) 'Medical and social needs of mentally subnormal patients', *British Journal of Preventative and Social Medicine*, *21*, 115-121

Lemkau, P., Tietze, C., & Cooper, M. (1942) 'Mental-hygiene problems in an urban district. Third paper', *Mental Hygiene*, *26*, 275-288

Lewis, E.O. (1929) *Report of the mental deficiency committee*, (parts I, II, III, IV), HMSO, London

Lewis, M.I., & Butler, R.N. (1974) 'Life-review therapy: Putting memories to work in individual and group psychotherapy', *Geriatrics*, *29*, 165-173

Libb, J.W., & Clements, C.B. (1969) 'Token reinforcement in an exercise program for hospitalized geriatric patients', *Perceptual and Motor Skills*, *28*, 957-958

Lilienfeld, A.M., & Lilienfeld, D.E. (1980) *Foundations of epidemiology*, Oxford University Press, Oxford

Linsk, N.L., Pinkston, E.M., & Green, G.R. (1982) 'Home-based behavioral social work with the elderly' in E.M. Pinkston, J.L. Levitt, G.R. Green, N.L. Linsk, & T.L. Rzepnicki (eds.), *Effective Social Work Practice: Advanced techniques for behavioral intervention with individuals, families and institutional staff,* Josey-Bass, San Francisco, CA

Looft, W.R. (1973) 'Reflections on intervention in old age: Motives, goals and assumptions', *The Gerontologist*, *13*, 6-10

Lopez, M.A., Hoyer, W.J., Goldstein, A.P., Gershaw, N.J., & Sprafkin, R.P. (1980) 'Effects of overlearning and incentive on the acquisition and transfer of interpersonal skills with institutionalized elderly', *Journal of Gerontology*, *35*, 403-408

Lourie, R. & Lourie, N.V. (1972) 'The new faces of advocacy', *Journal of the American Academy of Child Psychiatry*, *11*, 401-414

Lowenthal, M.F. (1965) 'Antecedents of isolation and mental illness in old age', *Archives of General Psychiatry*, *12*, 245-254

Lubin, R.A., & Kiely, M. (1985) 'Epidemiology of aging in developmental disabilities' in M.P. Janicki & H.M. Wisniewski (eds.), *Aging and developmental disabilities: Issues and trends*, Paul Brookes, Baltimore, MD

Lund, J. (1985) 'The prevalence of psychiatric morbidity in mentally retarded adults', *Acta Psychiatrica Scandinavica*, *72*, 563-70

MENCAP (1986) *Report of the Ad Hoc Leisure Committee to MENCAP*, MENCAP, London

MacDonald, M.L., & Butler, A.K. (1974) 'Reversal of helplessness: Producing walking behavior in nursing home wheelchair residents using behavior modification procedures', *Journal of Gerontology*, *29*, 97-101

Madison, H.L. (1964) 'Work placement success for the mentally retarded', *American Journal of Mental Deficiency*, *69*, 50-53

Malamud, N. (1972) 'Neuropathology of organic brain syndromes associated with aging' in C.M. Gaitz (ed.), *Aging and the brain*, Plenum Press, New York

Malin, N. (1980) 'Group homes', *E.R.G Report No.9*, Sheffield University, Sheffield

Malin, N., Race, D., & Jones, G. (1980) *Services for the mentally handicapped in Britain*, Croom Helm, London

Marlowe, R.A. (1976) 'When they closed the doors at Modesto' in P. Ahmed and S. Plog (eds.), *State mental hospitals: What happens when they close?*, Plenum Press, New York

Martin, A., & Millard, P.H. (1973) 'Cardiovascular assessment in the elderly', *Age and Ageing*, *2*, 211-217

McAllister, J. (1975) 'From the perspective of the President's Committee on Mental Retardation' in J. Hamilton & R. Segal (eds.), *Consultation-conference on the gerontologocal aspects of mental retardation*, Institute for the Study of Mental Retardation and Related Disabilities, University of Michigan, Ann Arbor, MI

McAvoy, L.H. (1976) *Recreational preferences of the elderly persons in Minnesota*, Unpublished Doctoral disseration, University of Minnesota, St. Paul, MN

McCall, G.J., & Simmons, J.L. (1978) *Identities and interactions*, Free Press, New York

McCarver, R.B., & Craig, E.M. (1974) 'Placement of the retarded in the community' in N.R. Ellis (ed.), *International review of research in mental retardation* (Vol 7), Academic Press, New York

McClannaham, L.E., & Risley, T.R. (1975) 'Design of living environments for nursing home residents: Increasing participation in recreation activities', *Journal of Applied Behavior Analysis*, *8*, 261-268

McConnell, S.R., Fleisher, D., Usher, C.E., & Kaplan, B.H. (1980) *Alternative work options for older workers: A feasibility study*, Ethel Percy Andrus Gerontology Center, Los Angeles, CA

McCormack, M. (1979) *Away from home - the mentally retarded in residential care*, Constable and Company, London

McCurley, R., Mackay, D.N., & Scally, B.G. (1972) 'The life expectation of mentally subnormal under community and hospital care', *Journal of Mental Deficiency Research*, *16*, 57-66

McDonald, E.P. (1985) 'Medical needs of severely developmentally disabled persons residing in the community', *American Journal of Mental Deficiency*, *90*, 171-176

McGuire, F.A. (1982) 'Constraints on leisure involvement in the later years', *Activities, Adaptation and Aging*, *3*, 17-24

McGuire, F.A., Dottavio, D., & O'Leary, J.T. (1986) 'Constraints to participation in outdoor recreation: A nationwide study of limitors and prohibitors', *The Gerontologist*, *26*, 538-544

McMahon, B., Pugh, T.F., & Ipsen, J. (1960) *Epidemiologic methods*, Little Brown, Boston, MA

Mechanic, D. (1974) 'Social structure and personal adaptation: Some neglected dimensions' in G.V. Coelho, D.A. Hamburg and J.E. Adams (eds.), *Coping and adaptation*, Basic Books, New York

Menolascino, F.J. (ed.) (1970) *Psychiatric approaches to mental retardation*, Basic Books, New York

Midwinter, R.E. (1972) 'Mental subnormality in Bristol', *Journal of Mental Deficiency Research*, *16*, 48-56

Miller, C. (1975) *Deinstitutionalization and mortality trends in profoundly mentally retarded*, Paper presented at the Western Research Conference on Mental Retardation, Carmel, CA

Miller, C., & Eyman, R. (1978) 'Hospital and community mortality rates among the retarded', *Journal of Mental Deficiency Research*, *22*, 137-145

Miller, E. (1977) *Abnormal ageing*, Wiley, London

Milne, J. (1983) 'Mentally handicapped people retiring in a residential setting: A program for developing opportunities for elderly mentally handicapped people and staff for their role in provision', Unpublished manuscript

Mitchell, A. (1984) *Elderly people who are mentally handicapped: Can they reminisce?*, Unpublished manuscript

Mittler, P. (1987) 'Staff development: Changing needs and service contexts in Britain' in J. Hogg and P. Mittler (eds.), *Staff training in mental handicap*, Croom Helm, London

Moller, B. (1965) *Om psykotiska barn. Fran inlagg vid rundabordssamtal om psykotiska barn*, Unpublished observations

Morris, M. (1985) 'Fowler urged to delay mental hospital closure', *Guardian*, 11th November 1985

Morse, D.W., Dutka, A.B., & Gray, S.H. (1983) *Life after early retirement: The experience of lower level workers*, Rowman and Allanhead, Totowa, NJ

Mueller, E., & Gurin, G. (1962) *Participation in outdoor recreation: Factors affecting demand among American adults*, U.S. Government Printing Office, Washington, D.C.

Muir-Gray, J.A. (1985) 'Social and community aspects of ageing' in M.S.J. Pathy (ed.), *Principles and practice of geriatric medicine*, Wiley, Chichester

Murphy, L.B., & Moriarty, A.E. (1976) *Vulnerability, coping, and growth from infancy to adolescence*, Yale University Press, New Haven, CT

Mutran, E., & Reitzes, D. (1981) 'Retirement, identity and well-being: Realignment of role relationships', *Journal of Gerontology*, *36*, 733-740

Myers, G.C. (1985) 'Aging and worldwide population change' in R.H. Binstock & E. Shanas (eds.), *Handbook of aging and the social sciences, second edition*, Van Nostrand Reinhold, New York

National Council on the Aging (1981) *Aging in the eighties: America in transition*, Washington, DC

National Development Team (1985) *Fourth report 1981/84*, HMSO, London

Nelson, R.P., & Croker, A.C. (1978) 'The medical care of mentally retarded persons in public residential facilities', *New England Journal of Medicine*, *299*, 1039-1044

Newcomer, R.J., Estes, C.L., & Freeman, H.E. (1985) 'Strategies of research for program design and intervention' in R.H. Binstock & E. Shanas (eds.), *Handbook of Aging and the Social Sciences, second edition*, Van Nostrand Reinhold, New York

Newman, E.S., Sherman, S.R., & Frenkel, E.R. (1985) 'Foster family care: A residential alternative for mentally retarded older persons' in M.P. Janicki and H.M. Wisniewski (eds.), *Aging and developmental disabilities: Issues and approaches*, Paul Brookes, Baltimore, MD

Nihira, K. (1969a) 'Factorial dimensions of adaptive behavior in adult retardates', *American Journal of Mental Deficiency*, *73*, 868-878

Nihira, K. (1969b) 'Factorial dimensions of adaptive behavior in mentally retarded children and adolescents', *American Journal of Mental Deficiency, 74*, 130-141

Nihira, K. (1976) 'Dimensions of adaptive behavior in institutionalized mentally retarded children and adults: Developmental perspective', *American Journal of Mental Deficiency, 81*, 215-226

North Western Regional Health Authority (NWRHA) (1985) *Run-down of hospitals for people with mental handicap in the North Western Region*, NWRHA, Manchester

Office of Population Censuses and Surveys (1984) *Census of England and Wales, 1981*, HMSO, London

Ohara P.T. (1972) 'Electron Microscopical Study of the brain in Down's syndrome', *Brain, 95*, 681-684

Oldham Social Services Department (1984) *Parents' Handbook*, OSSD, Oldham

Oliver, J. (1987) 'Personal communication'

Olson, M.I., & Shaw, C.M. (1969) 'Presenile dementia and Alzheimer's disease in mongolism', *Brain, 92*, 147-156

Osgood, N.J. (ed.) (1982) *Life after work*, Praeger, New York

Oster, J. (1953) *Mongolism: A clinicogeneological investigation comprising 526 mongols living on Seeland*, Danish Science Press, Copenhagen

Oswin, M. (1982) 'Nobody for me to look after', *Parents Voice, March*, 10

Oswin, M. (1983) *Bereavement and mentally handicapped people*, Paper presented to the 16th MENCAP Spring conference on mental handicap, University of Exeter, Exeter

Owens, D., Dawson, J.C., and Losin, S. (1971) 'Alzheimer's disease in Down's syndrome', *American Journal of Mental Deficiency, 75*, 606-612

Pagani, A. (1962) 'Social isolation in destitution' in C. Tibbitts & W. Donahue (eds.), *Social and psychological aspects of aging*, Columbia University Press, New York

Palmore, E.B. (1978) 'Compulsory versus flexible retirement: Issues and facts' in V. Carver and P. Liddiard (eds.), *An ageing population*, Hodder and Stoughton, Sevenoaks

Palmore, E.B. (1979) 'Predictors of successful aging', *The Gerontologist*, *19*, 427-431

Palmore, E.B., George, L.K., & Fillenbaum, G.G. (1982) 'Predictors of retirement', *Journal of Gerontology*, *37*, 733-742

Parker, S., & Smith, M. (1976) 'Work and leisure' in R. Dubin (ed.), *Handbook of work, organization and society*, Rand McNally, Chicago, IL

Parnes, H.S. (1981) 'Inflation and early retirement: Recent longitudinal findings', *Monthly Labor Review*, *103*, 27-30

Parsons, P.L. (1965) 'Mental health of Swansea's old folk', *British Journal of Social and Preventative Medicine*, *19*, 43-47

Pasmanick, B., Roberts, D.W., & Lemkau, P.W. (1959) 'A survey of mental disease in an urban population: Prevalence by race and income' in B. Pasmanick (ed.), *Epidemiology of mental disorder*, American Association for the Advancement of Science, Washington, DC

Payne, R. (1968) 'The psychotic subnormal', *Mental Subnormality*, *14*, 25-34

Penrose, L.S. (1938) *A clinical and genetic study of 1280 cases of mental defect* (MRC Special Report no. 229), HMSO, London

Penrose, L.S. (1972) *The biology of mental defect*, Sidgwick and Jackson, London

Philips, I. (1967) 'Psychopathology and mental retardation', *American Journal of Psychiatry*, *124*, 29-35

Pinkston, E.M., & Linsk, N.L. (1984a) 'Behavioral family intervention with the impaired elderly', *The Gerontologist*, *24*, 576-583

Pinkston, E.M., & Linsk, N.L. (1984b) *Care of the Elderly: A family approach*, Pergamon, New York

Polednak, A.P. (1975) 'Respiratory disease mortality in an institutionalised mentally retarded population', *Journal of Mental Deficiency Research*, *19*, 165-172

Pountney, M. (1987) *The Employment Preparation Unit, Birmingham*, Paper given at the MENCAP Spring conference, University of Exeter, Exeter

Powell-Proctor, L., & Miller, E. (1982) 'Reality orientation: A critical appraisal', *British Journal of Psychiatry*, *140*, 457-463

Praderas, K., & MacDonald, M.L. (1986) 'Telephone conversational skills training with socially isolated, impaired nursing home residents', *Journal of Applied Behavior Analysis*, *19*, 337-348

Primrose, D.A. (1966) 'Natural history of mental deficiency in a hospital group and in the community it serves', *Journal of Mental Deficiency Research*, *10*, 159-189

Primrose, D.A. (1971) 'A survey of 502 consecutive admissions to a subnormality hospital from 1st January 1968 to 31st December 1970', *British Journal of Mental Subnormality*, *17*, 25-28

Primrose, E.J.R. (1962) *Psychological illness: A community study.* (Mind and medicine monographs), Tavistock, London

Pyron, H.C., & Manion, U.V. (1970) 'The company, the individual and the decision to retire', *Industrial Gerontology*, *4*, 1-26

Quinn, J.F. (1977) 'Microeconomic determinants of early retirement: A cross-sectional view of white married men', *Journal of Human Resources*, *12*, 329-346

Quinn, J.F. (1981) 'The extent and correlates of partial retirement', *The Gerontologist*, *21*, 634-643

Rapoport, R., & Rapoport, R.N. (1975) *Leisure and the family life cycle*, Routledge and Kegan Paul, London

Ray, R., Payne, M., & Stryker, M. (1978) 'They only live for today', *Parents Voice*, *June*, 10-11

Raynes, N.V. (1987) 'Adaptive behaviour scales' in J. Hogg and N.V. Raynes (eds.), *Assessment in mental handicap: A guide to assessment practices, tests and checklists*, Croom Helm, London

Record, R.G., & Smith, A. (1955) 'The incidence, mortality, and sex distributions of mongoloid defectives', *British Journal of Preventative Social Medicine*, *9*, 10-15

Redick, R.W., Kramer, M., & Taube, B.A. (1973) 'Epidemiology of mental illness and utilization of psychiatric facilities among older persons' in E.W. Busse & E. Pfeiffer (eds.), *Mental illness in later life*, American Psychiatric Association, Washington DC

Reid, A.H. (1972a) 'Psychoses in adult mental defectives: I. Manic-depressive psychoses', *British Journal of Psychiatry*, *120*, 205-212

Reid, A.H. (1972b) 'Psychoses in adult mental defectives: II. Schizophrenic and paranoid psychoses', *British Journal of Psychiatry*, *120*, 213-218

Reid, A.H. (1982) *The psychiatry of mental handicap*, Blackwell, Oxford

Reid, A.H. (1983) 'Psychiatry of mental handicap: A review', *Journal of the Royal Society of Medicine*, *76*, 587-592

Reid, A.H. & Aungle, P.G. (1974) 'Dementia in ageing mental defectives: A clinical psychiatric study', *Journal of Mental Deficiency Research*, *18*, 15-23

Reinhart, R.A., & Sargent, S.S. (1980) 'The humanistic approach: The Ventura County Creative Aging Workshops' in S.S Sargent (ed.), *Nontraditional Therapy and Counselling with the Aged*, Springer, New York

Reiss, S. (1982) 'Psychopathology and mental retardation: Survey of a developmental disabilities mental health program', *Mental Retardation*, *20*, 128-132

Reiss, S., & Benson. B.A. (1985) 'Psychosocial correlates of depression in mentally retarded adults: 1. Minimal social support and stigmatization', *American Journal of Mental Deficiency*, *89*, 331-337

Richards, B.W. (1969) 'Age trends in mental deficiency institutions', *Journal of Mental Deficiency Research*, *13*, 171-183

Richards, B.W. (1976) 'Health and longevity' in J. Wortis (ed.), *Mental Retardation and Developmental Disabilities: An Annual Review* (vol. 13), Brunner/Mazel, New York

Richards, B.W., & Siddiqui, A. (1980) 'Age and mortality trends in residents of an institution for the mentally handicapped', *Journal of Mental Deficiency Research, 24*, 99-105

Richards, B.W., & Sylvester, P.E. (1969) 'Mortality trends in mental deficiency institutions', *Journal of Mental Deficiency Research, 13*, 276-292

Richardson, A., & Ritchie, J. (1986) *Making the bread: Parents' perspectives on adults with mental handicap leaving home*, King Edward's Hospital Fund for London, London

Richardson, A., & Ritchie, J. (1987) 'Unpublished work', London

Richardson, S. (1981) 'Living environments: An ecological perspective' in H.C. Haywood & J.R. Newbrough (eds.), *Living environments for developmentally retarded persons*, University Park Press, Baltimore, MD

Richardson, W.P., & Higgins, A.C. (1965) *The handicapped children of Almanace County, North Carolina*, Nemours Foundation, Wilmington, DE

Rinke, C.L., Williams, J.J., & Lloyd, K.E. (1978) 'The effects of prompting and reinforcement on self-bathing by elderly residents of nursing homes', *Behaviour Therapy, 9*, 873-881

Rinsky, L. (1981) 'Perspectives on surgery for scoliosis in mentally retarded patients', *Orthopedic Clinics of North America, 12*, 113-126

Robinson, M., & Steward, J. (1985) *The Homemaking scheme: Progress report*, Oldham Social Services, Oldham

Robinson, P.K., Coberly, S., & Paul, C.E. (1985) 'Work and retirement' in R.H. Binstock and E. Shanas (eds.), *Handbook of aging and the social sciences, second edition*, Van Nostrand Reinhold, New York

Rodstein, M. (1956) 'Heart disease in the aged' in I. Rossmann (ed.), *Clinical geriatrics*, J.B. Lippincott, Philadelphia, PA

Rosen, M., Floor, L., & Baxter, D. (1972) 'Prediction of community adjustment: A failure at cross validation', *American Journal of Mental Deficiency, 77*, 111-112

Rosen, M., Stallings, L., Floor, L., & Nowakiwska, M. (1968) 'Reliability and stability of Wechsler I.Q. scores for institutionalized mental subnormals', *American Journal of Mental Deficiency*, *73*, 218-225

Rosen, W.G. (1983) 'Neuropsychological investigation of memory visuoconstructional and visuoperceptual and language abilities in senile dementia of the Alzheimer type', *Advances in Neurology*, *38*, 65-73

Rosenstein, J.C., & Swenson, E.W. (1980) 'Behavioral approaches to therapy with the elderly' in S.S. Sargent (ed.), *Nontraditional therapy and counseling with the aging*, Springer, New York

Rosow, I. (1974) *Socialization to old age*, University of California Press, Berkeley, CA

Rowitz, L. (1979) *Who are the elderly developmentally disabled? A matter of definition*, Paper presented at a symposium on the 'Gerontological aspects of developmental disabilities', Omaha, NE

Rudelli, R.D. (1985) 'The syndrome of musculoskeletal aging' in M.P. Janicki, & H.M. Wisniewski (eds.), *Aging and developmental disabilities: Issues and trends*, Paul Brookes, Baltimore, MD

Rudie, R., & Riedl, S. (1984) 'Attitudes of parents and guardians of mentally handicapped former state hospital residents towards current community placement', *American Journal of Mental Deficiency*, *89*, 295-297

Rutter, M., Graham, P., & Yule, W. (1970) *A neuropsychiatric study in childhood*, Spastic International Publications, Heinemann Medical, London

Saleem, K. (1985) 'Mentally handicapped adults living at home: Perceptions of their lives', *Undergraduate thesis submitted to Psychology Department*, University of Manchester, Manchester

Sanario, E. (1981) 'Toilet retraining psychogeriatric residents', *Behaviour Modification*, *5*, 417-427

Sanctuary, G. (1983) *MENCAP information sheet*, MENCAP, London

Sanctuary, G. (1984) *After I'm gone* (What will happen to my handicapped child), Souvenir Press, London

Sandler, I.N. (1980) 'Social support resources, stress, and maladjustment of poor children', *American Journal of Community Psychology*, *8*, 41-52

Sarason, S.B. (1974) *The psychological sense of community*, Jossey-Bass, San Francisco, CA

Sargent, S.S. (1980) 'Introduction: Why nontraditional therapy and counselling with the aging?' in S.S. Sargent (ed.), *Nontraditional therapy and counseling with the aging*, Springer, New York

Schaie, K.W. (1983a) 'The Seattle longitudinal study: A 21-year exploration of psychometric intelligence in adulthood' in K.W. Schaie (ed.), *Longitudinal studies of adult psychological development*, Guilford Press, New York

Schaie, K.W. (1983b) 'What can we learn from the longitudinal study of adult psychological development?' in K.W. Schaie (ed.), *Longitudinal studies of adult psychological development*, The Guilford Press, New York

Schatz, G. (1983) 'The problem of preparing mentally handicapped people adequately for the future', *International Journal of Rehabilitation Medicine*, *6*, 197-199

Scheerenberger, R.C. (1983) *A history of mental retardation*, Paul Brookes, Baltimore, MD

Schloss, P.J. (1982) 'Verbal interaction patterns of depressed and nondepressed institutionalized mentally retarded adults', *Applied Research in Mental Retardation*, *3*, 1-12

Schnelle, J.F., Traughber, B., Morgan, D.B., Embry, J.E., Binion, A.F., & Coleman, A. (1983) 'Management of geriatric incontinence in nursing homes', *Journal of Applied Behavior Analysis*, *16*, 235-241

Schulz, J., Carrin, G., Krupp, H., Peschke, M., Sclar, E., & Van Steeberge, J. (1974) *Providing adequate retirement income - pension reform in the United States and abroad*, New England Press for Brandeis University Press, Hanover, NH

Schulz, J.H. (1980) *The economics of aging*, Wadsworth Press, Belmont, CA

Schulz, R., & Brenner, G. (1977) 'Relocation of the aged: A review and theoretical analysis', *Journal of Gerontology*, *32*, 323-333

Scott, F., & Zoernick, D.A. (1977) 'Exploiting leisure needs of the aged', *Leisurability*, *4*, 25-31

Scottish Health Service (1981) *Scottish Health Statistics*, (1979 Vol 2), HMSO, Edinburgh

Seltzer, G.B. (1981) 'Community residential adjustment: The relationship among environment, performance, and satisfaction', *American Journal of Mental Deficiency*, *85*, 624-630

Seltzer, G.B., & Seltzer, M.M. (1976) *The Community Adjustment Scale*, Educational Projects, Cambridge, MA

Seltzer, M.M. (1984a) *Older mentally retarded persons: Demographic profile and service requirements*, Paper presented at the 37th annual scientific meeting of the Gerontological Society of America, San Antonio, TX

Seltzer, M.M. (1984b) *What is successful aging for mentally retarded persons? A definition and strategy for measurement*, Unpublished manuscript

Seltzer, M.M. (1985a) 'Informal support for aging mentally retarded persons', *American Journal of Mental Deficiency*, *90*, 259-265

Seltzer, M.M. (1985b) 'Research in social aspects of aging and developmental disabilities' in M.P. Janicki & H.M. Wisniewski (eds.), *Aging and developmental disabilities: Issues and trends*, Paul Brookes, Baltimore, MD

Seltzer, M.M., Seltzer, G.B., & Sherwood, C.C. (1982) 'Comparison of community adjustment of older vs. younger mentally retarded adults', *American Journal of Mental Deficiency*, *87*, 9-13

Seltzer, M.M., Sherwood, C.C., Seltzer, G.B., & Sherwood, S. (1981) ' Community adaptation and the impact of deinstitutionalization' in R.H. Bruininks, C.E. Meyers, B.B. Sigford and K.C. Laskin (eds.), *Deinstitutionalization and Community Adjustment of Mentally Retarded People*, American Association on Mental Deficiency, Washington, DC

Shamoian, C.A. (1985) 'Assessing depression in elderly patients', *Hospital and Community Psychiatry*, *36*, 338-339

Shepherd, M., & Gruenberg, E.M. (1957) 'The age for neuroses', *Milbank Memorial Fund Quarterly*, *35*, 258-265

Shepherd, M., Cooper, B., Brown, A.C. (1966) *Psychiatric illness in general practice*, Oxford University Press, Oxford

Sherwood, S., Greer, D.S., Morris, J.N., Mor, V., & Associates (1981) *An alternative to institutionalization*, Ballinger, Cambridge, MA

Siegel, J.S. (1980) 'On the demography of aging', *Demography*, *17*, 345-364

Siegel, S., & Rives, J. (1980) 'Preretirement programs within service firms: Existing and planned programs', *Aging and Work*, *3*, 183-191

Siegler, I.C. (1983) 'Psychological aspects of the Duke longitudinal studies' in E.W. Schaie (ed.), *Longitudinal studies of adult psychological development*, The Guilford Press, New York

Silverstein, A.B. (1979) 'Mental growth from six to sixty in an institutionalized mentally retarded sample', *Psychological Reports*, *45*, 643-646

Sim, M. (1965) 'Alzheimer's disease: A forgotten entity', *Geriatrics*, *20*, 668-674

Simpson, I., Back, K., & McKinney, J. (1966) 'Exposure to information on, preparation for, and self-evaluation in retirement' in I. Simpson & J. McKinney (eds.), *Social aspects of aging*, Duke University Press, Durham, NC

Sjogren, H. (1950) 'Twenty-four cases of Alzheimer's disease: A clinical analysis', *Acta Medica Scandinavica*, *Suppl.*, 245-247

Slater, J., Fitzpatrick, S. & Carrins, D. (1981) 'Helping to overcome fears for the future', *Social Work Today*, *12(30)*, 11-12

Smith, D.C., Decker, H.A., Herberg, E.N., & Rupke, L.K. (1969) 'Medical needs of children in institutions for the mentally retarded', *American Journal of Public Health*, *59*, 1376-1384

Solitaire, G.B. and Lamarche, J.B. (1966) 'Alzheimer's disease and senile dementia as seen in mongoloids: Neuropathological observations', *American Journal of Mental Deficiency*, *70*, 840-848

Somerset County Council Social Services Department (1976) 'Survey of Mental Handicap - Stage One: Adults living at home', SCCSSD, Taunton

Sovner, R., & Hurley, D.A. (1983) 'Do the mentally retarded suffer from affective illness?', *Archives of General Psychiatry*, *40*, 61-67

Sparks, P.M. (1973) 'Behavior versus experimental aging: Implications for intervention', *The Gerontologist*, *13*, 15-18

Sperbeck, D.J., & Whitbourne, S.K. (1981) 'Dependency in the institutional setting: A behavioral training program for geriatric staff', *The Gerontologist*, *21*, 268-275

Streib, G., & Schneider, C. (1971) *Retirement in American society*, Cornell University Press, Ithaca, NY

Stromgren, E. (1963) 'Epidemiology of old-age psychiatric disorders' in R.H. William, C. Tibbitts, & W. Donahue (eds.), *The Process of aging* (Vol 2), Atherton, New York

Stroud, M., Murphy, M., & Roberts, R. (1984) *The Aged Mentally Retarded/Developmentally Disabled in Northeast Ohio: Access Research*, ACCESS, Akron, Ohio

Struwe, F. (1929) 'Histopathologische untersuchungen uber entstehung und weses der senile plaques', *Zeitschrift fur des gesamtes Neurologie und Psychiatrie*, *122*, 291-307

Stuckey, P.E., & Newbrough, J.R. (1981) 'Mental health of retarded persons: Social-ecological considerations' in H.C. Haywood & J.R. Newbrough (eds.), *Living environments for developmentally retarded persons*, University Park Press, Baltimore, MD

Sutton, E. (1986) *Planning for Developmentally Disabled Older Adults to Access Community Based Activities*, ACCESS, Akron, OH

Svanborg, A. (1977) 'Seventy-year-old people in Gothenburg. A population study in an industrialized Swedish city. II. General presentation of social and medical conditions', *Acta Medica Scandinavica*, *Supp 5*, 1-37

Sweeney, D.P., & Wilson, T.Y. (eds) (1979) *Double jeopardy: The plight of aging and aged developmentally disabled persons in mid-America*, Exceptional Child Center, Utah State University, Logan, UT

Tait, D. (1983) 'Mortality and Dementia among Ageing Defectives', *Journal of Mental Deficiency Research*, *27*, 133-142

Tarjan, G., Brooke, C.E., Eyman, R.K., Suyeyasu, A., & Miller, C.R. (1968) 'Mortality and cause of death in a hospital for the mentally retarded', *American Journal of Public Health*, *58*, 1891-1900

Tarjan, G., Wright, S.W., Eyman, R.K., & Keeran, C.V. (1973) 'Natural history of mental retardation: Some aspects of epidemiology', *American Journal of Mental Deficiency*, *77*, 369-379

Taylor, J.R. (1976) 'A comparison of the adaptive behavior of retarded individuals successfully and unsuccessfully placed in group living homes', *Education and Training of the Mentally Retarded*, *11*, 56-64

Thase, M.E. (1982) 'Longevity and mortality in Down's syndrome', *Journal of Mental Deficiency Research*, *26*, 177-192

Thase, M.E., Liss, L., Smelzer, D., and Maloon, J. (1982) 'Clinical evaluation of dementia in Down's syndrome: A preliminary report', *Journal of Mental Deficiency Research*, *26*, 239-244

Theil, G.W. (1981) 'Relationship of IQ, adaptive behavior, age and environmental demand to community-placement success of mentally retarded adults', *American Journal of Mental Deficiency*, *86*, 208-211

Thomae, I., & Fryers, T. (1982) *Ageing and mental handicap: A position paper*, International League for Persons with Mental Handicap, Brussels

Tinto, R. (1987) *Development of day services in statutory strategy*, Paper given at the MENCAP Spring conference, University of Exeter, Exeter

Tizard, J. (1964) *Community services for the mentally handicapped*, Oxford University Press, Oxford

Townsend, P. (1957) *The family life of old people*, The Free Press, Glencoe, IL

Tredgold, A.F. (1908) *A textbook of mental deficiency*, Balliere, Tindall & Cox, London

Tunstall, J. (1966) *Old and alone*, Routledge and Kegan Paul, London

Tyne, A. (1978) Cited in Wertheimer (1981)

Vaillant, G.E. (1977) *Adaptation to life*, Little, Boston, MA

Vallery-Masson, J., Poitrenaud, J., Burnat, G., & Lion, M.R. (1981) ' Retirement and morbidity: A three year longitudinal study of a French managerial population', *Age and Ageing*, *10*, 271-276

Vayhinger, J.M. (1980) 'The approach of pastoral psychology' in S.S. Sargent (ed.), *Nontraditional Therapy and Counselling with the Aging*, Springer, New York

Veall, R.M. (1974) 'The prevalence of epilepsy among mongols related to age', *Journal of Mental Deficiency Research*, *18*, 99-106

Waern, U. (1978) 'Health and disease at the age of sixty. Findings in a health survey of 60 year old men in Uppsala and a comparison with men 10 years younger', *Uppsala Journal of Medical Sciences*, *83*, 153-162

Walker, A. (1981) 'Community care and the elderly in Great Britain: Theory and practice', *International Journal of Health Services*, *11*, 541-557

Wang, H.S. (1981) 'Neuropsychiatric procedures for the assessment of Alzheimer's disease, senile dementia, and related disorders' in N.E. Miller and G.D. Cohen (eds.), *Clinical aspects of Alzheimer's disease and senile dementia*, Raven Press, New York

Ward, R.A. (1984) *The aging experience: An introduction to social gerontology*, Harper and Row, New York

Warren, S.F., & Mulcahey, M.A. (1984) *Life planning for handicapped adults in Tennessee: Research findings and recommendations*, John F. Kennedy Center for Research on Education and Human Development, Peabody College, Vanderbilt University, Nashville, TN

Watts, C.A.H., & Watts, B.M. (1952) *Psychiatry in general practice*, Churchill, London

Wells, A. (1983) Letter to 'Parents Voice', *33*, 21

Wells, L., & McDonald, G. (1981) 'Interpersonal networks and post-relocation adjustment of the institutionalized elderly', *The Gerontologist*, *21*, 177-183

Wertheimer, A. (1981) *Living for the Present: Older parents with a mentally handicapped person living at home. Enquiry paper no.9*, Campaign for People with Mental Handicap, London

Whelan, E., & Speake, B. (1977) *Adult Training Centres in England: Report of the first national survey*, Hester Adrian Research Centre, University of Manchester, Manchester

Whelan, E., Speake, B., & Strickland, T. (1984) 'The Copewell Curriculum: Development, content and use' in A. Deane & S. Hegarty (eds.), *Learning for Independence: Post 16 educational provision for people with severe learning difficulties*, Further Education Unit, London

Whittick, J.E. (1985) 'Attitudes to Caregiving', *Paper presented at the Scientific Meeting of Lothian Psychologists, 6th November 1985*

Wilkin, D. (1979) *Caring for the mentally handicapped child*, Croom Helm, London

Willer, B., & Intagliata, J. (1984) 'Residential care settings for the elderly' in B. Willer and J. Intagliata (eds.), *Promises and realities for mentally retarded citizens: Life in the community*, University Park Press, Baltimore, MD

Williams, C.E. (1971) 'A study of the patients in a group of mental subnormality hospitals', *British Journal of Mental Subnormality*, *17*, 29-41

Williams, P. (1985) 'Evidence to the House of Commons SSC on community care, (letter)', *Bulletin of the British Psychological Society*, *38*, 14-15

Williamson, J., Stokoe, I.H., Gray, S., Fisher, M., Smith, A., McGhee, A., & Stephenson, E. (1964) 'Old people at home: Their unreported needs', *Lancet*, *1*, 1117-1120

Willis, S.L. (1985) 'Towards an educational psychology of the older learner: Intellectual and cognitive bases' in J.E. Birren & K.W. Schaie (eds.), *Hanbook of the Psychology of Aging, second edition*, Van Nostrand Reinhold, New York

Wilson, L.A., & Brass, W. (1973) 'Brief assessment of the mental state in geriatric domicilary practice. The usefulness of the Mental Status Questionnaire', *Age and Ageing*, *2*, 92-101

Wisneiwski, K., Jervis, G.A, Moretz, R.C, & Wisniewski, H.M. (1979) 'Alzheimer neurofibrillary tangles in diseases other than senile and presenile dementia', *Annals of Neurology*, *5*, 288-294

Witt, P.A., & Goodale, T.L. (1981) 'The relationships between barriers to leisure enjoyment and family stages', *Leisure Sciences*, *4*, 29-49

Wolf, L.C., & Whitehead, P.C. (1975) 'The decision to institutionalize retarded children: Comparison of individually matched groups', *Mental Retardation*, *13*, 3-11

Wolfensberger, W. (1972) *The principle of normalization in human services*, Leonard Cranford, Toronto

Wolfensberger, W. (1985) 'An overview of social role valorisation and some reflections on elderly mentally retarded persons' in M.P. Janicki & H.M. Wisniewski (eds.), *Aging and developmental disabilities: Issues and trends*, Paul Brookes, Baltimore, MD

Wolfensberger, W., & Glenn, L. (1975) *Pass III: A method for qualitative evaluation of human services*, National Institute on Mental Retardation, Toronto

Wolfson, I.N. (1970) 'Adjustment of institutionalized mildly retarded patients twenty years after return to the community', *Mental Retardation*, *8*, 20-23

Wolverhampton Social Services Department (1982) *Adult mentally handicapped people living at home: Their future care - a guide for parents and relatives*, WSSD, Wolverhampton

Wood, S., & Shears, B. (1986) *Teaching children with severe learning difficulties: A Radical reappraisal*, Croom Helm, London

Wright, S., Valente, M., & Tarjan, G. (1962) 'Medical problems on a ward of a hospital for mentally retarded', *American Journal of Diseases of Children*, *104*, 142-148

Zetlin, A.G. (1986) 'Mentally retarded adults and their siblings', *American Journal of Mental Deficiency*, *91*, 217-225

Zigler, E., Balla, D, & Hodapp, R. (1984) 'On the definition and classification of mental retardation', *American Journal of Mental Deficiency*, *89*, 215-230

AUTHOR INDEX

SUBJECT INDEX